BEYOND BAGPUSS

BEYOND BAGPUSS

A History of Smallfilms Animation Studio

By Chris Pallant

THE BRITISH FILM INSTITUTE
Bloomsbury Publishing Plc
50 Bedford Square, London, WC1B 3DP, UK
1385 Broadway, New York, NY 10018, USA
29 Earlsfort Terrace, Dublin 2, Ireland

BLOOMSBURY is a trademark of Bloomsbury Publishing Plc

First published in Great Britain 2022 by Bloomsbury
on behalf of the
British Film Institute
21 Stephen Street, London W1T 1LN
www.bfi.org.uk

The BFI is the lead organisation for film in the UK and the distributor of Lottery funds for film. Our mission is to ensure that film is central to our cultural life, in particular by supporting and nurturing the next generation of filmmakers and audiences. We serve a public role which covers the cultural, creative and economic aspects of film in the UK.

Copyright © Chris Pallant, 2022

Chris Pallant has asserted his right under the Copyright, Designs and Patents Act, 1988, to be identified as author of this work.

For legal purposes the Acknowledgments on p. xv constitute an extension of this copyright page.

Cover design by Louise Dugdale
Cover images © Smallfilms

All rights reserved. No part of this publication may be reproduced or transmitted in any form or by any means, electronic or mechanical, including photocopying, recording, or any information storage or retrieval system, without prior permission in writing from the publishers.

Bloomsbury Publishing Plc does not have any control over, or responsibility for, any third-party websites referred to or in this book. All internet addresses given in this book were correct at the time of going to press. The author and publisher regret any inconvenience caused if addresses have changed or sites have ceased to exist, but can accept no responsibility for any such changes.

A catalogue record for this book is available from the British Library.

ISBN: HB: 978-1-8390-2239-5
PB: 978-1-8390-2238-8
ePDF: 978-1-8390-2241-8
eBook: 978-1-8390-2240-1

Typeset by Integra Software Services Pvt. Ltd.
Printed and bound in India

To find out more about our authors and books visit www.bloomsbury.com and sign up for our newsletters.

Dedication

To my mum and dad for introducing me to the Clangers *at an early age and starting all of this;*
to Lyndsey for supporting this journey through the realm of Smallfilms;
to Charlie and Evie for embracing these shows and allowing me to see them with fresh eyes.

CONTENTS

List of Illustrations	ix
Acknowledgments	xv

Chapter 1
INTRODUCTION 1

Chapter 2
THE WHIMSICAL AUTHENTICITY OF SMALLFILMS:
IVOR THE ENGINE (1959–64, 1975–7) 25

Chapter 3
BUILDING WORLDS: *THE SAGA OF NOGGIN THE NOG* (1959–65, 1982) 55

Chapter 4
AESTHETIC TRANSITION AND THE PERSISTENCE OF THE
HANDMADE IN *THE SEAL OF NEPTUNE* (1960),
THE MERMAID'S PEARLS (1962), AND *PINGWINGS* (1961–5) 77

Chapter 5
LOW-ANGLE PERSONS: *THE POGLES* (1965) AND *POGLES' WOOD* (1966–8) 101

Chapter 6
TECHNOLOGY AND INVENTIVENESS WITHIN SMALLFILMS ANIMATION:
CLANGERS (1969–74) 123

Chapter 7
THE FORGOTTEN HISTORY OF SMALLFILMS: *SAM ON BOFFS' ISLAND*
(1972–3) 143

Chapter 8
CREATIVE COLLABORATION AND THE BRICOLAGE OF *BAGPUSS* (1974) 167

Chapter 9
SMALLFILMS AT THE END OF THE ROAD? *TOTTIE* (1984, 1986),
LIFE ON EARTH PERHAPS (1985), AND *PINNY'S HOUSE* (1986) 195

Chapter 10
THE AFTERLIFE OF 'SMALLFILMS': ADAPTATION AND RENEWAL   225

Appendix A: Smallfilms – Statistical Perspectives   246
Appendix B: Examples of Oliver Postgate's Screenwriting Style   249
Works Cited   254
Filmography   262
Index   264

ILLUSTRATIONS

Figures

2.1	Composite image showing pan in *Ivor the Engine* (1959–64). © Smallfilms/Associated-Rediffusion Television	28
2.2	Ivor in his shed as seen in *Ivor the Engine* (1959–64). © Smallfilms/Associated-Rediffusion Television	29
2.3	Jones lights Ivor's boiler in *Ivor the Engine* (1959–64). © Smallfilms/Associated-Rediffusion Television	29
2.4	Jones pours a pot of tea in *Ivor the Engine* (1959–64). © Smallfilms/Associated-Rediffusion Television	29
2.5	Jones enjoys his morning tea in *Ivor the Engine* (1959–64). © Smallfilms/Associated-Rediffusion Television	29
2.6	Jones setting Ivor's controls as seen in *Ivor the Engine* (1959–64). © Smallfilms/Associated-Rediffusion Television	30
2.7	Point-of-view shot from Ivor's footplate as seen in *Ivor the Engine* (1959–64). © Smallfilms/Associated-Rediffusion Television	30
2.8	Stopping at the water tower as seen in *Ivor the Engine* (1959–64). © Smallfilms/Associated-Rediffusion Television	30
2.9	Ivor waiting at the signal as seen in *Ivor the Engine* (1959–64). © Smallfilms/Associated-Rediffusion Television	30
2.10	Approaching Dai Station as seen in *Ivor the Engine* (1959–64). © Smallfilms/Associated-Rediffusion Television	30
2.11	A breakdown for print adaptation of a story featuring Bluebell the Donkey, *c.* 1977. © Oliver Postgate Family Archive	34
2.12	Discussion of nuclear war written on the reverse of Figure 2.11, *c.* 1977. © Oliver Postgate Family Archive	35
2.13	The 1962 mapping of the Merioneth and Llantisilly Railway. Published by Abelard Schuman	37
2.14	The revised 1967 mapping of the Merioneth and Llantisilly Railway. Published by Abelard Schuman	38
2.15	Undated draft (*c.* 1974) showing fifty planned *Ivor the Engine* (colour) episodes; 'S' denotes standalone episodes. © Oliver Postgate Family Archive	41

2.16	Undated draft (*c.* 1974) recording re-sequencing of 'Unidentified Objects' from episode eight to thirteen. © Oliver Postgate Family Archive	42
2.17	The first script page for the first episode of the colour *Ivor the Engine* series. © Oliver Postgate Family Archive	43
2.18	*Ivor the Engine* (black-and-white) second series episode outline, 1962. © Oliver Postgate Family Archive	44
2.19	*Ivor the Engine* (black-and-white) third series episode outline, *c.* 1963–4. © Oliver Postgate Family Archive	45
2.20	Peter Firmin describes *Ivor the Engine* merchandising initiatives. © Peter Firmin Family Archive/BBC Written Archives Centre	47
2.21	Oliver Postgate maps out his vision for the *Ivor the Engine* cassette series. © BBC Written Archives Centre	48
2.22	The BBC and Smallfilms reach a truce. © BBC Written Archives Centre	51
3.1	Script material from Peter Firmin's original synopsis for *Noggin the Nog*. © Peter Firmin Family Archive	60
3.2	Live performance plans from Peter Firmin's original synopsis for *Noggin the Nog*. © Peter Firmin Family Archive	61
3.3	Previsualization sketches from Peter Firmin's original synopsis for *Noggin the Nog*. © Peter Firmin Family Archive	62
3.4	The inlet to Noggin's Fjord from *The Saga of Noggin the Nog* (1959–65). © Smallfilms/BBC	63
3.5	Oral saga tradition as seen in *The Saga of Noggin the Nog* (1959–65). © Smallfilms/BBC	63
3.6	Prince Noggin from *The Saga of Noggin the Nog* (1959–65). © Smallfilms/BBC	63
3.7	Noggin's coastal settlement as seen in *The Saga of Noggin the Nog* (1959–65). © Smallfilms/BBC	64
3.8	The castle of King Knut/Noggin the Nog from *The Saga of Noggin the Nog* (1959–65). © Smallfilms/BBC	64
3.9	King Knut walking to 'Knut's Seat' as seen in *The Saga of Noggin the Nog* (1959–65). © Smallfilms/BBC	64
3.10	King Knut sits and worries in *The Saga of Noggin the Nog* (1959–65). © Smallfilms/BBC	65
3.11	The castle of Nogbad the Bad as seen in *The Saga of Noggin the Nog* (1959–65). © Smallfilms/BBC	65

3.12	Villagers telling the King not to worry in *The Saga of Noggin the Nog* (1959–65). © Smallfilms/BBC	65
3.13	Noggin, Thornogsen, and Graculus take cover in *The Ice Dragon* (1961). © Smallfilms/BBC	68
3.14	The recurrent ritual of taking tea as seen in *The Ice Dragon* (1961). © Smallfilms/BBC	69
3.15	Explosion damage as seen in *The Firecake* (1965). © Smallfilms/BBC	70
3.16	A mushroom cloud as seen in *The Firecake* (1965). © Smallfilms/BBC	72
4.1	Cyrus meets a mermaid in *The Seal of Neptune* (1960). © Smallfilms/BBC	82
4.2	POV shot of a ship sailing on stormy seas in *The Seal of Neptune* (1960). © Smallfilms/BBC	84
4.3	Detailed establishing shot of the underwater city in *The Seal of Neptune* (1960). © Smallfilms/BBC	84
4.4	Drawing inspiration from everyday life as shown in *Pingwings* (1961–5). © Rediffusion/Smallfilms/ITV	90
4.5	The descriptive instructions provided by Oliver Postgate to Gloria Firmin, *c.* 1961. © Peter Firmin Family Archive	92
4.6	The hand-drawn aesthetic is self-reflexively foregrounded by the credits of *Pingwings* (1961–5). © Rediffusion/Smallfilms/ITV	94
5.1	Woodworking 101 as seen in *Pogles' Wood* (1965–8). © Smallfilms/BBC	104
5.2	*Pogles' Wood* unmade – draft synopsis, 6 June 1966. © Oliver Postgate Family Archive	113
6.1	Clangers inspect a mysterious object as seen in *Doctor Who* 'The Sea Devils' (1972). © BBC	124
6.2	Page 1 of Joan Firmin's *Clangers* knitting pattern. © Peter Firmin Family Archive	128
6.3	Page 2 of Joan Firmin's *Clangers* knitting pattern. © Peter Firmin Family Archive	129
6.4	An example of the unashamed and self-reflexive use of Meccano in *Clangers* (1969–74). © Smallfilms/BBC	135
6.5	*Pas de deux* – Smallfilms-style as seen in *Clangers* (1969–74). © Smallfilms/BBC	139
6.6	A bewildered astronaut discovers the magnetic appeal of *Clangers* (1969–74). © Smallfilms/BBC	140

7.1	Our first sight of the Say Birds as seen in *Sam on Boffs' Island* (1972–3). © BBC	150
7.2	Friendly Gurglers as seen in *Sam on Boffs' Island* (1972–3). © BBC	152
7.3	Crossed wires as seen in *Sam on Boffs' Island* (1972–3). © BBC	152
7.4	A crowd scene as seen in *Sam on Boffs' Island* (1972–3). © BBC	153
8.1	The ongoing cultural capital of *Bagpuss* as seen in *The Crown* (2016–present). © Left Bank Pictures/Sony Pictures Television Production UK/Netflix	167
8.2	Lady Diana Spencer (Emma Corrin) escapes into the realm of *Bagpuss* as seen in *The Crown* (2016–present). © Left Bank Pictures/Sony Pictures Telivision Production UK/Netflix	168
8.3	Professor Yaffle holds court – an example of stop-motion model-based animation in *Bagpuss* (1974). © Smallfilms/BBC	175
8.4	The hand-drawn cut-out Captain Duck as seen in *Bagpuss* (1974). © Smallfilms/BBC	175
8.5	Linda Birch's watercolour depiction of Captain Bagpuss as seen in *Bagpuss* (1974). © Smallfilms/BBC	175
8.6	Linda Birch's mermaids as seen in *Bagpuss* (1974). © Smallfilms/BBC	177
8.7	A sequence of metamorphic animation as seen in *Bagpuss* (1974). © Smallfilms/BBC	178
8.8	Page 1 of an early draft of a *Bagpuss* (1974) episode called 'Mill'. © Oliver Postgate Family Archive	184
8.9	Page 2 of an early draft of a *Bagpuss* (1974) episode called 'Mill'. © Oliver Postgate Family Archive	185
8.10	Page 3 of an early draft of a *Bagpuss* (1974) episode called 'Mill'. © Oliver Postgate Family Archive	186
8.11	Page 3 of a revised, clean draft of a *Bagpuss* (1974) episode called 'The Mouse Mill'. © Oliver Postgate Family Archive	187
8.12	Page 4 of a revised, clean draft of a *Bagpuss* (1974) episode called 'The Mouse Mill'. © Oliver Postgate Family Archive	188
9.1	The unambiguous attribution of *Life on Earth Perhaps* (1985) as a Smallfilms work. *Life on Earth Perhaps* (1985) directed by Oliver Postgate. © Smallfilms. All rights reserved	197
9.2	Apple, unsupervised by Marchpane, plays near the flame in *Tottie: The Story of a Dolls' House* (1984). © Goldcrest Films International/Smallfilms/BBC	202

9.3	Birdie deliriously lunges to save Apple from the flame in *Tottie: The Story of a Dolls' House* (1984). © Goldcrest Films International/Smallfilms/BBC	202
9.4	Mixed reactions to the sight of Birdie's melted remains in *Tottie: The Story of a Dolls' House* (1984). © Goldcrest Films International/Smallfilms/BBC	203
9.5	Despite the traumatic scenes, Marchpane remains unmoved in *Tottie: The Story of a Dolls' House* (1984). © Goldcrest Films International/Smallfilms/BBC	203
9.6	The art of war as seen in *Life on Earth Perhaps* (1985) directed by Oliver Postgate. © Smallfilms. All rights reserved	208
9.7	The human cost of modern war as seen in *Life on Earth Perhaps* (1985) directed by Oliver Postgate. © Smallfilms. All rights reserved	208
9.8	Red faces Blue in *Life on Earth Perhaps* (1985) directed by Oliver Postgate. © Smallfilms. All rights reserved	210
9.9	Red hits Blue in *Life on Earth Perhaps* (1985) directed by Oliver Postgate. © Smallfilms. All rights reserved	210
9.10	Blue hits Red in *Life on Earth Perhaps* (1985) directed by Oliver Postgate. © Smallfilms. All rights reserved	211
9.11	Mutually assured destruction as seen in *Life on Earth Perhaps* (1985) directed by Oliver Postgate. © Smallfilms. All rights reserved	212
9.12	Nuclear Winter as seen in *Life on Earth Perhaps* (1985) directed by Oliver Postgate. © Smallfilms. All rights reserved	212
9.13	Stockpiled nuclear weapons as seen in *Life on Earth Perhaps* (1985) directed by Oliver Postgate. © Smallfilms. All rights reserved	214
9.14	The penny begins to drop in *Life on Earth Perhaps* (1985) directed by Oliver Postgate. © Smallfilms. All rights reserved	214
9.15	Disjunkment as seen in *Life on Earth Perhaps* (1985) directed by Oliver Postgate. © Smallfilms. All rights reserved	215
9.16	Future world peace as imagined in *Life on Earth Perhaps* (1985) directed by Oliver Postgate. © Smallfilms. All rights reserved	215
9.17	Pinny and Victor as seen in *Pinny's House* (1986). © Smallfilms/BBC	218
10.1	Third Party Production's interpretation of *Noggin*. © Third Party Productions	229
10.2	Starting Ivor's engine in the iPad game. © Dreadnought Games	233

10.3	The minigame that challenges gamers to set Ivor's controls correctly. © Dreadnought Games	234
10.4	The Merioneth and Llantisilly Railway shown in the BBC's *Ivor the Engine* Annual of 1978	236
10.5	The final mapping of Ivor's Railway as drawn by Peter Firmin for the 2014 board game. © Esdevium/Surprised Stare Games	236
10.6	Distinct foreground, midground, and background focal points as seen in the new *Clangers* (2015–present). © Coolabi Productions/Smallfilms/Sprout	240
10.7	The BBC's *Clangers*-themed 404 webpage error screen (accessed in June 2021)	243
A.1	Total number of responses to a multiple-choice question that asked: 'Oliver Postgate and Peter Firmin created many imaginative worlds, but how many of these Smallfilms TV shows have you seen?'	246
A.2	Total responses to a single-choice question that asked: 'What is your favourite Smallfilms TV show?'	247
B.1	A sample script page from the production of *Alexander Mouse*. © The Oliver Postgate Family Archive	249
B.2	A sample script page from the production of *Ivor the Engine*. © The Oliver Postgate Family Archive	250
B.3	A sample script page from the production of *The Seal of Neptune*. © The Oliver Postgate Family Archive	251
B.4	A sample script page from the production of *Pingwings*. © The Oliver Postgate Family Archive	252
B.5	A sample script page from the production of *Clangers*. © The Oliver Postgate Family Archive	253

Tables

8.1	The rather limited screen credits associated with *Bagpuss* (1974). © Smallfilms/BBC	172
A.1	After coding the survey responses to remove non-significant words, this table shows the most frequently used words of significance by show	247
A.2	Comparison of approximate animation screen time	248

ACKNOWLEDGMENTS

Much of the writing of this book coincided with the first eighteen months of the Covid-19 pandemic. So, I want to acknowledge the many – far too many to mention – large and small gestures that family, friends, and colleagues made to ease the task of writing a book from home, through multiple phases of UK national lockdown, home-schooling, and working from home.

My thanks go to the Leverhulme Trust for their award of funding to support this project. Quite simply, without this funding a book of this ambition (spanning multiple archives and involving a substantial amount of fieldwork) would not have been possible.

I am truly grateful to both the Firmin and Postgate families for not only opening their family archives to me, but also for being generous hosts and allowing me to spend time in their homes and supplying rivers of tea.

Without the good will of the many interviewees that helped to bring the oral history of Smallfilms to life I would have been sunk. Over the several years that these interviews were conducted, some took place in person, some over the phone, and some on Zoom, Skype, and Teams as we all adjusted to Covid-19. In every instance, regardless of format, the conversations never felt hurried, so I thank my interviewees for this generous gift of time.

The staff at both the BBC and BFI archives really made my life very easy with their supreme knowledge and willingness to chase down long-forgotten details. Special thanks in particular are reserved for Kate O'Brien, from the BBC's Written Archives, who went out of her way on multiple occasions to help me.

I'm also very grateful to a number of friends who spent time discussing various aspects of this project, in particular: Rachel Moseley, Mitch Robertson, Steve Henderson, Nichola Dobson, Christopher Holliday ('the other Chris'), Caroline Ruddell, and Paul Ward.

Finally, I want to thank my editorial team at the BFI Publishing, namely Anna Coatman and Veidehi Hans, who have helped me steer through the choppy seas of Covid-19 book writing with endless patience, expertise, and support.

Chapter 1

INTRODUCTION

> I was also invited to give a couple of informal seminars to the Animation School at the RCA. These were so informal that they could hardly have been said to happen, but they taught me more than I really wanted to know about the way in which our simple craft had been inflated into a maniac pretentious pseudo-art.[1]
>
> —Oliver Postgate

At the start of a book dedicated to the serious study of the works of Smallfilms it is important to confront these views voiced by Oliver Postgate about the craft – animated storytelling – that brought him, and the viewers looking on, so much joy over multiple decades.[2] As an intellectual with pedigree spanning the creative, practical, and political spheres, the quotation that opens this book presents a moment of sharp dissonance.[3] Yet, at the same time, it reflects an important characteristic that runs through much of Postgate's work: an unrelenting desire to tell *his* story in *his* words. Confronted with the reality that others – and other intellectuals at that – were keen to take seriously an art form that, by his own admission, he had mastered only to the extent that enabled him to achieve his many creative visions via the path of least resistance, he retreated into spikey riposte.[4] To be clear, I have not written this book in a sensationalist manner, offering some trumped-up character assassination of Postgate to sell copies. Quite the opposite, for as you will see, I have employed a variety of research methods (detailed below) to provide a (re)balanced account of Postgate's work and how it contributed to the collaborative framework of Smallfilms more broadly.

Why, then, start with such a provocative quotation? The answer is threefold. First, it serves to emphasize the point made above that Postgate was a storyteller par excellence and this desire to create and control narrative extended to the world of Smallfilms beyond the frame of the small screen. Consequently, the multiple creative individuals who collaborated with Postgate over almost three decades – none more so than his partner-in-creation Peter Firmin – have seen their contributions recognized and regulated through the prism of Postgate's own autobiographical activity. Secondly, throughout his life, Firmin's own humility and reluctance to demand an equal share of the spotlight, as well as his own commitment to a similar 'it is what it is, we didn't over think it' attitude towards their creative labours, has served to support and reinforce the Postgate-centric version of Smallfilms history that circulates today. Lastly, there is the uncharitable description of Smallfilms' works as 'our simple craft', which emphatically mischaracterizes the unrelenting energy, continual creative reinvention, practical ingenuity, story craft, and ambition shown by Firmin and Postgate throughout their work together.[5] Therefore, this book offers an alternative to the prevailing – and unnecessarily narrow – Postgateian version of Smallfilms history.

Throughout the researching and writing of this book three core imperatives have shaped this endeavour:

1. to respond to the increasing risk of losing access to oral histories linked to the work of Smallfilms, and the wealth of perspectives that they bring, thereby prompting me to interview as many surviving Smallfilms collaborators as possible;
2. to use these newly gathered interviews, along with hitherto underused archival materials (both public and private), to expand our understanding of Smallfilms history; and
3. to better understand, through an analysis of Smallfilms' animated works and a 1,100-response audience survey, why the works of Firmin and Postgate have enjoyed such lasting appeal.

These core objectives are the foundation upon which this book rests. Stemming from this are nine chapters (not including this introduction), arranged in a loose chronology, each tackling a distinct moment of Smallfilms history. Informed by the data gathered as part of the primary research process (see Appendix A), these chapters, where appropriate, engage with themes identified as recurrent sources of appeal.

This current chapter sets out the underpinning agenda of the book, four important frames of reference, and the book's methodological footing. Chapter 2 starts with a discussion of Postgate and Firmin's creation of Smallfilms, before moving on to consider the development of their first animated series, *Ivor the Engine* (1959–64, 1975–7). Running throughout this chapter is a consideration of whimsical authenticity. Chapter 3 details the continued evolution of the Smallfilms project and focuses on the production of *The Saga of Noggin the Nog* (1959–65, 1982), with attention given to the theme of world building. Chapter 4 analyses a pivotal moment in the evolution of Smallfilms, when Firmin and Postgate transitioned from 2D cut-out cardboard animation to 3D stop-motion model-based animation and focuses on the shows *The Seal of Neptune* (1960), *The Mermaid's Pearls* (1962), and *Pingwings* (1961–5). Chapter 5 responds, in part, to the developing relationship between the BBC and Smallfilms and documents the creation of *The Pogles* (1965) and *Pogles' Wood* (1966–8). Taking the phrase low-angle persons, which was used by Postgate to describe the useful storytelling viewpoint afforded by the Pogles, this chapter engages with concept and establishes low-angle as a theme that can be seen to run throughout the works of

Smallfilms more broadly. Chapter 6 details the production of *Clangers* (1969–74) and considers the theme of technology. Here, the significance of technology is viewed from several perspectives, including the impact of changing television technology in the UK, how the overt low-tech construction of the show became a source of spectatorial appeal, and how Firmin and Postgate repeatedly engaged with the topic of the Space Race of the late 1960s and early 1970s. Chapter 7 serves to revise the Smallfilms timeline by providing hitherto absent detail about the marginalized show *Sam on Boffs' Island* (1972–3). Chapter 8 provides an opportunity to reconsider the development of *Bagpuss* (1974), arguably Smallfilms' most iconic production, in order to establish a clearer picture of its collaborative creation. The theme of bricolage provides a framework through which to look more closely at the collaborative contributions of Charlotte Firmin, Joan Firmin, John Faulkner, Linda Birch, and Sandra Kerr to the work of Smallfilms. Chapter 9 charts the final years of Firmin and Postgate's screen activity under the banner of Smallfilms. Challenging the prevailing view of this period as one of decline, this chapter highlights the continued ambition of Postgate and Firmin through their final works: *Tottie: The Story of a Dolls' House* (1984), *Life on Earth Perhaps* (1985), and *Pinny's House* (1986). Chapter 10 concludes our study of Smallfilms, bringing the discussion up to date, and revealing the ways that the themes of adaptation and renewal inform a range of recent Smallfilms reboots and spin-offs.

The themes of whimsical authenticity (Chapter 2), world building (Chapter 3), low-angle persons (Chapter 5), technology (Chapter 6), and bricolage (Chapter 8), which have been identified by my own close textual readings combined with the prevailing views returned by the survey data, are interwoven throughout the works of Smallfilms. The decision to tackle each theme separately, using specific Smallfilms productions as case studies, simply reflects a desire to establish these themes in a clear and systematic way. As the reader will find, cross-referencing to these themes occurs throughout the book as a whole, with the intention being to highlight the pervasive nature of these deep thematic undercurrents.

Frames of reference

Having established the underpinning agenda of this book, readers will find it helpful to take a moment to consider four key frames of reference that inform our understanding of Firmin and Postgate's work: the national context within which they operated, the significance of nostalgia and memory, the televisuality of their work, and the aesthetic particularities of their animation. These themes cut across the entirety of Smallfilms' output, so it is helpful to discuss them here, at the outset. It is also important to make clear that these themes are highlighted as a way to acknowledge their importance as frames of reference, but not as hard borders serving to contain or limit the analyses that follows throughout the book as a whole.

'Britishness'

Given the increasingly fractured notion of 'national identity', which, in recent years, has fuelled Brexit-related social division, the emboldening of far-right groups, and heated debates about how Britain's deeply problematic colonial history should be confronted, I would rather move this book away from the unhelpful narrowness and divisiveness of 'Britishness' as a conceptual touchstone.[6] However, as a proud Northerner now living in the South, as someone from a lower-middle-class background now bestowing an upper middle-class upbringing on my children, and as someone who detests un-critical, tub-thumping expressions of national pride, yet gives in to regrettable tribalism when the football is on, I simultaneously embody and confront the contradictoriness and complexity of Britishness on a daily basis and at a personal level. In a book about Smallfilms, it is impossible not to pick up the prism of Britishness and hold it to one's eye, if only to address it so that we might move beyond it.

Comedian Stewart Lee, a prolific interrogator of the contemporary British psyche, noted the following in a 2014 article for the *Big Issue*:

> Smallfilms makes me naively nostalgic for a world before free-market doctrines and focus groups, when a publicly funded body gave two indefatigable eccentrics and, we now realise, avatars of a distinctly British folk art, licence to pursue their particular and quietly subversive ideas, unencumbered by crass commercial expectations.[7]

Before concluding that in an age when 'our rulers struggle for a definition of Britishness' they 'could do worse than prescribe a study of the quirky, inventive, adaptable, liberal and profoundly humane back catalogue of Smallfilms'.[8] Lee is not alone in responding to the work of Smallfilms in this way, with many other mainstream publications spotlighting 'Britishness' as an important characteristic of Smallfilms' work.[9]

Some of the responses gathered through the audience survey also align with Lee's characterization. Featuring the words 'British', 'Britishness', and 'English' eighty-eight times, the responses suggested the various ways that these loaded terms can apply to the work of Smallfilms. Starting with the more matter-of-fact perspective that the works of Smallfilms are indelibly etched into collective British memory, some responses noted: 'Bagpuss and Clangers are both so iconicly [sic] British they're hard to not know' (Respondent 156); 'So British, so charming, so creative and iconic' (R198); and 'I like the innocence and the stop motion animation. It is quintessentially British and perhaps a bit crap – but I love it for that!' (R506). Others echoed Lee's focus on the quirkily inventive nature of Smallfilms: 'eccentricity and charm' (R22); 'Charm and British eccentricity' (R245); 'Charming, British and quirky' (R302); and 'Creativity, warmth, childhood wonder, inventiveness, Britishness' (R521). While others hint at a more layered, era-specific view of 'Britishness': 'Collectively Smallfilms gave me a sense of 1970s British (middle class) aesthetic which by the early 80s when they were still on TV a lot, could be contrasted against the newer British animation coming through to kids' TV' (R215); 'a particularly British tradition of animation and children's programming' (R174); and 'lots of earthy colours and the whole thing felt serene and British, a contrast to American content being imported then' (R744). Whereas some respondents began to engage with the slipperiness of 'Britishness' when used to refer to some sense of dominion: 'It's very British (not that I'm patriotic) but it makes me nostalgic' (R936); 'And when I say British, I mean English really, but the kind of English that unthinkingly thinks it's British. I suspect I always understood at some level these were very English programmes' (R215); and 'A touch of British – Kentish mischief?' (R288).

These responses confirm the prismatic nature of characterizing the works of Smallfilms as quintessentially British, whereby the individual perspectives, experiences, and expectations that we each bring will inevitably lead us to see the 'Britishness' of Smallfilms in different ways. Rather than revealing some perfectly measurable quality, these responses highlight the ambiguities – and potential shortcomings – of adopting such a register. Yes, we can find plenty of references to Heath Robinson-esque (or Oliver Postgateian) invention, dozens of cups of tea, an abundance of crafted items, literal scenes set in English villages and countryside, and a polite, gentle sensibility that runs throughout the writing, but are these superficial elements truly representative of 'Britishness'? For some viewers, and for some respondents to the audience survey, the answer will be yes. Yet, for others, being 'British' will mean something much more complicated and quite possibly less wholesome. Promoting a monocultural view of 'Britishness' runs the risk of marginalizing, or even erasing, the experiences of those who might identify with that second perspective.

Writing on the subject of national identity, Geoff Payne notes how it is a social division that operates at several levels:

> At the broadest level, it marks the boundaries that divide 'our nation' from those of others, and shapes the meanings that are attached to borders and those who do not live or were not born here. Within the British archipelago of islands it marks significant differences between the nations that together make up the UK state of Great Britain and Northern Ireland. With hindsight, its remarkable feature is that it has held together for so long, given the significance of national identities in these islands.[10]

Here, Payne usefully highlights the tensions – if not outright antagonisms – that still persist within the 'United' Kingdom. Perhaps then it is reasonable to argue that the work of Smallfilms is 'British', given the supreme – yet self-invested – storytelling power that the English Postgate and Firmin wield over their fictional dominion, which happens to include the top left-hand corner of Wales, a Scottish Hamish, an Irish Leprechaun, and several echoes of British Colonialism.

It is even more telling, though, that only eighty-eight references (contained within fifty-seven unique responses) were made to 'British', 'Britishness', and 'English' across the 1,100 total responses recorded in the survey. This comparatively small percentage (approximately 5 per cent) suggests that the overwhelming majority of responses (approximately 95 per cent) didn't value notions of 'Britishness' as being of sufficient significance to mention when discussing the appeal of Smallfilms works. As indicated above, while superficial associations to 'British' iconography are present in the works of Smallfilms, and shows such as *Bagpuss* and *Clangers* occupy a position in the UK's popular imagination, the concept of 'Britishness' represents something of an interpretational cul-de-sac. Given the fact that many of Smallfilms' works have enjoyed international distribution, with *Clangers*, at the time of writing, being the latest production to find new overseas audiences by debuting in China, it strikes me that the lasting appeal of Smallfilms resides in factors more universal than some hazy sense of 'Britishness'.[11]

Nostalgia and memory

Looking at the survey responses across two questions, one that asked respondents to describe what they liked about their favourite Smallfilms show, and another that asked what Smallfilms meant to them in more general terms, amongst the most common words were: (1) 'childhood' / 'child' (394 / 150 instances), (3) 'memories' (204), and (6) 'nostalgia' (131).[12] Similarly, conducting a word frequency review across seventy-five press articles returned by the British Library and Google's newspaper archives when searching the keyword 'Smallfilms' reveals a similar pattern, with the words 'childhood' and 'nostalgia' occurring at least once in each article.[13] Recent scholarship has also considered the function of nostalgia in relation to the work of Smallfilms, with Mark Whitehead suggesting that it has become 'a cliché for thirtysomethings to get misty eyed about the TV of their childhood, but Small Films [sic] output resists mere nostalgia',[14] and Kristyn Gorton and Joanne Garde-Hansen offering the example of a mother hesitating to introduce her son to *Bagpuss* because she 'wouldn't want him to not like it', and through his potential rejection of the show thereby dilute her own positive and nostalgic memories of *Bagpuss*.[15] Of all the extant Smallfilms scholarship – of which there is not a huge amount – it is Rachel Moseley who offers the most developed analysis. Invoking the work of Svetlana Boym (2001), and her reflective framework of reading nostalgia as an active, imperfect, and at times alienating way of remembering, Moseley highlights the risk of adopting an uncritical view of nostalgia, noting how the works of Smallfilms (and also Gordon Murray Puppets and FilmFair):

> emerge in a period frequently described as one of social upheaval (for some; of liberation, for others), and the enchanted, hand-made worlds they conjure look back to a moment of 'clear borders and values' (including a particular imagining of comforting, middle-class motherhood) before second-wave feminism and the other civil rights movements of their periods of production.[16]

In response, Moseley's book *Hand-made Television* (2016) seeks to 'unsettle the flattening out of these programmes through generalised notions of nostalgia'.[17]

The act of remembering the works of Smallfilms is aided, in part, by ongoing licensing and distribution agreements, first, in 2002, with the Dragons' Friendly Society, then in 2008, following Postgate's death, with Coolabi. As Stacey Abbott writes of these arrangements: 'Being a division of a global media outlet ensures a long "tail" for such apparently ramshackle productions.'[18] Ramshackle they might be, but it is worth noting that Coolabi came close to selling their Smallfilms licensing rights for £4.2 million in 2011.[19] With intellectual property valued as highly as this, it should come as no surprise that in addition to the TV shows themselves, hundreds – if not thousands – of Smallfilms tie-ins have been produced over the decades, both officially and unofficially, to please eager consumers.[20]

An aspect of this conversation that has remained ever-present, but, up to this point, been left implicit, is the role of collective memory (as the Social Sciences would characterize it) or shared individual memories (as psychologists might describe it) as an evolving social network that facilitates social contagion – the spread of memory. In 2009, Alin Coman et al. provided a useful comparison of how the notion of collective memory has been understood and applied within critical analysis to date across the disciplines of Social Science and Psychology. For Coman et al., Social Sciences scholars 'see commemorations and memorials as the *sine qua non* of the field, in that they are no doubt publicly available symbols that exist in large part to preserve the past'.[21] Meaning that 'the central question for students of collective memory is: how does society construct and maintain these symbols? They study the politics of memory, the memory practices of a community, and the resistance a community might raise to what is often the efforts of authority figures to shape a community's memory.'[22] While for psychologists, the role of schemas – individualized patterns of thought that allow us to organize our acquired knowledge in structured ways – occupy an important intermediary step, between the study of cognition at an individual level and the formation of 'shared individual memories'. Building on Frederick Bartlett's (1993) work on memory, Coman et al. suggest that 'memories are products of remembering, not stored representations of the past', which, depending on the context in which the memory is being generated, may draw upon any number of cognitive schemas, and therefore is not retrieved 'as a memory might be in a computer, but built out of the interaction between what is beneath the surface of the skin and the world beyond this surface'.[23] It is here that Coman and colleagues find the common ground between the social scientists and psychologists when it comes to understanding collective memory, suggesting that 'memorials can potentially change the memories of visitors one at a time, and thereby collectively all those who visit', meaning that if the 'change in individual memory is substantial, and similar across visitors, a memorial can effectively shape the collective memory'.[24]

This constant push and pull between individual and collective memory is particularly relevant when considering how the works of Smallfilms are *remembered* today. As the survey data reveals, many respondents presented opinions of shows such as *Bagpuss*, *Clangers*, and *Pogles' Wood*, for example, based entirely on memory. Given what has been noted above, it is perhaps unsurprising then that a general uniformity can be found in the responses. In addition to the high recurrence of words such 'childhood' (544 occurrences), 'memories' (204), and 'nostalgia' (131), many other positive words (and their stemmed variants) featured prominently, such as: 'lovely' (227), 'liked' (157), 'happy' (152), 'gentle' (82), 'charming' (80), and 'comforting' (69).[25] Yet, there is a conspicuous reluctance across the 1,100 responses to offer negative views of the works produced by Smallfilms. Even when asked to explain their choice of least favourite Smallfilms production, less than half of the respondents were able to identify a Smallfilms work that they disliked, and within the responses from those respondents that did identify a show their views were typically quite tame, with most negative responses focusing on personal motivations rather than issues rooted within the shows themselves. For example, multiple respondents pointed to their own lack of memory, or that they just preferred the other shows they had identified, or that they found the show in question a bit boring. The strongest negative response centred around the Witch that terrorized Mr and Mrs Pogle in *The Pogles* (see Chapter 3 for a more developed discussion of the Witch), with the words 'creepy' (5 occurrences) and 'scary' (8) being used to characterize her. While *Tottie: The Story of a Dolls' House* elicited the most memorable negative comment, with respondent number 279 writing: 'OMG *Tottie* land of nightmare fuel with scary doll murder' – which is a reasonable response given the malevolence of Marchpane.

It is not my intention to look for – and artificially amplify – things that do not exist within the works of Smallfilms, but rather the objective here, at the outset of this book, is to establish the ways that an unmistakable uniformity regarding the collective memory of Smallfilms has developed over time. As Michael Kammen writes: 'Nostalgia, with its wistful memories, is essentially history without guilt. … Although written history can never be complete, memory must inevitably be much less so. History and memory are not merely fractured. They are frequently at odds.'[26] Understanding memory and nostalgia in the ways outlined above, as active elements of cognition that work to structure our interaction with the world both individually and collectively, will help us as we move through our analyses of Smallfilms' many productions. Throughout this book, mixed research methods are used to navigate the inevitable biases that creep into a history of this kind. While nostalgia is undeniably an important shared experience for many when revisiting or remembering the works of Smallfilms, the homogenizing force of this collective nostalgia only takes us so far when attempting to better understand the lasting appeal of Smallfilms' works.

Smallfilms on television

To draw attention to the fact that the works of Smallfilms are, first and foremost, televisual texts might seem like a rather redundant activity. However, fully understanding their status as television episodes and series allows us to better understand the contexts of their original production, their broadcast, and why Smallfilms remains relatively neglected within extant scholarship.

If we think of television today, many readers will no doubt share an abstracted, distributed vision of what television has become. With shows and eyeballs no longer fixed to the television set, we are now able – internet connection permitting – to consume televisual content across a range of devices, wherever we choose, in a time-shifted manner. The development of on-demand services from companies such as Amazon, Disney, and Netflix, and highly popular amateur and consumer content platforms such as Instagram, TikTok, and YouTube, only serve to place extra stress on the role and place of 'television' in the twenty-first century. Furthermore, the *television set* of today, in all its flat, ultra-high-definition glory, dominating rooms with their 40+ inch span, may only occasionally bring real-time television broadcasts into the domestic space, instead functioning more as a multipurpose screen to play video games, conduct video calls with friends and family, and stream films. However, this was not the televisual experience for Postgate, Firmin, and the contemporary audiences of their Smallfilms productions.

Looking at the decades preceding the formation of Smallfilms, it is worth noting that while television services began in Britain in 1936, due to the prohibitive cost of early television sets, full 'investment in transmission and reception facilities did not occur until the late 1940s and early 1950s, but the growth was thereafter very rapid'.[27] Growing from less than 20,000 operational television sets in Britain in early 1947, largely clustered within Greater London, to 85 per cent of the population having domestic access to television by the early 1960s, with 10.5 million licenses issued and approximately sixteen hours of programming being made available to the majority of the UK viewership.[28] This dramatic increase in television ownership and viewing had a profound impact on 'domestic space, time, and other routine arrangements as TV "colonised" home life, "challenged" the centrality of the hearth, the wireless and the parlour and restructured the pre-existing flows of domestic leisure culture inside and outside the home'.[29]

While the physical size of television sets reduced during the time that Postgate and Firmin were making programmes, with the bulky cabinet-housed sets of the late 1950s giving way to sleeker, but still sizeable, sets of the late 1960s, the definition of the image increased, with the earlier 405 line black-and-white screens of the 1950s being replaced through the 1960s by slightly larger colour sets with screens capable of better image clarity. However, these newer television sets still relied on analogue broadcast technology, meaning that the quality of the image could vary daily, depending on localized environmental factors such as the weather and/or potential obstructions between the set's receiver and the nearby transmitter. These technological factors, coupled with the (slowly) evolving programming conventions of the 1950s to 1970s, provided the context for the oft-repeated distinction coined by John Ellis to describe the spectatorial difference between cinema and television:

> Cinema offers a large-scale, highly detailed and photographic image to a spectator who is engaged in an activity of intense and relatively sustained attention to it. Broadcast TV offers a small image of low definition, to which sound is crucial in

holding the spectator's attention. The spectator glances rather than gazes at the screen; attention is sporadic rather than sustained.[30]

While Ellis's distinction may not feel quite so apposite today, given the recent developments in *television* technology and viewership, his distinction does provide a useful framework through which to understand the viewing practices of audiences watching television during the time that Postgate and Firmin were active.

Another distinction that Ellis makes is between the narrative structures that served to distinguish cinema and television at the time that he was writing. Ellis suggests that these different forms of attention, the gaze of cinema, building on Laura Mulvey's work,[31] and the glance of television, enabled 'different modes of narrative to develop in each medium'.[32] He writes:

> Entertainment cinema characteristically adopts a tightly organised narration, organised around a particular problem or disruption that is resolved at the ending of the film. Events and characters are integrated into the continuous narration of this progression in its logical sequence. Broadcast TV normally does not adopt this self-enclosed narrational form. It is more concerned with open-ended forms like the series and serial, which run through a number of variations on the same basic narrative problem.[33]

This is a pertinent observation to the work of Firmin and Postgate, given that the bulk of their work offers narrative development in serial form. However, many Smallfilms works, such as *Ivor the Engine*, *Noggin the Nog*, *The Seal of Neptune*, and *The Mermaid's Pearls*, for example, provide sequences of introductory narration that recap events from previous episodes so that viewers are not disadvantaged if they have missed an episode or two – thereby allowing the episodes to become standalone to a degree. While *Clangers* also contains elements that develop in serial form – namely the steady expansion of the details known about the Clangers' moon and its fellow inhabitants – each episode starts with a passage of philosophical rumination rather than narrative recap.

It is also important to consider the institutional contexts within which Firmin and Postgate worked, with their work being commissioned and broadcast on both the BBC and Associated-Rediffusion. Different operational agendas informed the programming of the BBC and Associated-Rediffusion at the time of Smallfilms' inception, with the BBC guided by the Royal Charter, and Associated-Rediffusion, as a regional branch of the newly formed independent television network, bound by the needs to sustain commercial viability.[34] Crystalized during his tenure as the first Director General, John Reith gave shape to the BBC's public service remit, expanding the corporation's founding commitment to be a 'means of education and entertainment'[35] to the more familiar pledge to provide a 'means of information, education and entertainment'.[36] Since Postgate and Firmin produced work predominantly for BBC broadcast, it comes as no surprise to find the 'Reithian Trinity' permeating much of their work.

The final point that must be made is the invisible quality of certain types of television within extant scholarship. As Brett Mills notes,

> As we are academics, so we are audiences. It is unsurprising that we commonly choose to write about those programmes that we find interesting, or addictive, or pleasurable. Indeed, it is often the case that it is those interests that spark our desire to work as academics in the first place. And it is that enthusiasm which commonly informs our teaching and becomes an impetus to our work as a whole.[37]

Considering a range of factors that might result in certain programmes to become invisible, Mills provides a rallying cry to scholars to encourage the recovery of this invisible body of work. On this point, I agree with Moseley that the work of Smallfilms has remained largely invisible to scholars as consequence of the reasons outlined by Mills.

Mills also highlights issues of access as an important contributing factor when considering the invisibility of certain television works. As Dick Fiddy writes, 'early technical difficulties associated with the recording of live television programmes and the later injudicious wiping and junking policies of major British broadcasters has meant that hundreds of thousands of hours of precious television material is missing from the official UK television archives'.[38] This significant blind spot presents a very real barrier for UK television historians, and for scholars wishing to study the complete work of Smallfilms with the objective of making it more visible, this has been an obstacle that, until the publication of this book, has been impossible to fully overcome. Only as a result of the primary research carried out for this book have complete copies of *Sam on Boffs' Island* and *Pinny's House* been rediscovered (with the former having been long misplaced by the BBC and BFI archives until my viewing request was made, and the latter having resided unseen in the Firmin family's possession for several decades). These lacunas in the Smallfilms – and televisual – historical record can now be addressed.

The animation of Smallfilms

The animation seen across the works of Smallfilms is limited. Limited in a very literal sense, reflecting the economical constraints faced by Firmin and Postgate, and limited in the conceptual sense whereby Postgate deployed his animation in a very measured and calculated way to achieve the maximum impact from their labour. This is an important clarification to make, as neither should be seen as a negative criticism, since the economic and practical constraints faced by Smallfilms were fully embraced by both Postgate and Firmin and were interwoven into the fabric of their creative process.

The term limited animation is more commonly used to describe the style of animation popularized by United Productions of America (UPA) within the context of hand-drawn cel-based animation, which grew from a combination of factors: wanting to produce animation in a cost-conscious way and wanting to resist the push towards realism being promoted by Disney. Nichola Dobson notes that while 'limited animation can save time and money, it also creates a particular stylized effect on the finished animation'.[39] Despite working across both 2D and 3D types of animation, Postgate's animation continually adopts this limited approach, thereby stylizing the studio's animation along the intersecting axes of economy and artistic choice. Postgate is shown reflecting on his animation practice in the BBC's 2009 *Time Shift* documentary 'Oliver Postgate: A life in Small Films':

> Animation wasn't so much an imitation of life – it was a punctuation of conversation. We always stayed on the one who was talking. It made for a very simple film that was very clear, and there were no unnecessary things going on all around the edges. If I'm going to say something to you then I'm going to do it with a certain amount of gestures, in-between the times I'm completely still. This was how we managed to get through 120 seconds of footage a day, when most studios were getting through 10 seconds. We'd never move a mouth, we'd change the expression, because people were watching the hands.[40]

This approach to animation remained constant even when Firmin and Postgate switched from 2D cardboard cut-out animation, where whole hand-drawn heads and limbs would be swapped between exposures, to stop-motion 3D model-based animation, where magnetically mounted elements (such as moustaches and eyebrows) could be swapped to generate the same expressive quality.

The sum effect of this approach is a style of animation that intersperses longer passages of stillness with briefer flurries of animation, all stitched together by the dialogue of the characters, sound effects, music, and Postgate's omnipresent narration. Postgate and Firmin also frequently employ fully static images, panning and scanning, zooming, and cutting to suggest animation or movement. It is my view that this stillness is of profound significance when attempting to unpack the appeal of Smallfilms' limited animation. While the study of stillness, the freeze frame, and what comes between frames has been tackled before,[41] the agendas of these preceding works has been to reveal absences, such as the absence of recognized labour or the absence of indexicality. In the case of Smallfilms' animation, the held poses, which are held for the maximum reasonable duration, afford extended opportunities for the viewer to appreciate the material qualities of the objects on-screen, and to cognitively unpick their handmade construction. Furthermore, upon seeing Postgate's animation for the first time, our spectatorial understanding of how his animation is going to unfold for the remainder of that episode, allows the troughs of stillness to rapidly fill with anticipation for the next burst of animation.

This frequent stillness, the cornerstone of the Smallfilms aesthetic, distinguishes the studio's animation from that of its contemporary competitors. Gordon Murray's *Camberwick Green* (1966), *Trumpton* (1967), and *Chigley* (1969) series offer the viewer a more fluid style, with more frames per second being animated, and offering up characters with animated mouths. Fittingly, given the show's trippy energy, Serge Danot and Ivor Wood's *The Magic Roundabout* (ORTF, 1964–74; BBC, 1965–77) is the opposite of still, with each sequence bursting with activity and secondary animation. Although less paroxysmal than *The Magic Roundabout*, the multiple series that Ivor Wood directed and/or animated for FilmFair, which included the likes of *The Herbs* (1968), *Hattytown Tales* (1969–73), *The Adventures of Parsley* (1970), *The Wombles* (1973–5), and *Paddington* (1975–86), all feature a restlessness, whereby characters often pace back and forth, wring or wave their hands, and shake and wobble their heads, as a means of giving each scene extra dynamism. While Bob Godfrey's boiling animation style found in *Roobard* (1974), stood in stark contrast to the stillness of Firmin and Postgate's visual aesthetic. Add into the mix the numerous anarchic and zany North American cartoons that increasingly shared television schedules with Smallfilms productions, including the following shows that shared the daily listings with *Bagpuss* in the mid-1970s: *Dastardly and Muttley* (1969–70),[42] *Scooby-Doo, Where Are You?* (1969–78),[43] *Tom and Jerry* (1940–67),[44] *Wacky Races* (1968),[45] and *The Yogi Bear Show* (1961–2),[46] it is clear that the stillness of Smallfilms marks an aesthetic resistance of the busier tone of the productions noted here.

Connected to this stillness, and the spectatorial space that it creates, is the significance of the handmade aesthetic that it serves to reveal and, at times, emphasize. In recent years, the interconnectedness of craft and animation has also been explored in detail by Moseley (2016) and by Caroline Ruddell and Paul Ward in their edited collection *The Crafty Animator Handmade, Craft-Based Animation and Cultural Value* (2019).[47] Underpinning both is an awareness of the legacies of William Morris, John Ruskin, and the Arts and Crafts Movement, whose works of the late nineteenth century persistently provides the foundation for contemporary interpretations of 'craft'. As Christopher Frayling notes, before several new directions in craft practice began to emerge through the 1960s and 1970s (such as 'action-crafts', avante-garde crafts, and 'funk-crafts'), for many this legacy meant:

- Crafts must be made of natural materials, preferably in beige;
- Crafts must be functional;
- Crafts must be the work of one person, perhaps featuring visible thumbprints or surface imperfections to prove it;
- Crafts must be the embodiment of a traditional design (unless of a musical instrument);
- Crafts must be in the 'artisan' rather than the 'fine art' tradition;
- Crafts must be rural products;
- Crafts must be untouched by fashion (which, it went without saying, meant 'badly made fashion')
- Crafts must be easily understood;
- Crafts must last, like a brogue shoe or a fine tweed;
- Crafts must be affordable (even if, like William Morris's work, affordable mainly by Oxbridge colleges, Anglican churches, and collectors);
- Above all, crafts must provide a *solace*, in a rapidly changing world.[48]

These values accord closely with the principles, practices, and productions of Smallfilms, with the final bullet point especially evocative of the spirit of stillness discussed above.

Moseley situates the idea of craft at the heart of her discussion of the handmade aesthetic of Smallfilms. While the overtly crafted-ness of Smallfilms' works is a source of significant appeal, Moseley reveals how this quality presents something of a double-edged sword. Despite the popular appeal of Smallfilms' crafted-ness, this craft aesthetic has resulted in a conspicuous occlusion from scholarly study.[49] Reflecting on this predicament, which extends to the works of FilmFair and Gordan Murray as well as Smallfilms, Moseley writes:

> Although they are mentioned in popular histories of children's television and the memoirs of their makers and key personnel working in the industry during the period, they do not appear in the broader works on British television history, and are rarely mentioned in scholarly accounts of children's television. The programmes are missing, too, from work within the field of Animation Studies, and this consistent absence from scholarly literature across disciplines tells us much about their positioning in various hierarchies of cultural value. As animated television for children, characterised by a craft aesthetic which situates them outside of the discourses of 'art', these programmes have not been considered appropriate objects of study in any of these fields.[50]

Thankfully, Moseley's work, like that collected by Ruddell and Ward, goes some way to correct this imbalance.

In the introduction of their book, Ruddell and Ward unpick the duality of the word 'crafty', noting how this term can be applied usefully to animation. Drawing a connection with the performance of magic tricks, 'crafty' animation often deceives or misdirects its audience, which is characterized by Ruddell and Ward as being a central paradox of animation: 'that it simultaneously reveals and conceals its own construction'.[51] Ruddell and Ward write:

> Animation that 'shows us the wires', or revels in engaging the audience through a self-conscious disclosure of (parts of) the technique as part of its appeal. This does not mean that every animation mechanically talks us through 'how it was made', but rather that the 'hand of the artist', whether explicitly and literally shown or merely implied, is often fundamental to the form.[52]

Clearly, this view tallies closely with the self-aware and often playful tone that runs through much of Smallfilms' work. Overall, while the animation of Smallfilms may not be the most ambitious or sophisticated in terms of the quantity of animation per second or the amount of secondary action on-screen at any one time, the aesthetic fostered between 1959 and 1986 by Postgate and Firmin offered a great deal to the spectator in terms of stillness and handmade appeal.

From the outset, the primary objective of this book – and the underpinning research – was to go beyond the established understanding of Smallfilms and the dominant Postgateian version of the studio's history, so as to widen the frame and thereby allow other creative voices and hitherto marginalized creative contributions to become a more visible, and in doing so, to establish a more nuanced and even-handed history of this significant studio. By taking the time to consider the overarching themes detailed above – of 'Britishness', nostalgia, and memory, the televisual nature of Smallfilms, and the animation of Smallfilms – we are now better equipped to develop an expanded account, chapter by chapter, of each Smallfilms production, the collaborative activities that supported them, their surrounding contexts, and the themes that permeate within and between these shows. To deliver on this agenda a mixed research methodology has been adopted.

Notes on mixed methodology

To achieve the stated objectives, I have combined primary and secondary research to establish a mixed-method approach. The secondary research focused on surveying extant scholarship and materials published in the public domain (newspapers, magazines, online content) to establish a general understanding of how Smallfilms has been understood up to this point in both a scholarly and popular sense. Building on this preparatory work, the primary research then employed archival analysis, semi-structured key informant interviews, textual analysis, and a quantitative/qualitative audience survey, to enable, through their use in combination, the discovery and generation of new knowledge. What follows now is a short reflection regarding the application of these primary research methods.

Archival analysis

Throughout the researching and writing of this book I consulted the BBC's Written Archives, the BFI's Special Collections, and the private archives of the Firmin and Postgate families. The volume of material held across these four archival repositories is substantial, encompassing a wide range of document types and spanning from the late 1950s through to the early 2000s. With differing standards of archival management between the institutionally held archives and those held privately, these documents were treated with caution, with every effort made to triangulate interpretative acts using the other methods outlined below. Furthermore, given the visible/invisible power dynamics that determine which documents are preserved, either by active or passive acts (e.g. the originator of the document in question placing value in that particular item, or the fact that the storage environment privileged the survival of certain documents over others), these archival materials can never be seen as representing a complete picture of the associated production context.[53]

Throughout this book, Ian W. Macdonald's concept of the 'screen idea' informs the use of archival sources. Macdonald writes:

> The screen idea has multiple possibilities, even if it is written down and specified in great detail by those developing it. It is usually described in writing, in standardized forms, but it need not be. It is usually shared and developed verbally by several people, according to appropriate norms and assumptions, but again it could be developed entirely by one person on their own. [...] The value of this term is that it allows reference to a singularity (such as a film), without specifying pre-conditions for the existence of that singularity. The only rules are those which have been set by the conditions of production, at that time and in that place. A new singularity exists when those who name it decide it is new – one screen idea is abandoned in favour of another. The 'screen idea' is a conceit, a way of talking about a potential screenwork, not a concrete screenwork.[54]

Macdonald's 'screen idea' enables engagement with the material artefacts of the archive, but in such a way as to dethrone the material documents in favour of the ideas that are running through them – or are absent from them – so that the archive can be read as both simultaneously pulling towards and away from the final screenwork. In the context of Smallfilms, this is a valuable framework to adopt, given the many archival absences that exist, which provide opportunities to pause and recognize afresh how the screen idea was being controlled and constructed in those moments of archival absence.

Textual analysis

Here, my approach to textual analysis, which is fundamentally rooted in the need offer a close study of the screenworks of Smallfilms, is informed by the work of Ethan Thompson and Jason Mittell. Acknowledging that when studying televisual works a 'text' might be a single episode, or two, or an entire series, Thompson and Mittel note how textual analysis enables a 'close reading' of a programme 'to make a broader argument about television and its relation to other cultural forces, ranging from representations of particular identities to economic conditions of production and distribution'.[55] The goal of such an endeavour, write Thompson and Mittell, 'is to connect the program to its broader contexts, and make an argument about the text's cultural significance, thus providing a model for how you can watch television with a critical eye'.[56]

Of course, relying solely on textual analysis is liable to result in an interpretation that is indebted, either reflexively or unconsciously, to the existing world view of the researcher. Such a shortcoming is alleviated by the fact that textual analysis is rarely conducted in isolation and is almost always accompanied by other research methods that serve a complementary role within the overarching research process, with each method serving to compensate for whatever shortcoming the other might have.

As noted above, Fiddy's work highlights how current access to historic television is often patchy, with many shows either permanently or temporary lost. This is the case for some Smallfilms works, with series such as *Sam on Boffs' Island* and *Pinny's House* only accessible in full via the BFI archives and the Firmin family's private archive, respectively. Whereas a tranche of black-and-white *Ivor the Engine* episodes currently remains in a limbo state, resting on film reels within the Postgate Family archives, but awaiting the necessary funding to facilitate digital resurrection. The uneven availability of the complete Smallfilms oeuvre gave the textual analysis an essential secondary purpose: to help plug these gaps. Where the shows exist in archives but not in the public domain, the textual accounts and analyses offered in this book help to increase awareness of these hard-to-reach series. In the case of the black-and-white *Ivor the Engine* episodes, thankfully a substantial amount of production material and correspondence survives in the Postgate family's private archive, so these archival materials provided a way of gaining an approximate sense of those inaccessible shows.

Key informant interviews

Given the core objectives to gather oral history and expand the Smallfilms historical narrative, it was essential to gain new first-hand perspectives to help move our discussion beyond the received history. Consequently, twenty-one individuals, who could be characterized as key informants, were interviewed between December 2016 and March 2021. Many of the individuals interviewed were consulted more than once to allow follow-up questions to be asked. Key informants can be defined as 'individuals who are articulate and knowledgeable about their community',[57] and in the context of this project these individuals were members of the Firmin and Postgate families as well as creative collaborators who worked on the shows in question. Crucially, these twenty-one individuals provided many of the classic elements anticipated when working with key informants, including 'detailed historical data, photographs, manuscripts, knowledge about interpersonal relationships, a contextual framework in which to observe and interpret behaviour, and a wealth of information about the nuances of everyday life'.[58]

As a method for gathering qualitative information, interviewing key informants has the potential to be a high-value activity. Equally, though, it must also be acknowledged that of all the research methods employed here this approach carries the highest potential for bias. Biases introduced inadvertently by the interviewer, whereby personal appearance, facial expression, tone of voice, misrecording of answers, and ill-considered responses all have the potential to misdirect the informant.[59] Additionally, failure of memory, given the time spans being covered, and the natural editorialization of memory that occurs as we recall details from the past, all stand as possible obstacles for the researcher that is wholly reliant on key informants. As Stephen Frosh eloquently couches it, the human subject is never a whole, since it 'is always riven with partial drives, social discourses that frame available modes of experience, ways of being that are contradictory and reflect the shifting allegiances of power as they play across the body and the mind'.[60]

By studying the information gleaned from the key informants alongside the information gained from the other, complimentary research methods, it has been possible to go some way to mitigate against many of the issues noted above. Additionally, a semi-structured approach was adopted for at least the first half of every interview, thereby helping to assist memory and lessen the impact of completely unplanned interviewer interaction, whilst still allowing a degree of conversational interaction to be established.[61] Given the underpinning objective of this book to expand the Smallfilms narrative to plug gaps in the historical record, each interview also culminated with a phase of unstructured interviewing. The benefit of this, as Robert Atkinson highlights, is the ability to prompt the revelation of hitherto unknown details related to 'the most important influences, experiences, circumstances, issues, themes, and lessons of a lifetime'.[62] To ensure that the details of these interviews could be sufficiently considered, each interview was recorded, with informed consent secured on each occasion.

Quantitative/qualitative survey data

A variety of approaches face the researcher interested in learning more about the views of a specific community or population – in this case the views of Smallfilms audiences. Of course, the gold standard method for probabilistic statistical analysis is to employ a stratified random sampling method when surveying populations, thereby ensuring that all representative subgroups (varying across age, gender, and race, for example) are sampled. Given the prohibitive costs of collecting a truly stratified random sample that is representative of the UK population, coupled with the fact that the primary objective of this survey was to gain original qualitative information about how the works of Smallfilms have been understood and valued, a convenience model of snowball sampling was adopted instead.[63] Therefore, the quantitative and qualitative data gathered from the 1,100 respondent sample is only used in this book to speak with confidence about the preferences expressed by the respondents, and as a basis from which to make general inferences. However, even after choosing a convenience method, careful consideration was still given to the design of the survey, the dissemination method, and actions that could be taken to limit the generation of overly biased data.

Thanks to the momentum generated by Martin Barker over a number of years, the mass-audience projects centred around *The Lord of the Rings* trilogy, *Alien*, *The Hobbit* trilogy, and *Game of Thrones* provide a wealth of insight not just about the audiences of the works in question but also about research design. Other approaches were considered, such as the focus group and text-in-action methods used by scholars such as Helen Wood and Beverley Skeggs,[64] but the narrow sample sizes of these earlier studies were not desirable, given the emphasis placed here on the collection on large volumes of qualitative data.

A key objective was to collect over one thousand responses, thereby giving the opportunity to conduct a stratified *post hoc* internal sampling if desired.

1. Introduction 19

While someway short of the response rates secured by *The Lord of the Rings* (c. 25,000 overall),[65] *The Hobbit* (36,109 overall),[66] and *Game of Thrones* (c. 10,000)[67] projects, which had the advantage of a network of international scholars to champion each project, the figure of 1,100 responses for this Smallfilms project aligned closely with the participation rates secured by the *Alien* (1,125 overall),[68] *Star Wars* (c. 2,200 overall),[69] and *Monty Python* (1,123 UK responses – 6,120 overall)[70] projects. Within the Smallfilms survey, respondents were wide-ranging in age, and while the gender split was not 50/50, the split of 61 per cent female to 36 per cent male (and 3 per cent identifying across the nonbinary spectrum) was satisfactory.

When designing the questions, I adopted a mixed model similar to the projects noted above, whereby the combination of quantitative (closed, multiple choice responses) and qualitative (open, free-text responses) data generated what Barker and Mathijs characterize as a 'richly structured combination of data and discourses'.[71] Having settled on Google Forms as the platform best-suited to my needs (given the ability to embed, and link to, the Google Form across multiple social media services and standalone websites, as well as the in-built and real-time analysis functions), I wanted to avoid the questionnaire being too long, a factor that Barker and Mathijs reflected on following the closure of their 29-question *Hobbit* survey that took on average twenty minutes to complete.[72] With this in mind, I designed a thirteen-question survey, which contained eight multiple-choice questions and five free-text questions, and which could be completed in approximately five to ten minutes, depending on the detail included in the free-text responses. Having conducted some informal testing with earlier drafts of the survey amongst friends, I received feedback that most felt uncomfortable when answering questions of a personal nature, such as age, gender, level of education, and profession, so in the interest of gaining maximum participation, I limited the personal questions to just age, the type of environment in which they grew up, and their gender. Having this qualitative data was enough to gain a sense of how representative the responses were in terms of age and gender. Of course, this was a decision taken to ensure maximum completion, and we will never know whether the completion rate would have been as strong if additional personal questions had been included (although, anecdotally, I did see some comments on social media about the survey complaining about the need to state their age – by year, nothing more – so it is possible that more personal questions would have prompted some respondents to walk away without finishing the survey).

As noted above, the goal was never to generate a truly random sample, but rather to gather a sizeable amount of qualitative information that could help to inform my thinking, and to help balance out the other research methods and their own shortcomings. With that objective in mind, I sought to gather responses in an organic way over an eighteen-month period (between June 2019 and December 2020), thereby avoiding the potential exclusion of respondents who might not have online access for a period of time, or who might work 9.00 am to 5.00 pm each day (and might therefore be unable to participate if the survey was conducted via telephone during office hours). Ultimately, successful dissemination of the survey relied on the snowball effect facilitated by the swirling eddies of social media interaction. A single message with a link to the survey, posted on public Facebook subgroups, Twitter, and via emails to several media-related mailing lists generated the initial propulsion, and from that point on the survey found a life of its own. Twitter proved the most effective dissemination platform, with spikes of activity happening every so often as different localized groups picked up the survey and spun it into a different Twitter orbit.

Conclusion

This introduction began by quoting Postgate's incredulity at how his 'simple craft had been inflated into a maniac pretentious pseudo-art'.[73] Of course, as noted above, these words constituted an attempt by Postgate to control the Smallfilms narrative. However, as this introduction has set out, the history of Smallfilms is far greater than the singular contributions of one man, Postgate, let alone the focused contributions of two men, Postgate and Firmin. Having established some important frames of reference and having reflected on the methodological underpinnings of this book, it is now time to begin our journey through the many worlds of Smallfilms.

Notes

1. Oliver Postgate, *Seeing Things: An Autobiography* (London: Sidgwick & Jackson, 2000), pp. 410–411.
2. The public's joyful celebration of Smallfilms is readily evident, while Postgate makes it clear on a number of occasions throughout his autobiography, *Seeing Things* (2000), that he also enjoyed many joyful moments engaged in making animated stories.
3. Postgate's creative acumen is evident through his televisual works, while his practical ability can be seen through his persistent invention of Heath Robinson-esque devices throughout his life, and his political awareness and impact can be seen through his committed lobbying for nuclear disarmament during the second half of the Cold War.
4. For ruminations on Smallfilms' position with the animated film tradition and his pragmatic attitude to achieving a level of animation competence, see Postgate, *Seeing Things*, p. 225 and p. 364.
5. I will be using 'Firmin and Postgate' and 'Postgate and Firmin' interchangeable throughout this book to both draw attention to the hierarchy implied when Postgate's name is presented first, despite the alphabetical incongruity, and as a way to softly rebalance this dynamic by allowing both names to be first in equal measure throughout the book.
6. For example, see Marlene Miglbauer, Susanne Kopf, and Veronika Koller (eds), *Discourses of Brexit* (Oxford: Routledge, 2019); Tom Wall, 'The Day Bristol Dumped its Hated Slave Trader in the Docks and a Nation Began to Search its Soul', *The Observer* 14 June 2020, https://www.theguardian.com/uk-news/2020/jun/14/the-day-bristol-dumped-its-hated-slave-trader-in-the-docks-and-a-nation-began-to-search-its-soul (accessed 29 October 2021).

7 Stewart Lee, 'The Clangers are Truly British', *The Big Issue* vol. 51 no. 1123 (6 October 2014), p. 19.
8 Lee, 'The Clangers are Truly British', p. 19.
9 See Harry Harris, 'The Christmas Animation: A Brief History', *New Statesman* 19 December 2018, https://www.newstatesman.com/culture/tv-radio/2018/12/christmas-animation-brief-history (accessed 29 October 2021); Viv Groskop, 'Peter Firmin, the Man Behind Bagpuss and the Clangers', *The Observer* 13 March 2016, https://www.theguardian.com/tv-and-radio/2016/mar/13/interview-peter-firmin-co-creator-bagpuss-the-clangers (accessed 29 October 2021); James Palmer, 'The Clangers Celebrate 50 Years since the Apollo 11 Moon Landing', *The Sunday Times* 14 July 2019, https://www.thetimes.co.uk/article/the-clangers-celebrate-50-years-since-the-apollo-11-moon-landing-wr0h5nnlx (accessed 29 October 2021).
10 David McCrone, 'National Identity', in Geoff Payne and Eric Harrison (eds), *Social Divisions: Inequality and Diversity in Britain* (Bristol: Policy Press), p. 303.
11 Anon, 'Clangers Launches on 10 Major VOD Channels Across China', 25 May 2021, https://www.skwigly.co.uk/clangers-launches-on-10-major-vod-channels-across-china/ (accessed 13 December 2021).
12 Chris Pallant, *Smallfilms: Audiences – data set* (June 2019–December 2020) – results limited to nouns over five letters in length: https://docs.google.com/forms/d/e/1FAIpQLSdMaX_ZiSZMJcx4joTt3vpfUtL-alvFqbFn9W0JXeY7Prb1jw/closedform (accessed 15 November 2021).
13 Search conducted 25 August 2020, reviewing articles from the following publications: BBC News, *Big Issue*, *Telegraph & Argus* (Bradford), *Fantasy/Animation* blog, *Flux Magazine*, Ipswich Council, *Kent Online*, National Trust, *Radio Times*, and *The Telegraph*.
14 Mark Whitehead, *Animation* (Harpenden: Pocket Essentials, 2004), p. 11.
15 Kristyn Gorton and Joanne Garde-Hansen (eds), *Remembering British Television: Audience, Archive and Industry* (London: BFI, 2019), pp. 126–127.
16 Rachel Moseley, *Hand-made Television: Stop-Frame Animation for Children in Britain, 1961–1974* (London: Palgrave, 2016), p. 4.
17 Moseley, *Hand-made Television*, p. 4.
18 Tat Wood, 'The Cult of Children's TV', in Stacey Abbott (ed.), *The Cult TV Book* (London: I.B. Tauris, 2010), p. 175.
19 Alex Hawkes, 'Bagpuss Licensee to be Sold for £4.2m', *The Guardian* 20 September 2011, https://www.theguardian.com/business/2011/sep/20/bagpuss-owner-sold-venture-capital (accessed 29 October 2021).
20 While there might be a temptation to describe the many Smallfilms tie-ins as 'paratexts' this would not be accurate, for as Jonathan Gray notes, 'paratexts are not simply add-ons, spinoffs, and also-rans: they create texts, they manage them, and they fill them with many of the meanings that we associate with them' (Jonathan Gray, *Show Sold Separately: Promos, Spoilers, and Other Media Paratexts* [New York: New York University Press, 2010], p. 6), and while some Smallfilms tie-ins (such as the annuals) do contribute in an active sense to the management of the *text*, most Smallfilms tie-ins are commercially motivated.
21 Alin Coman, Adam D. Brown, Jonathan Koppel, and William Hirst, 'Collective Memory from a Psychological Perspective', *International Journal of Politics, Culture, and Society* vol. 22 no. 2 (2009), p. 126.
22 Coman et al., 'Collective Memory from a Psychological Perspective', pp. 125–141, p. 126; a good discussion of the collective inscribing and reinscribing of *Star*

Wars-related memories, which describes how *Star Wars* fan communities have, in multitudinous ways, resisted the authority of Lucas and Disney, to establish parallel collective memories of the film franchise can be found in: Colin B. Harvey, 'Binding the Galaxy Together: Subjective, Collective, and Connective Memory in *Star Wars*', in William Proctor and Richard McCulloch (eds), *Disney's Star Wars: Forces of Production, Promotion, and Reception* (Iowa City: University of Iowa Press, 2019), passim.

23 Coman et al., 'Collective Memory from a Psychological Perspective', p. 127.
24 Coman et al., 'Collective Memory from a Psychological Perspective', p. 128.
25 Pallant, *Smallfilms: Audiences – data set*.
26 Michael Kammen, *Mystic Chords of Memory: The Transformation of Tradition in American Culture* (New York: Vintage Books, 1993), p. 688.
27 Raymond Williams, *Television: Technology and Cultural Form*, 2nd edn (London and New York: Routledge, 2003), p. 23.
28 Tim O'Sullivan, 'Researching the Viewing Culture: Television and the Home, 1946–1960', in Helen Wheatley (ed.), *Re-Viewing Television History: Critical Issues in Television Historiography* (London: I.B. Tauris, 2007), p. 162.
29 O'Sullivan, 'Researching the Viewing Culture: Television and the Home, 1946–1960', p. 163.
30 John Ellis, *Visible Fictions: Cinema, Television, Video* (London and New York: Routledge, 2001), pp. 24–25.
31 See Laura Mulvey, 'Visual Pleasure and Narrative Cinema', *Screen* vol. 16 no. 3 (1975), passim.
32 Ellis, *Visible Fictions*, p. 25.
33 Ellis, *Visible Fictions*, p. 25.
34 The regional nature of Associated-Rediffusion also limited the national reach of those early Smallfilms shows broadcast by the channel, with the coverage being restricted to the South East of England.
35 British Broadcasting Corporation, *1927 Royal Charter* (London: British Broadcasting Corporation, 1927), p. 1.
36 British Broadcasting Corporation, *1937 Royal Charter* (London: British Broadcasting Corporation, 1937), p. 1.
37 Brett Mills, 'Invisible Television: The Programmes No-One Talks about Even Though Lots of People Watch Them', *Critical Studies in Television* vol. 5 no. 1 (2010), p. 5.
38 Dick Fiddy, *Missing Believed Wiped: Searching for the Lost Treasures of British Television* (London: British Film Institute, 2001), p. 3.
39 Nichola Dobson, *Historical Dictionary of Animation and Cartoons*, 2nd edn (Lanham, MD: Rowman & Littlefield, 2020), p. 150.
40 *Timeshift*, 'Oliver Postgate: A Life in Small Films', directed by Francis Welch (BBC Four, 2010)
41 See Norman McLaren in Georges Sifanos, 'The Definition of Animation: A Letter from Norman McLaren', vol. 3 no. 2 (1995), pp. 62–66; Laura Mulvey, 'Visual Pleasure and Narrative Cinema', *Screen* vol. 16 no. 3 (1975), pp. 6–18; Hannah Frank, *Frame by Frame: A Materialist Aesthetics of Animated Cartoons*, 1st edn (Oakland: University of California Press, 2019); and Garrett Stewart, *Between Film and Screen: Modernism's Photo Synthesis* (Chicago: University of Chicago Press, 1999).
42 BBC One TV schedule for 14 February 1975 retrieved from BBC Genome, https://genome.ch.bbc.co.uk/schedules/bbcone/london/1975-02-14#at-13.45 (accessed 13 May 2021).

43 BBC One TV schedule for 9 April 1975 retrieved from BBC Genome, https://genome.ch.bbc.co.uk/schedules/bbcone/london/1974-04-09#at-13.45 (accessed 13 May 2021).
44 BBC One TV schedule for 5 August 1975 retrieved from BBC Genome, https://genome.ch.bbc.co.uk/schedules/bbcone/london/1975-08-05#at-13.30 (accessed 13 May 2021).
45 BBC One TV schedule for 12 August 1975 retrieved from BBC Genome, https://genome.ch.bbc.co.uk/schedules/bbcone/london/1975-08-12#at-13.30 (accessed 13 May 2021).
46 BBC One TV schedule for 14 February 1975 retrieved from BBC Genome, https://genome.ch.bbc.co.uk/schedules/bbcone/london/1975-02-14#at-16.25 (accessed 13 May 2021).
47 Mosley, *Hand-made Television*; Caroline Ruddell and Paul Ward (eds), *The Crafty Animator Handmade, Craft-Based Animation and Cultural Value* (London: Palgrave, 2019).
48 Christopher Frayling, 'The Crafts', in Boris Ford (ed.), *Modern Britain: Cambridge Cultural History of Britain* (Cambridge: Cambridge University Press, 1992), p. 169.
49 For example, no mention is made to the work of Smallfilms across the following works: Maureen Furniss, *A New History of Animation* (New York: Thames & Hudson, 2016); Stephen Cavalier, *The World History of Animation* (London: Aurum Press, 2011); Giannalberto Bendazzi, *Animation: A World History – Volumes 1–3* (Boca Raton, FL: CRC Press, 2015).
50 Moseley, *Hand-made Television*, p. 9.
51 Caroline Ruddell and Paul Ward, 'Introduction', in Ruddell and Ward (eds), *The Crafty Animator*, p. 1.
52 Ruddell and Ward, 'Introduction', p. 2.
53 Many of these anxieties around archival research, particularly in the context of Television Studies, are covered in greater detail in: Christine Geraghty and David Lusted (eds), *The Television Studies Book* (London: Arnold, 1998); Helen Wheatley (ed.), *Re-Viewing Television History: Critical Issues in Television Historiography* (London: I.B. Tauris, 2007).
54 Ian W. Macdonald, *Screenwriting Poetics and the Screen Idea* (London: Palgrave, 2013), pp. 4–5.
55 Ethan Thompson and Jason Mittell, 'Introduction', in Ethan Thompson and Jason Mittell (eds), *How to Watch Television* (New York: New York University Press, 2020), p. 4.
56 Thompson and Mittell, 'Introduction', p. 4.
57 David M. Fetterman, 'Key Informant', in Lisa M. Given (ed.), *The SAGE Encyclopedia of Qualitative Research Methods* (Thousand Oaks, CA: Sage, 2008), p. 477.
58 Fetterman, 'Key Informant', p. 477.
59 Geoff Payne and Judy Payne, *Key Concepts in Social Research* (London: Sage, 2004), p. 131.
60 Stephen Frosh, 'Disintegrating Qualitative Research', *Theory & Psychology* vol. 17 no. 5 (October 2007), p. 638.
61 See Svend Brinkmann, 'Unstructured and Semi-Structured Interviewing', in Patricia Leavy (ed.), *The Oxford Handbook of Qualitative Research* (Oxford: Oxford University Press, 2014), p. 286.

62 Robert Atkinson, 'The Life Story Interview', in Jaber F. Gubrium and James A. Holstein (eds), *Handbook of Interview Research: Context and Method* (Thousand Oaks, CA: Sage, 2002), p. 125.
63 Based on pricing provided by Prolific, a public research consultancy firm, a UK-focused representative random sample survey of the kind described in this chapter would cost between £10,000 and £15,000.
64 Helen Wood, *Talking with Television: Women, Talk shows, and Modern Self-Reflexivity* (Illinois: University of Illinois, 2009); and Beverley Skeggs and Helen Wood, *Reacting to Reality Television: Performance, Audience and Value* (London: Routledge, 2012).
65 Martin Barker and Ernest Mathijs, 'Introduction: The World Hobbit Project', *Participation: Journal of Audience & Reception Studies* vol. 13 no. 2 (2016), p. 158.
66 Barker and Mathijs, 'Introduction: The World Hobbit Project', p. 159.
67 Martin Barker, Clarissa Smith and Feona Attwood, *Watching Game of Thrones: How Audiences Engage with Dark Television* (Manchester: Manchester University Press, 2021), p. 1.
68 Martin Barker, Kate Egan, Tom Phillips, and Sarah Ralph, *Alien Audiences: Remembering and Evaluating a Classic Movie* (London: Palgrave, 2016), p. 12.
69 Richard McCulloch (Co-Director of The World Star Wars Project) email correspondence with Chris Pallant, 24 August 2020.
70 Kate Egan, 'Memories of Connecting: Fathers, Daughters and Intergenerational Monty Python Fandom', in Kate Egan and Jeffrey Andrew (eds), *And Now for Something Completely Different: Critical Approaches to Monty Python* (Edinburgh: Edinburgh University Press, 2020), p. 207.
71 Barker and Mathijs, 'Introduction', p. 160.
72 Barker and Mathijs, 'Introduction', p. 161.
73 Postgate, *Seeing Things*, p. 411.

Chapter 2

THE WHIMSICAL AUTHENTICITY OF SMALLFILMS: *IVOR THE ENGINE* (1959–64, 1975–7)

All right, then. A Welsh railway engine. So what does a Welsh railway engine do for a living? Pulls trucks with things in. A bit dull, really. Hardly the stuff of legend…

The answer came – wait for it – while I was in the bath. I muttered 'Eureka', climbed out dripping wet, and telephoned Peter: 'He wants to sing in the choir'…

That single thought provided the touchstone for the world of *Ivor the Engine*, that ordinary world in which the extraordinary was just going to be part of the landscape.[1]

'Well, of course he does', was Peter Firmin's response to Oliver Postgate's Eureka phone call.[2] In this single moment the combined – and harmonious – creative ambitions of Firmin and Postgate were indelibly galvanized. While this was not their first production together, the birth of Smallfilms as we know it today can be traced back to this moment. But, before we continue down the tracks and explore the world of *Ivor* more fully, it is worth taking a moment to establish the experiences that drove Postgate towards his Eureka moment.

Having worked together on *Alexander the Mouse* (1958) for Associated-Rediffusion (the London-based ITV franchise at that time), Postgate's next commission for the franchise was *The Adventures of Master Ho* (1958), while Firmin picked up work on the franchise's 'Small Time' (1955–66) programming, namely working on *The Musical Box* (1959–66). These separate experiences provided valuable insights that would shape the early thinking behind *Ivor the Engine*. Firmin continued to work in the live medium and produced a series of 'hand-operated nursery rhyme card animations',[3] which provided visual accompaniment to the live musical performances of Rolf Harris and Wally Whyton. Although described as animations, these hand-operated cards required real-time manipulation so arguably fall somewhere between the categories of animation and puppetry.

Postgate, seeing the shortcomings of such live animation/puppet-based processes, moved into 'single-frame film animation', employing a 'film camera adapted to capture one frame at a time via bits of Meccano and pieces of string'.[4]

Crucially, while Postgate described his work animating *The Adventures of Master Ho* as 'slow and laborious', he also recalls that 'it was also tremendously exciting'.[5] The reason being, Postgate notes, was that once he reviewed his test footage he came to the following realization: 'It didn't matter what the picture was of. It didn't matter that Master Ho had stumbled rather than walked […] I had done something momentous. I had opened up another dimension to the still picture. I had given it the extra dimension of time. I had made it come to life.'[6] Having gained this understanding of the potent, metamorphic power of animation, when Postgate reunited with Firmin in late 1958, it was clear – at least to Postgate – that their next project would be animated via stop-frame means.

Reflecting on the challenge of the blank page, Postgate notes how sometimes 'a brainwave would come, but often I found myself scouring the inside of my head trying to imagine the *sort of thing* that heads of TV departments might fancy'.[7] Which, in turn, led Postgate to ask the question: 'Was there something somewhere that would surely touch their heartstrings? Not cuddly bunnies or cute dollies, that was for sure. Dogs? Horses? Hmmm… Cars? Motorbikes? Boats? What did every boy of my generation want to be when he grew up? An engine driver of course.'[8] Firmin's own memories of this development sheds light on an important practical consideration that Postgate leaves unsaid. Firmin recalls how Postgate realized that, after this successful animation of *The Adventures of Master Ho*, 'he could do it, and it worked, and they loved it, and what he was doing obviously had a future'.[9] Firmin then casts Postgate's series of character considerations, from dogs to steam engines, in a slightly different light, remarking: 'So he then thought, "oh, what's the best thing, what's the easiest thing to animate?" So, he thought, "Well it really needs something with wheels, because legs are hopeless to animate, very difficult", so he thought of something with wheels.'[10]

As is the case for much of this book, a key objective here is to peel back the layers of the show in question, in this case *Ivor the Engine*, in an attempt to better understand the show's production and lasting appeal. Looking at the language used by those survey respondents who selected *Ivor the Engine* (b/w and colour) as their favourite Smallfilms production (see Appendix – Figure A.3), it is clear that the combination of characters, setting, and story is key, with the interweaving of the more *authentic* locomotive-related features and processes with the more *whimsical* elements, such as dragons and singing trains, being at the heart of this appeal.[11] Of course, these concepts of *authenticity* and *whimsy* are italicized for good reason, given the very obvious artifice of *Ivor the Engine* as an animated text, which self-evidently imposes certain limits on any notion of *authenticity*, while at the same time paving the way for any manner of *whimsical* expression by virtue of the unbridled metamorphic potential of animation as an art form. With this in mind, it is the consistent way that Postgate and Firmin regulate the authentic and whimsical elements that gives rise to a specific internal logic that is an important part of the show's considerable appeal. This whimsical authenticity, as we shall define it here, is also a core element of the Smallfilms world-building process across much of their oeuvre.

This chapter focuses on three main objectives: to better establish the notion of whimsical authenticity through an analysis of the black-and-white and colour series of *Ivor the Engine*, focusing in turn on the importance of everyday routines, dual appeal, and the reimagined setting of Wales; to untangle a continuity issue found in the colour series, which, when analysed using archival sources, helps to reveal the extent to which the black-and-white and colour productions of *Ivor the Engine* differ; and to establish the ways that Firmin and Postgate sought to extend the life of this series beyond its initial broadcast context.

The whimsical authenticity of *Ivor the Engine*

As a result of the early successes of marionette series such as *Muffin the Mule* (BBC, 1946–55; ITV, 1956–7), *Andy Pandy* (BBC, 1950, 1952, 1970), *The Woodentops* (BBC, 1955–7), and *Flower Pot Men* (BBC, 1952–3), to name but a few, live, puppet-based performance had become the orthodoxy of contemporary domestically produced children's television. Additionally, Neville Wortman, who competed with Postgate and Firmin for 'Small Time' bookings, recalls how 'America was ruling the roost in those days, so everything was American, cartoons, animation, everything, and we had no equivalent to it.'[12] In this context, with the prevailing broadcast logic favouring domestic puppet-based productions, combined with the importation of American hand-drawn animation, to satisfy the children's scheduling remit, Firmin and Postgate's decision to produce *Ivor the Engine* as a cut-out stop-frame animation with a detailed aesthetic, clearly marked them as a studio – regardless of size and location – to watch (reinforced by the fact that they were also working in parallel on *The Saga of Noggin the Nog*, which employed the same aesthetic, but which they were making for the BBC – discussed in Chapter 3).

Our introduction to the world of *Ivor the Engine*, narrated with characteristic Postgatean charm, sets a tone that would become a lyrical constant of almost all of the Smallfilms creations that followed:

> Not very long ago, in the top left-hand corner of Wales, there was a railway. It wasn't a very long railway or a very important railway, but it was called The Merioneth and Llantisilly Rail Traction Company Limited, and it was all there was. And in a shed, in a siding at the end of the railway, there lived Ivor the Engine, the locomotive of the Merioneth and Llantisilly Rail Traction Company Limited.[13]

Here, the mismatch between grand titles and humble reality not only offers an early moment of humour but also hints to the viewer that through the power of storytelling – or self-determination, in the case of Ivor and the Merioneth and Llantisilly Rail Traction Company Limited – this will be a world of surprising contrasts.

As dramatist and playwright Goran Stefanovski once remarked: 'One can make a powerful script without using words at all. There is a substance in scriptwriting which precedes "the word" and which is stronger than words. These primary scripting elements are dramatic opposites, contrasts, contradictions and mismatches.'[14] In *Ivor the Engine*, Postgate and Firmin create a world – and story – that fuses the everyday routines of steam locomotion and village life with singing trains and utilitarian dragons. Both parts of this equation carry equal weighting in the construction of *Ivor the Engine*, and the quotidian details we encounter in the opening two minutes of the first episode are just as important as the thrill of being introduced to Idris the dragon. It is this combination of carefully managed tensions that generates the whimsical authenticity found in *Ivor the Engine*.

Everyday routines – building an authentic picture of steam locomotion

Both Firmin and Postgate were able to draw upon personal knowledge to help establish the intimate nuances of Ivor's world. For Firmin, these details stemmed from his father who worked as a railway telegraphist,[15] while Postgate drew upon the stories told by his drama school friend Denzil Ellis, who had been an engine fireman.[16] Reflecting on this connection, Postgate writes:

> He once told me how his day used to start. At some unearthly hour in the morning he would have to go and wake up the engine, clear out the firebox, take paper and wood and ignite its fire, just as you or I would light a stove or a kitchen range, so that the engine would be boiling nicely by the time it was due to set off for Edinburgh. I had been touched by that story because it seemed to give a human dimension to the glowing hundred-ton steel power-machine thundering up the main line.[17]

While the speeds of locomotion on display in *Ivor the Engine* are much less modest than this vision of industrial velocity, Firmin and Postgate do make a highly successful job of translating these daily preparations to the small screen.

The first episode of *Ivor the Engine* starts with an establishing shot of a semi-rural landscape, complete with railway water tower and distant church spire. This shot is held for twenty-seconds, before the camera pans to the right to reveal Ivor's shed, and then zooms into the scene before fading to black (Figure 2.1).

Figure 2.1 Composite image showing pan in *Ivor the Engine* (1959–64).

Figure 2.2 Ivor in his shed as seen in *Ivor the Engine* (1959–64).

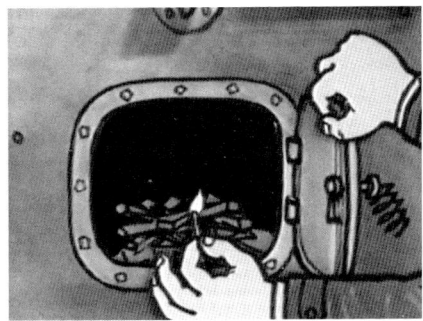

Figure 2.3 Jones lights Ivor's boiler in *Ivor the Engine* (1959–64).

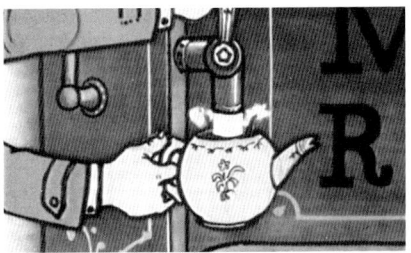

Figure 2.4 Jones pours a pot of tea in *Ivor the Engine* (1959–64).

Figure 2.5 Jones enjoys his morning tea in *Ivor the Engine* (1959–64).

This fade facilitates a transition to the inside of the shed where we are introduced to Ivor for the first time (Figure 2.2). We then cut back outside to see Jones the Steam opening the doors ready to begin the day, and remarking: 'Morning Ivor, jumping cold this morning.'[18] At this moment, Jones lights Ivor's fire with a match and begins to ready the engine's boiler for the day (Figure 2.3).

Then, the narrator (Postgate) notes that at this point 'Jones the Steam would make his pot of tea, and then he would sit, on the step of the engine, and drink his cup of tea. Oh, very nice a cup of tea in the morning' (Figures 2.4 and 2.5).[19] Postgate's repetition of the word tea functions here to help establish the routine nature of this act. After finishing his cup of tea, Jones climbs Ivor's footplate to open the regulator a little, thereby allowing the steam from Ivor's heated boiler to begin driving his pistons. As Ivor trundles out from his shed, the image switches to a point-of-view (POV) shot, first showing Jones operating Ivor's controls (Figure 2.6), before shifting to a view from his footplate, looking over Jones's shoulder and down the track (Figure 2.7). After stopping to fill up at the water tower (Figure 2.8) they move down the rails to the signal box. Upon reaching the signal box, the narrator proclaims: 'Oh, there was trouble, the signal was set

Figure 2.6 Jones setting Ivor's controls as seen in *Ivor the Engine* (1959–64).

Figure 2.7 Point-of-view shot from Ivor's footplate as seen in *Ivor the Engine* (1959–64).

Figure 2.8 Stopping at the water tower as seen in *Ivor the Engine* (1959–64).

Figure 2.9 Ivor waiting at the signal as seen in *Ivor the Engine* (1959–64).

Figure 2.10 Approaching Dai Station as seen in *Ivor the Engine* (1959–64).

against them, they couldn't go past' (Figure 2.9). After waking Owen the Signal, via a few sharp toots from Ivor's whistle, they make their way down the rails towards Llaniog Station. Approaching via another POV shot from Ivor's footplate, we see Dai Station waiting on the platform (Figure 2.10).

Within this sequence, lasting approximately three minutes, we get a sense of the narrative tone that will run throughout the series. Here, equal emphasis is placed on the microdetails of the functioning world, which are squarely grounded in reality, thereby endowing the story world with a sense of interior authenticity, alongside hints of the whimsical ingredients that circulate around this (seen in this opening sequence through Jones's conversation with Ivor).

While the sequence described above presents a series of routine details in the life of a steam engine, the process of animating this sequence presented a number of challenges for Postgate and Firmin. Smallfilms was certainly not a big-budget studio, no large crews of animation specialists were hired to help support the production, and Firmin and Postgate resisted the pull of London to remain firmly independent in the quiet woodland of Kent. These circumstances meant that *Ivor the Engine*, and the work of Smallfilms more broadly, is characterized by high levels of economy, ingenuity, and craft.[20] How then did Firmin and Postgate go about imbuing the flat, cut-out world of *Ivor the Engine* with a sense of energy and life. Two key characteristics that they considered from the outset were achieving convincing sensations of speed and depth.

The visualization of speed, namely the locomotion of Ivor, was tackled through a combination of approaches. Firmin recalls how he developed Ivor's wheels as 'proper wheels, and they were on little pins, so they could go round', and when Ivor travelled particularly fast he 'did them out of focus, so [Postgate] could just whizz them along'.[21] Firmin explains:

> Yes, just draw a wheel and a blur, with speed lines [...] Because, in fact, turning it, at speed, is a bit distracting – because you know what happens when wheels on cowboy films start going backwards, so it was a much better idea to do a blur. In fact, a lot of the principle that Oliver worked out, was that you have faith that the eye will fill in the gaps. That sort of leaving a certain amount to the imagination, and not trying to do everything, because he couldn't afford to do single frames.[22]

This aesthetic strategy works well in the show, and this approach to blurring wheel rotation when at speed is applied to all other vehicles that feature in the series.

Regarding depth, Firmin notes how he and Postgate shared the same desire to 'get a different shot from the sideways shot'.[23] Moreover, Firmin notes how, connected to the need for aesthetic variety, he wanted to find a way to get 'the perspective of [Ivor]'.[24] The solution, he notes, was to put Ivor's footplate, the platform where Jones the Steam stands, on the camera itself. Firmin recalls:

> I made an outline of the cabin on a, we called it a camera piece, on the front of the camera, and we went down the line and the important thing was to make the centre of gravity, the vanishing point, dead centre of the picture, so that, and I drew the lines going dead centre, going to that point, so the vanishing point was always in the centre of the picture so the camera could go down there and it was so convincing. That you could go down that line that it looked like you were really travelling down that line. And you know, those sort of simple things, if it had been off centre it would have been slightly disturbing, but little things like: perspective.

Likewise, describing the iconography of Ivor, Firmin notes how 'there was also the smoke, out of the funnel, that was cotton wool, bits of cotton wool'.[25] Postgate's approach to the animation of these bits of cotton wool adds another level of real-world correspondence, by depicting Ivor's steam drifting with the wind whenever the engine decelerates or having it slowly evaporate when Jones uses Ivor to make a pot of tea.

Consulting the survey data, it becomes clear that this attention to detail regarding Ivor's steam was not lost on the audience. Respondent 17 writes: 'The animation was fab (the steam made out of cotton wool) and the stories were quaint. Reminds me of happy times when I was a child. I love steam engines too.' While Respondent 538 adds: 'I was a fan of Thomas the Tank Engine as a kid, Ivor was similar and I enjoyed the fact that it looked like you could make it yourself, they were drawings alive and the cotton wool as puffs of smoke set my imagination into gear.'[26]

Other comments capture a more emotive response to *Ivor the Engine*: 'Love trains' (R320); 'it has trains!' (R213); 'Interest in railways and Wales' (R416); 'When I was growing up I was fascinated by vehicles of all kinds, so a show centred around a train was perfect' (R84); and 'Because I have childhood memories of watching this and visiting Narrow gauge railways in Wales' (R328). For others, it was the evocative soundscape of *Ivor the Engine* that proved to be the big attraction: 'To be honest it was very hard to choose but its narration that sticks in my head – and the sounds of the train' (R443); 'I loved Ivor, his noises, his character. The music so evocative. The sounds have never left me, and I get a glow of reassuring nostalgia just thinking about them' (R559); and simply 'pssht-i-co pssht-i-co' (R193).

For others, there was a family association with the world of *Ivor the Engine*: 'My grandad drove steam trains. I associated Ivor with him and his world when I was a child, and still do. Precious memories' (R385); and 'My Grandpa (who was a metallurgist on the railways) always said it was his favourite programme and watched it with me and my brother' (R491). While others reveal a more direct professional association: 'Well going on to work for the Railway, then it must have put it in my mind!' (R212); 'I watched this growing up and later became a train driver' (R370); and 'I loved the whole universe created by the stories… I ended up working on the railway… I blame Ivor' (R562). Comments, such as these, confirm an assertion made by Postgate in 1993: 'What is it that the English are unashamedly sentimental about in those days […] and the answer has got to be railway engines.'[27]

These considerations and motivations elevated *Ivor the Engine* beyond merely a cheaply made animated novelty, serving only to help fill the 'Small Time' schedule. As a consequence of these motivations, Postgate and Firmin successfully established a character with which audiences of all ages could identify, and through whose eyes/windows we were granted a new, whimsically authentic way of looking at the top left-hand corner of Wales.

Dual appeal storytelling

When asked at what age range he was aiming when writing *Clangers*, Postgate responded:

> The films we made were aimed at the Head of Department at the BBC, who was about 57 at the time, and she was a nice lady called Ursula Eason, and very humane and ordinary, and full of fun. If we had studied children in anyway, apart from having children, we wouldn't necessarily have succeeded in selling the films, because the woman at the BBC had fairly clear opinions of what she would find acceptable, and these were conditioned in some ways by the fact she was a middle-aged, English (well, Irish-actually, if you go all the way back) lady, who was brought up as I was on Beatrix Potter, A.A. Milne, and Lewis Carroll, and all the sort of 'Founding Fathers' of English Tweeness.[28]

Although responding to a question about *Clangers*, Postgate's response reveals a universal principle. The balance, to which Postgate's words point, has faced storytellers throughout history, whether working in oral, written, or visual mediums. Casie Hermansson and Janet Zepernick suggest that film-makers 'creating children's film and television must anticipate and cater to the adult gatekeeper in order for their work to have a chance of reaching its intended child audience. These complex production and consumption power dynamics are "hidden," but they, too, factor into the DNA of all children's film and television and govern most aspects of its marketing and distribution.'[29] This attitude informs all of Smallfilms' work, but our concern here is *Ivor the Engine*, so how then did Firmin and Postgate translate this dual appeal agenda into stories located in Merioneth and Llantisilly that could achieve this objective?[30]

Ivor the Engine is full of examples of this approach, but to help illustrate this point we will focus on the episode 'Unidentified Objects' (first broadcast February 1976), which offers a particularly acute example of this dual address. The episode begins with Ivor waiting at Llaniog Station, with Postgate's narration stating: 'Oh, I suppose there's not a lot to do today, or he'd be somewhere with his little flat truck. I wonder where Jones the Steam and Dai Station are? Oh, sitting in deck chairs on the platform, look, having a cup of tea: there's luxury now!' This moment of relaxation prompts Jones to ruminate existentially: 'I wonder sometimes, Dai, looking up in the sky, about, you know, life on other planets, and that.' To which Dai responds confidently, 'Yes, there is, I've got a book about it', before spotting a flying saucer in the sky at that very moment and thereby bringing their tea break to an abrupt end. There is considerable potential for dual appreciation in this sequence, with adult audiences likely recognizing the all too fleeting moment of relaxation as a feature of adult working life, and the response of Dai Station, as the behaviour of a professional know-it-all.

From a child's perspective, it is likely to be equally relatable; readers of this book can surely recall moments from their childhood where they battled to rouse a grown-up from their moment of relaxation. While the mystery and excitement of aliens and flying saucers would surely capture the attention of a young mind. Yet, for an older viewer, watching this episode in 1976, the sudden appearance of UFOs could be taken as a reference to the escalating tensions of the Cold War – a dual reading that is made all the more potent given that Postgate's personal archive contains a handwritten story breakdown for an *Ivor the Engine* print adaptation, *c.* 1977 (Figure 2.11), on the reverse of which we find a draft document concerning the subject of nuclear warfare (Figure 2.12).

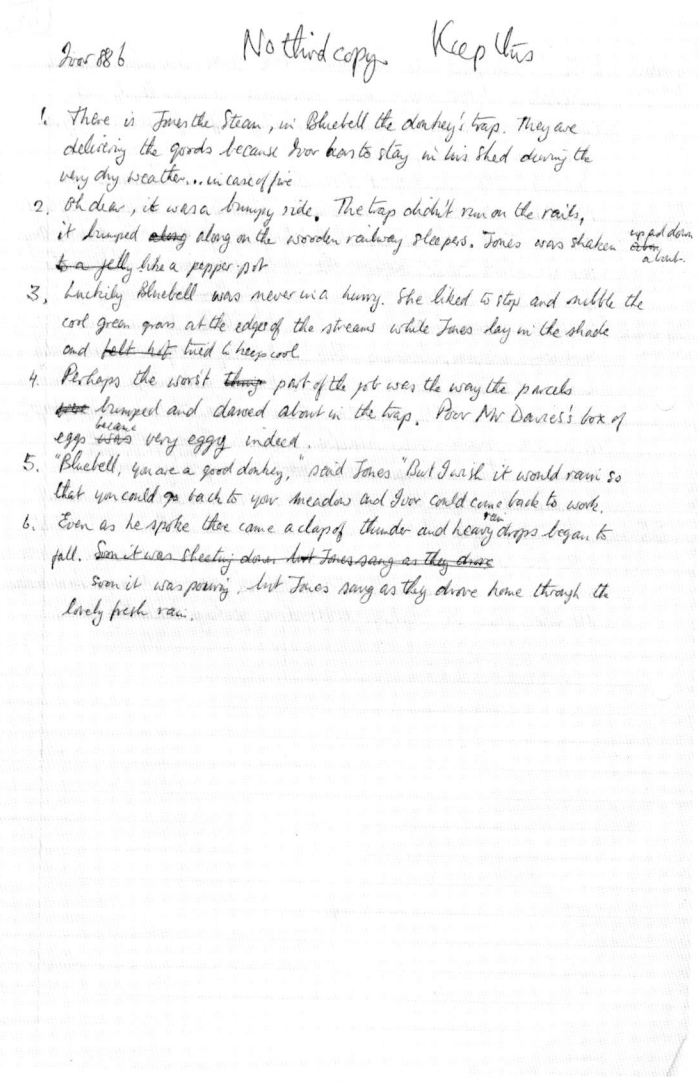

Figure 2.11 A breakdown for print adaptation of a story featuring Bluebell the Donkey, *c.* 1977.

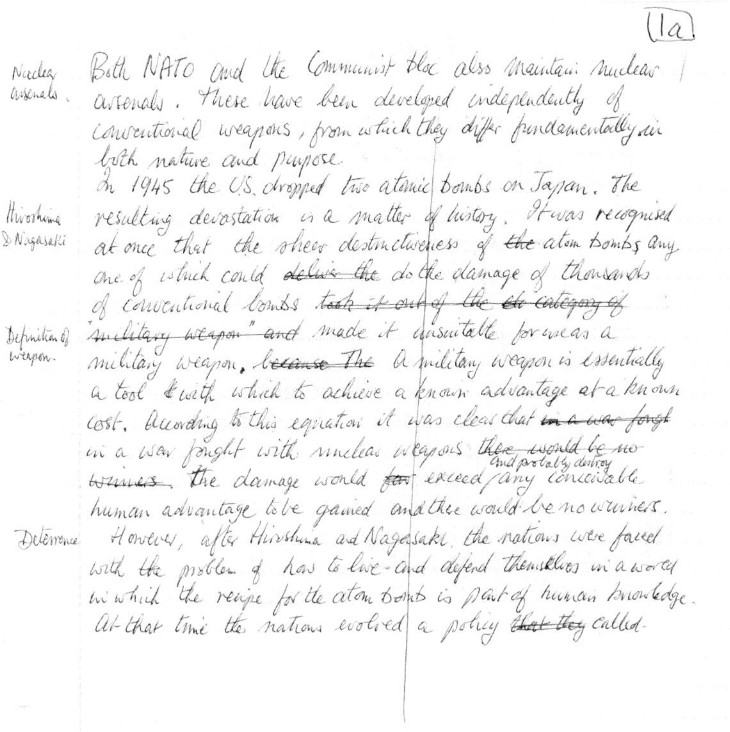

> (1a)
>
> **Nuclear arsenals.** Both NATO and the Communist bloc also maintain nuclear arsenals. These have been developed independently of conventional weapons, from which they differ fundamentally in both nature and purpose.
>
> **Hiroshima & Nagasaki** In 1945 the U.S. dropped two atomic bombs on Japan. The resulting devastation is a matter of history. It was recognised at once that the sheer destructiveness of ~~the~~ atom bombs any one of which could ~~deliver the~~ do the damage of thousands of conventional bombs ~~took it out of the~~ ~~category of~~
>
> **Definition of weapon.** "military weapon" ~~and~~ made it unsuitable for use as a military weapon, ~~because The~~ A military weapon is essentially a tool ~~&~~ with which to achieve a known advantage at a known cost. According to this equation it was clear that ~~in a war fought~~ in a war fought with nuclear weapons ~~there would be no winners,~~ the damage would ~~far~~ exceed and probably destroy any conceivable human advantage to be gained and there would be no winners.
>
> **Deterrence** However, after Hiroshima and Nagasaki, the nations were faced with the problem of how to live - and defend themselves in a world in which the recipe for the atom bomb is part of human knowledge. At that time the nations evolved a policy ~~that they~~ called

Figure 2.12 Discussion of nuclear war written on the reverse of Figure 2.11, *c.* 1977.

Fittingly, the episode first provokes a sense of trepidation, as Jones and Dai approach the source of the apparent alien invasion, hearing a seemingly distressed Mr Dinwiddy in the midst of it all, before delivering a classic comic reversal. Rather than being an alien invasion, we discover that the UFOs are simply an armada of soap bubbles, generated by Mr Dinwiddy, using a repurposed 'blower from the old smelting oven' powered by a lever-driven hammer. This comedic reversal is completed with Dinwiddy celebrating his achievement with the remark: 'There you are, up it goes, a perfect soap bubble.' While Jones is similarly awestruck, Dai punctures the euphoria, interjecting: 'Silly, I call it, wasting time like that, blowing bubbles all day, you're supposed to be a Gold Miner, not a Bubble Blower.' In itself, this moment offers broad appeal, by lampooning a grown-up (Dai) intent on quashing fun in favour of regulations, in this case insisting upon what job Dinwiddy should be doing, a moment that surely resonates with audiences young and old alike.

With audiences accustomed to what is and what isn't within the realms of possibility within the narrative world of *Ivor the Engine*, coupled with the fact that viewers are encouraged to take their cue from Jones the Steam and Dai Station's responses to the mysterious sighting, the well-established expectations of whimsical authenticity function here to create a space for uncertainty. Ultimately, the bubble blower is discovered, and the tensions are reconciled, with the narrative serving to reinforce both the whimsical nature of this idea, as well as the suggested authenticity of its mechanical workings.

Wales: Reimagined

The intersecting appeal of North Walian geography and dragon-related content is a strong feature of the survey data. Several respondents focus on the Welshness of the show: 'Lovely portrayal of Wales' (R165); 'It depicts a small but eccentric community in rural Wales; I loved the accent of the narration' (R171); 'I love the animation style and the setting. It reminds me of our childhood holidays in Wales' (R144); 'Such great characters and stories – always liked railways too! The illustrations were fantastic, bringing to life Wales' (R294); 'So hard to choose. I loved all three as a child, but there was something rather glorious about the mix of industrial heritage (a steam train) and beautiful Welsh countryside. I have particularly fond memories of the one where Ivor goes on holiday and ends up swimming in the sea – such a wonderfully incongruous image!' (R135); and 'pastoral, lyrical, transcendental, anti-capitalist, mystical, Celtic and V.Elliott's oboe is utterly magical' (R343). Whereas the majority of respondents who highlighted the intersection of Wales/Dragons as a significant point of appeal, some combined the appeal of steam trains and dragons, while others simply highlighted the appeal of dragons: 'I loved the dragon, Idris, the Welsh accents and the steam engine. I think it made me think of going on holidays (we used to travel through Wales on our way to Ireland every summer)' (R70), 'It was Welsh based and appealed to a small South Walian girl, even though it was set in North Wales. I also loved Idris the dragon' (R229), and 'loved the accents. adore how the baby dragons are looked after' (R169); 'Wales, dragons and small railway engines' (R177), 'You can't beat a steam train and a dragon' (R83), and 'The dragons in the firebox' (R29); 'Dragon episode stayed with me' (R383), and, succinctly, 'Idris' (R437).

In light of these statements, it is clear that the imagined adventures of Ivor the Engine, gained added appeal by virtue of their occurrence in an exaggerated – but recognizable – version of North West Wales. More precisely, it was the fixed and knowable nature of Ivor's landscape that proved a compelling bedrock upon which the more fantastical elements could be constructed, encountered, and developed. Postgate remarks:

> When we were working on Ivor the Engine, when I said I'd like [Peter] to go from somewhere to somewhere, he would say 'no, he can't go there, because he'd get out the map' [Figures 2.13 and 2.14], and say 'it isn't possible from Llanmad to Yn Leach, because you've got to go through Tan yr Gyllch', and I would argue with him and point out to him that this was only a film and it didn't matter. [Peter's] not going to give me the backgrounds with which to do it, because he couldn't, you know, he [Ivor] was as real as that. So, one went on with this particular level of incongruity where you propose one single magical faculty, as it were, one single deviation from normality, and everything else is perfectly normal.[31]

Here, we can see that Firmin played a critical role in championing the importance of fixed and knowable space, actively prohibiting Postgate's more relaxed approach to screen continuity.

While points of geographic interest emerged iteratively as more *Ivor the Engine* series were completed, these two evolutions of the map (Figures 2.13 and 2.14), which adopt differing graphic styles, demonstrate the fixed nature of each location once mapped by Firmin. So, for example, while Tewyn (Figure 2.14, bottom right) is added in the 1967 map, this does not alter the comparative locations of Llaniog,

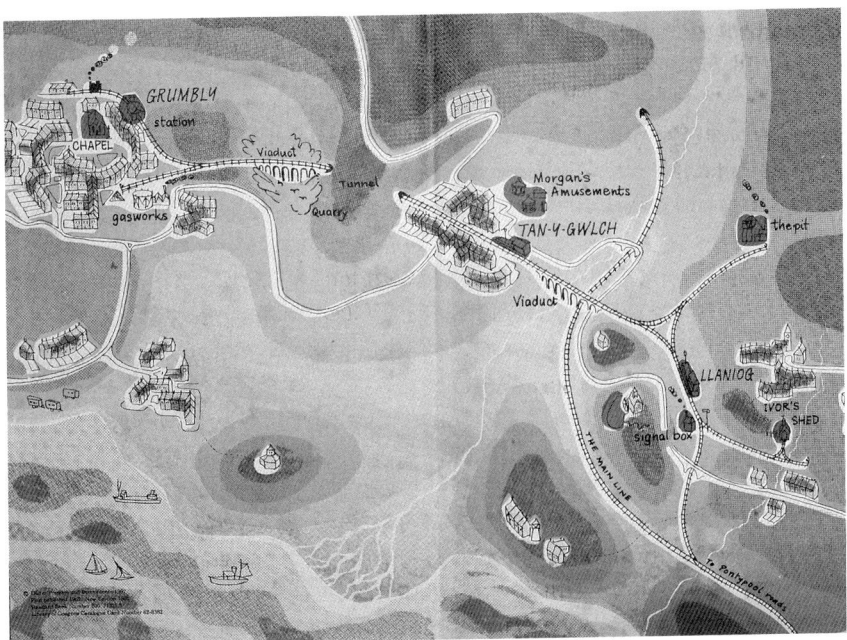

Figure 2.13 The 1962 mapping of the Merioneth and Llantisilly Railway. Published by Abelard Schuman.

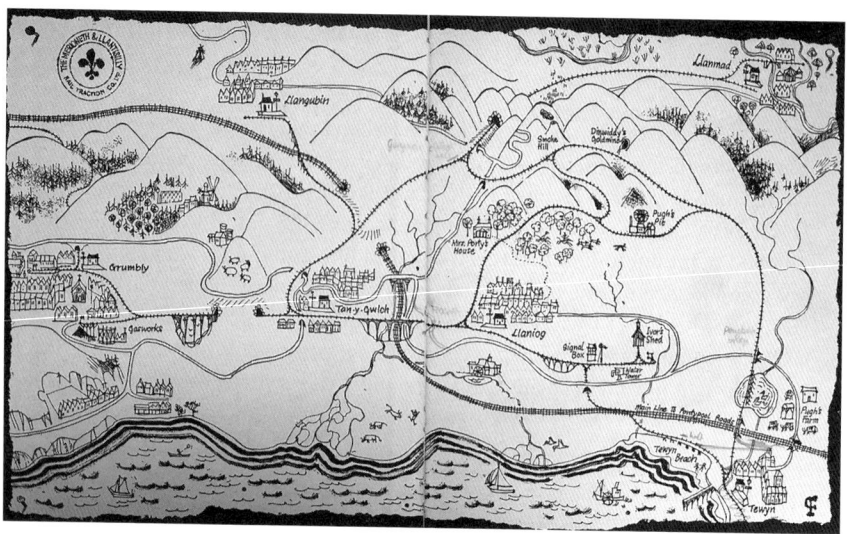

Figure 2.14 The revised 1967 mapping of the Merioneth and Llantisilly Railway. Published by Abelard Schuman.

Tan-Y-Gwlch or Grumbly, as they had been established in the 1962 map, which was based solely on the landscape established in the 1959 series. With the location of *Ivor the Engine* so carefully mapped and guarded by Firmin, it meant that the whimsical characters and incidents conjured by Postgate would always occupy the same relatable – authentic – space.

Idris the dragon, while fulfilling the role of Welsh symbol, also functions much like Ivor, with his storylines rooted firmly in the day-to-day business of the community and surrounding region. Describing the function of Idris, Postgate notes how 'dragons and things turn up, but they are commonplace in Wales anyway, so one doesn't count those as being magical'.[32] This attitude is clearly evident in the show's writing. Idris first makes an appearance in 'The Egg' (episode five, broadcast 2 February 1976), with the audience hearing the following narration after Idris hatches, once the egg is placed inside Ivor's furnace chamber: 'There, looking out of Ivor's funnel, was a dragon, not one of your lumping great fairy-tale dragons, but a small, heraldic Welsh dragon, glowing red hot and smiling.'[33] At which point Idris the dragon repeats his opening question, asking the choirmaster: 'Do you know Land of My Fathers?' These remarks identify Idris as part of the Welsh contemporary, not a figure of an imagined mythical or fairy-tale tradition, as Postgate notes in the narration, but an everyday dragon, wishing to hear the local choir's rendition of the Welsh National Anthem.

Idris's integration into the everyday drama of Merioneth and Llantisilly is quickly cemented within the series, as episode seven ('The Alarm', broadcast 5 February 1976) sees the dragon come to the community's aid. The episode opens with a scene of the choir singing, accompanied by Idris and Ivor. After the song finishes and the choir practice ends, Mr Evans, the choirmaster, suggests that, given the cold weather, they 'repair to Mrs Thomas's establishment and take nourishment'. Upon arrival, we discover that Mrs Thomas's gas fryer is 'playing up' and she can't get it hot enough to fry. After a moment of collective disappointment at the thought of not getting their cod and chips, Jones has an idea. The narration explains:

> Jones the Steam ran up on to the siding and had a word with Idris, who said he would be happy to oblige and then he flew straight down over the town and sat himself under Mrs Thomas's fish fryer. Idris blew and blew and blew. The fats began to sizzle and soon Mrs Thomas's shop was full of the lovely smell of frying fish and chips.

At the end of this episode, Mr Evans makes a discovery. Reading from the newspaper that is wrapped around his cod and chips, he shares with the gathered audience, including Idris, an article titled 'Dragons at Llaniog: Are Dragons Really Extinct?', in which it states that 'the Welsh Antiquarian Society […] is proposing to make a full investigation'. Mr Evans finishes by telling Idris that this will surely make him famous. Hearing this news, Idris reacts with the following outburst, before flying away: 'Oh dear, oh no, no, not that, not that, oh dear!' Witnessing Idris's distress at the prospect of becoming an object of public attention, Jones and Mr Evans suggest that the community forget their encounters with Idris, with the hope of protecting his anonymity. In this episode, Postgate and Firmin actively resist fantastical fairy-tale-based associations of dragons, first by having Idris help to fix a fish and chip shop fryer (a greasy and particularly un-folkloric device), and then by having the community resist the opportunity to mythologize the existence of Idris, again, an action that runs counter to folk tradition, especially that of Wales, where *The Mabinogian* features no less than three dragon-related stories ('Peredur [Son of Evrawc]', 'The Story of Lludd and Llevelys', and 'Vortigern'). Again, this is an example of Postgate and Firmin actively regulating the balance between whimsy and authenticity.

More than just colouring in – 'The Dinwiddy conundrum'

The production of the colour *Ivor the Engine* series is often presented as a straightforward project of taking the two thirteen-episode series, which were made in black-and-white, and simply remaking the works in colour. For example, Jonny Trunk and Richard Embray's beautiful coffee-table book *The Art of Smallfilms* only offers the following account of this work: 'Very few *Ivor* artworks survive from the three ITV series, but in the 1970s the BBC asked for more *Ivor* episodes and Peter and Oliver remade the second and third series in colour, again with Peter painting and cutting out the backgrounds and characters.'[34] This characterization of the work involved implies continuity and reproduction with the original black-and-white works. Oliver Postgate's own account of this work, penned in his autobiography, goes some of the way towards more fully establishing the work involved in this project, but, for the non-specialist reader, this still suggests a relatively linear and uncomplicated process of self-adaptation. Recounting a phone call from Monica Sims, Head of Children's Television in 1975, Postgate writes: 'She told me that what the BBC wanted, and had wanted for years, was *Ivor the Engine*. She didn't just want brand-new films. If I could make them again from scratch in colour, she would be delighted to have all the old black and white films, as well as any new ones I could think of.'[35] Postgate's words, while offering more than Trunk and Embray's, still suggests a simple colour revamp of the black-and-white work done fifteen years earlier for Associated-Rediffusion.

A number of factors highlight that remaking *Ivor the Engine* in colour was, in fact, much more labour-intensive than these accounts suggest. First, looking at the runtimes involved in this conversion to colour, it is hard to imagine this project being a simple one, given that series two and three of the black-and-white *Ivor the Engine* both comprised thirteen ten-minute episodes, totalling 260 minutes of runtime, and Smallfilms ultimately producing forty five-minute episodes, totalling 200 minutes of runtime, for the BBC. Evidently, with a 60-minute shortfall, this conversion project would have required careful work to maintain the balance of the main and sub narratives, and the extensive development process can be seen across several series planning documents that have survived in Postgate's personal archive (Figures 2.15 and 2.16). Plans that also reveal that Firmin and Postgate initially conceived the colour series as a fifty-episode sequence.

Furthermore, the production of *Ivor the Engine* in colour required the series to be completely rescripted, so as to record the adapted storyline (a product of the new runtime format for the series), and to support the reanimation of the series. It was not possible for Postgate to simply reuse the original script pages from the black-and-white series. This fresh labour is captured in the script pages – or, more accurately, in the production markings made upon these new script pages (Figure 2.17).

If we return to the colour episode 'Unidentified Objects', discussed earlier in this chapter, we find an unusual example of series discontinuity that reveals the challenges and complexities of maintaining their storytelling ambition across this major readaptation project. We can call this discontinuity 'the Dinwiddy conundrum'. What do we mean by this? Well, in response to Dai Station's disparaging account of Dinwiddy's machine, 'Silly, I call it, wasting time like that, blowing bubbles all day, you're supposed to be a Gold Miner, not a Bubble Blower', Dinwiddy retorts: 'Silly? Well, I don't know. I dig up all this gold and then *they just put it in the ground again*. No, I reckon it's just as silly digging gold as blowing bubbles. Only blowing bubbles is easier and more fun.'[36] Why the conundrum? The answer: Dinwiddy's comments about putting the gold back into the ground in 'Unidentified Objects' (episode thirteen) is a reference to a turn of events featured in episodes 'Gold' (seventeen) and 'Mrs Porty' (eighteen). Here lies the conundrum. Clearly, Postgate and Firmin are attempting to weave this subplot across multiple episodes, which is hardly remarkable in itself, given that many Smallfilms works offer similar continuous narratives across multiple episodes. What is noteworthy is the faulty continuity of this reference. There are three possible scenarios that might explain this.

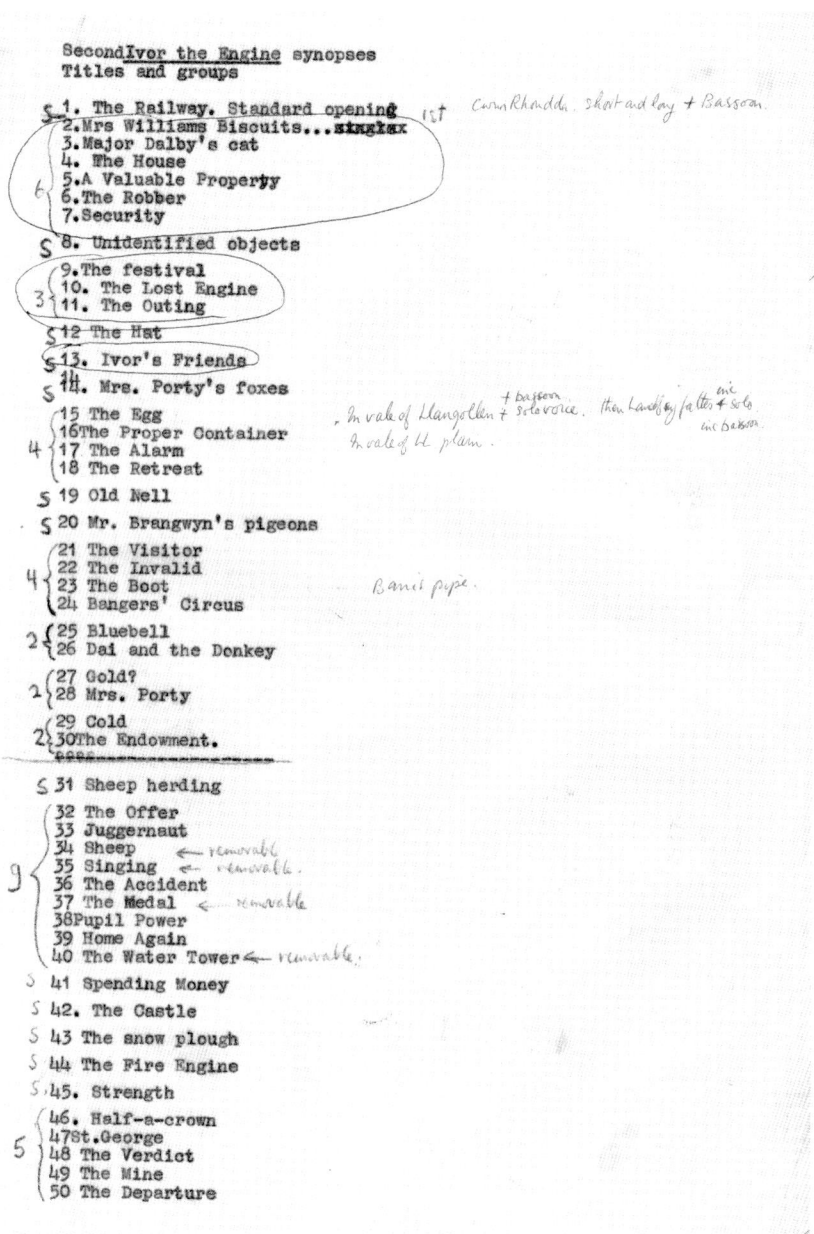

Figure 2.15 Undated draft (*c.* 1974) showing fifty planned *Ivor the Engine* (colour) episodes; 'S' denotes standalone episodes.

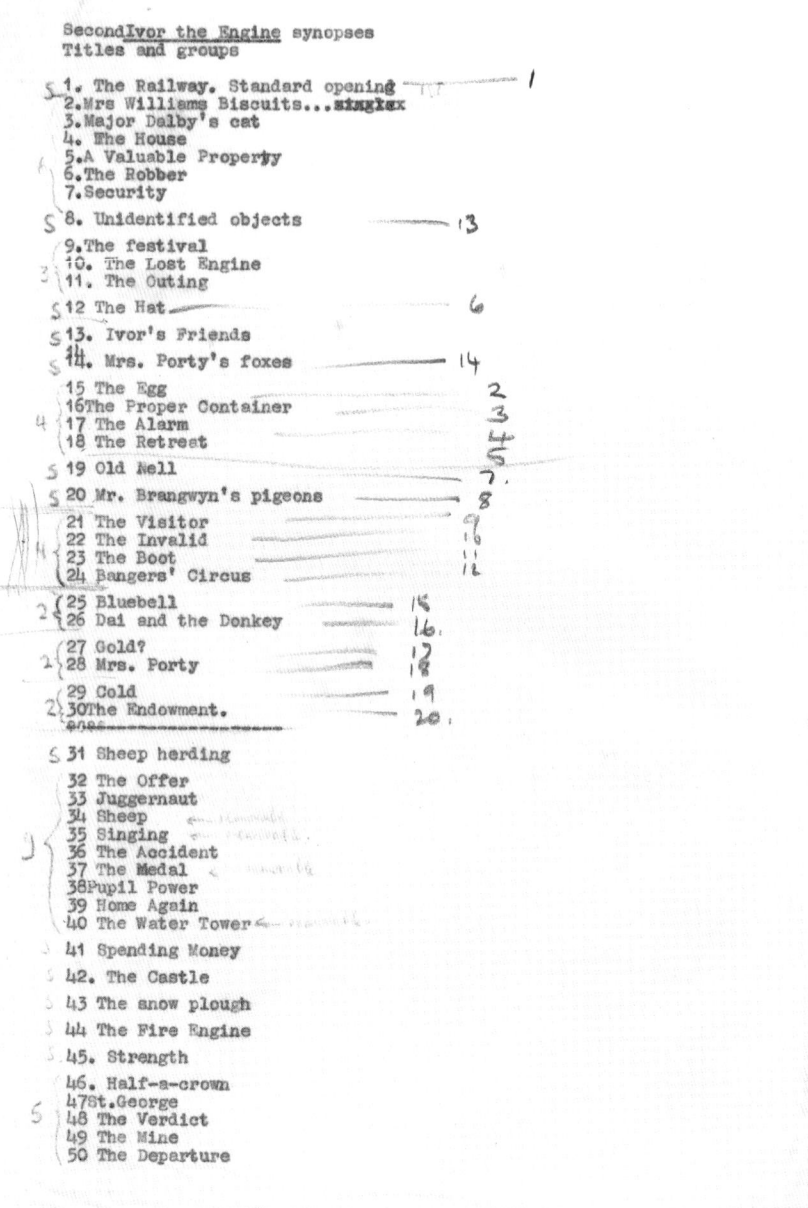

Figure 2.16 Undated draft (*c.* 1974) recording re-sequencing of 'Unidentified Objects' from episode eight to thirteen.

2. The Whimsical Authenticity of Smallfilms   43

Figure 2.17 The first script page for the first episode of the colour *Ivor the Engine* series.

First, we must note that 'Unidentified Objects' was a new episode created solely for the colour series of *Ivor the Engine* (see Figures 2.18 and 2.19 for full episode listings of the black-and-white and second and third series). Therefore, it is possible to see in this episode a reference back to the black-and-white

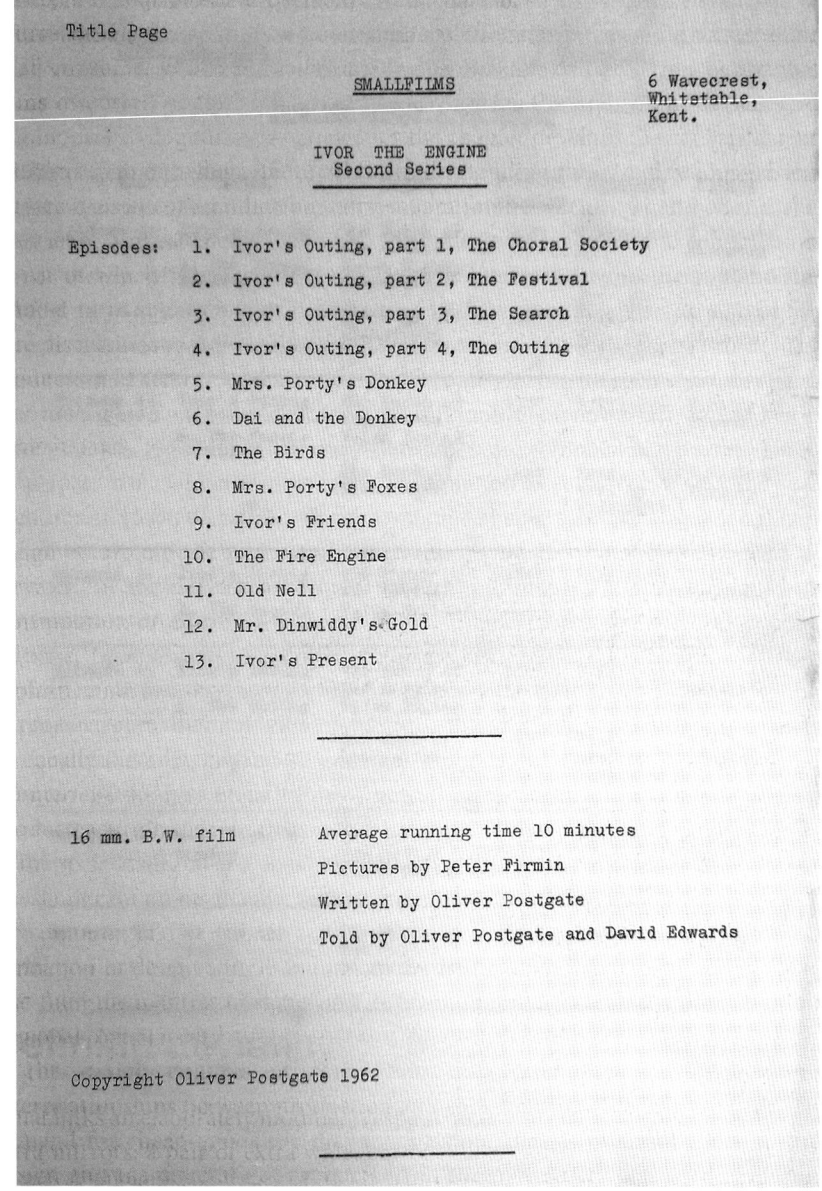

Figure 2.18 *Ivor the Engine* (black-and-white) second series episode outline, 1962.

Ivor the Engine series, in which the 'Gold' / 'Mrs Porty' plotline had been previously explored, but which had not yet occurred in the colour series at the time that 'Unidentified Objects' was broadcast. This would constitute a rather remarkable act on Postgate's part, trusting that some portion of the adult viewership would have sufficient recollection of the black-and-white *Ivor the Engine* series to make this connection, and thereby justify the incongruity of Dinwiddy's remarks.

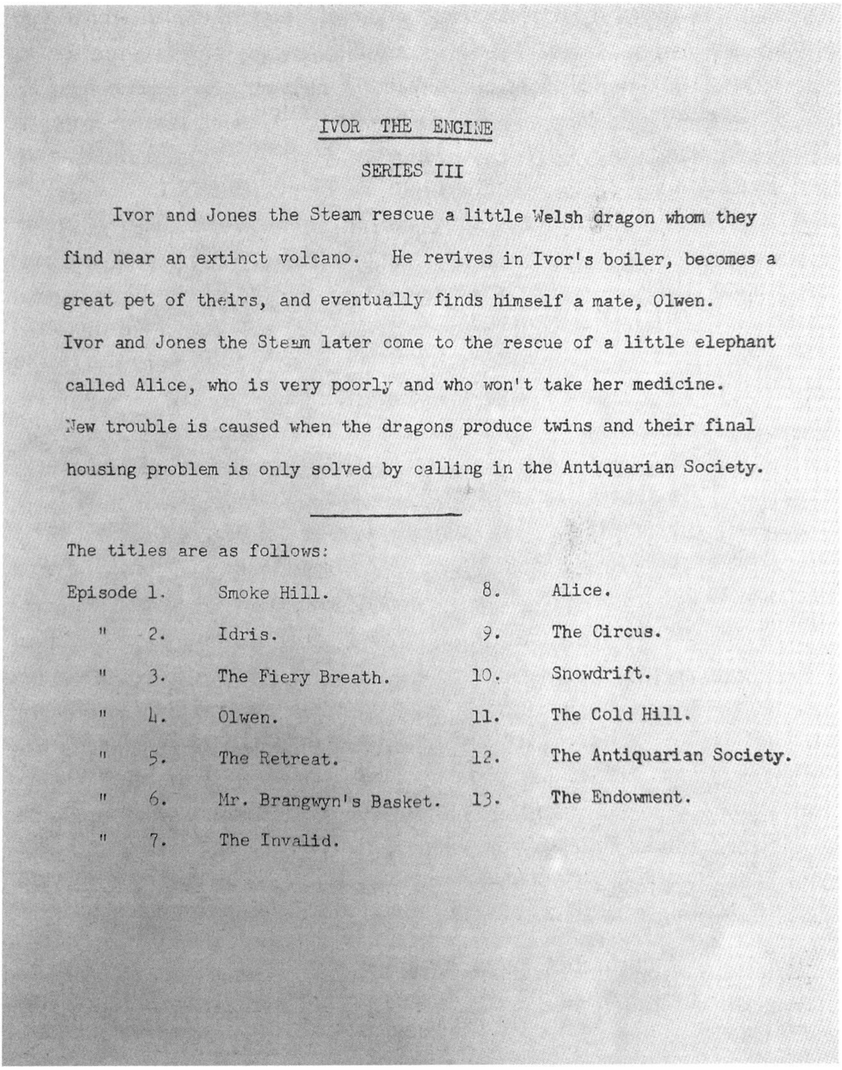

IVOR THE ENGINE

SERIES III

Ivor and Jones the Steam rescue a little Welsh dragon whom they find near an extinct volcano. He revives in Ivor's boiler, becomes a great pet of theirs, and eventually finds himself a mate, Olwen.

Ivor and Jones the Steam later come to the rescue of a little elephant called Alice, who is very poorly and who won't take her medicine.

New trouble is caused when the dragons produce twins and their final housing problem is only solved by calling in the Antiquarian Society.

The titles are as follows:

Episode				
1.	Smoke Hill.	8.	Alice.
2.	Idris.	9.	The Circus.
3.	The Fiery Breath.	10.	Snowdrift.
4.	Olwen.	11.	The Cold Hill.
5.	The Retreat.	12.	The Antiquarian Society.
6.	Mr. Brangwyn's Basket.	13.	The Endowment.
7.	The Invalid.		

Figure 2.19 *Ivor the Engine* (black-and-white) third series episode outline, *c.* 1963–4.

Another possible explanation to this conundrum is that, given the standalone nature of 'Unidentified Objects', which means that it could feasibly fit almost anywhere in the overarching series narrative, is that following the delivery of the episode by Firmin and Postgate, the BBC chose to air the episode at an earlier time than originally suggested by the Smallfilms duo. This explanation can be ruled out, given the materials that have survived in Oliver Postgate's personal archive, which includes the original episode synopsis and the final run schedule for the colour series. In this document, Postgate eventually lists 'Unidentified Objects' as episode thirteen, matching the sequencing broadcast by the BBC.[37]

Then there is the most likely explanation: Postgate and Firmin made a continuity mistake. It is reasonable to see how the writing of a new episode, in this case 'Unidentified Objects', by drawing upon two distinct narrative threads, spanning the black-and-white and colour *Ivor* series, coterminous in their overarching objective, but divergent in their pacing, might result in such an error in script continuity. Regardless of the conundrum, the fact that Postgate has Dinwiddy make these remarks shows a high degree of narrative ambition to weave a subplot across multiple episodes, and potentially multiple decades, thereby revealing the colour *Ivor the Engine* episodes as much more than just straightforward adaptations of the earlier black-and-white episodes.

Branch lines and sidings

During Postgate's lifetime, extending Ivor beyond the realm of TV proved a mixed experience. Reflecting on the early promise of BBC merchandising initiatives set in motion in 1967, Postgate writes in his autobiography: 'for reasons I have never fathomed, our characters didn't really take off into the big time of merchandising'.[38] Contained in the BBC archive is a letter written by Firmin to Roy Williams, then Commercial Manager at the BBC, which provides an update on merchandising activity related to the colour Ivor (Figure 2.20).

Simply dated 13 February, it is likely that Firmin wrote this letter in early 1976, not early 1975 (when pre-production agreements for the colour Ivor were initiated), because Firmin makes reference to his hope that videotapes will be available for potential clients to see, at the time of writing. In another letter, written by Postgate, dated 22 December 1975, we can see that negatives were to be 'cassetted' by the BBC for Smallfilms to send out to their foreign agents. It is probable, then, that Firmin's letter (Figure 2.20) postdates that of Postgate. In the letter we can see the ambition of Firmin and Postgate to merchandise *Ivor the Engine*, with potential deals noted with Rovex (a toy manufacturer based in Margate who owned the Hornby brand), ICI (who at that time were invested in domestic decoration products such as wallpaper and paint), Liberta Imex (a generalist print company), and two publishers Abelard Schuman and Collins. Some products alluded to in Firmin's letter did come to fruition, such as ICI's wallpaper and multiple picture books, but for the most part, Firmin and Postgate were left frustrated on this front.

2. The Whimsical Authenticity of Smallfilms

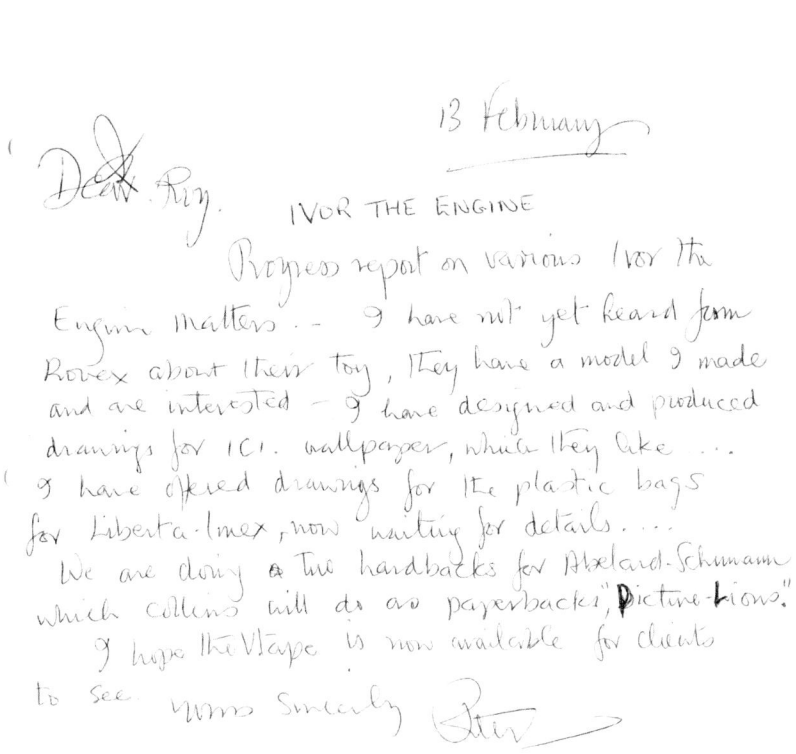

Figure 2.20 Peter Firmin describes *Ivor the Engine* merchandising initiatives.

Returning to *Ivor the Engine* in 1984, the BBC's Written Archives holds a collection of letters that details the production of another offshoot: a four-cassette audio series. These letters are exchanged between Firmin and Postgate, Vernon Elliott (the composer for the original TV series), and the BBC Records team, comprising Sylvia Cartner (overseeing the project), Maggie West (dealing with the contract), William Gregson (initially managing the recording process), and Mehmet Arman (who succeeded Gregson). These letters record a strained process, during which the creative vision of the BBC Records Team gradually begins to diverge from that of Firmin and Postgate.

The earliest letter held by the BBC from this production is dated 25 January 1984, from Postgate to Gregson, and serves to initiate the project. Much of this letter is matter-of-fact in tone, detailing what has been sent along with the letter (tape recordings and musical cue sheets), but Postgate also takes this opportunity to provide Gregson with 'some notes about selection', qualifying gently that they are 'only ideas'.[39] Notes these might be, but, because they occupy a full side of A4, these also contain detailed references to timings, and suggest episode selections, meaning that from the outset Postgate establishes a clear agenda: to craft a bespoke and appropriate narrative experience for the cassette series (Figure 2.21).

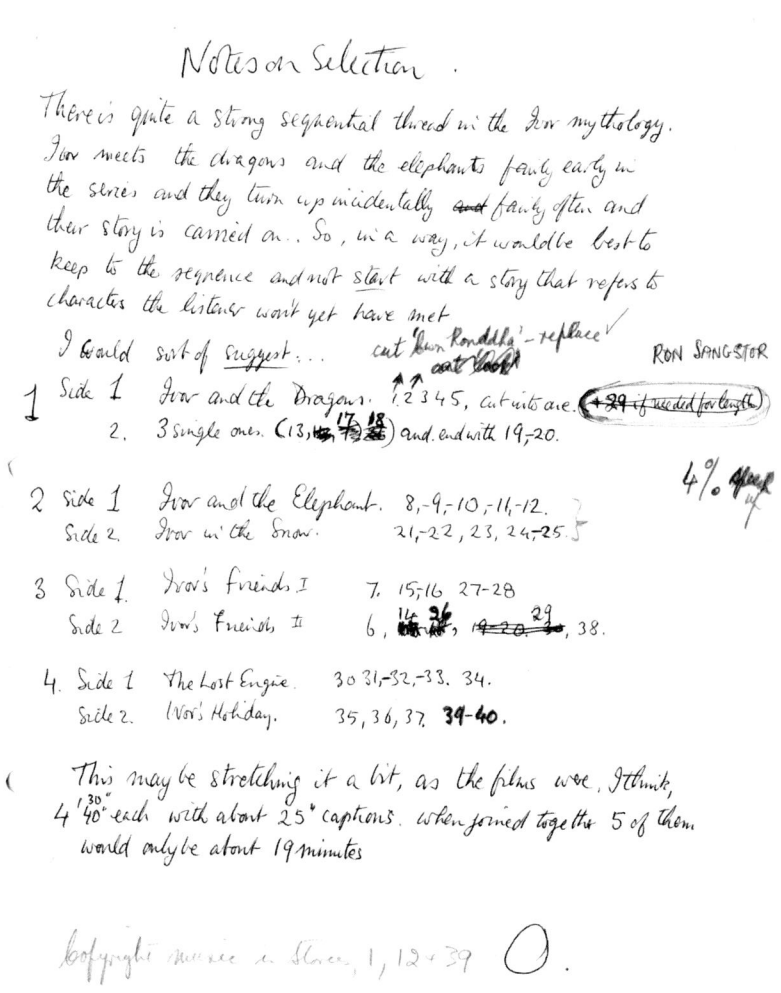

Figure 2.21 Oliver Postgate maps out his vision for the *Ivor the Engine* cassette series.

This is made explicit in Postgate's preamble to his page of 'notes' (transcribed here in case readers struggle to decipher Postgate's handwriting):

> *Notes on selection*
>
> There is quite a strong sequential thread in the Ivor mythology. Ivor meets the dragons and the elephants family early in the series and they then turn up incidentally fairly often and their story is carried on. So, in a way, it would be best to keep to the sequence and not <u>start</u> with a story that refers to characters the listener won't yet have met.[40]

Furthermore, the episodes suggested by Postgate – and the manner in which he describes how they could be cut – reveals his desire to see this cassette rendition of *Ivor the Engine* offer something new to the listener, while at the same time retaining the principles of whimsical authenticity that unpinned the series' success on television. This is most acutely evident in the suggestion to have cassette three comprise of a collage of encounters with 'Ivor's Friends', drawing upon sequences taken from episodes seven, fifteen to sixteen, twenty-seven to twenty-eight (side one) and six, fourteen, twenty-six, twenty-nine, thirty-eight (side two), thereby presenting the listener with a balanced diet of the everyday routines of the Merioneth and Llantisilly Rail Traction Company alongside the more fantastical events and encounters that happen along its lines.

The next two letters held by the BBC, another from Postgate (22 March 1984) and one from Firmin (24 April 1984), both focus on contractual discussions. After that, a letter from Postgate to Arman (5 May 1984), which begins: 'Sorry to have been so long coming back to you about this', voices his and Firmin's reservations about the BBC's plans to reproduce *Ivor the Engine* script materials verbatim, as an accompaniment to the cassette series. Postgate states unequivocally that 'to put the exact wording of the film scripts out as if they were a book would be a very bad idea', before offering the solution: 'I would of course be happy to write and record some of our work for that purpose.'[41]

Following this we find a letter from West (10 May 1984) that confirms certain contractual matters, a letter from Postgate (8 August 1984) following up a query from his accountant, and a letter from Elliott (undated, but stamped on receipt as 7 December 1984), which thanks West for sending complimentary copies of the cassettes to him following their general release. Shortly after this, Postgate writes to Arman (24 January 1985) to express his disappointment – and, more significantly, his disapproval – of the cassette series in its released form. Postgate opens his letter with a note of surprise, stating that, until he 'heard by chance' about the cassette's release (perhaps tipped off by his friend and long-time collaborator Elliott), he 'had assumed that the project had become side-tracked' and was still expecting to have an opportunity to 'hear the compilation before it was finally pressed'.[42] Postgate makes it clear to Arman that he was under the impression that the format proposed in his letter dated 25 January 1984, was the agreed format for the project, stating: 'If you remember we discussed this at some length when the project began.'⁴³ While Postgate's letter of 25 January 1984, was sent to Gregson, his reference to lengthy discussions, of which there is no record held by the BBC, suggests these were meetings in person and telephone conversations between Postgate and Arman after the exit of Gregson from the production. Postgate restates his view that the BBC has deviated from the agreed vision throughout this letter. Closing the letter, Postgate invites Arman to comment on the situation.

Postgate's letter prompted a busy period of internal fact-checking and contractual scrutiny. Cartner, the project lead, contacted Arman, opening her internal BBC memo thus:

> If you didn't agree to assemble the stories into 2 or 3 longish episodes, then you are in the clear. No-one told me to do it and Oliver Postgate didn't mention it to me. If he had I would have pointed out to him that by editing the stories and reassembling them we will not be putting out the original soundtracks of the films as stated on the record sleeve, we would have to say 'based on the original stories from the TV series' and that would not be the same as the TV series. I would also have pointed out that children want the stories as they have seen them on TV, that is why all our children's records are the complete story as in each episode of the TV series and we keep them separate so that they can pick out their favourite story on the record.⁴⁴

Cartner then goes on to highlight 'Clause 7' of the contract agreed with Smallfilms, which grants the BBC 'complete control over the content and format', before highlighting their compliance with Postgate's preferred ordering of the episodes, as well as the unexpected amount of technical work required to accommodate the 'extremely poor' quality of the tapes provided by Postgate.⁴⁵

In response, Arman drafted a letter following Cartner's guidance.⁴⁶ However, this letter, which adopts a robust tone, was never sent, and instead Arman called Postgate on 31 January 1985, to seek a resolution verbally.⁴⁷ The phone call worked and the last letter in this file, dated 9 February 1985, which comes from Postgate adopts a conciliatory tone (Figure 2.22).

These letters, while not a complete historical record (since they do not capture the meetings in person, phone calls, and any letters that may have been misfiled, damaged, or lost), provide an insight into the interpersonal dynamics of this project, and their desire to see the tone – of whimsical authenticity – translated in a meaningful way over to the audio series. As we will see throughout this book, both Postgate and Firmin placed extremely highly value on having creative control over their projects, and, at times, such as the example discussed here, it is possible to see how this exacting approach to the merchandising/extension of their TV works might have placed occasional strain on professional relationships.

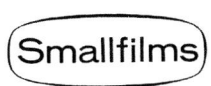

OLIVER POSTGATE & ASSOCIATES
76 HONEY HILL, NEAR WHITSTABLE, KENT CT5 3BP
TELEPHONE: BLEAN (STD CODE 022777)......305.
VAT REGISTRATION NO. 202 1102 56

REGISTRY
RH25
General

new phone number
Canterbury (0227) 471305

Mehmed Arman
BBC Enterprises (Records)

9 2 85

(1) Sylvia.
(2) Maggie - for file

Dear Mehmed Arman,

IVOR THE ENGINE

Thankyou for telephoning me about the Ivor record.

As you said, the whole thing does seem to have resulted from an initial misunderstanding that somehow survived the various discussions.

Such things just have to be weathered, so I thought I had better write and formally confirm that I find the record acceptable and, apart from a slight tendency to repeat itself in places, very clean and enjoyable. Perhaps you and all concerned will also accept my apologies for being so peevish about it.

with best wishes,
yours sincerely,

Oliver Postgate

Figure 2.22 The BBC and Smallfilms reach a truce.

Conclusion

This chapter has charted the evolution of *Ivor the Engine*, from the point of conception (and at the same time the inception of Smallfilms), through two TV series, one made in black and white that broke new ground for Associated-Rediffusion, and one made in colour for the BBC that secured the show's large and loyal fanbase, through various offshoots in the years following. Over the course of this chapter we have highlighted the concerted development of whimsical authenticity as a theme that is both a core component of *Ivor the Engine*'s appeal, as well as being a feature of much of Smallfilms' work in a broader sense. Of course, this is just one element of appeal found within the work of Smallfilms, and the chapters that follow will serve to emphasize a number of other key characteristics. Resisting the urge to stand still, never afraid to journey to uncharted lands in search of new characters and stories to tell, and always to adapt to new processes of animation. Leaving the top left-hand corner of Wales, our attention now turns to the northern lands of another Smallfilms realm.

Notes

1. Postgate, *Seeing Things*, p. 210; as noted in the introduction, we must remember that there is inevitably a degree of self-editorialization that occurs when working from memory, either in response to an interview question or as part of the process of writing an autobiography, so, whenever possible, this book seeks to draw upon as many perspectives as possible as a countermeasure to the editorialized quality of recollection.
2. Peter Firmin, interviewed by Chris Pallant, Canterbury, UK, 19 October 2017; Postgate, *Seeing Things*, p. 210.
3. Postgate, *Seeing Things*, p. 205.
4. Alistair McGown, 'Oliver Postgate and Peter Firmin', http://www.screenonline.org.uk/tv/id/562266/index.html (accessed 17 May 2021).
5. Postgate, *Seeing Things*, p. 207.
6. Postgate, *Seeing Things*, p. 208.
7. Postgate, *Seeing Things*, p. 209, italics in original.
8. Postgate, *Seeing Things*, p. 209.
9. Peter Firmin, interviewed by Chris Pallant, Canterbury, UK, 19 October 2017.
10. Peter Firmin, interviewed by Chris Pallant, Canterbury, UK, 19 October 2017.
11. Edith K. Ackerman provides a useful definition of whimsy, suggesting that it 'points to a quaint, fanciful, and mostly gentle form of humour that arises from treating "glitches," or quirks, as serendipitous "overtures" to unexpected possibilities'. See Edith K. Ackerman, 'Amusement, Delight, and Whimsy: Humor has its Reasons that Reason Cannot Ignore', *Constructivist Foundations* vol. 10 no. 3 (2015), p. 406. The wording used by Ackerman dovetails closely with that language found within the audience survey. Yet, as Moseley convincingly argues, building on the work of Warren S. Poland, when taken in isolation, the notion of whimsy is too 'light, sweet and quickly disappearing' to do justice to the depth of Smallfilms works. See Moseley, *Hand-made Television*, and Warren S. Poland, 'Whimsy', *Psychoanalytic Quarterly* vol. 79 no. 1 (2010), p. 236. Following this cue, and also the work of Philip Hayward,

who leverages the notion of whimsy in conjunction with concept of complexity to reveal the layered musical aesthetic of *Clangers,* the concepts of whimsicality and authenticity are twinned in this study to appropriately reflect both the textual qualities of the Smallfilms screen works themselves and also the overwhelming mood of the responses captured by the survey data. See Philip Hayward, 'Whimsical Complexity: Music and Sound Design in the Clangers', in K. J. Donnelly and Philip Hayward (eds), *Music in Science Fiction Television: Tuned to the Future* (New York and London: Routledge, 2013), pp. 72–86.

12 Neville Wortman, interviewed by Chris Pallant, London, UK, 15 July 2019.
13 Author's transcription from broadcast episode, available on Smallfilms' Facebook page, posted 18 September 2020, https://www.facebook.com/419889534720570/videos/352936362560732 (accessed 18 May 2021).
14 Goran Stefanovski, 'Teaching the "Unteachable"', Canterbury Christ Church University, 30 June 2015, pp. 5–6.
15 Peter Firmin, interviewed by Chris Pallant, Canterbury, UK, 19 October 2017.
16 Postgate, *Seeing Things*, p. 209.
17 Postgate, *Seeing Things*, p. 209.
18 Author's transcription from broadcast episode, available on Smallfilms' Facebook page, posted 18 September 2020, https://www.facebook.com/419889534720570/videos/352936362560732 (accessed 18 May 2021).
19 Author's transcription from broadcast episode, available on Smallfilms' Facebook page, posted 18 September 2020, https://www.facebook.com/419889534720570/videos/352936362560732 (accessed 18 May 2021).
20 For a deeper consideration of the craft traditions bound-up in the work of Smallfilms, see Postgate, *Seeing Things*, and Moseley, *Hand-made Television*, and for a more broad-base study of the interlinked concepts of craft and animation, see Ruddell and Ward, *The Crafty Animator*.
21 Peter Firmin, interviewed by Chris Pallant, Canterbury, UK, 19 October 2017.
22 Peter Firmin, interviewed by Chris Pallant, Canterbury, UK, 19 October 2017.
23 Peter Firmin, interviewed by Chris Pallant, Canterbury, UK, 19 October 2017.
24 Peter Firmin, interviewed by Chris Pallant, Canterbury, UK, 19 October 2017.
25 Peter Firmin, interviewed by Chris Pallant, Canterbury, UK, 19 October 2017.
26 Pallant, *Smallfilms: Audiences – data set*.
27 Oliver Postgate, interviewed by Tim Jones, Canterbury, UK, 14 July 1993.
28 Oliver Postgate, interviewed by Tim Jones, Canterbury, UK, 14 July 1993.
29 Casie Hermansson and Janet Zepernick, *The Palgrave Handbook of Children's Film and Television* (Basingstoke: Palgrave, 2019), p. 9.
30 The function of dual appeal is discussed widely under a variety of names, such as: 'Double Coding', a concept derived from the architectural scholarship advanced by Charles Jencks in *The Language of Post-Modern Architecture* (New York: Rizzoli, 1991); 'Narrative Layering', used by Adam Chapman to describe an approach to the tension of designing video game experiences that balance story/play, in *Digital Games as History* (New York and London: Routledge, 2016); and as 'Bi-Modal Address' by Carol A. Stabile and Mark Harrison in *Prime Time Animation* (Abingdon, UK: Routledge, 2003).
31 Oliver Postgate, interviewed by Tim Jones, Canterbury, UK, 14 July 1993.
32 Oliver Postgate, interviewed by Tim Jones, Canterbury, UK, 14 July 1993.
33 Author's transcription from broadcast episode, available on Smallfilms' Facebook page, posted 18 September 2020, https://www.facebook.com/419889534720570/videos/352936362560732 (accessed 18 May 2021).

34. Jonny Trunk and Richard Embray, *The Art of Smallfilms* (London: Four Corners Books, 2014), p. 200.
35. Postgate, *Seeing Things*, p. 320.
36. Author's transcription from broadcast episode, available on Smallfilms' Facebook page, posted 18 September 2020, https://www.facebook.com/419889534720570/videos/352936362560732 (accessed 18 May 2021), italics added for emphasis.
37. Ivor the Engine, colour series episode schedule, *c.* 1975, Ivor the Engine Folder, Oliver Postgate Archive, Postgate Family private collection.
38. Postgate, *Seeing Things*, p. 265.
39. Correspondence from Oliver Postgate to William Gregson, 25 January 1984, WAC R/125/401/1, Ivor the Engine, BBC Written Archives, UK.
40. Correspondence from Oliver Postgate to William Gregson, 25 January 1984, WAC R/125/401/1, Ivor the Engine, BBC Written Archives, UK.
41. Correspondence from Oliver Postgate to Mehmet Arman, 5 May 1984, WAC R/125/401/1, Ivor the Engine, BBC Written Archives, UK.
42. Correspondence from Oliver Postgate to Mehmet Arman, 24 January 1985, WAC R/125/401/1, Ivor the Engine, BBC Written Archives, UK.
43. Correspondence from Oliver Postgate to Mehmet Arman, 24 January 1985, WAC R/125/401/1, Ivor the Engine, BBC Written Archives, UK.
44. Correspondence from Sylvia Cartner to Mehmet Arman, 31 January 1985, WAC R/125/401/1, Ivor the Engine, BBC Written Archives, UK.
45. Correspondence from Sylvia Cartner to Mehmet Arman, 31 January 1985, WAC R/125/401/1, Ivor the Engine, BBC Written Archives, UK.
46. Unsent correspondence from Mehmet Arman to Oliver Postgate, no date, WAC R/125/401/1, Ivor the Engine, BBC Written Archives, UK.
47. Correspondence from Sylvia Cartner to Mehmet Arman, 31 January 1985, WAC R/125/401/1, Ivor the Engine, BBC Written Archives, UK.

Chapter 3

BUILDING WORLDS: *THE SAGA OF NOGGIN THE NOG* (1959–65, 1982)

> The obvious next move would be to expand. I could take on capital and form a proper film company, with a studio, employees and new, state-of-the-art equipment. That was the conventional approach and I could see that if I had personal ambition, if I wanted to make a name for myself in the field of film-making, if I wanted my work to become recognized as world-leading in its excellence and win Oscars, that was the way I would have to go.[1]

For readers familiar with the world and works of Smallfilms, you already know what is coming next, but for those readers who are discovering this story for the first time, Oliver Postgate's words are full of wry self-awareness. Postgate and Peter Firmin never did get an invite to the Oscars, their studio never grew beyond the walls of Firmin's repurposed farm sheds, yet their work, which spanned four decades, never once lacked ambition. Rather than driving towards restless expansion, glitzy recognition, and untold riches, Firmin and Postgate held an unwavering ambition to continually rewrite the Smallfilms narrative through their work, inventing a string of original worlds that captivated audiences across several generations.

Like *Ivor the Engine*, which was running on parallel tracks to *The Saga of Noggin the Nog* through 1959 into 1960,[2] it enjoyed a double life: being first broadcast in black and white between 1959 and 1965, before being rejuvenated in colour in 1982.[3] Unlike *Ivor the Engine* though, which enjoyed a comprehensive revival in colour, Smallfilms only produced a colour version of the second *Noggin* saga, 'The Ice Dragon', and a two-part colour adaptation of their 1971 *Noggin* book *The Pie*. Therefore, while the colourized world of *Ivor* expanded upon the original black-and-white narrative, the colour *Noggin* episodes offered a more concentrated return to the 'Lands of the North' and the show's cut-out animation style. Given that both colour reboots were commissioned and funded by the BBC, this difference in approach reflects the shifting attitudes of the BBC towards the work of Postgate and Firmin in the early 1980s (see Chapter 9). In his own words, Firmin suggested that 'being an old-fashioned method' he didn't think the BBC 'were very keen' because Smallfilms 'didn't fit in with the modern tone of things'.[4]

Looking at the survey responses associated with both versions of *The Saga of Noggin the Nog* (Figure A.3), once again elements such as 'characters', 'story', and 'setting' are revealed as pervasive markers of appeal. Digging deeper into the data highlights the importance of the Norse mythology and the sense of history that Firmin and Postgate evoked throughout the series. Taken in combination, these elements all feed one common agenda: world building. Just like the quality of whimsical authenticity, established in the previous chapter, which informs almost all of Smallfilms' work, so does the desire to create and explore their imagined worlds, whether they are located in North Wales, the Nordic fjords, the ice sheets of Alaska, the deep sea, Kentish woodlands, outer space, the inner space of a doll's house, or the storefront of Bagpuss & Co. this focus on world building will be considered in detail here, using *The Saga of Noggin the Nog* as a case study. Divided into three main sections, this chapter offers: a discussion of the shifting domestic and production contexts within which Postgate and Firmin operated at the time of the show's creation; an analysis of the world-building strategies employed for this show; and a discussion of Firmin and Postgate's attempts to engage allegorically with contemporary sociopolitical tensions linked to nuclear arms.

1959

It is important that this history does not give an impression of a planned, predictable, linear march through time, with each new Smallfilms production following neatly on from the one before. This is not how we experience life, and any retelling of history along those lines should be treated with suspicion. This early chapter in the history of Smallfilms certainly resists chronological sequencing, as several significant and overlapping events happened in 1959 that are worth elaborating here. First, work on *Ivor the Engine* for Associated-Rediffusion continued through to spring of that year, coinciding with Prue Myers's due date (Myers being married to Postgate). With the arrival of twin boys in June 1959, the Postgate family clearly had new, domestic responsibilities to fulfil. Having concluded the production of *Ivor the Engine*, Postgate, who was then living in a modest flat in London, recalls how the arrival of twins 'and all their paraphernalia meant the camera and animation table were summarily banished from the bedroom'.[5] With the arrival of Simon and Stephen, the family numbered seven, with Postgate already stepfather to Prue's children: Kevan (fourteen in 1959), Kerris (twelve that year), and Krispian (six that year). The Firmin family numbered five in 1959, with Peter and Joan Firmin having welcomed three daughters between 1954 and 1958: Charlotte, Hannah, and Josephine. (By the end of 1964, the Postgate family would include another son, Daniel, while the Firmins would have three more daughters between 1960 and 1965: Katherine, Lucy, and Emily.) The blossoming nature of both the Postgate and Firmin families prompted a re-evaluation of their living arrangements, with both families deciding to move down to Kent in 1959.

Joan notes how they were familiar with the area, having visited on a number of occasions to meet up with old friends from their Central Arts days: 'we used to come down quite often and see them, and the distance between London and here isn't huge, and there is a decent railway, it's not too far. So, we knew what it was like, and the primary school up here was very well spoken about, so it seemed like reasonable place to go.'[6] Having discovered the favourable credentials of the area, the next step was to acquire property. While the Postgate family settled into a fairly conventional house, Peter and Joan opted for something more substantial: a small farmstead. The combination of the modest farmhouse and several dilapidated outbuildings, all connected by a sizeable garden, provided the impetus and opportunity for Smallfilms to grow. Joan recalls:

> The big barn had a thatched roof and the thatch had disappeared down the middle, so they saw the potential in it. It was ok for Peter because he was in that barn, he made that into his studio right from the beginning, and then Oliver quickly converted the cowshed. It was good getting out of the house, and actually having a space, because if you were in the house you get involved in things, not just telephone calls and things like that, but kids coming up and asking you to do this and do that, and there was always one that wasn't at school.[7]

This farmstead setup has provided inspiration for numerous headline writers over the decades,[8] yet this rather pastoral-romantic account of their creative process does not fully convey the mechanical ingenuity of their production setup.

Postgate notes how the cowshed was divided to allow close and complimentary working, with Postgate's equipment being housed in 'the dairy part', while Firmin had 'his studio and desk in the end where the cows had lived'.[9] This might seem a trivial detail, to note that the two inhabited adjacent workspaces, but this is an important transition to mark, given that prior to moving down to Kent, both families were based in London. Their newly established proximity meant that there would be 'no more tube journeys across London to fetch a carboard leg, or half a dozen tiny hands'.[10] This might seem like a small concern, yet such journeys were a routine inconvenience for Firmin and Postgate in their early days, given the fundamentally iterative nature of their creative process. While their stories were carefully scripted, and the animation timings were calculated in advance, the absence of a detailed storyboarding or pre-visualization meant there was still significant room for improvisation – improvisation that typically required the creation of a new or replacement object by Firmin.[11] Whilst this process was a significant hindrance, arguably even a shortcoming, when based in different boroughs of London, when housed in the same cowshed, this ability to extend their creative freedom deep into the production of their shows, directly fuelled the handcrafted aesthetic that came to typify the work of Smallfilms.

> One of the virtues that Peter and I have when working, is that while we collaborate a lot in the conception and originally what is going on, he has his department and I have mine, and within reason we are very critical of what each other does, but we don't have any sovereignty over each other's department. So, most of our conversations take place by way of argument, which is fine. So, what we do,

when we get the first tape finished, the cassette tape (I make a cassette of the finished take), we then sit down together with this tape recorder and we play it backwards and forwards and backwards and forwards and we try to see what the pictures are, and unfortunately, he sees, being left-handed, moving from right to left, while I, being right-handed, move from left to right, and we got over this by sitting at opposite sides of the table.[12]

Once in the cowshed, Postgate set about building his animation studio. Built 'mainly out of scaffold poles and pieces of bicycle', Postgate remarked how it had 'several sophisticated facilities, like a piece of dressmaker's tape-measure glued to the back wall to show the height of the camera, side rollers to carry very long backgrounds and a new Meccano drive mechanism for the camera that had an electrically operated release', which gave 'an exposure of about three-quarters of a second for each frame'.[13] While these details are established in Postgate's autobiography, and they are a feature of the popular history of the studio, an important part of this history that has yet to be fully articulated is the role that Joan played in managing this domestic-professional spatial dynamic. Clearly, having a stop-frame setup that included elements such as Meccano, in a setting where young children lived and played, is a good way to endanger the continuity of your production – for example, it would take less than a minute (perhaps during a tea or toilet break) for a little Postgate or Firmin child to peep into the cowshed and spot the perfect piece of Meccano to complete a creation of their own, and in the process disrupt many hours' worth of stop-frame endeavour. The fact that no examples of such innocent interference have ever been put on record suggests that the Firmin and Postgate children were impeccably behaved. Perhaps. Or, more likely, that Joan, who ran the household, was ever-present and was therefore able to guide and supervise the children's play.[14]

As will be noted at multiple points later in this book, Joan Firmin contributed in various ways to the sustained success of Smallfilms, expertly fulfilling both domestic and creative roles. In recognizing these roles, it is not my intention to suggest a mutually exclusive dichotomy between Joan Firmin's running of the Firmin household and her contribution to Smallfilms' screen craft, and where one activity supersedes the other, rather, it is my intention to value both undertakings equally, and to acknowledge the blurred boundary between these arenas of activity. Ensuring the efficient running of the Firmin farmstead (which was the location for both the Firmin family home and the Smallfilms studio) did not preclude Joan from taking on screen-related labour (e.g. helping to design the Clangers), correspondingly, undertaking fabrication work to support the production of *Bagpuss* did not mean that she gained any extra support domestically. To use a term popularized by Penny Summerfield in her work on women's wartime lives, Joan's career can be seen as 'episodic', with her priorities and focus perpetually shifting between family and creative expression.[15] Furthermore, and borrowing from the work of Melanie Bell, it is essential to embrace both aspects of Joan's life and reconsider the terms by which we judge career success – terms that are often uneven by virtue of their patriarchal origin.[16]

3. Building Worlds

With the cowshed set up for production, work on *Noggin* began in earnest in the summer of 1959. While the popular perception of Postgate and Firmin casts Postgate as the author and animator, and Firmin as the one responsible for illustration and fabrication, it was actually Firmin who penned the first synopsis for *Noggin*, in the shape of the multi-page treatment that he produced for Associated-Rediffusion:

> I remember trying something out, I wrote a sort of outline of the first two stories, where he goes off in his long ship and, I was thinking of doing it as a live programme, you know, live cardboard animations, as it was in those days, and Associated-Rediffusion said 'No, no, this is not at all suitable for our audience, this is not suitable for children, they are too young for it, this is too sophisticated.' So I put it aside, talked to Oliver about it and he said 'I thought those chessmen have got story to tell', and he asked me if he could work on it, and I said fine, well I'm not going to be able to do anything with it. So, he said, 'why don't we try to produce it as a film and show it to the BBC'.[17]

Firmin's humility, here, has resulted in this extensive and detailed double episode treatment (Figures 3.1 to 3.3) being reframed as merely an 'outline':

> I did a sort of outline, I'm not really a writer, my attempts at humour and satire aren't very clever, so Oliver took it over and added those extra characters and brought in the king of walruses and developed the character of Nogbad, and things like that, and we did a few sort of sketches, and Oliver wrote a couple of scripts and we took them to the BBC, and they said 'yes, we'd like to try this'. [...] We sold Noggin on a very rough book, with a few drawings and script or two. Because we'd done Ivor, and they'd all liked Ivor [...] the BBC tended to trust Oliver, he had that sort of amazing confidence to explain what he was doing and they realized that.[18]

Seeing the detail of these treatments, it is clear that Firmin's writing did contribute significantly to the tonal development of *Noggin*, and while there is no doubt that Postgate's writerly labour was ultimately greater than Firmin's, this should not erase the fact that Firmin did more than just provide the illustrations for the show.

Establishing the world of Noggin: *Norse authenticity and sagic whimsy*

As noted at the start of this chapter, a range of respondents highlighted specific Nordic elements as being central to the appeal of the series in question. For example: 'Amazing re-imaging of nordic sagas' (R591); 'Loved the Norse myths' (R324); 'Was always fascinated by Norse myths and loved Thornogsson [*sic*]' (R57); with one respondent even drawing parallels with contemporary Scandinavian programming, noting the 'almost scandi-noir feel to the stories' (R129). Responses also point to the ambition of Firmin and Postgate to forge connections between their imagined realm and surviving details of twelfth-century Norse culture: 'I was immersed in Nogland. My father had a model of one of the Lewis chessmen,

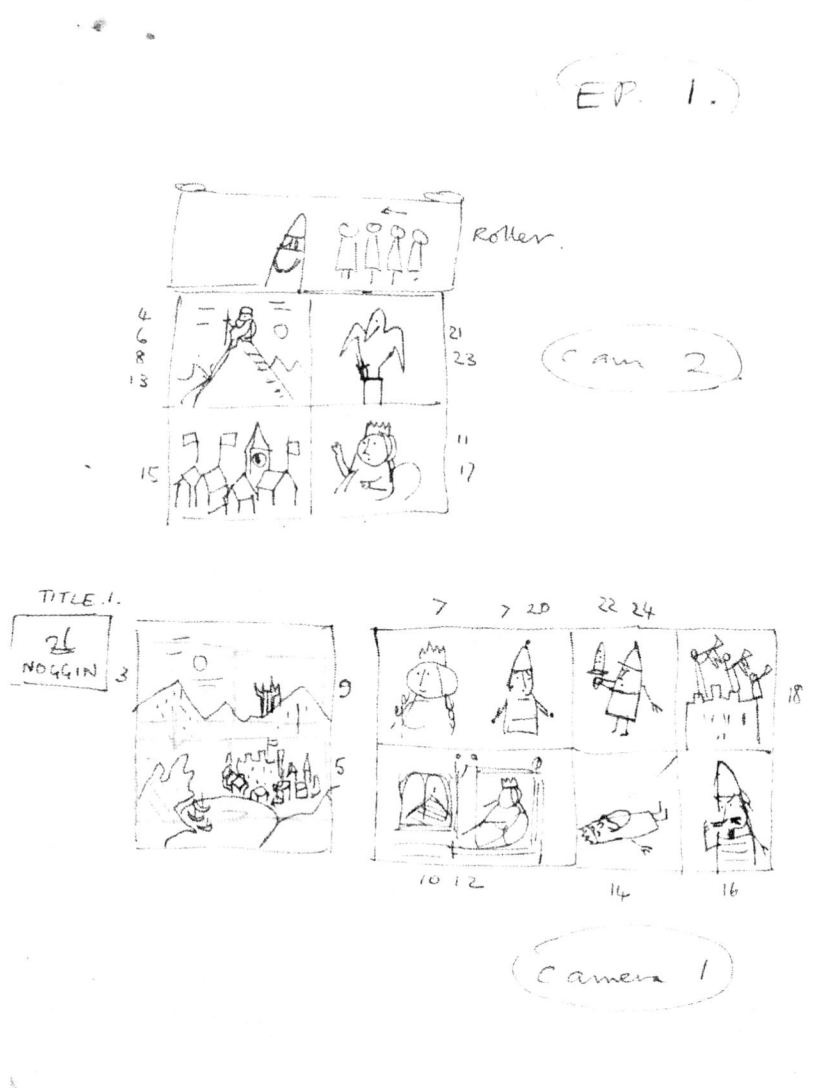

Figure 3.1 Script material from Peter Firmin's original synopsis for *Noggin the Nog*.

which I loved as a child, and that may have had something to do with it too.. and as I got older and learned about Norse mythology, I saw how clever it was and loved it more' (R127); 'It uses an epic Icelandic Saga structure cleverly undercut by Postgate's naturalistic writing and delivery' (R152); and 'It was true to the Norse mythology it represented and sparked in the infant me a thirst for knowledge.

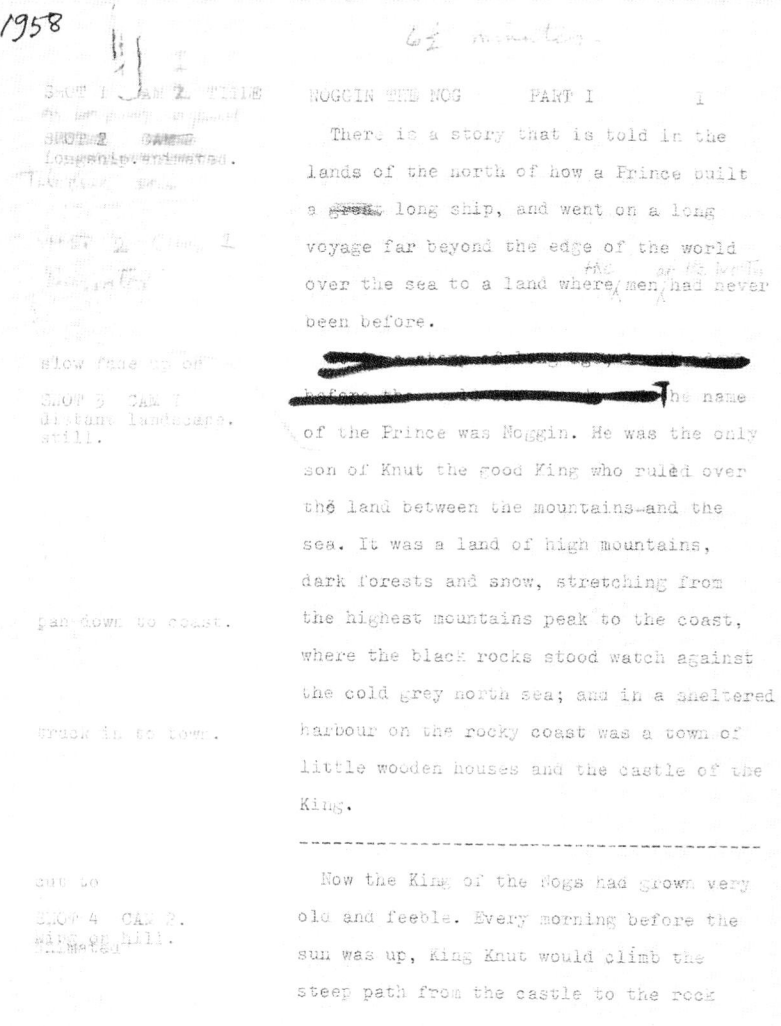

Figure 3.2 Live performance plans from Peter Firmin's original synopsis for *Noggin the Nog*.

As with all Smallfilms stuff, it wasn't patronising and used language that caused young minds to ask questions. It was deep rather than shallow (as also was *Trumpton*, etc) and quietly passed on its moral message in a subtle way' (R173).

To help contextualize these responses – especially for readers who might be unfamiliar with the precise details of the show – it is worth taking a moment to provide an account of how the first episode begins. In a nod to the oral traditions

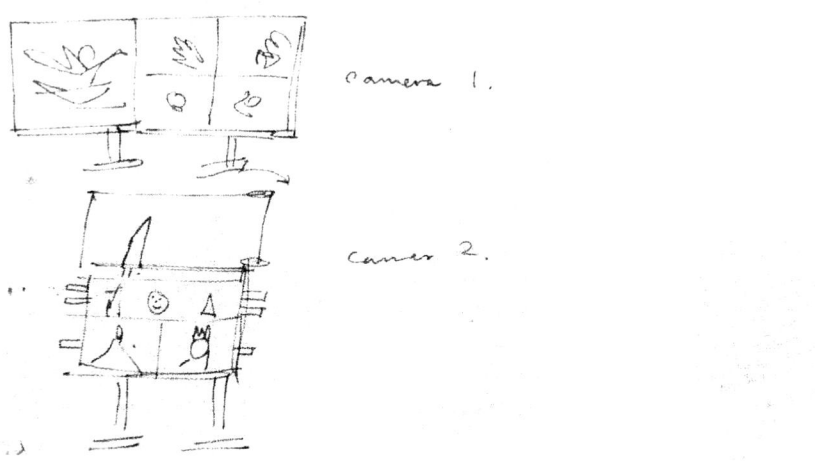

Figure 3.3 Previsualization sketches from Peter Firmin's original synopsis for *Noggin the Nog*.

of storytelling that preceded the written Nordic sagas,[19] Postgate serves as narrator and tells *The Saga of Noggin the Nog*:

> In the lands of the North, where the black rocks stand guard against the cold sea [Figure 3.4], where the dark night is very long, the men of the northlands sit by the great log fires, and they tell a tale [Figure 3.5]. They tell how a Prince built a

3. Building Worlds   63

Figure 3.4 The inlet to Noggin's Fjord from *The Saga of Noggin the Nog* (1959–65).

Figure 3.5 Oral saga tradition as seen in *The Saga of Noggin the Nog* (1959–65).

Figure 3.6 Prince Noggin from *The Saga of Noggin the Nog* (1959–65).

long ship and sailed in it beyond the black ice at the edge of the world to bring home his bride from the land of the midnight sun. Noggin the Nog [Figure 3.6] was the name of the Prince, young and strong and fair as men of the northlands are, and he was the son of Knut, King of the Nogs, ruler of this land of dark forest and snow.

This land of mountains and valleys and deep narrow bays where the sea roars between the black rocks and the wind howls cold in the night. There was the little town of wooden houses, clustered by a bay where the sea was calm [Figure 3.7]. And there above it was a small castle, the castle of King Knut [Figure 3.8]. Now, every morning as the sun rose, King Knut put on his crown and took his morning walk, up the steep paths beside his castle to the rock above the town, the rock which was known as 'Knut's Seat' [Figure 3.9].

There he sat [Figure 3.10], and as the sun rose behind the mountains to melt away the black clouds and night, King Knut would begin to worry. He would look down on the harbour and the houses and he would worry about his people and what they would eat in winter, and whether their roof's leaked, and whether

Figure 3.7 Noggin's coastal settlement as seen in *The Saga of Noggin the Nog* (1959–65).

Figure 3.8 The castle of King Knut/Noggin the Nog from *The Saga of Noggin the Nog* (1959–65).

Figure 3.9 King Knut walking to 'Knut's Seat' as seen in *The Saga of Noggin the Nog* (1959–65).

they had warm socks in this cold weather. He would look down on his castle and worry about his queen, Grunhilde, and who would look after her when he died for he was a very old king and not at all well. And then he would think about his son, Noggin, and he would worry about Noggin, because it was a custom in the northland that the kind should be married, and if not Noggin had chosen a maiden to be his queen within six weeks of his father's death then he could not be king, and then the crown would go to his wicked uncle, Nogbad the Bad. And then the kind would look out over the town and the bay and see beyond it the forbidding turrets of the castle of Nogbad [Figure 3.11], towering above the forest and he would worry about Nogbad and what would happen to his beloved peoples if the wicked Nogbad should ever become King of the Nogs. And the people of the town would look up at the rock and see their king sitting their worrying, and they would say 'don't worry old king, it'll be alright' [Figure 3.12]. But, of course, the King went on worrying just the same.

Figure 3.10 King Knut sits and worries in *The Saga of Noggin the Nog* (1959–65).

Figure 3.11 The castle of Nogbad the Bad as seen in *The Saga of Noggin the Nog* (1959–65).

Figure 3.12 Villagers telling the King not to worry in *The Saga of Noggin the Nog* (1959–65).

By detailing the introductory narration of *The Saga of Noggin the Nog*, it is possible to identify several roots of the audience appeal noted above. It is also possible to identify formative characteristics that would develop across the series as a whole, which refer back to twelfth-century Nordic culture; notable also are the number of these characteristics that were introduced by Firmin in his original treatment, which becomes clear if we compare Firmin's synopsis (Figures 3.1 to 3.3) with certain details featured in the opening monologue as written by Postgate.

In the introduction, we hear of 'how a Prince built a long ship and sailed in it beyond the black ice at the edge of the world to bring home his bride from the land of the midnight sun'. Here, Postgate and Firmin (Figure 3.1) seek to evoke a range of influences. The undertaking of such a voyage draws parallels with the Vinland Sagas, which centred on the settling of Greenland and the exploration of landmasses around Newfoundland, Baffin Island, and Labrador.[20] Firmin was certainly aware of Erik the Red's story, referring to it as an early source of inspiration, alongside the Lewis Chessmen, for his Noggin synopsis.[21] Postgate, by identifying the destination of Noggin's quest as 'the land of the midnight sun', further extends the correspondence between these formative plotlines in *The Saga of Noggin the Nog* and the voyage to Greenland – and beyond – in the Vinland Sagas. Furthermore, the process by which the exact details of Noggin's bride-to-be are revealed, courtesy of the walrus-tusk blade carried by Graculus, which bears an image of Nooka, daughter of Nan of the Nooks, offers additional associations with the Inuit culture. While the association of the walrus-tusk blade with ancient Inuit culture is more straightforward, with such items being useful tools and commodities for trade, the significance of Nooka's name is perhaps less obvious.[22] Postgate recalls how this part of the plot was suggested by Hannah Firmin, Peter and Joan's four-year-old daughter, as she 'had seen the famous film *Nanook of the North* [1922] which was about the home life of Eskimos and had decided she was a Nook and could not therefore be expected to wear pyjamas in bed'.[23] *Nanook* is a much-discussed film, in so much as it represents an early keystone for the documentary form, yet the film-maker Robert Flaherty, through his uncompromising efforts to secure a record of ethnographic *fact*, frequently takes *Nanook* into the territory of *fiction*.[24] Ultimately, while generated by a myriad of inspirational forces, this predicament – the need to voyage the seas to unite with Nooka – establishes the overriding narrative tension that runs through the first saga: will Nogbad prevent the union of Noggin and Nooka?

Another passage of the introduction that establishes significant historical detail refers to the Nog's settlement, describing 'the little town of wooden houses, clustered by a bay where the sea was calm', above which is 'a small castle'. These details, which were established in Firmin's synopsis and developed by Postgate, and their depiction on-screen, closely links the Nog settlement with that of Norwegian coastal habitations during the medieval period. Jesse L. Byock, contrasting Icelandic and Norwegian defensive philosophies of the medieval period, notes how, by being so remote and thereby free from the threat of invasion, 'Iceland was left alone to develop a societal structure corresponding to its internal needs. In this respect it was completely different from the rest of the Norse cultural area (or form all of Europe for that matter), where attack could be frequent and swift.'[25] In Norway, 'whose long coastline and numerous fjords approximate Iceland's coast, the fear of surprise attacks bound the regional communities into a cohesive military, and hence political, units which could successfully defend their borders'.[26] Furthermore, comparing the iconography of King Knut's castle (Figure 3.8) with that of defensive architecture from the early to mid-medieval period, reveals a rather incongruous detail: machicolated upper battlements. Machicolations (gaps in the battlement floor that purposefully overhung the outer castle wall) allowed those defending the castle from attack to retain a line of sight – and firing line for their archers – upon their assailants, who would otherwise reach a shielded angle at the base of the castle's outer wall. Rainet Atzbach notes how, by around the fourteenth century, 'machicolations were known throughout Europe, but the use of both machicolations and bretèches declined in parallel to the spread of hand firearms in the 15th and 16th centuries', because 'the advantage of defending a castle by means of gravity simply turned into a disadvantage when attackers became able to fire directly at their enemies through these wall openings'.[27] Of course, *The Saga of Noggin the Nog* takes place in an imagined past, so there is no requirement that the architecture or military customs of Noggin's land should be historically appropriate to the *c.* 900–1100 time period of the story. Instead, it is useful to establish the amount of medieval reference points that Firmin, through his synopsis and visual work, and Postgate, through the narrative, embed within *The Saga of Noggin the Nog*. It is the presence of these details that serves to establish a sense of composite authenticity regarding Norse identity that was a key appeal for many of the viewers.

While the elements discussed above situate the appeal of *Noggin* in recognizable historical details, the following serves to highlight the importance of the whimsical/authentic coupling as a site of considerable appeal within *Noggin*. Within the survey we can see how notions of surrealism, magic, absurdity, and humour feed into the overarching Smallfilms constant of whimsical authenticity. One respondent writes: 'Very positive main character, fabulous voice over (probably the main reason – I'm a natural storyteller myself and this was a great role model for me), and what I now think of as a surreal mix of myth and history but at the time seemed like highly probable history!' (R124). Contained in this single response are the two prevailing themes identified by respondents: story craft and humour, and the more magical and surreal passages that punctuate Noggin. Stating what they like most about Noggin, the following comments highlight these themes of story craft and humour: 'Great storytelling' (R410); 'Because it was funny' (R31); 'Fun. Historical' (R146); and 'Style, atmosphere and wit' (R15). While other responses highlight the more magical and surreal qualities of Noggin as key elements of appeal: 'Seemed magical' (R430); 'Magical realism' (R386); 'It was so surreal, which was wonderful when I was a kid' (R280); and 'The deadpan delivery of ironic humour, the absurdism and the gentle pacing' (R286).

A good example of this whimsical storytelling can be seen in episode three of the second saga, *The Saga of Noggin the Nog: Noggin and the Ice Dragon* (1961). Midway through this episode, Noggin and his expeditionary group are carried through the air by Graculus's family to the Hot Water Valley, but upon arrival they find it deserted:

Ronf   Welcome to the Hot Water Valley.
Noggin   Thank you, Ronf, and thank you birds for carrying us.
Ronf   This is my valley and the home of my people.
Noggin   Well, there don't seem to many people about.
Ronf   Oh, they're there alright, hiding in caves and holes in the ground for fear of the dragon. Come down to my house, it isn't far from here, only keep very quiet, and if you hear the dragon you must hide at once.
At which point the party descends into the valley and arrives at Ronf's house.
Ronf   I don't think it's big enough for you to come indoors, but in any case, it isn't very safe in house, let's go into the trench at the end of the garden. That's where I've lived mostly since the dragon came.
Narrator   Noggin, Thornogsen, and Graculus hid in the trench at the end of the garden and Ronf went into the house to make a pot of tea.

Figure 3.13 Noggin, Thornogsen, and Graculus take cover in *The Ice Dragon* (1961).

At this moment the camera frame begins to shake, and we hear the distant rumble of heavy footsteps. Hearing this, the party responds with a reasonable degree of trepidation (Figure 3.13). Crouching deeper into the trench, we see Ronf make a desperate dash for cover, spilling his tea tray in the process.

> **Ronf** It's coming, keep down.
> *At which point the dragon comes into view, walking though the village in search of the Hot Valley's inhabitants.*
> **Ice Dragon (Groliffe)** There must be some somewhere, there must be. There must be some somewhere, oh dear.
> *Unable to find anyone, the dragon then turns and begins to leave.*
> **Noggin** Fly up and see where it goes, Graculus.
> **Graculus** It's flying up into a valley on the side of the mountain. Look over there, you should be able to see it.
> **Noggin** Well, let's have that cup of tea, and we'll think about what to do next.
> **Narrator** Fortunately, the teapot wasn't broken and hadn't spilled much, so they had a cup of tea and thought [Figure 3.14].[28]

This sequence combines all of the elements noted by the respondents, resulting in a sequence that oscillates between fantastical adventure, mild peril, everyday routine (tea drinking) pathos, and humour, thereby evoking a strong sense of whimsy.

Figure 3.14 The recurrent ritual of taking tea as seen in *The Ice Dragon* (1961).

As we find throughout the Smallfilms universe, there is a recurrent recognition that flights of fantasy must be counterbalanced with details of the everyday – we found this in *Ivor the Engine* (detailed in Chapter 2), and we find it again here. Defining whether this approach to storytelling represents something of a guaranteed magic formula, allowing audiences to invest themselves fully into fantasy spaces, by virtue of repeated encounters with familiar and quotidian events (such as eating fish and chips and drinking cups of tea), is beyond the remit of this book. Yet, by bringing recognizable details of everyday life into their whimsical worlds, Firmin and Postgate allow audiences to relate to – and invest in – characters that might otherwise be seen as two-dimensional distractions.

Reflections of the contemporary world: Firecake as nuclear allegory

The final saga in the initial black-and-white series, *The Saga of Noggin the Nog: Noggin and the Firecake* (1965), sees Firmin and Postgate push their work in a more politically minded direction. Spanning three episodes, *Noggin and the Firecake* tells a cautionary tale of how an explosive invention, called 'Firecake', can cause tremendous damage and harm if used without care. Invented by Olaf the Lofty, the episode starts with Noggin running to meet Olaf on his castle battlements, prompted by the sound of a huge explosion and Olaf's

Figure 3.15 Explosion damage as seen in *The Firecake* (1965).

exuberant cries of 'marvellous, marvellous, oh it's marvellous'. Described as the 'most powerful stuff in the world' by Olaf, the destruction caused by 'only half a teaspoon' is substantial (Figure 3.15). After making sure that Olaf is ok, Noggin decrees: 'If you're going to do demonstrations of your stuff, whatever you call it […] You will have to demonstrate it somewhere else, somewhere a long way away, up in the hills or somewhere.' Excited by this suggestion, Olaf immediately schedules a demonstration up in the mountains, in a place called Roundhead Valley.

The story then moves to Roundhead Valley and we see Olaf making final preparations to test his new batch of Firecake. Keen to ensure a more controlled outcome than his first destructive test, Olaf asks the attendees to take cover; however, like his first test, this second explosion draws a similarly horrified response from Noggin:

Olaf Everybody take your places please, hide behind the rocks, please. Ladies and gentlemen, here you see the most powerful invention in the whole world, this is Firecake, this is the stuff that will change the face of the world!
The Firecake explodes with enormous force, shattering rocks and sending debris high into the air.
Noggin No, most definitely no!
Olaf But with that stuff you could change the face of the world.

Noggin   Could! You already have. Goodness knows what damage you have done already! Look, that rock, it's cracked clean in half. No, Olaf, you were very clever to have invented it, it's marvellous stuff, but now you're going to something much more clever and marvellous.

Olaf   Oh yes?

Noggin   You are going to forget all about it. You are going to forget you ever invented it, destroy whatever is left, and burn the papers. I want no trace of it left in the world.[29]

At this point, Olaf appears to acquiesce. As the Nogfolk begin to make their way back to the village, only Prince Knut senses something has changed in Roundhead Valley as a consequence of Olaf's Firecake detonation. We soon discover that the large boulders that populate Roundhead Valley are in fact the tops of the heads of ancient giants, who have buried themselves deep into the ground to guard a magic sword.

That night, one of the giants, still in rock form, comes to the village and sits against the wall of Noggin's castle. Time passes and Knut becomes fond of this silent, unmoving stone giant. One evening, Knut is unable to sleep and is looking out of his window when he hears the sound of a song coming from inside the stone giant. After climbing down from his window to replenish the giant's crown of flowers, he is unable to reach back up to his bedroom window, so he settles in the giant's arms for the night. The stone giant transforms into his regular giant form and carries Knut off into the night. Waking, Knut is reassured by the giant, who shows Knut the world from his high vantage point. Knut also gains the power of penetrating sight, by virtue of being in the giant's arms, and as the giant carries him to Roundhead Valley, Knut is able to see sleeping villagers through the walls of their homes, sleeping birds through the branches of their trees, sleeping rabbits through the earth walls of their warrens, and sleeping fish deep beneath the surface of their fjords.

Arriving in Roundhead Valley, the giant shows Knut what lies beneath the ground, as the narrator recounts: 'The sword was driven through five gold rings deep in the earth, each gold ring led through the earth to one of the five round-topped stones. Knut saw that each stone was really a giant, a calm, sad, gentle-faced giant, like the one who carried him.' The action then cuts back to Noggin, who, after realizing that Knut and the stone giant are missing, gathers a search and rescue party. Eventually, they spot the giant approaching and ready themselves to attack. At the last moment, Nooka spots that Knut is safely in the giant's arms and calls off the attack, allowing the giant to return Knut safely to the village.

Fearing the unpredictable nature of the giant, Olaf reveals to Graculus that he ignored Noggin's command to destroy the Firecake recipe, arguing that Noggin will surely be glad to have more Firecake to deal with the giant that took his son the night before. One of Nogbad's crows overhears this conversation and a short while later returns with reinforcements to steal Olaf's recipe. Graculus finds the crows in a forest gathering charcoal (one of the Firecake ingredients) and follows them back to Nogbad's ruined black castle, where he finds him making Firecake. After being informed of Nogbad's devious activities by Graculus, Noggin assembles his troops and makes for the black castle. After being spooked by clattering noises, Noggin and Thornogson lead an assault on the black castle, only to find it deserted. A note left by Nogbad which states: 'Sorry to have missed you. I have gone to fetch the sorcerer's sword. Love to all, Nogbad. P.S. Hope you enjoyed the music. P.P.S Thanks for the Firecake recipe, it has been very useful.'

At this point, Thornogson recites the legend of the magic sword, which he reveals once belonged to a powerful sorcerer, and how the holder of the sword can command obedience from anything in sight. Thornogson tells of how the giants buried it deep under a rock and guarded the rock forever. At that moment they hear an enormous explosion and see a giant mushroom cloud towering above Roundhead Valley (Figure 3.16). Working out that Nogbad must be plotting to use the Firecake to help acquire this sword, Noggin travels to Roundhead Valley in Olaf's flying boat, but crashes in a nearby lake after Nogbad's crows spring a mid-air attack. Nogbad is indeed in Roundhead Valley, readying a wide array of Firecake buckets, and when Graculus arrives, Nogbad tells the bird that he has enough Firecake 'to blow this whole valley, and everything in it, to a heap of rubble'.

Figure 3.16 A mushroom cloud as seen in *The Firecake* (1965).

Just as Noggin and his troops arrive, Nogbad frees the sword from the ground, freezing Noggin's army, rendering them powerless. Holding the sword and freezing all living things in sight, Nogbad announces his intentions:

> Now at last is Nogbad's hour, across the whole world, the power of the sword will bring me everything that I have always wanted. First of all the crown of the Northlands will be mine. Then, the crown of all the world. A world that moves at my command, or is still at my command, as now in the silence, the stillness, that I, Nogbad, have commanded.[30]

At this point, the stone giants emerge from the ground. Nogbad is powerless to stop them as the stone giants are neither living nor dead, they are godlike in their existence. As they group around Nogbad, pinning him, Knut, who had been carried to Roundhead Valley by the giant in the village, commands Nogbad to drop the sword. Nogbad obeys, allowing Knut to pick up the sword and smash into pieces, thereby breaking the enchantment.

Noggin's army then wakes, and the giants emerge from their stone form. The giants warn everyone not to touch the sword fragments as it is full of evil magic. Noggin instructs Olaf to use up the last of the Firecake to destroy the final fragments of the sword. Turning to Graculus, Noggin reflects on the events that have happened over the course of this saga: 'You know Graculus, I wonder which was more dangerous in the end, Olaf's Firecake or that magic sword? Olaf's invention I think, because the sword is broken forever now. But anybody can invent Firecake again if they're fool enough. Oh well, let's hope it won't be for a long time. Let's go home now, I'm hungry.'

For audiences at the time, and for readers now, the allegory of this saga is probably fairly easy to decode, with the Firecake representing the threat of nuclear weapons. Following the use of nuclear weapons in World War II, testing continued through the 1950s, with the explosive potential of the nuclear bombs increasing dramatically over the decade. In the United States, between 1951 and 1963, 'over a hundred aboveground atomic tests occurred at the Nevada Test Site. Each burst produced clouds that rose many thousands of feet, then tracked across the country, leaving a path of fallout in its wake.'[31] As well as the Soviet Union, which was equally committed to nuclear testing, many other countries began to conduct their own nuclear weapons research. Sarah J. Diehl, James Clay Moltz, and Mildred Vasan note:

> In October 1952, the United Kingdom joined the nuclear club by testing a plutonium fission bomb off the coast of Australia. France tested its first nuclear weapon in February 1960 at a site in the Sahara Desert. Several other states, including India, Israel, and China, also began research into nuclear weapons during the 1950s. In 1958, Washington began deploying nuclear-tipped cruise missiles on Taiwan and in South Korea for possible use against Chinese conventional (and future) forces.[32]

As Diehl, Moltz, and Vasan identify, towards the end of the 1950s tensions began to escalate as a result of such widespread nuclear activity. This nuclear testing reached its height with the detonation of the 50 megaton 'Tsar Bomba' in October 1961. Already double the size of any nuclear bomb detonated by the United States, the 'Tsar Bomba' was only partially filled, given concerns of fallout radius, it had the potential to deliver a detonation of 100 megatons if so desired. Regardless, the detonation of the 'Tsar Bomba' 'was more than a thousand times as powerful as the two bombs that were dropped on Japan, or ten times the yield of all conventional explosives used in the Second World War, or a quarter of the estimated yield of the eruption of Krakatoa in 1883'.[33] Almost exactly one year after the detonation of 'Tsar Bomba' the inevitable crisis point was reached.

That moment, the Cuban Missile Crisis of October 1962 was triggered by the brinksmanship of the Soviet Union and the United States. Thankfully, nuclear Armageddon was averted. Understandably, the sociocultural backdrop to all this military nuclear posturing was vocal public protest. Popular opposition to nuclear weapons research grew particularly visible in the United States in the late 1950s, 'when health officials revealed the presence of radio-nucleids in cow's milk as far east as New York as a result of nuclear testing in Nevada'.[34]

Living through such times, it is tempting to ask not whether Postgate and Firmin sought to offer their support to the Complete Nuclear Disarmament (CND) movement with this heavily allegorical *Noggin* saga, but rather, how could they ignore it? Complete with mushroom clouds, flower rings (evoking thoughts of the peace movement), sword fragments that remain dangerous after breaking (representing a magic half-life), and the desire for a shared Firecake amnesty, the symbolism of *Noggin and the Firecake* is hardly subtle. Yet, in typical Postgateian fashion, he publicly denied any such intent:

> When I showed her the script Ursula Eason, the Deputy Head of Children's Programmes at the BBC, looked at me quizzically. 'Social comment now, is it?' she growled.
> 'No, not especially,' I replied, lying. 'Just another saga, like the others.' Ursula laughed and commissioned the films.[35]

This was a consistent feature of Postgate's public articulation of his creative works – they were just stories. However, as he indicates in this exchange with Eason, drawn from his autobiography, on this occasion he allowed some recognition of subtext to filter through to the surface. Firecake is an exception in this regard, and that he was willing to acknowledge this social commentary with regard to CND serves as an early indicator of a path he would follow much more publicly just over a decade later (see Chapter 9).

Conclusion

As we have seen over the course of this chapter, the subject of world building was something that both Postgate and Firmin took very seriously, and it is also a theme that is repeatedly shown to be a key source of appeal within the survey data. Having constructed the worlds of Ivor the Engine and Noggin the Nog, as well as successfully establishing Smallfilms as a purveyor of compelling animated television, they faced a question: what next? The answer, as was always the answer, was to look around themselves to find inspiration for their next imagined world. As the next chapter reveals, not only did these new worlds introduce viewers to new Smallfilms characters, Firmin and Postgate also expanded their approach to animation and took audiences beyond their well-established 2D hand-drawn style into the realm of stop-motion 3D model-based animation.

Notes

1. Postgate, *Seeing Things*, p. 221.
2. It should be noted that Postgate and Firmin also worked on other comissioned projects during this time, such as 'Benjy and Bolt' (1960), which was an episode supplied for the BBC's *For Deaf Children* programming. It is unlikely that 'Benjy and Bolt' was a formal Smallfilms production, and no reference is made to it in Postgate's autobiography. At present, all we know about this show is contained in the BBC Genome entry for it: https://genome.ch.bbc.co.uk/search/0/20?order=first&filt=service_bbc_television_service&q=benjy+and+bolt#top (accessed 10 Dec 2021).
3. There is a common factual error that claims *The Saga of Noggin the Nog* was broadcast in colour on the BBC between 1979 and 1980. I have attempted to trace the origin of this factual error, but the precise origin is unclear. This error, at the time of writing, is repeated on the BBC's website ('The Saga of Noggin the Nog First Transmitted', https://www.bbc.com/historyofthebbc/anniversaries/september/noggin-the-nog [accessed 24 May 2021]), in a *Radio Times* article ('The 50 Greatest Children's TV shows of all Time', *Radio Times* 13 January 2018), and on numerous personal blogs. The correct broadcast year, 1982, is stated – albeit rather buried – in Postgate's autobiography, is recorded on BBC Genome, and on the BFI's ScreenOnline database (Alistair McGown, 'The Saga of Noggin the Nog (1959)', http://www.screenonline.org.uk/tv/id/562377/index.html [accessed 8 June 2021]). IMDB offers both versions of history, citing 1979 to 1980 as the headline broadcast dates, but then only citing 1982 as the credit for all of the individuals involved.
4. Peter Firmin, interviewed by Chris Pallant, Canterbury, UK, 2 November 2017.
5. Postgate, *Seeing Things*, p. 217.
6. Joan Firmin, interviewed by Chris Pallant, Canterbury, UK, 4 October 2019.
7. Joan Firmin, interviewed by Chris Pallant, Canterbury, UK, 4 October 2019.
8. See 'Ivor the Engine Lost shows found in Pig Sty', *Express* 26 October 2010, https://www.express.co.uk/news/uk/207541/Ivor-The-Engine-lost-shows-found-in-pig-sty (accessed 8 June 2021); 'Lost Ivor the Engine Reels found in a Pig Sty', *WalesOnline* 26 October 2010, https://www.walesonline.co.uk/news/wales-news/lost-ivor-engine-reels-found-1893448 (accessed 8 June 2021); Nick Hartley, 'Cartoons: Inside the Cow Shed Where Classics were Made', *BBC News* 28 December 2019, https://www.bbc.co.uk/news/av/uk-wales-50906949 (accessed 8 June 2021).
9. Postgate, *Seeing Things*, p. 222.
10. Postgate, *Seeing Things*, p. 222.
11. For more detail regarding the tradition of storyboarding, see Chris Pallant and Steven Price, *Storyboarding: A Critical History* (Basingstoke: Palgrave, 2015).

12 Oliver Postgate, interviewed by Tim Jones, Canterbury, UK, 14 July 1993.
13 Postgate, *Seeing Things*, p. 222.
14 Joan Firmin, interviewed by Chris Pallant, Canterbury, UK, 4 October 2019.
15 Penny Summerfield, *Reconstructing Women's Wartime Lives* (Manchester: Manchester University Press, 1998).
16 Melanie Bell, 'Movie Workers: Women's Labouring Bodies in Britain's Film Studios', British Association of Film, Television and Screen Studies Annual Conference, 7–9 April 2021.
17 Peter Firmin, interviewed by Chris Pallant, Canterbury, UK, 2 November 2017.
18 Peter Firmin, interviewed by Chris Pallant, Canterbury, UK, 2 November 2017.
19 Theodore M. Andersson notes that the dating and ordering of written sagas is difficult, 'but more difficult still is any attempt to imagine their oral prehistory', and that while 'scholars agree that there was such a prehistory: that is, that the sagas were told in some form before they were written down. Just what that form may have been, however, is a matter of perennial debate.' See Theodore M. Andersson, *The Growth of the Medieval Icelandic Sagas (1180–1280)* (Ithaca, NY: Cornell University Press, 2006), p. 3.
20 Patricia D. Sutherland, Peter H. Thompson, and Patricia A. Hunt, 'Evidence of Early Metalworking in Arctic Canada', *Geoarchaeology: An International Journal* vol. 30 no. 1 (January 2015), passim.
21 Peter Firmin, interviewed by Chris Pallant, Canterbury, UK, 31 August 2016.
22 Christine Hatt, *The Peoples of North America before Columbus* (Milwaukee, WI: Raintree, 1999), p. 50.
23 Postgate, *Seeing Things*, p. 220.
24 See John W. Burton and Caitlin W. Thompson, 'Nanook and the Kirwinians: Deception, Authenticity, and the Birth of Modern Ethnographic Representation', *Film History* vol. 14 no. 1 (1 January 2002), pp. 74–86.
25 Jesse L. Byock, *Feud in the Icelandic Saga* (Berkeley: University of California Press, 1993), p. 77.
26 Byock, *Feud in the Icelandic Saga*, p. 77.
27 Rainer Atzbach, 'The Legend of Hot Tar Or Pitch as a Defensive Weapon', in Rainer Atzbach, Lars Meldgaard Sass Jensen, and Leif Plith Lauritsen (eds), *Castles at War* (Bonn: Hablet, 2015), p. 128.
28 Author's transcription from broadcast episode, available on YouTube, posted 22 November 2014, https://www.youtube.com/watch?v=zoq7qwTC1SU (accessed 1 June 2021).
29 Author's transcription from broadcast episode, available on YouTube, posted 22 January 2021, https://www.youtube.com/watch?v=WHOa-rJ-DDw (accessed 10 Dec 2021).
30 Author's transcription from broadcast episode, available on YouTube, posted 22 January 2021, https://www.youtube.com/watch?v=WHOa-rJ-DDw (accessed 10 Dec 2021).
31 Richard L. Miller, *Under the Cloud: The Decades of Nuclear Testing* (Texas: Two-Sixty Press, 1991), p. 8.
32 Sarah J. Diehl, James Clay Moltz, and Mildred Vasan, *Nuclear Weapons and Nonproliferation: A Reference Handbook* (Santa Barbara, CA: ABC-CLIO, 2002), p. 11.
33 Rodric Braithwaite, *Armageddon and Paranoia: The Nuclear Confrontation since 1945* (Oxford: Oxford University Press, 2018), p. 276.
34 Diehl, *Nuclear Weapons and Nonproliferation*, p. 10.
35 Postgate, *Seeing Things*, p. 247.

Chapter 4

AESTHETIC TRANSITION AND THE PERSISTENCE OF THE HANDMADE IN *THE SEAL OF NEPTUNE* (1960), *THE MERMAID'S PEARLS* (1962), AND *PINGWINGS* (1961–5)

Mr Pingwing   Television? What's television?
Penny Pingwing   Oh, Papa, you're so old-fashioned. You know, television, that box in Mrs. Farmer's sitting room. They all sit in front of it in the evenings and it shows them bright pictures.
Mr Pingwing   What, inside the box?
Paul Pingwing   Yes, Papa.
Mr Pingwing   Oh, whatever will they think of next![1]

Buoyed by the early successes of *Ivor the Engine* (for Associated-Rediffusion) and *The Saga Noggin the Nog* (for the BBC), the temptation to slide into a steady rotation of *Ivor* and *Noggin* productions would surely have prompted many an independent studio to settle. However, the domestic demands facing Peter Firmin and Oliver Postgate, who, at the start of the 1960s, were new homeowners with rapidly growing families, provided a steady dose of reality to fuel their creative drive. Consequently, Smallfilms produced three additional animated productions in the early 1960s taking them beyond their existing *Ivor* and *Noggin* commitments: *The Seal of Neptune* (1960 – employing cut-out animation), *The Mermaid's Pearls* (1962 – also cut-out animation), and *Pingwings* (1961–5 – introducing stop-frame model-based animation).[2] However, unlike *Ivor* and *Noggin*, which garnered a sizeable fanbase and thereby became prominent shows in the Smallfilms oeuvre, *The Seal of Neptune*, *The Mermaid's Pearls*, and *Pingwings* did not.

Reviewing the survey data gathered during the writing of this book, when looking at what percentage of respondents have knowledge of the shows in question, we find that *Ivor* was the most known in this grouping (colour: 84.6 per cent awareness; black and white: 50.8 per cent), with *Noggin* second (colour: 57.6 per cent; black and white: 45.2 per cent), *Pingwings* a distant third (10 per cent), and *The Seal of Neptune* and *The Mermaid's Pearls* suggesting less than 2 per cent awareness. Of course, when divorced of context, this data can take us only so far. Yes, *The Seal of Neptune*, *The Mermaid's Pearls*, and *Pingwings* are amongst the least well-known Smallfilms shows, but this does not make them any less important to the overarching historical narrative that this book is seeking to offer.

In fact, that *The Seal of Neptune* and *The Mermaid's Pearls* are still remembered at all is rather remarkable in itself.

For much of its early development, 'the television industry paid scant regard to preservation', partly due to the lack of recording technologies 'and partly because, until 1955, the majority of material was transmitted live'.[3] As Dick Fiddy notes, 'TV was thought of as an ephemeral medium, with no need of a history and the telerecording technique of archiving was rarely used and then mostly for items of outstanding historic interest or for sports and prestigious arts events.'[4] Running parallel to this were professional anxieties regarding the reuse of recorded broadcasts, resulting in 'union concerns about repeats displacing new output and therefore reducing work for cast and crew'.[5] These factors, coupled with a general apathy shown by both the BBC and ITV towards self-archiving through the 1950s, resulted in a huge slice of the televisual record being lost to time.

This remained the state of affairs even after the development of videotape technology in the late 1950s. Even though the adoption of videotape could have led to extensive archiving, 'the fact that videotape could be used again (and was extremely expensive at the time) meant that often, once a programme had had its customary repeat, the tape was wiped and used for something else'.[6] To reinforce Fiddy's point, Chris Perry and Simon Coward have costed the investment in videotape during the late 1950s at approximately '£500 per reel'.[7] To put that cost in context, at that time it would have been possible to buy a small car, such as a Ford Anglia or Prefect, for less than £500.[8]

A gradual shift in attitude began with the launch of a national television collection by the British Film Institute's National Film Archive (NFA) in 1959. For the first few years this was an informal initiative because, as Lisa Kerrigan notes, while 'the National Film Archive began preserving television programmes in 1951, it was not until 1961 that the BFI's Memorandum of Association was altered officially to include television as part of the Institute's remit'.[9] Subsequently, a 'Television Acquisitions Officer' was appointed to guide the selection of material for inclusion, and agreements were made between 'the NFA, BBC, Television Rota Services (covering the Royal Family) and two ITV companies, Granada and Associated-Rediffusion'.[10] However, the initial impetus proved impossible to sustain, resulting in a rather lean acquisition programme over the first years of the archive's life, with 158 programmes acquired in 1962–3, declining to 40 in 1963–4, and falling to just 27 in 1964–5.[11] It is important to re-establish this context given the pervasive, often automatic, digital archives that exist today both in the professional and personal arena.[12] That was not the reality for Firmin and Postgate and it is therefore largely due to the committed self-archiving of Smallfilms that we still have access to the majority of their early televisual works.

In fact, for a long time, both *The Seal of Neptune* and *The Mermaid's Pearls* were considered *lost* since no material from either show could be found in the BBC or BFI archives. Having been stored for considerable time in one of the old Smallfilms studio spaces on Firmin's property, over the years they gradually disappeared from view behind piles of boxes and paraphernalia. Following a clear-out, the film reels emerged, and archival specialists Kaleidoscope offered their services to both review the footage and provide safe storage. Containing black-and-white episodes of *Ivor the Engine* that had not been seen for several decades, as well as *The Seal of Neptune* and *The Mermaid's Pearls*, the rediscovery prompted a variety of sensationalist headlines in the press, such as: '1960s' Ivor the Engine episodes unearthed in Kent' (BBC News), 'Lost episodes of Ivor the Engine discovered in "priceless" haul found in pig shed' (*Daily Mail*), 'Episodes of Children's TV classic discovered' (*Kentish Gazette*), and 'Lost Ivor the Engine reels found in a pig sty' (*WalesOnline*).[13] Regardless of whether these shows were lost or simply misplaced, the awareness raising of the BFI's 'Missing Believed Wiped' initiative, and the proactive work of Kaleidoscope, helped bring them back into public view.

Having established this context of archival inconsistency and textual scarcity, this chapter serves two purposes: the first being to provide a detailed account of the three shows in question, *The Seal of Neptune*, *The Mermaid's Pearls*, and *Pingwings*, which have hitherto evaded detailed scrutiny; and, secondly, to bring into focus the importance of the handmade – or craft – aesthetic, which carries across the shows in question, and that characterizes the work of Smallfilms more broadly. The shows featured in this chapter span a five-year period and two distinct styles of animation, revealing a studio in transition, with Postgate and Firmin remaining committed to the creative renewal of their work alongside their desire to establish Smallfilms as a reliable production hub within the UK's children's television industry. Working show-by-show, this chapter offers a significant expansion of the Smallfilms production history, by focusing on these hitherto marginalized works.

Foregrounding the handmade

As noted in Chapter 1, notions of craft and the handmade are linked powerfully with the work of Smallfilms, albeit more commonly with their model-based works rather than their cut-out animation. Across the survey responses, thirty-three references are made to the handmade/handcrafted quality of Smallfilms' work, with ten of these references making explicit connections with the predominantly model-based productions '*Clangers*', '*Pingwings*', and '*Pogles*', and with only one reference to a cut-out production, '*Noggin*'. Of course, the references to '*Pogles*' within this slice of the data should be treated with caution, since *Pogles' Wood* was a mixed-media production with numerous cut-out animation sequences, but each reference to '*Pogles*' in the data explicitly links the show to the 3D model-based animation realm, not the 2D cut-out realm. Furthermore, for Moseley, who writes at length about craft in relation to Smallfilms in her own work, the predominant association is with the studio's stop-frame model-based animation, not their cut-out works.[14] Similarly, all of the references to the work of Smallfilms within Caroline Ruddell and Paul Ward's *The Crafty Animator: Handmade, Craft-Based Animation and Cultural Value* (2019), exclusively privilege their stop-frame works as sites of craft association and appeal. However, as this chapter seeks to establish, although the mode of animation favoured by Firmin and Postgate may have changed through the first half of the 1960s, the importance of the handmade aesthetic *remained* constant despite this shift in process, rather than being a by-product of this transition, and should be seen as an equally key source of appeal in their early hand-drawn, cut-out works.

While there is an established discourse that draws connections between craft and cut-out animation, with the likes of Lotte Reiniger's *The Adventures of Prince Achmed* (1926), Gordan Murray's early black-and-white *Captain Pugwash* (1957–66) episodes, or Richard Williams's *The Little Island* (1958), which all debuted prior to the inception of Smallfilms, provoking debate along this interpretational continuum. Reiniger's cut-out silhouette animation offers an unlikely but arguably compelling comparison for the cut-out works of Smallfilms. As Rachel Palfreyman notes, the reception of Reiniger's animated film-making tends to focus on praising her work, rather than analysing it in depth, suggesting that 'such neglect is in part due to the difficulty of contextualising Reiniger combined with her technical virtuosity which sees her relegated to "craft" rather than art'.[15] Palfreyman zooms in on this virtuosity, commenting on how 'Reiniger is universally acknowledged as a kind of goddess of the scissors. Her cuts are nothing short of miraculous. And so, animator and cutter, Reiniger, patiently nudging and illuminating her creatures, is a giver of life, and cutter of life.'[16] Paradoxically, as Palfreyman highlights, Reiniger's skill, displayed explicitly on-screen, actually served to divert sustained study of her work into the register of superficial praise. While it is unfair to compare the skill displayed by Firmin through his cut-out technique and illustration to that of Reiniger, given the very different aesthetic objectives of their respective works, the same hand-made and craft associations have led Firmin's work – and by extension that of Smallfilms – to be situated outside discourses of 'art', resulting, as Moseley notes, in these programmes not being 'considered appropriate objects of study'.[17] To extend this comparison, the production setting provides a more direct link between the handmade work of Reiniger and Firmin. As Tashi Petter remarks: 'It is the very handcrafted and homemade quality of Reiniger's animations that renders her films so powerful. Her creative practice specifically flourishes within a "domestic" environment, rather than being inhibited by these conditions.'[18] Here, there is a strong similarity with how the potency of the domestic space both informed and imbued the work of Smallfilms with a related homemade appeal.

It remains open to debate whether the handmade aesthetic cultivated by Smallfilms resulted from a proactive and consistent stylistic choice, or was an outcome – or side-effect – of Postgate and Firmin's deft appropriation of readily available – and often domestic – materials, as well as their collective confidence to find inventive solutions to whatever production challenges presented themselves. That said, associations of craft and the handmade are highly valued and fetishized by those respondents who have shown a passion for the works of Smallfilms. The following discussions of *The Seal of Neptune* and *The Mermaid's Pearls* therefore seek to provide a detailed account of the series narratives, given their limited visibility, as well as highlighting moments whereby the combination of stillness and their explicit 'handmade-ness' offers a site of particularly Smallfilmsian spectatorial pleasure.

4. Aesthetic Transition and the Persistence of the Handmade

The Seal of Neptune (1960)

Looking across all of Smallfilms' works at total animation screen time and the ratio of how much animation features per episode (see Appendix A – Figure A.4), despite the historic marginalization of these two shows, when viewed as a couplet they rank as one of the highest productions measured by the ratio of animation versus live action per episode and featured over one hundred minutes of animation over the two series. Told over six episodes, we follow a young seahorse called Cyrus as he journeys to return the lost Seal of Neptune. The story begins with Cyrus receiving a warning from his mother. Aware that he is getting older and more adventurous, Cyrus's mother urges him not to venture too far. Predictably, the game of hide and seek that follows, between Cyrus and his shrimp friend (called Bartholomew, but this is considered too long a name, so he is just called shrimp by his friends), inadvertently takes Cyrus, by way of a mysterious cave, into view of a shipwreck, where Cyrus subsequently finds a golden seal. Although he does not know what this seal is, he recognizes that it might be important, so he brings it back to the cave and hides it there for safe keeping.

Following in a linear manner, episode two begins with Cyrus showing shrimp the seal, with shrimp then suggesting that they take it to a wise old monkfish to find out what it is. This journey, which employs a similar tracking shot technique as seen in *Ivor the Engine*, sees multiple layers of drawings used to create both a sense of parallax and depth. The monkfish explains that all the power and authority of Neptune are contained in the seal and that Cyrus should return it:

> That which you hold, Seahorse, is the Royal Seal of Neptune, King of the Sea, Emperor of the fishes, the monsters, and the microbes, and all things that live in the sea. Master of the waves, wrecker of sail ships of men, Lord of the Crowned Dolphins, etc., etc., and you'd better put it back where you found it before the trouble starts.[19]

Voiced by Postgate, this short monologue delivered by the wise old monkfish follows the established Smallfilms paradigm of juxtaposing the magical with the mundane – the twin foundations of whimsical authenticity. On this occasion, the monkfish abruptly undercuts his grand proclamation with the 'etc., etc.,' as if becoming bored with his own solemnity, before rapidly bringing the narrative back to the consequences of a juvenile seahorse not following his mother's advice. Heeding the monkfish's words, Cyrus and the shrimp head back to the wreck, yet find their way blocked by a frenzy of sharks. Having broken up the wreck in search of Neptune's Seal, the sharks circle the area, forcing Cyrus and the shrimp to take shelter. Eventually, the sharks disperse, but worried that a sea creature with bad intent might take the Seal from where it now lies, Cyrus decides to return the Seal to Neptune himself.

Episode three opens on an increasingly despondent Cyrus. Unsure where he needs to go, he regains his composure, and decides to surface in an attempt to

Figure 4.1 Cyrus meets a mermaid in *The Seal of Neptune* (1960).

reorient himself. Cyrus hears singing and decides to follow the sound, which results in an encounter with a mermaid (Figure 4.1):

>**Mermaid** Well, you're a strange looking thing, to be sure! You're half horse and half fish by the look of it. What are you?
>**Cyrus** I'm a seahorse and I'm lost.
>**Mermaid** Well, of course you're not lost, silly, you're here with me, you can't be lost.
>**Cyrus** Yes, but what are you? I can see you are half fish, but what the other half is I don't know. But you're very beautiful and I love to hear you sing.
>**Mermaid** I'm a mermaid. I'm half fish and half maiden, and I live here on this rock.
>**Cyrus** My name is Cyrus, I live by a rock quite a long way from here, close to the shore. What's your name?
>**Mermaid** My name? Oh, I haven't got a name yet, I'm too young, I'm only three hundred years old.
>**Cyrus** I should have thought was very, very, very old.
>**Mermaid** Oh no, that is not old for a Mermaid, and anyway, Mermaids don't get names until they are at least five hundred, or until they do something special.[20]

4. Aesthetic Transition and the Persistence of the Handmade

This exchange offers another good example of whimsical authenticity, with the matter-of-fact tone of the mermaid serving to regulate the fantastical narrative being established (such as an encounter between a talking seahorse and a mermaid, and the revelation that mermaids live for many centuries being accepted quite straightforwardly by Cyrus). Furthermore, the sequence also showcases Firmin's attention to detail, with his hand-drawn cut-out illustrations not only offering an anatomic detailing but also skilfully suggesting underwater shadow and the ocean's tidal ripples.

After the mermaid has confirmed that Cyrus does indeed hold the Seal of Neptune, she offers to shelter him for the night. As Cyrus gets ready to set off again, the mermaid reveals that he must head west to find Neptune's Kingdom. Significantly, she tells Cyrus that while he carries the Seal of Neptune, he will be safe from danger, before tying the Seal on to Cyrus's tail with a strand of her mermaid hair (which, she tells him, will not break until Cyrus commands it).

Episode four sees Cyrus encounter a shoal of flying fish. Talking to the flying fish, Cyrus learns he still has a long way to go, but the fish suggest that he might speed up his journey by hitching a ride on a nearby sail ship. Working as a team, the flying fish propel Cyrus at speed to the ship's hull. Once there, Cyrus finds a dormant barnacle for shelter and rides for two days on the ship's hull. When the ship comes to rest, a storm hits and we see the crew listen keenly for the ringing of the red buoy bell, so they can navigate away from the flat-topped rocks. During the storm we see more examples of Firmin's skill to create cut-outs that, while clearly hand-drawn, contain a range of illustrative techniques to help give the sequence a real sense of drama, such as drawing exaggeratedly jagged waves, showing the ships sails full of the storm's wind, and offering another example of the POV technique initially developed during the production of *Ivor the Engine*, which allows Postgate to give a sense of the rise and fall of the ship as it lurches over the waves (Figure 4.2). Hearing the bell, Cyrus leaves the protection of the barnacle and enters the frothing, stormy seas. Remembering the Mermaid's words about the protection afforded by the seal, Cyrus commands the sea to be calm. Exhausted, Cyrus sleeps on the chain that trails beneath the buoy.

At the start of episode five we hear the sounds of nearby singing, which, in turn, wake Cyrus from his sleep. Following the sound, Cyrus finds the flat-topped rocks and meets a Mermaid there. Cyrus shows the Seal of Neptune to the mermaid and is told to wait until the full moon. The mermaid informs Cyrus that if, at that point, the sounds of Neptune's courtly bell can be heard, then Cyrus will be able to follow the crowned dolphins down to meet Neptune at the city gates. The mermaid tells of how the city once stood above the sea and was populated with evil men, until one day it sunk beneath the waves. Those who enter the evil city now will lose their minds and be lost forever. The mermaid takes great care to make these details clear to Cyrus: that Neptune only holds court at the city's gates and only when the bell can be heard. Predictably, at full moon impatience gets the better of Cyrus, and, after not hearing any sounds coming from the deep, he decides to swim down to investigate. Finding the city (Figure 4.3), he enters and

Figure 4.2 POV shot of a ship sailing on stormy seas in *The Seal of Neptune* (1960).

Figure 4.3 Detailed establishing shot of the underwater city in *The Seal of Neptune* (1960).

4. *Aesthetic Transition and the Persistence of the Handmade*   85

almost immediately loses his memory, thereby forgetting his task and becoming disorientated and tired.

The level of oceanic detail conveyed through the hand-drawn visuals, as seen across Figures 4.1 to 4.3, reveals how Firmin's own knowledge of seafaring and sea mythology, drawn from his own interest in Oceanography and his time spent completing National Service in the Royal Navy, helped to regulate the whimsical authenticity of the show.[21] Luckily, having anticipated Cyrus's wilfulness and knowing the importance of Neptune's Seal, the mermaid comes to the city wall and beckons the little seahorse. Cyrus, having forgotten his name, ignores the Mermaid's call. Persisting, the Mermaid tricks Cyrus to come to her, thus rescuing him from the city. As the episode closes, Cyrus recovers his memory, and they hear the sound of the city bell.

The final episode in the series features a bemused Neptune, who praises Cyrus for the determination and courage he has shown by returning his Seal. Neptune offers to reward Cyrus, but Cyrus states that he doesn't need anything (apart from a safe homestead), asking instead that Neptune grants the mermaid from episode three, who gave him shelter and guidance, a name. Neptune agrees and hands Cyrus a magic locket containing a name. Escorted by mermaids and crowned dolphins, Cyrus delivers the magic locket to the mermaid. When Cyrus asks what her name is, she tells him it is a secret, 'but a nice name'. The final scene of the series sees the crowned dolphins setting up signs around Cyrus's home that read 'SEAHORSE ROCK. NO SHARKS. BY ORDER'.

The Mermaid's Pearls (1962)

Picking up where *The Seal of Neptune* left off, episode one of *The Mermaid's Pearls* opens with Postgate's narration re-establishing the underwater terrain where Cyrus the seahorse lives with this family and friends. After Cyrus hears a mermaid singing, we learn that tomorrow is the mermaid's 300th birthday – as we know from the previous series this is a significant age for mermaids – and she is expecting to receive a crown from King Neptune to commemorate the occasion. Cyrus and the shrimp ask her what throne she will sit on, to which the mermaid replies that she was just planning to decorate her rock with a bit of seaweed. Hearing this, Cyrus tells the mermaid that all the rock-dwelling creatures will help to make her a throne. Postgate's narration describes this throne-crafting activity in characteristic style:

> So, Cyrus and shrimp fetched all their friends and they gathered soft seaweed and laid it on the rock. They fetched silver sea berries and the sea spider strung them on a thread. They fetched fans of scarlet coral, which the lobsters fitted into the back of the throne with their cunning claws. The white mother of pearl on the inside of the long razor shells, they laid in patterns around the throne, and over the top of the throne they hung threads of golden ringers from the seabell tree. The arms of the throne were woven seagrass, with a perfect alive, white clam at the end of each.[22]

Given the importance and pervasiveness of the handcrafted aesthetic throughout the work of Smallfilms, it is tempting to see this sequence as a rather self-reflexive acknowledgment by Postgate and Firmin of the role played by found objects as forces of inspiration during their early pre-production ideation work. Shortly after the throne is finished King Neptune arrives. He makes a grand entrance, riding in a giant shell pulled by two crowned dolphins and flanked by two mermaids. Neptune beckons the mermaid; however, the mermaid can't be found. Neptune, remembering Cyrus, calls him over to learn what is going on and tasks him with finding the errant mermaid. Finding the mermaid crying, we learn that she has dropped her locket into a great sea trench. Without hesitation, Cyrus and shrimp volunteer to search for it.

Episode two begins with Cyrus and shrimp descending into the trench, where they find a shipwreck that hides the chain from the mermaid's necklace. Unfortunately, the necklace is broken and only the chain can be found. To their surprise, the chain is being held by a 'nasty looking crab'.[23] Shrimp tries to get the necklace but the crab wakes and fends him off. Cyrus comes up with a plan: using a strand of mermaid hair he fixes one end of the chain to a hook in the shipwreck, thereby using the magical, unbreakable properties of the hair to prevent the crab making off with the chain. Shrimp then takes the initiative and acts as bait, taunting and luring the crab away, thus leaving the chain bound to the wreck and unattended. Cyrus and the shrimp continue their search of the wreck, looking for the missing pearls and locket. While searching, Cyrus gets trapped in a treasure chest, forcing shrimp to put the mermaid hair to use again as a pulley to lift the lid. When Cyrus emerges, he reveals he has found one of the four pearls.

Episode three opens with Cyrus and shrimp wondering where they can store the chain and the pearl safely while they search for the other missing pieces. A giant clam offers to store the broken necklace, and while doing so reveals that he knows many things about the ocean by virtue of the fact that he is always listening to the events of the aquatic realm. Cyrus and shrimp are told by the clam to search a nearby field of sea grass. While searching in the thick sea grass they encounter a herd of sea cows who agree to help search for the missing pearls and locket (after Cyrus and Shrimp perform a short song to alleviate the cows' boredom). Their combined efforts prove fruitful and they unearth a range of forgotten treasures, including a pocket watch, gold coins, a rusty nail, a padlock, a spoon, and an unassuming glass bottle. When they tip the bottle, a missing pearl rolls out.

Returning to the wise clam with the freshly retrieved pearl, episode four begins with the clam telling Cyrus and Shrimp that next they must search the 'black deep'. Cyrus asks if it is possible to swim down there, to which the clam replies:

> You can try. Seahorses can swim very deep, but not shrimps. Also, you must get a long strand of spun sea web from the seaspider, and as Cyrus goes down he must tie the end around his middle, and Shrimp must hold the other end, because, sometimes, if you swim very deep you get dizzy and you don't know which way up you are, then you might swim down instead of up and never be found again.[24]

4. Aesthetic Transition and the Persistence of the Handmade

After asking whether the seaspider will give them web freely, the clam tells Cyrus and shrimp that they should bring the spider something nice in exchange. Offering one of the gold coins found in the previous episode, they successfully secure the web, and Cyrus embarks on his descent into the black deep. After a failed first attempt, shrimp suggests they could enlist the help of some of the creatures living in the black deep. They decide to drop some of the found items into the black deep as a way of enticing the deep-sea creatures to come to their aid, and consequently a flat-looking deep-sea creature rises up to meet them. After shrimp negotiates with the creature, offering up the gold pocket watch, the remaining pearls are recovered from the black deep. Returning the pearls to the clam for safe keeping, they hear the sound of the locket singing in the distance.

The penultimate episode begins with Cyrus and Shrimp spotting a seabream in possession of the missing locket. They give chase but the seabream is too fast for them. From a distance, they spot the seabream drop the locket as it passes a ship's hull, with the locket getting tangled in some seaweed. Eventually, the ship stops and the locket dislodges from the seaweed, but drifts down into the sunken city of evil men, first encountered by Cyrus during *The Seal of Neptune*. Shrimp volunteers to retrieve the locket, but Cyrus retells of his earlier misadventure and the dangers of losing your memory. Shrimp suggests tying the spiderweb line around his waist as he goes in, so that Cyrus can pull him out if he gets into distress. Inevitably, the shrimp forgets his purpose once in the city. Stumbling upon the locket, the shrimp admires its beauty, but becomes distracted as he notices a line tied to his middle. Having forgotten its purpose and finding it uncomfortable he unties it. Seeing the jeopardy of the situation, Cyrus comes up with a plan – he ties the web to a loose statue high on the city wall and pushes it off, as the web catches, the statue swings into the giant city bell causing it to chime.

The final episode opens with the large city bell ringing out across the ocean. Hearing the bell, Neptune quickly arrives. Cyrus confronts Neptune and explains the situation. Impressed with Cyrus's bravery again, Neptune overlooks the fact that the mermaid had lost her necklace. Neptune goes to the city wall and begins to serenade the locket, prompting it to gravitate to him. Neptune then turns his attention to shrimp, devising a plot to get the helpless crustacean out:

> **Neptune**   You know, little seahorse, even I, Neptune, can't go in there to fetch him out. There is only one thing in there that belongs to me still, that throne in the shape of shell in the middle of the square. That throne was dedicated to me when men lived in the city, so it still belongs to me. Now, everybody be quiet while I talk to this shrimp.
> Hi there, King of the Shrimps, where are you? Hail, oh King of the Shrimps. Do you hear me calling?
> **Shrimp**   Perhaps I am a shrimp? Perhaps I am King of the Shrimps? I wonder if I am? I wonder who is calling?
> **Neptune**   Hail, King of Shrimps.
> **Shrimp**   Hail, fat old person, with a beard and fork, who are you calling?

Neptune I am calling you, oh King of the Shrimps. Come here to the wall, I have a jewel to show you.
Shrimp No thanks, I don't want to a jewel. The King of the Shrimps is tired and wants to sleep.
Neptune Then sit on your throne and sleep oh mighty king. Your throne is in the place of honour, there in the square behind you.[25]

Shrimp then goes to sleep on the throne and is transported by magic into Neptune's hand, safe outside the city. After a full explanation, Cyrus and shrimp return to the clam to piece the necklace back together, before returning to the mermaid. In a whirlwind of final activity, Neptune then visits the mermaid to bestow a crown upon her. Then, in thanks for their heroic efforts, Neptune bestows little fairy gold crowns upon Cyrus and shrimp, proclaiming: 'little fishes, you are brave and strong and I am proud to have you in my kingdom. You will have many adventures before you are old. I have made you these crowns of fairy gold, wear them, all fish will honour you, and the crowns will guard you from danger.' With this the story ends.

The focus across these first two sections of the chapter has been to establish the narrative tone, structure, and ambition of these two lesser-known Smallfilms productions, not only for the benefit of readers who know little about them but also to help position them more visibly within the Smallfilms oeuvre. As noted previously, after completing work on *The Seal of Neptune* and *The Mermaid's Pearls* Postgate and Firmin changed their animation style for their next seven original productions (excluding their work colourizing *Ivor* and *Noggin*), only returning to 2D hand-drawn cut-out animation for a new production a quarter of a century later with *Pinny's House* (1986 – see Chapter 9).

Pingwings (1961–5)

Due to the fact that *Pingwings* was only broadcast once by Associated-Rediffusion as part of their 'Small Time' programming, and was then considered lost between 1965 and 2007,[26] with no pre-production materials surviving in the BFI's Associated Rediffusion archive, it is hardly surprising that this show is often marginalized in historical accounts of the studio, especially when other more colourful and accessible shows, such as *Bagpuss* (see Chapter 8) and *Clangers* (see Chapter 6), enjoy such popular adoration and widespread circulation. This is unfortunate because in several ways *Pingwings* is a remarkable and important series: it was the first British TV series to be filmed using stop-motion animation; it represents and reflects a moment of transition for Postgate and Firmin, when their Smallfilms operation began to shift from 2D hand-drawn cut-out animation to 3D model-based animation; and it remains a rare example of a TV series employing stop-motion model-based animation to be filmed outdoors (and therefore at the mercy of the natural elements).

As has been noted earlier in this chapter, this moment of shift – from cut-out to model-based animation – should not be understood as a linear progression. For example, between 1961 and 1963, Firmin and Postgate juggled work on four shows, across both forms of animation: *Ivor the Engine*, *Noggin the Nog*, *The Mermaids Pearls*, and *Pingwings*. This was less a eureka moment, with stop-motion representing a certain path to fame and fortune, but rather another example of Postgate and Firmin's appetite to try new things, to find inspiration in the currents of their everyday life, and to embrace the art of creative problem-solving.

The spark for *Pingwings* came from a chance encounter between Postgate and a freshly washed children's toy. While walking through the Firmin's back garden, Postgate noticed a knitted penguin suspended by its beak, hanging from the washing line. Struck by this image, Postgate began to imbue this scene with creative potential:

> I thought how uncomfortable it must be to be pegged out on the line by one's beak with one's stuffing sopping wet. A stuffed knitted penguin would hardly be seaworthy. It would have to be a land bird, unless the wool was very special. Wasn't there some French knitting wool named *Pingouin*? Perhaps the uncomfortable bird was a pingwing. The Firmins kept goats, chickens, ducks, all sorts of livestock in their farmyard-garden. Maybe they also kept pingwings, or possibly they didn't keep them, they just lived there.[27]

Interviewed in 1993, Postgate embellished this account of the *Pingwings*' conception, revealing how his first encounter with the recently washed toy also directly inspired the narrative:

> They were woolly penguins, about so high, with half-pound weights in their bottoms, and little cardboard feet that you tucked in when you remembered to do it. These Pingwings waddled about outdoors and had a grand life. There was a sort of family situation – a nuclear family of Pingwings. The first one was that mama has laid an egg, and there was a tremendous sort of fuss, they went to fetch father Pingwing who had just been washed and was held on the line by his nose, pegged on the line [Figure 4.4], so he couldn't come straight away, but they managed to get him down. Eventually mama hatches this egg and there was quite a lot of ordinary life and times, kind of like a very simplified family story, I can't think of one [long pause], *The Archers*, or something of this sort, you know. Just living in the underworld of the farm, which is, again, a different view of looking at life, from really low down.[28]

The diminutive stature of the pingwings afforded Firmin and Postgate an alternative frame through which to look at the world, taking them beyond their previously wide-angled views of the locomotive, Norse, and deep-sea worlds that had gone before to a more close-up, intimate engagement with the natural world that surrounded their studio. Of course, pingwings are not *real* or *natural*, but

Figure 4.4 Drawing inspiration from everyday life as shown in *Pingwings* (1961–5).

the matter-of-fact register with which they are introduced, typical of Smallfilms, grants them a zoological authenticity. Our acceptance of the pingwings as a hitherto unseen farmyard creature is perhaps supported by the stop-motion process of their animation, with viewers in possession of adequate resolution television sets being able to recognize their material composition as knitted wool, thereby hinting at what it would be like to touch a pingwing. Their physicality, which is foregrounded repeatedly throughout the series, also promotes a greater appreciation of the weight and tactility of these creatures.

The foregrounded tactility of *Pingwings* certainly constitutes an appealing characteristic of the series, and, it could be argued, of stop-motion animation more broadly. Moseley points to a double layered appeal rooted in the physical construction of the pingwings. Noting the shift that occurred in the first half of the twentieth century to synthetic products and processes such as Lycra, aerosols, disinfectants, frozen foods, and new plastics, Moseley highlight that 'a key ethos of 1960s counter-culture was [a] rejection of the mass-produced and manmade, in conjunction with a re-embracing of natural materials and the made-by-hand'.[29] Produced in the early 1960s, and within a rural setting, it is possible to read *Pingwings* as representing an extension of the counterculture ethos in stop-motion form. Highlighting the importance of this stop-motion aesthetic, Moseley notes how similarly produced children's programmes of this period 'often speak to this contemporary interest in hand-made objects and aesthetics, to the culture of the workshop rather than the factory, as well as articulating a counter-cultural politics which echoes Western hippie philosophies of the mid-1960s'.[30] Beyond these broad sociocultural connections, Moseley also identifies how the knitted bodies of the pingwings provide a more intimately rooted source of appeal, noting how the

> 'hand-made' quality of the *Pingwings* is evident in every close shot, and as the episodes progress across three series, the pingwings' knitted bodies become increasingly piled or 'bobbled'. This increasing 'woolliness' across their surfaces is the visual and virtually tactile evidence of the repetitive touch of the maker as the puppets have been handled, repositioned and moved over and over again in the stop-frame process. It is also a powerful evocation of the comforting intimacy of hand-made, well-worn, much-loved soft toys.[31]

Moseley's observations are well-judged and helpfully re-establish the contemporary cultural backdrop surrounding the production of *Pingwings*.

The material production of the pingwing armatures and knitted bodies also provides an opportunity to extend the production narrative beyond the core partnership of Postgate and Firmin. As the previous chapter noted, other individuals, such as Joan Firmin, deserve credit, whether directly or indirectly, for the success of Smallfilms. While Joan's contributions are discussed at multiple points throughout this book, with regards to the production of *Pingwings*, Gloria Firmin (Peter's sister) played an important role in their inspiration and fabrication. Having encountered Gloria's handiwork hanging from the washing line, Postgate then wrote to her to request additional pingwing family members be knitted. As we can see in the original letter to Gloria (Figure 4.5), Postgate offers instruction about colour composition, approximate sizes, and the type of wool ('mo-hair' – for its 'fluffy' quality and likely also for its durability). Clearly, compared to a conventional knitting pattern designed to be followed, Postgate's sparse instructions relied upon Gloria's knitting skill to fill in a considerable amount of missing detail.

While Gloria provided the knitted pingwing exteriors, Postgate devised a homemade armature:

> The Clerkenwell Screw Company in Hatton Garden kept every imaginable shape and size screw and screw-related object in stock. There I found some 3/8in (1cm) diameter brass balls with 1/3in (3mm) threaded screw-holes in them. I have no idea what they were originally meant for, but for me they were to be the artificial hips, elbows, shoulder and neck-joints of the pingwings. I made each joint by clamping the ball between holes drilled in flat steel strips (Meccano) and I made the limbs and body and beak out of wood.[32]

With the pingwing puppets fabricated, all that was left was to bring them to life. Whereas the cut-out production method used for all of the Smallfilms works up to that point necessitated Firmin and Postgate working in close proximity,

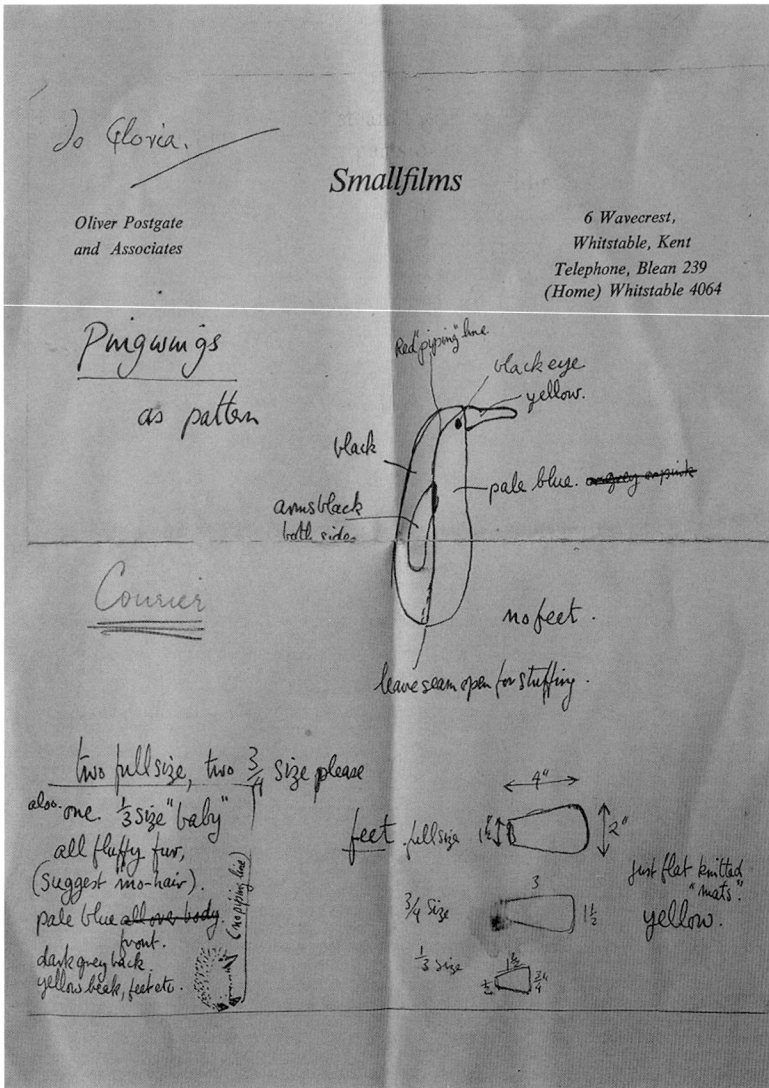

Figure 4.5 The descriptive instructions provided by Oliver Postgate to Gloria Firmin, c. 1961.

with Firmin continually feeding Postgate with planned and un-planned cut-out elements, with the shift to stop-motion, puppet-based animation, a more linear production arrangement began to emerge, with Firmin occupying more of the pre-production realm (and some on-screen cameos during production), and with Postgate coming to dominate the production and post-production processes. As discussed at various other points in this book, Firmin's responsibilities also began to include the afterlife of each Smallfilms production, taking the lead for marketing and merchandising initiatives, as well as policing copyright compliance.

Postgate and Firmin, anticipating the more labour-intensive nature of filming stop-motion model-based animation outside, also sought to adjust audience expectations, using the narrator's introduction to establish the shy nature of the pingwings, and therein the fact that standard live-action footage, without pingwings – or other stop-motion elements – would be commonplace:

> Then there are ducks, they don't seem to do anything much except walk about and quack; and of course Mini the cat, Mini is a lady, 'hello Mini'; and Sammy, he's a guinea pig, he likes to hide in the long grass; and Gay the goat, if she'll stand still for a minute; and of course the pingwings, if we can find the pingwings. There's the big barn, look, there a usually pingwings in the big barn, but of course it's no use going charging in looking for them because they will hide. No, we will have to wait here and see if we can see one.[33]

This also establishes a blueprint that is used for most of Smallfilms' subsequent stop-motion productions, whereby the first sixty to seventy seconds of every episode either repeats a standard visual sequence with interchangeable narration, or live-action footage is used to set the scene before the stop-motion animation begins. In the case of *Bagpuss*, this opening title sequence, which contains no animation, runs over two minutes. Beginning the vast majority of their stop-motion productions in such a way allowed important narrative information to be conveyed through the narration, while keeping the production costs as economical as possible by limiting the time spent animating, as well as paving the way for judicious use of live-action footage.

As noted, a key shift that can be seen throughout the series, compared to their concurrent cut-out productions, is the emphasis placed on the semi-rural landscape, the lived environment of Buckleberry Farm (really the Firmin's farm), and the everyday misadventures of the pingwing family. The Postgate's family archive also reveals that there was a phase, early in production, when the name of the farm was still up for debate, with multiple references to both Bankside Farm and Buckleberry Farm featuring interchangeable as the name of the Pingwing's home. This relaxed approach to the fictional naming of the farm space is perhaps illustrative of the real-world certainty with which Postagte and Firmin operated at this moment, knowing that practically the farm space would be that of Firmin's, so the fictional name could be finalized later.

The importance of the hand-made and the everyday farm environment is signified immediately, with the opening credits (Figure 4.6) being scrawled in chalk onto the side of a farm building (in reality, this was the side of the cowshed, in which a large proportion of Smallfilms production took place, thereby adding an extremely exclusive inside joke into the credits).

Figure 4.6 The hand-drawn aesthetic is self-reflexively foregrounded by the credits of *Pingwings* (1961–5).

Furthermore, across several episodes, we encounter members of the family living at Buckleberry Farm, all of which are played by members of the Firmin and Postgate families. The narrator, the farmer, is played on-screen by Firmin, but voiced by Postgate, the 'man who comes every day to work' is played by Postgate (again, another inside joke, given the reality of his daily commute to the Firmin's farm to bring life to the imagined worlds of Smallfilms), while Joan Firmin plays Mrs Farmer. The blending of the real and the imaginary, first explored by Postgate and Firmin in *Pingwings*, certainly proved appealing, with one respondent enjoying seeing 'the simplicity of their little knitted bodies set in the real world' (R384), while another respondent found the juxtaposition 'completely hilarious' (R606). For the Firmin and Postgate families, there was an added layer of pleasure to be had:

> Kay Laboratories used to process the films. So, he'd do a few days filming, about two and half minutes on a reel, so he'd a few reels then send them up to town and we'd wait. We had this marvellous sort of meeting, he say 'come on, we're going to show some rushes', and we'd go over into the pig sty, and he had a great big cinema and a big old car seat on the floor and the girls would go and sit in that, and there was great excitement, and we'd sit there and watch these rushes coming back, and see what he'd got – and it was miraculous.[34]

While the process of finding inspiration in their everyday lives and filming in the Firmin farmstead brought homespun charm to the series, and, perhaps even more importantly, established a highly economical means of production, filming stop-motion, model-based animation in such a way brought certain challenges.

If, during their lifetime, you were lucky enough to hear Postgate or Firmin talk about the production of *Pingwings*, you will almost certainly have heard the anecdote about the caterpillar. Across the several occasions that I had the chance to see Firmin speak publicly, as well as in the interviews that I conducted with him privately, this anecdote was repeatedly told:

> What was sometimes the case, especially while we were doing *Pingwings*, which was the first outdoor animation, was the trouble with insects coming into shot! Caterpillar walking across a wall, I remember this particularly, baby Pingwing was in front of this wall, and he [Postgate] was doing the animation and he didn't notice that there was a caterpillar creeping along the top of the wall, so in the hour or so he did perhaps a minute of film, 'whoosh-whoosh-whoosh', this caterpillar was all over the place.[35]

What is remarkable about this story is that it is rooted in production memory, as no other evidence of this sequence survives. As Postgate notes in his autobiography: 'So on the film the caterpillar dominated the scene by performing a frenzied fandango. It had to be re-shot.'[36] This sequence, which we can only imagine today, reveals a defining characteristic of all of Smallfilms' work: the desire to carefully regulate the levels of whimsy and authenticity, so that they could tell compelling and entertaining stories with the minimum of extraneous distraction. For others, working with similar financial restraint, the opportunity for a cheap laugh from the frenetic caterpillar might have seen this sequence make the final cut (and thereby save the costs of reshooting), but for Postgate and Firmin, the caterpillar ruptured the internal logic of the narrative world they had so carefully handcrafted. Inevitably, for a production filmed largely outdoors, other features of the natural world did invade the frame and, due to their pervasive quality, made it into the final series.

The first, unshackled natural element that can be seen in *Pingwings* is the slow but continuously changing quality of sunlight. Writing in his autobiography, this factor alone prompts Postgate to warn his readers '*do not try to make single-frame films out of doors*', giving the reason that '*the light keeps changing*'.[37] Throughout the series we see shadows moving around objects, which, for longer scenes, also jump from place to place on occasion, offering an unintentional glimpse of what Norman McLaren considered the most important part of the animating process, the in-between, or, as Firmin and Postgate would probably describe it, a tea break.[38] Clouds also have a habit of obscuring the sun in the UK, even in sunny Kent, thereby causing the light level to vary more radically between exposures. Postgate writes: 'The effect on the film, as you can imagine, is weird, like neon lights flashing on and off at irregular intervals.'[39]

The second example of the stop-motion process introducing unintended outcomes into the filmed footage relates back to the in-between activities of Postgate:

> Some of the shots revealed the presence of the omnipotent ghost that causes everything to happen. The first time I saw this puzzling manifestation I couldn't think what it was. As the Pingwings walked away from the camera they left behind them a wake of crushed, heaving grass. Then I realised what it was – my footprints, which I had left as I walked backwards and forwards between the camera and the puppets.[40]

While the infamous caterpillar was easily cut, being an isolated incident in a short scene, these natural arrythmias that permeate through most scenes were beyond editorial control. However, because of their abstract quality (unlike the literalness of the caterpillar), rather than being an overt distraction, these *flaws* lend a magical quality to the landscape, giving it an energy, a sense of life, that is not often seen in everyday, real-time existence.[41]

Having opened this chapter with a typically knowing reference, embedded within the final *Pingwings* episode, to the rapid growth of television, we now end the chapter by unpacking the significance of this reference in more detail. This final episode begins with Mabel (Mrs Pingwing) feeling unwell. Concerned for her well-being, Mr Pingwing visits Pog, an ornamental pig that intermittently features throughout the series, doling out various pieces of wisdom. On this occasion, Pog offers the following advice: 'keep her warm, out of drafts, plenty of hot mint tea made with fresh mint and don't let her run about'.[42] Taking a different approach to their mother's care, Paul and Penny suggest that Mrs Pingwing might be soothed by watching some television. After explaining what television is to their father they set about making a TV from an old cardboard box. Upon completion, they ponder what to do next:

> **Penny**   Isn't it exciting, Paul, what shall we do?
> **Paul**   Well, I suppose we'd better sing a song, we know we can do that.
> **Penny**   But we ought to have cowboys and Indians, and baddies, and a lady that tells you how to do cooking.[43]

Through Penny's clear awareness of contemporary television programming trends, we are left in little doubt that *Pingwings* is set in the contemporary moment of the late 1950s or early 1960s, yet affording a new way of looking at this familiar world by virtue of seeing it afresh through the eyes of the newly discovered pingwings.

At the end of the episode, it transpires that Paul and Penny's idea to comfort their mother with television proves more effective than the remedy suggested by Pog. However, the television show that Mrs Pingwing enjoys is not some remote broadcast, but rather a live performance by her family staged within the handcrafted cardboard 'TV'. Introduced by Mr Pingwing, Paul and Penny then sing a short folk song, before Baby Pingwing provides a fittingly grand finale to the series. Assuming the title of Sir Ambrose Pingwing, Baby Pingwing proceeds to display a range of kitchen utensils with great earnestness. However, his cooking show rapidly descends into farce as, punctuated by his high-pitched squeaks, he first sits haphazardly in a saucepan, then tumbles back with the saucepan now on his head, before steadying himself, only to then tip a bowl of sugar over himself. This performance brings laughter from Mrs Pingwing, who declares, 'Oh children, I'm not ill anymore, I've laughed so much I've laid an egg!' With this revelation of what has been ailing Mrs Pingwing through the episode the series closes. Moseley writes:

> It is significant for the text's ambivalent oscillation between ideas of a traditional past and modernity that Mabel is comforted not by actual television, by 'the new', but rather by a mediatory form of entertainment which presents the new medium in a more palatable fashion: as a game of Charades; as hand-made television.[44]

It is fitting then that *Pingwings* concludes in such a way, pointing, quite knowingly, towards the new form of overtly handmade television – stop-motion model-based animation – that would usurp cut-out animation as the dominant mode of animation for Smallfilms in the coming years.

Conclusion

This chapter has focused on an important moment in Smallfilms history, being when the studio shifted from 2D cut-out hand-drawn to stop-motion 3D model-based animation, while retaining across this transition the unashamedly handmade aesthetic that made the work of Smallfilms so appealing. Continuing with stop-motion for their next production, Postgate and Firmin also sought to channel a dynamic that had been established in their earlier works, a dynamic that gave the characters that populated the worlds of Smallfilms a fresh – and frequently useful – perspective on the world around them.

Notes

1 Author's transcription from *Pingwings* episode 16, 'Entertainment', viewed on DVD (Dragons' Friendly Society).
2 During this period Postgate also worked for the BBC on the show *Little Laura* (1960), which, while not a Smallfilms production, provided a welcome payday. The forgotten nature of *Little Laura* is evident in the survey data, with only one respondent, from the 1,100 responses, claiming knowledge of the show.
3 Chris Perry and Simon Coward, 'Swiped or Wiped? Kaleidoscope's Part in the Recovery of Lost Television Programmes', *Critical Studies in Television* vol. 5 no. 2 (2010), p. 49.

4   Fiddy, *Missing Believed Wiped*, p. 6.
5   Perry and Coward, 'Swiped Or Wiped?', p. 49.
6   Fiddy, *Missing Believed Wiped*, p. 7.
7   Perry and Coward, 'Swiped Or Wiped?', p. 49.
8   Derek Tait, *1950s Childhood: Spangles, Tiddlywinks and the Clitheroe Kid* (Stroud: Amberley, 2013).
9   Lisa Kerrigan, 'Stories that Never End: Television Fiction in the BFI National Archive', *Critical Studies in Television* vol. 5 no. 2 (2010), p. 73.
10 Perry and Coward, 'Swiped Or Wiped?', p. 50.
11 Paul Madden, *Keeping Television Alive* (London: British Film Institute, 1981), p. xii.
12 Of course, the pervasive and automatic nature of current digital archival systems does not mean they offer the best long-term solution, given the precarity of electronically stored information. Without careful maintenance, the software and hardware required to store and retrieve digital archives can become a significant barrier, with incompatibility issues stalking even the most well-resourced endeavour. See, for example, the British Library's web resource: 'The challenges of digital preservation', https://www.bl.uk/digital-preservation/challenges (accessed 1 June 2021).
13 See '1960s' Ivor the Engine Episodes Unearthed in Kent', *BBC News* 26 October 2010, https://www.bbc.co.uk/news/uk-england-kent-11626470 (accessed 8 June 2021); Katie Alston, 'Episodes of Children's TV Classic Discovered', *Kentish Gazette* 4 November 2010, https://www.pressreader.com/uk/kentish-gazette-canterbury-district/20101104/281835755078248 (accessed 10 June 2021); 'Ivor the Engine Lost shows found in Pig Sty'; 'Lost Ivor the Engine Reels found in a Pig Sty'.
14 Moseley, *Hand-made Television*, passim.
15 Rachel Palfreyman, 'Life and Death in the Shadows: Lotte Reiniger's Die Abenteuer Des Prinzen Achmed', *German Life and Letters* vol. 64 no. 1 (2011), p. 6.
16 Palfreyman, 'Life and Death in the Shadows', pp. 16–17.
17 Moseley, *Hand-made Television*, p. 9.
18 Tashi Petter, '"In a Tiny Realm of Her Own": Lotte Reiniger, Domesticity and Creativity', *Animation Studies 2.0*, 9 October 2017, https://blog.animationstudies.org/?p=2166 (accessed 1 November 2021).
19 Author's transcription from *The Seal of Neptune* episode 2, viewed on DVD (Dragons' Friendly Society).
20 Author's transcription from *The Seal of Neptune* episode 3, viewed on DVD (Dragons' Friendly Society).
21 Peter Firmin, interviewed by Chris Pallant, Canterbury, UK, 3 December 2016.
22 Author's transcription from *The Mermaid's Pearls* episode 1, viewed on DVD (Dragons' Friendly Society).
23 Author's transcription from *The Mermaid's Pearls* episode 2, viewed on DVD (Dragons' Friendly Society).
24 Author's transcription from *The Mermaid's Pearls* episode 4, viewed on DVD (Dragons' Friendly Society).
25 Author's transcription from The Mermaid's Pearls episode 6, viewed on DVD (Dragons' Friendly Society).
26 Amid Amidi, 'Pingwings Rediscovered', *Cartoon Brew* 30 May 2007, https://www.cartoonbrew.com/classic/pingwings-rediscovered-3402.html (accessed 8 June 2021).
27 Postgate, *Seeing Things*, p. 225.
28 Oliver Postgate, interviewed by Tim Jones, Canterbury, UK, 14 July 1993.
29 Moseley, *Hand-made Television*, p. 25.

30 Moseley, *Hand-made Television*, p. 25.
31 Moseley, *Hand-made Television*, p. 76.
32 Postgate, *Seeing Things*, p. 227.
33 Author's transcription from *Pingwings* episode 1, viewed on DVD (Dragons' Friendly Society).
34 Peter Firmin, interviewed by Chris Pallant, Canterbury, UK, 2 November 2017.
35 Peter Firmin, interviewed by Chris Pallant, Canterbury, UK, 2 November 2017.
36 Postgate, *Seeing Things*, p. 228.
37 Postgate, *Seeing Things*, p. 228.
38 Sifanos, 'The Definition of Animation', pp. 62–66.
39 Postgate, *Seeing Things*, p. 228.
40 Postgate, *Seeing Things*, p. 228.
41 For an extended analysis of the active role often played by animated landscapes, see Chris Pallant, *Animated Landscapes: History, Form and Function* (New York: Bloomsbury Academic, 2015).
42 Author's transcription from *Pingwings* episode 18, viewed on DVD (Dragons' Friendly Society).
43 Author's transcription from *Pingwings* episode 18, viewed on DVD (Dragons' Friendly Society).
44 Moseley, *Hand-made Television*, p. 47.

Chapter 5

LOW-ANGLE PERSONS: *THE POGLES* (1965) AND *POGLES' WOOD* (1966–8)

> Then you will tell me, won't you, little Mrs Pogle, or must I shake you a little? Then I shall turn you into frogs, slimy frogs on the bank of a dry river you shall be, turned by me on the count of three![1]
>
> —The Witch (*The Pogles*, episode 4)

As noted in Chapters 3 and 4, both the Firmin and Postgate families grew dramatically through the early 1960s, with Peter and Joan Firmin having six daughters (and a large variety of livestock) by mid-decade, while Oliver Postgate and Prue Myers's blended family also included six children by the end of 1964 (although their eldest, Kevan, was twenty by mid-decade). Given the pressures of raising such large families, it is hardly surprising to see the juggling of productions, which characterized the first five years of Smallfilms activity, give way to a more focused, single-production mentality. The second-half of the 1960s, therefore, was dominated by the production of the stop-frame model-based animation series *The Pogles* (1965) and *Pogles' Wood* (1966–8), which were filmed in the woodland around the Firmin farm.

To a certain extent, the success of Smallfilms' animated productions through the late 1950s and early 1960s paved the way for others to follow. While Firmin and Postgate were not the only ones making animation for children's programming in the UK, they remained outliers, with the bulk of productions made for child audiences at this time instead favouring either live action or puppetry. As television commissioners began to recognize the successes of shows like *Ivor the Engine* and *Noggin the Nog*, the number of animated television productions broadcast for young audiences began to increase, with the number of productions rising steadily through the early 1960s and then more sharply between 1965 and 1969. Alongside the work of Smallfilms, several other familiar shows emerged: *The Magic Roundabout* (ORTF, 1964–74; BBC, 1965–77), *Camberwick Green* (BBC, 1966), *Trumpton* (BBC, 1967), *Bizzy Lizzy* (BBC, 1967),[2] *The Herbs* (BBC, 1968), *Chigley* (BBC, 1969), and *Mary, Mungo and Midge* (BBC, 1969). Perhaps as a consequence of a growing sense of competition, and a need to respond to the likes of Gordon Murray and Ivor Wood, *The Pogles* pushed Smallfilms into darker territory (of which the opening quote from the Witch is emblematic), while the production history behind *Pogles' Wood* reveals an attempt, by Postgate, to embrace the psychedelia of the late 1960s (which was a popular aesthetic feature of *The Magic Roundabout*).

Divided into four main sections, this chapter begins with a discussion of the titular theme of 'Low-Angle Persons', which, on this occasion stems from a thematic concern established by Postgate himself. Following this we look at *The Pogles*, placing equal emphasis on Firmin's pre-production work and Postgate's narrative ambition. Then, through a close reading of documents held in the BBC's Written Archives, we will unpack the choppy pre-production journey behind *Pogles' Wood*. Finally, and sticking with the BBC archive, we study the work undertaken by Firmin to extend the commercial potential of all things Pogle.

In search of low-angle persons

Reflecting on his experiences of making *Pingwings*, Postgate writes in his autobiography that, in spite of all the continuity troubles caused by the natural conditions, he enjoyed making the show: 'Filming single-frame puppets was less fiddly than filming cutout cartoons. There were no backgrounds to set up, no figures to assemble and joint, no cotton-wool puffs of steam to move. The puppets were just there. I could choose the shots and camera angles as I went along.'[3] Having settled on the idea of another stop-motion model-based series, Postgate recalls the creative thought process that led to the development of *The Pogles*: 'I was sure there were other small persons about, persons not in Peter and Joan's farmyard, but somewhere. People had gnomes in their gardens, of course, but they were a bit sedentary and rarely seemed to do anything except fish. Maybe there were low-angle persons in the forest.'[4] Postgate's imagination duly obliged and these persons were discovered and subsequently named Pogles.

Tantalizingly, Postgate doesn't elaborate more fully on what he means by 'low-angle persons'. In the most literal sense, which is perhaps the meaning Postgate was intending, this term might refer to the diminutive characters that populate the many worlds of Smallfilms, sometimes hidden in the undergrowth, underwater, outer space, or in plain sight, whose upward view provided low-angle perspectives. By virtue of their size, their low-angle viewpoint affords new and often unexpected ways of looking. For example, Idris (*Ivor the Engine*), Graculus (*Noggin*), Romf (*Noggin*), Cyrus (*Seal of Neptune* and *Mermaid's Pearls*), the Pingwings, the Pogles, and the various toys that populate *Bagpuss* all bring low-angle perspectives to bear on their respective narratives. A case could also be made to see the Clangers as being low-angle characters, by virtue of their comparative size to the many recognizable human-made objects that land on their planet.

Postgate's term might also suggest the fact that the 'low-angle persons' within the works of Smallfilms frequently reveal a lack of knowledge related to specific acts, items, or situations, thereby setting up convenient narrative tensions that are typically resolved with the 'low-angle persons' acquiring new knowledge. To use a term favoured by David Baboulene, this tension results in 'knowledge gaps'.[5] While

Baboulene's work interrogates the principles of story design in contemporary cinema, it is possible – and useful – to map his notion of 'knowledge gaps' onto the work of Smallfilms. Writing in his 2017 doctoral thesis, Baboulene states that a knowledge gap exists 'whenever there is a difference in the knowledge held between any of the respondents in a narration'.[6] Disparities of this kind are everywhere when you start to look for them: *L'Arroseur Arrosé* (1895), *The Cabinet of Dr. Caligari* (1920), *North by Northwest* (1959), *The Jungle Book* (1967), *Toy Story* (1995), and every episode of every TV detective/sleuth show ever made. When looking at the work of Smallfilms, the notion of the knowledge gap aligns neatly with the construction and function of Postgate's low-angle characters. The low-angle characters that populate the works of Smallfilms all prompt knowledge gaps. For example, characters such as Cyrus, the Pingwings, the Pogles, the Clangers, and the toys that populate *Bagpuss*, frequently lack knowledge, and therefore spend their respective narratives seeking answers. While other characters have more knowledge than the rest of the characters in their story, leading to narrative tensions, such as Idris's fear of the Antiquarian Society and his subsequent hiding, or when Cyrus returns to the sunken city with the shrimp in *The Mermaid's Pearls*, and, as a result of the shrimp's lack of knowledge, we share Cyrus's unease at the prospect of the shrimp venturing into the city.

In the case of *The Pogles* and *Pogles' Wood*, this was an important dynamic given their positioning within the *Watch With Mother* programming, and the expectation that young viewers would be watching the series, broadcast by the BBC, to be entertained and educated. A particularly layered example of this trope can be seen in the *Pogles' Wood* episode 'Woodwork' (BBC1, 12 December 1967). At the start of the episode we learn that Mr and Mrs Pogle are about to visit their fairy friends. In fact, this is a pretence to draw Mrs Pogle away from the family home so that Pippin and Tog, who are staying behind, can make a chair and table for her birthday. With the coast clear and before beginning the job, Pippin tells Plant, 'look, we've got some pieces of real cut wood, we found them near where the sawmill used to be'.[7] After which the following exchange plays out:

Pippin Tog, have you got the saw and the nails, would you see if you could find the hammers. I know how we're going to make it, Plant.
Plant Good, I will watch you.
Pippin Making things with wood is easy! You just stand the bits up together and knock in nails.
Plant Oh, yes?[8]

Paying no attention to the Plant's sceptical response, Pippin begins hammering in nails and attaching legs. Without the use of glue or any kind of temporary fixings to hold the materials steady, Pippen's woodworking leaves a lot to be desired. After attaching the fourth leg, Pippen proclaims: 'there it is, a table!' However, as Figure 5.1 shows, the table is quite poorly made.

Full of naïve confidence, Pippen states, 'you don't need to hold it anymore, Tog', to which Tog replies with a hesitant 'ogglug?', before Pippen commands 'let go of it'.

Figure 5.1 Woodworking 101 as seen in *Pogles' Wood* (1965–8).

Of course, as Tog suspected, the table isn't able to stand unaided and immediately slumps over. Undeterred, Pippen resumes:

Plant   It's a bit wobbly, ins't it, Pippen?
Pippen   Oh, it just wants a few cross pieces. Here, for instance.
[*Pippen picks up a cross piece and attempts to hammer it directly onto the unsupported leg. The table collapses completely. Pippen then become cross and hammers madly at the table.*]
Oh, its silly! The rotten thing, it isn't trying!
Plant   [*Laughing*] Hehe. Oh, Pippen, you mustn't go hitting things with a hammer just because what you're trying to make doesn't come right. Making things in wood is not easy, it is quite difficult, and you must learn how to use the wood the proper way if you want to make things properly.
Pippen   But I want to get the chair and table ready before Mrs Pogle comes home.
Plant   Well, this time I will see if I can help you with a little magic, but first I want to tell you an old story about a carpenter.[9]

At this point Plant narrates the story of a carpenter who struggles to make a living, but who receives a royal commission to make a matching chair and table.

The catch: the furniture must be made in one day. Falling asleep on the job, the carpenter's tools become animated magically (via stop-motion) and complete the job. The Plant's morality tale, by virtue of the step-by-step woodworking shown in the sequence, also offers both the audience within the narrative (Pippen and Tog) and the audience of *Watch With Mother* the chance to learn something of the skills and processes involved in woodworking a table and chair. Such sequences, which are common throughout *Pogles' Wood*, are examples of low-angle persons prompting a knowledge gap, which in turn are exploited to deliver educational content via entertaining narratives.

Without wishing for this to become tenuous, there is also one more way that Postgate's term can be understood: as a characterization of power relationships. A common tendency throughout the work of Smallfilms is a desire to destabilize – and on occasion invert – the power relationships revealed between conceptually low-angle persons and those characters portrayed as being superior. For example, in the *Ivor the Engine* episode 'Mrs Porty's Foxes', we see Jones the Steam dupe a group of aristocratic fox hunters by hiding their quarry in Mrs Porty's fancy hat, and thereby saving it from their murderous intentions. Then there is Olaf the Lofty, who, throughout *The Saga of Noggin the Nog*, repeatedly invents weird and wonderful contraptions, announcing their arrival with habitual self-aggrandizement before their eventual failure or misappropriation (by Nogbad). Similarly, many of Major Clanger's inventions, introduced with the sense that 'Major knows best', typically result in periods of disequilibrium on the Clanger's moon, before another member of the Clanger family – or supporting character – restores order. Additionally, there are moments when seemingly all-powerful beings are reduced in stature, as is temporarily the case when a disorientated shrimp insults Neptune (*The Mermaid's Pearls*) or the Witch (*The Pogles*) is reduced to 'no-thing'. This is a constant of Smallfilms: poking fun at the high and mighty, and placing value in a sense of common good, community, and equality. Whether Postgate had one or all of the above in mind when offering the term 'low-angle persons' is impossible to know, but what is undeniable is the utility of this perspective, when evaluating the appeal of Smallfilms' works.

The Pogles *(1965)*

Fully aware of the potential challenges to be faced if *The Pogles* was to be filmed outside, Postgate tasked Firmin with the job of fabricating not just the Pogles, but also a woodland set inside their studio. Postgate notes:

> The house-in-the-tree-root that Peter built for the Pogles in my studio was particularly realistic and handsome. It had a stout wooden door with a bell beside it which the hedgehog who called in the mornings would ring, and an upstairs window with shutters. Real ivy was growing up it and the garden was

greengrocer's grass. Like all of their kind, Mr and Mrs Pogle were short and stocky and wore very large boots with hinged toe-caps. These contained lumps of lead to stop them falling over.[10]

While Postgate's words do give a sense of Firmin's finished work, this account is characteristic of how Firmin's labour is sometimes minimized or marginalized in accounts of the studio's history. Repeatedly, Firmin's own modesty when talking about Smallfilms has resulted in an elevation of Postgate's narrative achievements at the expense of his own contributions to the studio's productions.

When interviewing Firmin, I asked about the fabrication processes required before production of *The Pogles* could begin. Firmin began by retracing familiar stories of repurposed bits of Meccano, before moving to a discussion of the lead-weighted boots. Offering more depth than Postgate's summary of the Pogles' boots, Firmin revealed that the design was rooted in an awareness of how they were to be animated, and – more significantly – *where* they were to be animated:

> Their boots are hollow, with a big lump of lead in the boot. You know when a puppet moves from one step to the next, you could have them spiked to the ground, but this was a matter of just weight, so, in the big boot, the toe-cap lifts up and there is a great lump of lead in there, and the other one is empty. So, Oliver would do the animation and one boot would go down and he'd have to take that lead from the other boot and put it in that one, ready for the next step, that was our answer to using puppets on natural ground where you couldn't always spike. I built the set in the barn, the woodland set was in the barn, so that was a polystyrene-type base for that, so that's alright for spikes, but in the open air you just relied on their weight.[11]

Within Firmin's words, we can see evidence of the careful design work that took place before Postgate's camera began to roll. Firmin's boot design, with swappable lead weights, reveals an expert understanding of the animation procedure to be followed by Postgate. Firmin not only designed models that could perform on a variety of surfaces (a lesson learned from their work on *Pingwings*) but also, by having a hinged toe-cap, he ensured that the process of switching the weights could be done without disturbing the animation flow, and would therefore not introduce any unwanted disruptions of continuity, which could have been the case had he designed fully swappable boots or legs.

Given the gradual increase in picture quality of television sets in the mid-1960s, and with the decision being taken to film much of *The Pogles* inside the Smallfilms studio, Firmin also recognized the value of having convincing settings:

> Most of it was done in the barn, so I built sets with real bits of tree, real bits of ivy and grass. I mean, there was the grocer's grass, the imitation grass, but there was also real grass, and things which would last a couple of days and then went yellow and streaky, because they were in the dark, so they would have to be replaced a lot. That was all pretty basic, but it worked well. I also did enormous twelve-foot square backdrops of woodland scenes, for the backgrounds of Pogle shots.[12]

As well as giving attention to backgrounds that were destined to serve as backdrops to the main action, Firmin also made sure the sets were practical. For example, when crafting the Pogle's treehouse, he worked to combine durability with flexibility: 'I made the treehouse that they lived in, it was sort of Papier-mâché, but giant corrugated carboard-mâché. It had a door, and I had to do an interior, and the interior had stairs.'[13] These production insights reveal the wide variety of materials and considerations confronted by Firmin as he worked to establish the foundation for Postgate's stop-motion animation.

The first episode of *The Pogles* begins with introductory narration presented over live-action footage of the wood in which the Pogles live. As has been noted in previous chapters, this is common feature of Smallfilms productions, and serves the dual purpose of establishing the story via Postgate's narration and filling time with economical footage (with live action being quicker to shoot than animation). The introduction informs the viewer that hedgehogs play an important role in the daily routine of Pogles: 'You see, hedgehogs go to bed in the early mornings, and Pogles get up in the mornings and Pogles are very heavy sleepers and have to be woken up in the mornings otherwise they sleep all day', and this confuses them, 'so every Pogle's house has a bell, outside the front door', which, it transpires, the hedgehogs ring.[14]

After some unpalatable exchanges between Mr and Mrs Pogle, with Mr Pogle tipping his wife out of bed and then demanding breakfast, followed by Mrs Pogle accusing Mr Pogle of overeating, Mr Pogle is sent on an errand to find some 'dwarf beans' to be planted in their garden. Unable to find them, Mr Pogle instead finds a single, large bean. Returning home, we learn that the bean is not what it initially seems, since it can be heard snoring in Mr Pogle's barrow. At this point Mr and Mrs Pogle debate whether the bean will wake up if they plant it, which leads them to bury it deep in their garden. Once in the ground, the bean sprouts into a magical talking plant which, after taking some nourishment in the form of bilberry wine, grants Mrs Pogle her wish of having a line of 'dwarf beans' in her garden.

Episode two opens with a group of fairies noisily circling around the plant, waking the Pogles from their sleep. After dispersing the fairies, Mr Pogle notices that the magic plant has grown a flower and is swaying gently while humming. Fetching a ladder and climbing up to investigate, Mr Pogle realizes that the plant is in fact cradling a baby and the humming is a lullaby. Taking responsibility for the baby, Mrs Pogle brings it inside while Mr Pogle is sent to fetch some milk from the dairy. Failing in his mission and falling clumsily into a milk pale in the process, Mr Pogle returns home empty-handed. In the meantime, the magic plant has conjured a bottle of warm milk for Mrs Pogle to feed the baby with. As the episode ends, the Pogles find a silver crown in the baby's basket.

Following Mrs Pogle's suggestion to ask the plant, they learn that the fairies had something to do with the appearance of the baby. Dutifully, Mr Pogle sets off to find a fairy to interrogate, but before he has chance to put his questions to the fairies, the fairies urge him to return home. Upon his return, Mr Pogle finds the house seemingly deserted, eventually discovering Mrs Pogle trapped in a magic sack beneath a trapdoor. We learn that a Witch raided the house while Mr Pogle was gone, and while the Witch didn't find the silver crown, which she presumably sought, she did take the baby.

Having been magically transported by the plant to help her husband in his pursuit of the Witch, Mrs Pogle finds him trapped in a wooden cage. The Witch, who has been watching, then appears and confronts the Pogles, quickly imprisoning Mrs Pogle in another cage. Following a threatening speech delivered by the Witch, we learn that the crown is in fact the Crown of the King of Fairy Land. After the Witch threatens to turn Mr and Mrs Pogle into frogs, Mrs Pogle uses a magic flower, given to her by the plant at the start of the episode, to burn the Witch to a pile of ashes. Having rescued the baby, they return to find their home ransacked, but with the crown still safely hidden away.

The final two episodes see the Witch employ several tricks (including Trojan-style stealth and the impersonation of a police officer) in an attempt to infiltrate the Pogle's tree home. Finally, after breaking the door, the Witch confronts the Pogles. Following an exchange of threats a wind-up bird retrieves the crown and places it on to Mr Pogle's head. Sensing the crown's power, Mr Pogle goads the Witch, quickly revealing that there is no power to match that of the crown. Freezing the Witch as she attempts to escape, Mr and Mrs Pogle debate what to do with her:

Mrs Pogle   Can you turn her into something like she's turned others into in her time? Something, I don't know?
Mr Pogle   Trouble is, that don't seem to stop her. She's been a jug of milk, an old boot, and a bonfire, and she just turns herself back into herself again.
Mrs Pogle   Well, it looks like there's nothing we can do.
Mr Pogle   That's it! Nothing. Witch, hag of the night, dream-creeper, be 'no thing' at all, be nothing.[15]

With that the Witch vanishes into a swirling ball of black nothing. This proves a fitting act given Postgate's desire to find – and establish – new low-angle persons in *The Pogles*, with this victory extending the multifaceted low-angle quality of the Pogles beyond just their physically diminutive stature, to also include their inversion of the power dynamic established throughout the series via their defeat of the seemingly superior Witch. Taking the crown off, Mr Pogle gives it to the wind-up bird. With this act, the bird transforms into the King of the Fairies. The Fairy King reveals that the baby is his child, and that the fairies owe a great debt to the Pogles for keeping the baby safe and defeating the Witch. The final act sees the King remove the gold shackle from the plant, then task the fairies with supplying as much bilberry wine as they can muster, before feeding it to the plant and thereby rejuvenating it. The series ends with chants of 'all is well' and the Pogles dancing with the plant and the fairies in celebration.

Having written a story that took Smallfilms into new, darker territory, the stop-motion model-based animation employed for *The Pogles* also represented an evolution, in terms of confidence, sophistication, and ambition, over the animation found in *Pingwings*. In Postgate's own words, the animation of the Pogles and their fellow woodland inhabitants, only accounted for 'about 10 per cent' of the footage that is seen on-screen (see Appendix – Figure A.4 for a wider analysis of animation screen time).[16] However, this did not limit the impact of the animation that was used:

> All the way through, if you look at my films, you will see that my animation is very economical, but very powerful. Because, I'm not recreating life, I am illustrating a story and telling a story by an extension of the pen. I'm coming at it from the other direction, and what is the minimum amount of visual delivery that I have to do to get this to appear to be alive, which one has accepted more or less anyway that they're there, and to convey the movements, and it is surprising how much one needn't do, and how much better it is from *not doing those things that animation doesn't do well*. I mean, when they have to change an expression, I change the whole head, and take the head off and put another one on, most of the time, just to change an expression. I go to Peter and say give me 'oh' expression, and he'd say 'stay there', and then five minutes later he'd be back here with a head, which I'd then have to dry under the lights, because it was still wet [Postgate chuckles]. For the Mr Pogle, Peter also had magnetic eyebrows and bushy moustache, and Mrs Pogle had a 'woo' and a smile as well, but she had wire eyebrows, which sort of moved up and down, which was quite adequate for the purpose, because we never attempted lip-sync, and I don't think anybody has ever said to me, 'I'm sorry, I want to see the mouths move', because it really is awfully unnecessary. And once you don't see it, you don't look for it.[17]

In this statement, Postgate articulates the creative production philosophy that underpinned the animated works of Smallfilms as a whole, highlighting the constant tension between – and consideration of – the demands of the narrative and the need to maintain visual interest. Postgate's words also reinforce the point made in the introduction of this book regarding the prevalence and importance of stillness within the work of Smallfilms.

Within the responses of those respondents identifying *The Pogles* or *Pogles' Wood* as being their favoured Smallfilms show, beyond the more general comments that discussed the appeal of the 'world of the wood', 'surreal qualities', 'memorable characters, accents and catchphrases', or the 'glow of childhood nostalgia', there is a clear preference for – and recollection of – *Pogles' Wood* over *The Pogles* (at a ratio of 4:1).[18] Although the survey data offers little by way of comment on the low-angle qualities of these productions, that *Pogles' Wood* gave Postgate far greater scope to invest the world and its characters with low-angle potential, by increasing the educational remit considerably from *The Pogles*, perhaps contributed to *Pogles' Wood*'s more universal appeal by virtue of the series' deeper connection with Postgate's own multifaceted low-angle ambitions. Ultimately, Postgate's assertions about the power of story transcending any sense of procedural limitation were proved correct, with the survey data confirming one specific aspect of *The Pogles'* legacy: the impact of the Witch narrative. Tellingly, every response that favoured *The Pogles* identified the 'sinister' or 'scary' witch and 'creepy location' as key elements that left a lasting impression.[19]

The combination of Firmin's model work and Postgate's narrative design resulted in a witch that was so unsettling that when the BBC approached Smallfilms to commission a follow-up, there was little appetite to see her return. In his autobiography, Postgate recalls the initial meeting with Doreen Stephens, Head of Family Programmes at the BBC, as occurring in 'the middle of 1965'; however, the BBC's written archives show correspondence between Postgate and Stephens, regarding the development of *Pogles' Wood*, commencing in February of 1965, suggesting that while Postgate's characterization of their initial is meeting is fair, he has misremembered the timing of this encounter. Postgate writes: '[Stephens] told me that the Corporation's view, which was that Mr and Mrs Pogle were very welcome at the BBC, and that the friendly magic, as practised by the plant, was perfectly acceptable, but the Witches screaming in the back garden were definitely *non grata*'.[20] Postgate and Firmin did not object to this stipulation and work began on devising *Pogles' Wood*.

Pogles' Wood (1966–8)

The BBC's Written Archives contain a steady stream of correspondence between Postgate, Firmin, and various individuals working at – and with – the BBC. These letters and internal memos record the process by which *The Pogles*, with its multi-episode narrative, was reconfigured into *Pogles' Wood*, which adopted a more standalone episodic structure (albeit with some narrative continuity across episodes). They reveal a moment of creative flirtation, on Postgate's part, between series two and three of *Pogles' Wood*, which was left unrealized, and they show how this particular Smallfilms production was almost cut short by the national wage freeze imposed by the Labour Government in 1966. Beyond the production realm, they reveal the efforts made by Firmin to commercialize all things Pogle. Therefore, to better establish these industrial subplots and contexts, which have not been interrogated in the works published on Smallfilms to date, this final section of the chapter draws upon the BBC's archived correspondence.

The earliest letter held by the BBC related to *Pogles' Wood* is from Postgate to Stephens, dated 20 February 1965, and documents an acceptance of the new format being proposed, with Postgate noting that there 'should be small adventures, nothing dangerous of course, and a fair amount of visits to real places to see real things going on'.[21] In reply, Stephens writes to Postgate on 22 February 1965 to suggest that the new series would fit well within the *Watch with Mother* (BBC, 1953–73) programming. Stephens also takes the opportunity to inform Postgate that Producer Ursula Eason and Purchasing Assistant V. Maccoby would be helping to take the series into production and contractual agreement.[22]

For readers unfamiliar with *Watch with Mother*, it represented a well-matched home for *Pogles' Wood*, given the emphasis now being placed on having the low-angle characters encountering unfamiliar everyday situations or objects, and thereby learning about these subjects through the episode. By turning the characters of *Pogles' Wood* into on-screen proxies for the young *Watch with Mother* audience, Stephens sought to deliver on the BBC's commitment to disseminate 'information, education, and entertainment', as codified in the 1964 Charter.[23] With these institutional pressures at play, the very title of *Watch with Mother* was 'intended to deflect fears that television might become a nursemaid to children and encourage "bad mothering"'.[24] However, as Sarah Godfrey and Su Holmes note, in their article that tracks the evolution of familial representation through the history of BBC's preschool programming, the suggested 'containment within the domestic, and the discursive and institutional emphasis on the mother–child relationship', which was core to *Watch With Mother*, 'only enjoyed dominance for a short period, as more mothers sought paid employment, as more children were in childcare, and as more and more children viewed on their own'.[25]

In a letter from Stephens, dated 10 August 1965, we find an example of the BBC's attempted administration of the Charter's principles. Having received episode synopses from Postgate, Stephens suggests 'one or two small changes', related to concerns about inaccurate seasonal depictions and the use of incorrect nomenclature:

> I think we need to be careful about some of the references to blackberrying, particularly in Scripts 8, 9, &10. Sheep shearing and birds' eggs are surely not normally found in the countryside at the same time as ripe blackberries. [...]
>
> In No.3 would you check whether it is correct to use the word 'hive' in connection with wild bees. I thought they 'nested' and that a hive was man-made for the domestic variety.[26]

Stephens' point about beehives is correct, yet the completed episode (*Pogles' Wood*: episode 3: 'Honey Bees', 21 April 1966) features the word hive used throughout. There is no correspondence on file that suggests this was a contested matter, so it is possible to see this as an example of Postgate's confidence and persuasive power as a rhetorician, or the tolerance of Stephens, or as an example of creative autonomy enjoyed by Smallfilms by virtue of their relative geographic remoteness, or a mixture of all three.

Having offered direction to Postgate, Stephens then writes to the Controller of BBC One on 11 August 1965: 'You asked me to find out whether it would be possible to offer "THE POGLES" [*sic*] in January/March in place of "CAMBERWICK GREEN". I have discussed this with Oliver Postgate. As his series is being purchased with rights of repeats over seven years he is unwilling to be rushed.'[27] Stephens goes on to write:

> To produce the series in time to start transmission in Week 1 would be at the expense of the kind of careful checking and thinking which he wants to do as the programmes develop. I have agreed the scripts in principle, but he plans to let us hear each tape as he does it before he gets involved in filming, and each film in the series at the rough-cut stage. This type of careful checking would be impossible if the series had to be ready by January.[28]

Stephens's position held and *Camberwick Green* aired at the start of 1966, not *Pogles' Wood*. What is clear, having read all of the Smallfilms-related correspondence held by the BBC, is the nurturing, protective, and peacekeeping role played by Stephens, while helping to bring the work of Smallfilms to the screen.

As the first broadcast of *Pogles' Wood* series one (17 April 1966–30 June 1966) approached its conclusion, Postgate contacted Eason on 6 June 1966 to open discussions regarding a second series. Always looking to flex his creative muscles, Postgate opened his letter with a suggested change of direction for *Pogles' Wood* series two:

> Not the same as the first lot. My idea was that we should dodge the purely educational emphasis and, keeping the Pogle Establishment as a basis, go for things which are fun and stimulating to the imagination. Musical stories from the plant, jokes, mischief, scrapes, a bit more magic, one or two more characters, and I hope, a complete puppet world of the plant's contriving inhabited by earnest ludicrous antic characters living in their own preposterous world.[29]

Within Postgate's words we can see an aspiration to return to the playfulness of Smallfilms' earlier works, such as *Ivor the Engine*, *The Saga of Noggin the Nog*, and *Pingwings*, to name but a few, which embraced whimsical authenticity throughout their narratives. We also see a desire to expand the settings to include the 'complete puppet world of the plant' and to place less emphasis on education and more emphasis on 'jokes, mischief, scrapes'.

Accompanying his letter dated 6 June 1966, Postgate attached typed, half-page synopses for six new *Pogles' Wood* episodes. While some of these early synopses did evolve into broadcast episodes, others, like synopsis number six (Figure 5.2), did not. In the synopsis pictured in Figure 5.2 we can see a clear example of Postgate's desire to move *Pogles' Wood* away from an educational footing, to a show that indulges in entertainment for its own sake. For those with prior knowledge of Disney's *Fantasia* (1940) or *The Band Concert* (1935), when reading this synopsis it is difficult not to see the influence of these works, films of which Postgate was surely aware.[30] The opening scene depicting the Pogles' house 'in more than usual pandemonium', with Pippin and Tog contributing the beating of a honey-can and the whistling of a two-note flute, respectively, evokes the musical unruliness of *The Band Concert*, in which Mickey Mouse battles in the role of conductor to keep his band in check as well as halting the unwelcome interjections of Donald Duck, who, after entering the short animation in the role of snack seller, plucks a flute from his tunic and plays it disruptively. Of course, the bedlam that evolves throughout *The Band Concert* aligns neatly with the rising intensity of Rossini's 'William Tell Overture', which is the score being conducted by Mickey. In fact, Postgate's suggestion that the robber is chased 'into the arms of the park keeper' prompting a very fortissimo ending echoes the 'Mickey Mousing' that occurs throughout *The Band Concert*.[31] The parallels with Disney's *Fantasia* are perhaps even more striking, with the magic conjured by youthful hands (those of Pippin and Tog in *Pogles' Wood* and Mickey

> POGLES' WOOD Second Series   Episode 2
>
> STRONG MUSIC
>
> It is raining. In the Pogle's house there is more than the usual pandemonium. Pippin is beating time on the honey tin, the milk-jug and the staircase while Tog plays his flute and dances on the landing. Most of the ground floor is occupied by Mr Pogle who is making a sort of summer-house frame out of twigs. Mrs Pogle is picking her way through this lot trying to cook the dinner. She appeals to the Plant who tells her to open the front door. She does this. The Plant then tells Pippin and Tog to play the Pied Piper tune. They do so. At once, to Pogle's surprise, the pieces of twig and string that Pogle was using dance out into the garden. There the twigs assemble themselves into a sort of pavilion. The Plant covers the pavilion with handsome conjured material, finishing with gold fringing and a gold ball on the top. Mr Pogle, Pippin and Tog occupy this. Mr Pogle mentions the resemblance between this pavilion and the bandstand in Episode 1. Pippin says this is more gorgeous than the bandstand because of the gold ball on the top. The Plant tells them another musical story about the bandstand with the new gold ball on the top. A Peter-and-the-Wolfish story about a robber who plans to steal it and how the instruments, solo and in concert foil his dastardly plans and chase him into the arms of the Park keeper. Very ffortissimo ending.
>
> Mrs Pogle hears the strong music and scolds them for making loud music. She says that music is pretty, sweet and sad, not noisy and rough and rushing wildly about. The Plant obligingly conjures some instruments and they play a sweet schmalzy piece for Mrs Pogle who is entranced... until she remembers her cake in the oven.

Figure 5.2 *Pogles' Wood* unmade – draft synopsis, 6 June 1966.

Mouse in *Fantasia*) spiralling out of control, before a masterly intervention (by the plant in *Pogles' Wood* and the wizard Yen Sid in *Fantasia*) restores order.

Having received Postgate's synopses, Eason sent them on to Joy Whitby, a Children's Television Producer who was working on *Jackanory* (BBC1, 1965–96) at the time, for comment. Whitby, writing to Stephens's division ('A.H.F.P.Tel' –

Assistant Head of Family Programmes Television), notes her unfamiliarity with 'any of Oliver's current Pogles' and how she is unaware of 'how well they have been received', before offering the following critique of the synopses:

1. He is imaginative and original. I love the fantasy of (2), (3), (5) (leaving out the Roundabout start).
2. The other plots seem weaker at this stage – I agree about avoiding overlaps with *Magic Roundabout* as in (4) and the opening of (5).
3. I'm always suspicious of contrived musical stories like (1) and (6) because so many hacks have exploited the same idea. But Oliver may well be able to give it a face-lift.
4. When he talked about Plant at that lunch we had over a year ago, I remember suggesting it might seem too like Weed. I still think there's that danger. Can't he find an alternative?[32]

Although Whitby closes by saying that she'd 'give him the go-ahead', her memo highlights a concern that would have been widely shared: potential overlap with *The Magic Roundabout*.

Originally created for French television, *The Magic Roundabout* was discovered by Stephens and brought over to the BBC, where *Playschool* presenter Eric Thompson was assigned to write and narrate the English version.[33] *The Magic Roundabout* rapidly gained a broad audience, airing late in the afternoon, 'just before the 5.55pm main early-evening news bulletin on BBC 1', therefore meaning that 'many adults caught the program while waiting for the news'.[34] Furthermore, as *Pogles' Wood* began its third rerun in January 1967, the two series were scheduled in close proximity, with *The Magic Roundabout* enjoying a second rerun at that time. For example, on 4 January 1966, audiences young and old could have settled down to watch *Pogles' Wood – 1: 'Grains of Wheat'* at 1.30 pm and then *The Magic Roundabout – 5: 'Dancing Brooms'* at 5.45 pm.[35] With *Pogles' Wood* being broadcast weekly, rather than daily, this pattern of both shows airing on the same day repeated every seven days, as their schedules aligned.

It is impossible to know if Postgate viewed *The Magic Roundabout*'s more prime-time scheduling with envy, yet it is clear from his letter and synopses dated 6 June 1966 that he was keen to push the second series of *Pogles' Wood* in a new, zanier direction. By suggesting this change, it was inevitable that the BBC Commissioners and Producers, responsible for handling the business of Smallfilms and the adaptation of *The Magic Roundabout*, would draw comparisons between the two shows. The fact that Thompson, like Postgate, specialized in crafting child-friendly worlds that were laced with overt and covert adult references, would not have been lost on Eason, Stephens, and Whitby. Ultimately, series two of *Pogles' Wood* charted a course somewhere between the show's first series and the more psychedelic tone embraced by *The Magic Roundabout*.

With the conceptual parameters for series two established, Firmin and Postgate encountered a fresh challenge that threatened to sink their production of *Pogles' Wood* series two: the Prices and Incomes Bill of 1966. Under the

Labour Governments of 1964–70, George Brown gave incomes policy added bite, with increasingly elaborate mechanisms for monitoring wages and pricing being introduced through the second half of the decade.[36] It was against this backdrop of economic restraint that Postgate and Firmin attempted to negotiate the finances of their second *Pogles' Wood* series. Almost in parallel, Postgate started discussions with the BBC about the new series in early July 1966, while the government's Prices and Incomes Bill was put before Parliament that same month (gaining Royal Assent in August of 1966).[37] As Alec Cairncross notes, a 'wage-freeze in July 1966' had a 'marked effect on wage-bargains and helped to limit the rise in hourly wages' over the following six months to less than 1 per cent.[38] Firmin and Postgate, having pitched a more ambitious second series to the BBC, consequently found themselves in a battle to adequately finance their proposed production.

Throughout the second half of July, Postgate and Macooby exchanged letters regarding the contractual details of the *Pogles' Wood* second series. With the BBC adopting the position that the series should be costed at the same rate as the first, Postgate wrote to Macooby to explain why such an arrangement would leave Smallfilms out of pocket:

> I have got the bills from the first lot so there is no reason why I shouldn't do some accurate costings for this lot. In fact I see no reason why I shouldn't show you the estimates – if only to prove that I am not buying Cadillacs.
>
> Attached is a sheet showing what the last lot cost and what I expect the next lot to cost. The new lot aren't exactly like the first lot. They are to have much more different art-work, puppets and cartoons and a lot more different music. Hence the higher costs for these films. The lab charges went up last year by about 25 per cent.[39]

Despite Postgate making it clear that the costs to produce *Pogles' Wood* had increased due to a variety of factors, the BBC maintained a firm stance and continued to negotiate pricing as per the government's policy.

Ultimately, it was Stephens's decisive action that facilitated a resolution. In a letter to Postgate, dated 12 August 1966, Stephens included a copy of a memo that she had sent to Gordon Smith, Head of Purchasing for BBC Enterprises, who was at the heart of the BBC's hard-line approach to this particular recommission. In her memo, Stephens restates the appeal of *Pogles' Wood* and how well it fits with the *Watch with Mother* programming, she highlights where the pricing mismatch stems from (being the BBC's attempt to cost the new, more expensive series, at the same rate as the earlier, less-costly series), and takes personal responsibility for giving Postgate and Firmin the notion that a higher price would be available for their second series.[40] Stephens writes:

> Earlier this summer before he started working on a synopsis for the new WATCH WITH MOTHER series, it was agreed verbally between Oliver Postgate and myself that when the contract was issued for the new series, the price would be

higher and could be related to the actual costs of the first series plus an allowance for the increase in laboratory charges and further costs that might result from the added complications included in the new series.[41]

Stephens's intervention was successful, and, after receiving the internal memo on the 12 August, Smith immediately issued his own memo, circulated to a number of senior BBC Controllers, Heads and one Assistant General, that lobbied for approval of the show at the new rate: 'The cost of the new series represents a slight increase (£210 per programme) on the price paid under the early agreement but essentially we are acquiring a different produce, which is designed to be more ambitious production format and involved more complicated and elaborate art work with additional puppet characters and more varied music.'[42] As noted earlier in this chapter, once again Stephens's support for the Smallfilms cause, which is unrecognized in existing historical accounts of the studio, was key.

Smith then wrote to Stephens a few days later to apologise for the contractual tensions that had been created over the previous weeks. Smith writes, 'I'm sorry if our well intentioned efforts to implement the Corporation policy and indeed comply with Government edict caused you any embarrassment', before concluding: 'Ah well; they say the road to hell is paved with good intentions and I have certainly contributed my share. I hope all will now be tranquil in POGLES WOOD.'[43] Shortly after, on 5 September 1966, the BBC issued a contract to Smallfilms for the delivery of a second *Pogles' Wood* series. With that, Firmin and Postgate were able to complete production without jeopardizing the financial health of their studio.

Beyond the wood

Securing a broader commercial return from their television work became a key focus for Firmin both during and after the production of *Pogles' Wood*. Having tried unsuccessfully to develop merchandise for their previous shows, namely *Ivor the Engine*, *Noggin the Nog*, and *Pingwings*, it is clear from the correspondence held in the BBC's archive that Firmin held more hope that *Pogles' Wood* could be their commercial breakthrough. Firmin's hope was well founded. When Smallfilms first began production in 1959, approximately 58 per cent of UK households owned a television, compared to 84 per cent in 1965, meaning that the number of viewers seeing *Pogles' Wood* on a regular basis would have been potentially much greater than the number of viewers of their earlier shows.[44] An additional limiting factor for *Ivor the Engine* and *Pingwings* was the fact they were broadcast by Associated-Rediffusion and Southern Television, respectively, thereby limiting their geographic reach. While Postgate was busy animating the models that Firmin had made earlier in the production cycle, Firmin proposed, received, and developed a number of commercial extensions to the *Pogles* brand.

Between 1964 and 1967, we can see Firmin's responsibility for managing the commercialization of Smallfilms' shows become increasingly formalized, complementing the well-established working routines that saw Postgate – for the most part – devise the stories and animate the show, and with Firmin providing the lead for visual design, illustration, and fabrication. As Postgate playfully expressed to Harry Lowe, the BBC Assistant Commercial Manager handling *Pogles*-related matters, in February 1966, 'my henchman, Peter Firmin […] is in charge of the merchandising side'.[45] Postgate's characterization of Firmin in such a way is a reflection of Firmin's dual appetite to expand the commercial potential of Smallfilms' television work, yet also maintain his exacting design standards across all of this spin-out activity.

In letters dated March to July of 1966, we see a glimpse of this activity, with references to potential 'Vinyl Squeakers' being manufactured by Pedigree Dolls,[46] a 'Nite-lite' in development for Cobex,[47] 'three licence applications approved' for Sto-Rose Toys,[48] and a 'children's range of tea set' with Gaydon.[49] In a letter to Firmin, dated 19 October 1966, Howe establishes the full extent of this activity, noting: Thomas Hope & Sankey Hudson Ltd. 'are still definitely interested in manufacturing POGLES JIGSAWS'; 'B.I.P. Gaydon Ltd. are very pleased with the art work you supplied and over lunch last week they confirmed they would be sending the contracts any day now'; 'I have also enclosed approval forms for wallpaper and a set of 3 puzzles and games booklets'; 'Contracts have been issued to both Pelham Puppets Limited and Deans Child Play Toys Limited and I am still awaiting their return for counter for countersignature'; and 'Finally, I am sorry for the delay in forwarding to you the advance royalty received from Mettoy Limited in respect of Vinyl Toys but this should be in your hands within the next few days.'[50] Howe concludes by stating that there is 'no doubt at all that these manufacturers will go ahead'.[51] While all of this para-televisual commercial activity would have undoubtedly boosted Smallfilms' finances, there is little suggestion that Firmin and Postgate were interested in making a quick buck.

In fact, the BBC archive reveals that Firmin remained constantly vigilant throughout all of this para-televisual activity, working hard to ensure that standards did not slip. This is most clearly articulated in the early correspondence between Firmin and Lowe related to the development of print annuals, which would eventually be published by Hamlyn through the late 1960s and into the 1970s. In a letter dated 26 November 1966, Firmin writes:

> [I]n the matter of these publications, as in all the products, we care very strongly about the accuracy of the artwork. We would be grateful if you would impress upon their minds that we are fussy. (The German publisher of Ivor the Engine, Engelbert Verlag, was forced to withdraw an edition of the books and I eventually illustrated the new ones, because he went ahead and published using his artist, who had his own ideas of what Ivor looked like.)
>
> I only mention this because we have had several occasions in the past, apart from the extreme one, to realise that many people in the publishing business think that as long as the money rolls in we don't care about the product. Some people don't. We do.[52]

The tone of Firmin's letter is firm, while remaining reasonable, revealing a desire, shared by Postgate, to ensure that all Smallfilms-related activities maintained a degree of integrity. Seeking to dispel any potential ambiguity, Firmin closes this letter by referring to other products in development at that time: 'It seems a long time since you saw the mock-up of the cloth doll. We still have not seen any products, neither the balloons nor even the Vinyl dolls although the designer came here to draw the puppets. I hope they are not getting too far without consulting us because a lot of work might be wasted.'[53]

As well as looking to find a domestic market for *Pogles*-related merchandise, Firmin also maintained steady pressure on their Commercial Manager at the BBC, Lowe. Over a series of letters, we see Firmin press Lowe for details of any deals being struck with overseas markets, who, in turn, presses his Manchester-based franchising agent, John Pemberton, of World Distributors Ltd., for similar detail. In a letter from Pemberton to Lowe, dated 25 October 1966, there is a tantalizing suggestion that some inroads were made on the international scene, with Australia, Canada, South Africa, and New Zealand all named as countries in which Pemberton would like to licence rights for *Pogles' Wood* fun books.[54]

Conclusion

Despite the challenges identified in this chapter, the time spent working on *The Pogles* and *Pogles' Wood* was one of comparative stability and consistency, compared to the years previous and the split energies of parallel productions. During the mid-1960s, we can see Postgate and Firmin attain a level of confidence that would see them continue to thrive creatively. As production on *Pogles' Wood* concluded, nether Postgate or Firmin could have imagined the lasting cultural legacy that their next project would have. Leaving behind the black-and-white, pastoral surrounds inhabited by the Pogles, Smallfilms left Earth's orbit, embarking on a voyage to discover a colourful and technological moon, which reverberated with the sounds of whistles and clangs.

Notes

1 Author's transcription from *The Pogles* episode 4, viewed on DVD (Dragons' Friendly Society).
2 *Bizzy Lizzy* was a recurrent part of the Picture Book programming within *Watch with Mother*, but was turned into a standalone, short-running series in 1967.
3 Postgate, *Seeing Things*, pp. 250–251.
4 Postgate, *Seeing Things*, p. 251.
5 David Baboulene, 'Knowledge Gaps in Popular Hollywood Cinema Storytelling: The Role of Information Disparity in Film Narrative' (University of Brighton, 2017).
6 Baboulene, 'Knowledge Gaps in Popular Hollywood Cinema Storytelling', p. 19.
7 Author's transcription from Pogles' Wood episode 'Woodwork', viewed on DVD (Dragons' Friendly Society).

8   Author's transcription from Pogles' Wood episode 'Woodwork', viewed on DVD (Dragons' Friendly Society).
9   Author's transcription from Pogles' Wood episode 'Woodwork', viewed on DVD (Dragons' Friendly Society).
10 Postgate, *Seeing Things*, pp. 253–254.
11 Peter Firmin, interviewed by Chris Pallant, Canterbury, UK, 3 December 2016.
12 Peter Firmin, interviewed by Chris Pallant, Canterbury, UK, 3 December 2016.
13 Peter Firmin, interviewed by Chris Pallant, Canterbury, UK, 3 December 2016.
14 Author's transcription from *The Pogles* episode 1, viewed on DVD (Dragons' Friendly Society).
15 Author's transcription from *The Pogles* episode 6, viewed on DVD (Dragons' Friendly Society).
16 Oliver Postgate, interviewed by Tim Jones, Canterbury, UK, 14 July 1993.
17 Oliver Postgate, interviewed by Tim Jones, Canterbury, UK, 14 July 1993.
18 Chris Pallant, *Smallfilms: Audiences – data set*.
19 Chris Pallant, *Smallfilms: Audiences – data set*.
20 Postgate, *Seeing Things*, p. 255.
21 Correspondence from Oliver Postgate to Doreen Stephens, 20 February 1965, File T2/299/1, 'Watch with Mother, Joe & Sir Prancelot & Pogles', BBC Written Archives Centre (WAC), Reading, UK.
22 Correspondence from Doreen Stephens to Oliver Postgate, 22 February 1965, File T2/299/1, 'Watch with Mother, Joe & Sir Prancelot & Pogles', BBC Written Archives Centre (WAC), Reading, UK.
23 British Broadcasting Corporation, *1964 Royal Charter* (London: British Broadcasting Corporation, 1964).
24 Alistair McGowan, 'Watch With Mother', Screenonline, http://www.screenonline.org.uk/tv/id/445994/index.html (accessed 8 June 2021).
25 Sarah Godfrey and Su Holmes, 'Surely the most Natural Scenario in the World': Representations of "Family" in BBC Preschool Television', *Critical Studies in Television* vol. 11 no. 1 (2016), p. 60.
26 Correspondence from Doreen Stephens to Oliver Postgate, 10 August 1965, File T2/299/1, 'Watch with Mother, Joe & Sir Prancelot & Pogles', BBC Written Archives Centre (WAC), Reading, UK.
27 Correspondence from Doreen Stephens to the of Controller of BBC One, 11 August 1965, File T2/299/1, 'Watch with Mother, Joe & Sir Prancelot & Pogles', BBC Written Archives Centre (WAC), Reading, UK.
28 Correspondence from Doreen Stephens to the of Controller of BBC One, 11 August 1965, File T2/299/1, 'Watch with Mother, Joe & Sir Prancelot & Pogles', BBC Written Archives Centre (WAC), Reading, UK.
29 Correspondence from Oliver Postgate to Ursula Eason, 6 June 1966, File T2/299/1, 'Watch with Mother, Joe & Sir Prancelot & Pogles', BBC Written Archives Centre (WAC), Reading, UK.
30 Postgate refers to the quality of Disney's animation in his autobiography (*Seeing Things*, p. 324).
31 For an excellent discussion of Mickey Mousing, see Andy Birtwistle, *Cinesonica: Sounding Film and Video* (Manchester: Manchester University Press, 2010), pp. 184–236.
32 Correspondence from Joy Whitby to Doreen Stephens, 20 June 1966, File T2/299/1, 'Watch with Mother, Joe & Sir Prancelot & Pogles', BBC Written Archives Centre (WAC), Reading, UK.

33 Horace Newcomb, *Encyclopedia of Television*, 2nd edn (London: Routledge, 2004), p. 1395.
34 Newcomb, *Encyclopedia of Television*, p. 1395.
35 TV schedule for 4 January 1966 retrieved from BBC Genome, https://genome.ch.bbc.co.uk/schedules/bbcone/london/1967-01-04#at-13.30 (accessed 4 November 2021) and Lost Media Wiki, https://lostmediawiki.com/The_Magic_Roundabout_partially_found_French_stop-motion_animated_series;_1963-1990 (accessed 4 November 2021).
36 Alec Cairncross, *Managing the British Economy in the 1960s* (London: Palgrave, 2016), p. 17.
37 Her Majesty's Government, 'Sitting of 12 August 1966', Hansard 12 August 1966, https://api.parliament.uk/historic-hansard/sittings/1966/aug/12 (accessed 8 June 2021).
38 Cairncross, *Managing the British Economy in the 1960s*, p. 17.
39 Correspondence from Oliver Postgate to V. Macooby, 21 July 1966, File T2/299/1, 'Watch with Mother, Joe & Sir Prancelot & Pogles', BBC Written Archives Centre (WAC), Reading, UK.
40 Correspondence from Doreen Stephens to Gordon Smith, 12 August 1966, File T2/299/1, 'Watch with Mother, Joe & Sir Prancelot & Pogles', BBC Written Archives Centre (WAC), Reading, UK.
41 Correspondence from Doreen Stephens to Gordon Smith, 12 August 1966, File T2/299/1, 'Watch with Mother, Joe & Sir Prancelot & Pogles', BBC Written Archives Centre (WAC), Reading, UK.
42 Correspondence from Gordon Smith to BBC Controllers, Heads and one Assistant General, 12 August 1966, File T2/299/1, 'Watch with Mother, Joe & Sir Prancelot & Pogles', BBC Written Archives Centre (WAC), Reading, UK.
43 Correspondence from Gordon Smith to Doreen Stephens, 17 August 1966, File T2/299/1, 'Watch with Mother, Joe & Sir Prancelot & Pogles', BBC Written Archives Centre (WAC), Reading, UK.
44 Broadcasters' Audience Research Board (BARB) and the CLOSER Research Centre based in UCL's Institute of Education, 'Television ownership in private domestic households', https://www.closer.ac.uk/data/television-ownership-in-domestic-households/# (accessed 31 October 2021).
45 Correspondence from Oliver Postgate to Harry Lowe, 20 February 1966, File R120/39/1, 'Pogles Wood Merchandising: General', BBC Written Archives Centre (WAC), Reading, UK.
46 Correspondence from K.P Mackenzie to Harry Lowe, 15 March 1966, File R120/40/1, 'Pogles Wood Merchandising: Licences A – Z', BBC Written Archives Centre (WAC), Reading, UK.
47 Correspondence from Peter Firmin to Harry Lowe, no date, File R120/39/1, 'Pogles Wood Merchandising: General', BBC Written Archives Centre (WAC), Reading, UK.
48 Correspondence from Peter Firmin to Harry Lowe, 2 May 1966, File R120/39/1, 'Pogles Wood Merchandising: General', BBC Written Archives Centre (WAC), Reading, UK.
49 Correspondence from Peter Firmin to Harry Lowe, 2 July 1966, File R120/39/1, 'Pogles Wood Merchandising: General', BBC Written Archives Centre (WAC), Reading, UK.

50 Correspondence from Harry Lowe to Peter Firmin, 19 October 1966, File R120/39/1, 'Pogles Wood Merchandising: General', BBC Written Archives Centre (WAC), Reading, UK.
51 Correspondence from Harry Lowe to Peter Firmin, 19 October 1966, File R120/39/1, 'Pogles Wood Merchandising: General', BBC Written Archives Centre (WAC), Reading, UK.
52 Correspondence from Peter Firmin to Harry Lowe, 26 November 1966, File R120/39/1, 'Pogles Wood Merchandising: General', BBC Written Archives Centre (WAC), Reading, UK.
53 Correspondence from Peter Firmin to Harry Lowe, 26 November 1966, File R120/39/1, 'Pogles Wood Merchandising: General', BBC Written Archives Centre (WAC), Reading, UK.
54 Correspondence from John Pemberton to Harry Lowe, 25 October 1966, File R120/40/1, 'Pogles Wood Merchandising: Licences A – Z', BBC Written Archives Centre (WAC), Reading, UK.

Chapter 6

TECHNOLOGY AND INVENTIVENESS WITHIN
SMALLFILMS ANIMATION: *CLANGERS* (1969–74)

The Clangers watch from under their lids and behind rocks as an astronaut comes out of the space module. His intercom is heard chatting astronauts' chat as he lopes across the planet's surface setting up a piece of equipment like a parking meter. He brings out a large flag and sets it up on a pole. He steps back and salutes the flag. He turns and lumbers off into his space craft. The Clangers watch him climb in. They come out and watch it go. They look at the flag.
    Tiny Clanger: Oh! It's a tablecloth.
    Small Clanger: Yes, yes, a tablecloth.
    Major Clanger: Yes of course!
          —Excerpt from 'Tablecloth' script by Oliver Postgate (1969)[1]

In the first episode of the six-part *Doctor Who* serial 'The Sea Devils' (1972), we find the Master seemingly imprisoned at a naval base in the English Channel. Viewers quickly discover, however, that this is just a ruse, and the Master, with the help of his apparent jailor Colonel Trenchard, is actually repurposing equipment from the naval base as part of another dastardly scheme to become all-powerful. Knowing that the titular Sea Devils have been encountered near this naval base, the Master uses his staged imprisonment to get close to them, and – crucially – to secure the materials he believes will control them. Ultimately, as always happens, the Master's plan backfires and the Doctor must save the day. All very exciting, but what stands out about the episode given the focus of this book is the fact that the Master also encounters other 'interesting extra-terrestrial life' by virtue of the television in his cell: *Clangers*.

  Tuning in, the Master sees the start of 'The Rock Collector' (BBC, 25 April 1971), an episode of the stop-motion model-based animation series *Clangers* that features an astronaut conducting fieldwork. While the Master only sees a 45-second glimpse of the episode, during which the Clangers scrutinize an unfamiliar object (Figure 6.1), had he watched the episode in full he would have seen the hapless astronaut encounter the Clangers, several Froglets, and the Soup Dragon – prompting the intrepid explorer to black out with shock.

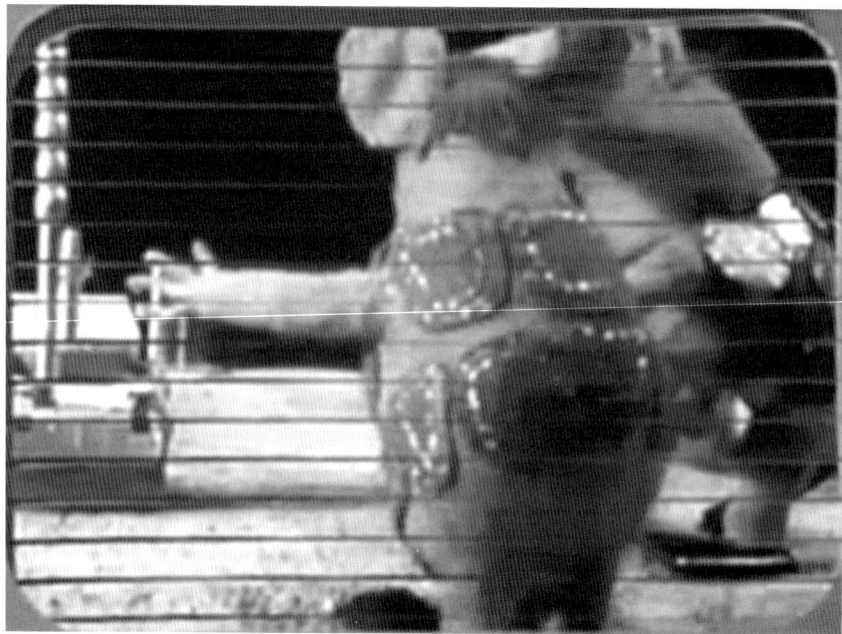

Figure 6.1 Clangers inspect a mysterious object as seen in *Doctor Who* 'The Sea Devils' (1972).

At the end of the 'The Rock Collector', the Clangers clean the astronaut – who is all soupy after falling into the soup wells – and bundle him back into his Lunar Lander. Despite the brevity of their appearance within 'The Sea Devils', this glimpse of *Clangers* offers attentive viewers plenty to consider. First, there is the immediacy of the lunar landscape and the mysterious object – subject matter that fits well with the overarching themes of *Doctor Who*. Then there is the Master's initial response, looking on with cheerful interest, seemingly imitating the Clangers' whistles. Until, that is, Trenchard asks what he is watching, to which the Master responds by describing the Clangers as 'interesting extra-terrestrial life', prompting Trenchard to abruptly retort: 'Only puppets, you know? For children.'[2] A perfect encapsulation of the spectatorial tensions faced by both *Clangers* and *Doctor Who* – being shows that attracted audiences of all ages, while also being characterized as 'for "children's TV"'.

This sequence also foregrounds the centrality of technology as a key theme within *Clangers* – as well as the work of Smallfilms more broadly. The episode shown focuses on the topic of lunar technology, and the misadventures of a bewildered astronaut. We are shown this as if it is being broadcast live and being viewed on a television screen by the Master. Furthermore, the fact that this specific screened media exists within the diegetic framework of an episode of *Doctor Who*, a show that places an acute emphasis on scientific ingenuity and outer space-based technology, implies that *Clangers* provided an appropriate thematic match for this cameo appearance.

It is this concern with technology that provides the focus for this chapter, and the core association of inventiveness (as highlighted by the survey data – see Appendix – Figure A.3). After establishing the context of *Clangers*' production, including a more in-depth consideration of the contribution of Joan Firmin than has been attempted before, this chapter will consider: the influence that contemporary developments in screen technology exerted over the inception and production of *Clangers*; how the overt low-tech fabrication of *Clangers* constitutes a source of spectatorial appeal; and how Firmin and Postgate repeatedly engaged with the Space Race of the late 1960s and early 1970s within the series.

Clangers: *In the beginning*

Approximately ten years after the start of their Smallfilms journey, Postgate and Firmin faced the challenge of creating yet another original story. Postgate offers a rather ambivalent account of this challenge in his autobiography: 'They [the BBC] wanted something completely new and quite astonishing. Oh, yes. Well, that was a challenge. For me it meant another piece of paper to sit and look at. Once again we were going to have to pull our living out of the sky.'[3] While Postgate does acknowledge the perpetual demands placed on their creativity in order to make a living, his tone implies this was a challenge that was met without much struggle. However, speaking more candidly in his interview with local filmmaker Tim Jones in 1993, Postgate gave a greater sense of the strain involved in such an existence:

> Being creative, having to do something new, invent something, alter things, in order to show you're still there is a personality fault, basically. I think a lot of people who have done creative things do so because if they don't, they cease to exist. This, I know, is true of myself, and I wouldn't wish it onto other people. There is nothing quite like as frightening as having a wife and six children and a blank piece of paper, which is your next year's feeding, and you have to pull out of the sky your livelihood. The idea of being able to live on one's creativity, where you are dubious of its continuity, is a recipe for terrible anxiety.[4]

The contrasting nature of these accounts of the same predicament, offered by the same person, reveals the value of drawing upon multiple perspectives. In this case, by placing Postgate's more candid account alongside his editorialized view of the creative life, gives a greater appreciation of the collective appetite of both Firmin and Postgate, to repeatedly put themselves through the process of creating new stories – rather than settling into a life of sequels and spin-offs.

Given the pressure of confronting the blank page, it is hardly surprising to see that the pre-production of *Clangers* (through ideation, visual design, writing, and fabrication) followed a similar pattern to their previous shows. Like with *The Saga of Noggin the Nog* and *Pingwings*, Postgate and Firmin found inspiration at home. Writing in his autobiography of his familiarity with the science fiction genre and the works of H. G. Wells, Postgate also tells of an occasion when his twin sons Simon and Stephen told him a tale about the moon:

> Apparently there was a giant called Edward on the other side of the moon who lived on soup, hot soup. I asked how he obtained the soup and they explained that as the moon was quite full of soup, all he had to do was unscrew a volcano and suck it out through a straw. I mentioned that I thought the other side of the moon was thought to be very, very cold and they pointed out that the soup was very, very hot. That was all useful information.[5]

Inspired by this reimagining of the moon, Firmin and Postgate then revisited their past work, 'looking for old ideas to recycle'. As a result, they returned to the *Noggin* 'First Readers' book series and the story of *Noggin and the Moonmouse*. From this combination of influences, Postgate and Firmin found their spark.

Quickly establishing the basic premise that the Clanger family lived on a moon, not dissimilar to our own moon, and encountered unfamiliar objects and creatures on an episodic basis, thereby generating narrative momentum, the task of designing and fabricating the precise details of the Clanger's world fell to Firmin. After sketching out some rough impressions of the cavern, Postgate waited for Firmin to work his magic:

> These must have triggered off Peter's imagination because the places he eventually built, with things that could be put together from existing materials but set in incongruous situations – wheel-bushes, copper-leaf tress, and small thickets of drinking-straws – far outstripped, in originality and completeness of conception, anything I could have thought of.[6]

It is important to highlight this particular creative contribution by Firmin, so unequivocally offered by Postgate, since it provides a glimpse of Firmin's own capacity to expertly channel the whimsical impulse.

Compared with the effusive praise lavished on Peter Firmin by Postgate, regarding the design and creation of the Clangers' realm, his account of Joan Firmin's contribution is much more economical: 'Joan Firmin knitted them and she dressed the ladies, Mother Clanger, Tiny Clanger and the aunts, in patchwork coats.'[7] With Postgate dedicating just nineteen words and less than two lines to Joan Firmin's contribution to the creation of one of British television's most iconic families, it is easy to see why her part of the Smallfilms narrative is often marginalized. Despite Joan's influential contribution, helping to define the look of the Clangers, her name is often omitted as a consequence of the focus placed on both Postgate and her husband Peter. Within academic discourse, even where attempts have been made to raise her status, such as in Rachel Moseley's book *Hand-made Television: Stop-Frame Animation for Children in Britain, 1961–74* (2016), this still feels tentative, with just five references made to Joan's work throughout the book. While in Caroline Ruddell and Paul Ward's otherwise excellent edited collection, *The Crafty Animator: Handmade, Craft-Based Animation and Cultural Value*

(2019), even though importance is placed on the knitted craft aesthetic of *Clangers* on several occasions throughout the book, no connection is made between these significant material artefacts and the labour of Joan Firmin.

Within popular discourse, two *Woman's Weekly* articles, timed to promote the return of *Clangers* on BBC CBeebies with the titles 'Clangers return with free knitting pattern' (29 June 2015) and 'Peter Firmin: My wife knitted the original Clangers and dressed the girls like Twiggy' (14 July 2015), reveal a similar tendency to relegate the contributions of Joan Firmin.[8] Beyond the prosaic title of the June article and the uncomfortable omission of Joan's name from the second title, both articles also share a similar structure that privileges the contributions of Postgate and Peter Firmin to the design and creation of the Clangers over and above that of Joan Firmin. In the June article, we encounter five references to Peter, three references to Oliver, and a reference to Michael Palin's vocal performance, before we read Joan's name in the seventh paragraph of an article ostensibly about a knitting pattern that she played a key part in creating. Similarly, in the July article, Joan's name is first introduced in paragraph six of the twelve-paragraph article. Having met with Joan on a number of occasions through the process of researching and writing this book, her self-deprecating nature sees her shy away from taking any credit for her creative and craft-based contributions to the success of Smallfilms. It is quite possible that over the years people have approached Joan to try to tell her story, or at least bring her more fully into the Smallfilms story, but these attempts have been thwarted by Joan's own modesty. Even so, the (Peter) Firmin/Postgate bias of the *Woman's Weekly* articles reveals how challenging it can be to move beyond the orthodox (Postgateian) account of Smallfilms history.

Characteristically, when asked to give more detail of the design process, Joan offered the following summary: 'I'd knit a bit, and he'd [Postgate] say, "can it be a bit fatter round here", you know, and you alter it a bit.'[9] Such a matter-of-fact account takes for granted the expertise of Joan as a knitter. Moreover, the fact that Joan would knit for a while on her own, working from her own instincts, and then check-in with Postgate to make sure that the work matched his needs, reveals the trust placed by Postgate in Joan to conceive and fabricate the Clangers, and also the skill of Joan to adjust her work following feedback from Postgate. Given Joan's centrality within the fabrication process, it is unfortunate to find her name omitted from the typed knitting pattern that, pre-World Wide Web, was sent to viewers interested in knitting their own Clanger (Figures 6.2 and 6.3).

What compounds the unfortunate omission of Joan's name from the knitting pattern, is how prominently Postgate's name is presented, erroneously, suggesting that he was the sole creator of *Clangers*. This misrepresentation of authorship by the BBC, also sets up the possibility for misunderstanding on the part of those receiving the knitting pattern, as they might also reasonably – but falsely – assume that Postgate was the sole creator of the knitting pattern in question.

Joan also recalls how the Clangers would need to be unpicked regularly so that the Meccano armatures could be extracted, thereby allowing for the joints to be re-tensioned. After handing over the armature for maintenance, Joan would then take that opportunity to clean the knitted elements. Noting that the Clangers 'only

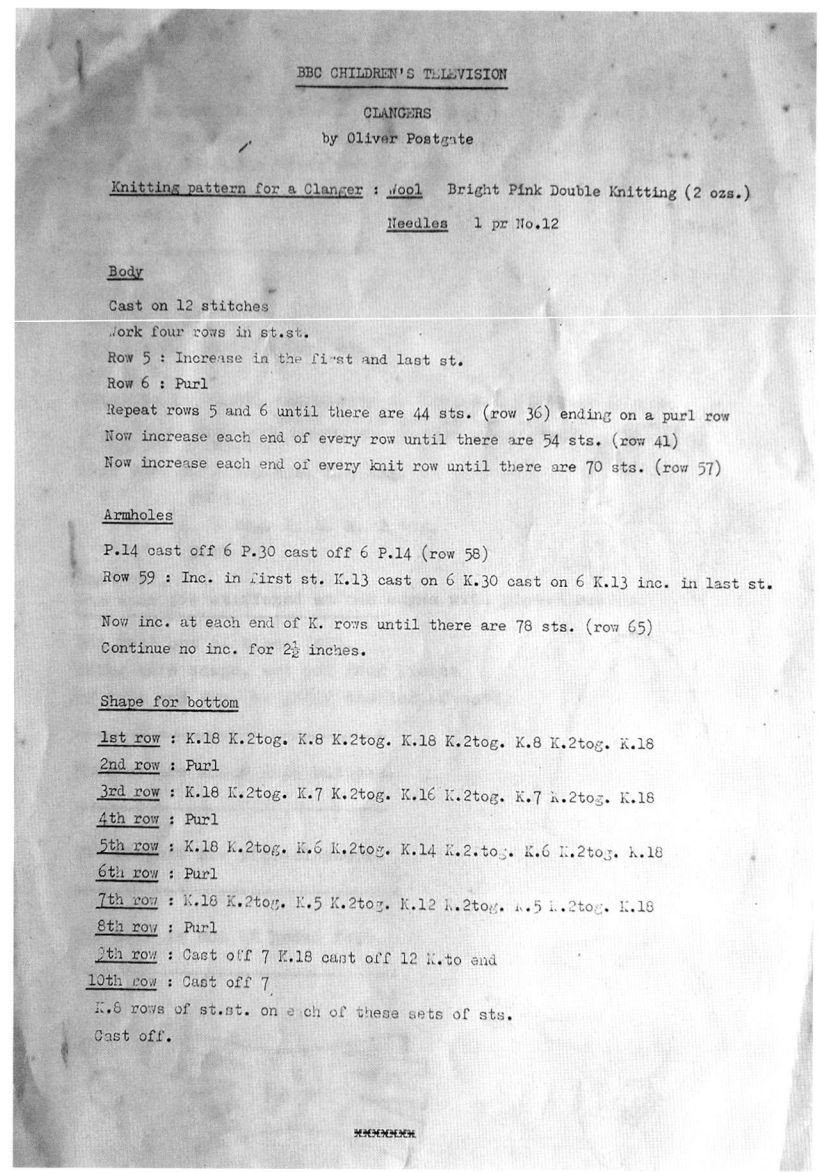

Figure 6.2 Page 1 of Joan Firmin's *Clangers* knitting pattern.

had one set of clothes', Joan recalls how 'with them handling them out there in the barn, they did get quite dusty, dirty, and looking manhandled'.[10] This was an activity that Joan undertook without prompting: 'they didn't notice things like that, they would give it to me if one had to be undone because its joints needed tightening, or something, and I'd give them a wash. And that acrylic wool, the

6. Technology and Inventiveness within Smallfilms Animation 129

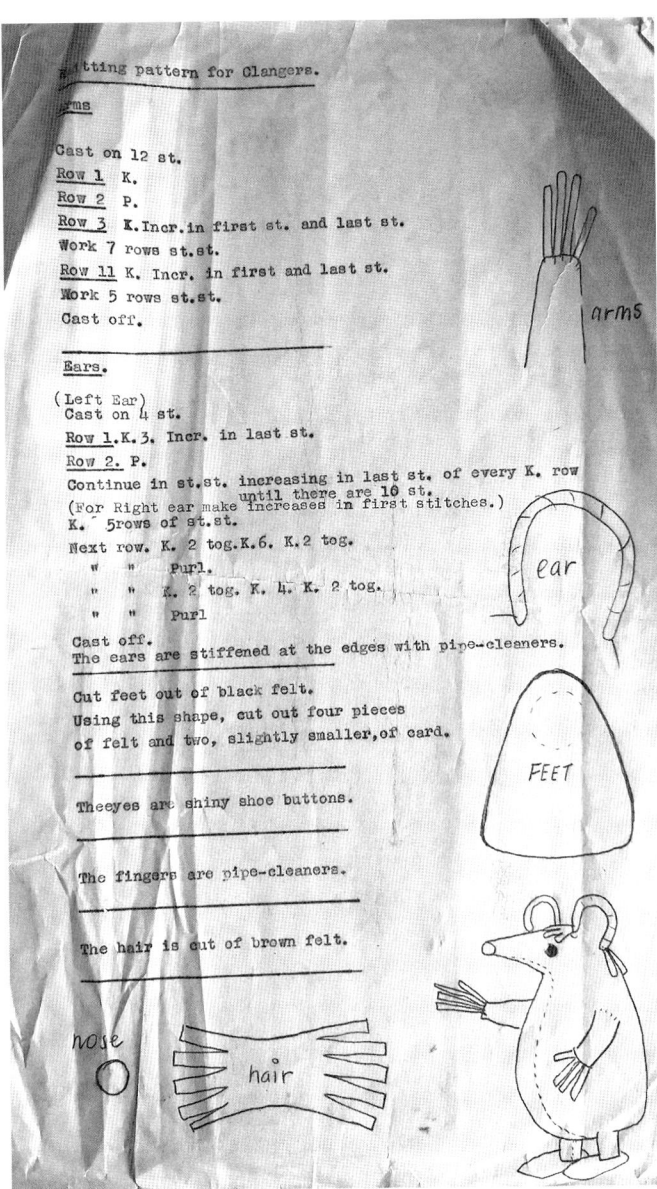

Figure 6.3 Page 2 of Joan Firmin's *Clangers* knitting pattern.

colour doesn't run. I could wash them and hang them on the line, and it didn't shrink or anything'.[11] Regardless of potential continuity issues, with Clangers suddenly becoming much cleaner and thereby pinker between scenes, Joan notes how 'there were a couple of series, so there were plenty of times when I'd be washing them'.[12] Given the importance placed by the BBC on Clangers being a colourful show, Joan's frequent washing of the knitted elements constitutes an important – but hitherto neglected – production process. It is not an exaggeration to see Joan's labour, on multiple levels, as contributing significantly to the show's iconic visual appeal.

Screen technologies: Pink to make the BBC wink

Reflecting on their shift from Pogles to Clangers, Postgate writes: 'In 1968 the BBC issued a decree which put paid to our ambitions to make any more *Pogles' Wood* type films. In future all bought films were to be in colour – not only "in colour" but "colourful". They wanted something completely new and quite astonishing.'[13] Despite Postgate's characterization of this moment as being something of a Big Bang for colour television in the UK, in actual fact, the transition from black and white to colour was gradual. As Iain Logie Baird, grandson of John Logie Baird, notes, colour TV sets 'did not outnumber black-and-white sets until 1976, mainly due to the high price of the early colour sets', and that by the end of 1969 only 200,000 sets were in use in the UK.[14] Sales data confirms Baird's assessment of the steep price differential between colour and monochrome at the time of colour's introduction, whilst also showing how colour television deliveries overtook monochrome deliveries for the first time in 1973.[15]

This gradual shift in consumer behaviour, from monochrome to colour technology, prompted the BBC to conduct a series of audience studies in an attempt to better understand how viewer behaviours might be changing with the introduction of colour broadcasts. For example, in a 1968 Audience Research Report, titled 'A Pilot Survey of Colour Television Owners', 2,668 colour television owners were questioned about their viewing habits. The summary of responses to questions 7 and 8 gives a clear indication that, despite the higher cost, the introduction of colour broadcasting was proving a success:

> 7. Most of the sample agreed that their choice of programme was to some extent determined by whether it was in colour of not, but the degree of influence was not, in their opinion, over-riding. About one in three said their choice was 'always' or 'frequently' determined in this way, a half that 'sometimes' it was, whilst a sixth answered that they 'never' let this consideration influence them.
>
> 8. 61% would definitely advise a friend in similar financial circumstances to get a colour receiver <u>now</u>. Virtually all the remainder would do so when there are more hours of colour programming.[16]

With early audience data suggesting that the appetite for colour transmission was likely to grow, and that for many viewers, colour programming was preferred to monochrome, it is clear why Postgate and Firmin received the BBC's decree for a more colourful production when enquiring about a follow-up to *Pogles' Wood*.

As well as the internal activity, recorded within Audience Research Reports, the BBC also hosted the external-facing International TV Design Conference in

1968, which was devoted to the subject of colour. Leah Panos discusses this event in her article about the BBC's development of colour television drama, noting that 'this five-day conference, held at Television Centre, was attended by nearly 150 delegates from more than 20 countries', and provided an opportunity for 'showcasing achievements in colour design, showing compilations of graphics and excerpts from various genres, including light entertainment, drama and live events'.[17] Panos notes how Richard Levin, who served as Head of Design at the BBC between 1953 and 1971, 'attempted to lay down some guidelines on restricting colour usage', calling for programme makers to: 'Think in colour – but before you commit yourself, think in black and white [...] Keep it all restrained. It's easier, quicker and more effective to add colour than to take it out. Don't work at colour – make colour work for you. In other words, keep it sparse and make it significant and not irrelevant to the performance.'[18] Consequently, with such attention being focused on the shift to colour transmission and programming, it is easy to see why a show centred on the adventures of a family of bright pink moon mice would have appealed to the BBC.

Without wishing to labour this point, it is important to acknowledge how wholeheartedly the shift to colour was embraced within *Clangers*. Beyond the iconic pink of the Clangers, the first two series offer up, to name just a few of the most prominent examples: a green Soup Dragon, blue Sky Moos, orange Froglets, the silver and gold Iron Chicken, brass Hoots, an orange television set, a brass musical boat, red and yellow Glow Honey, and a mountain of colourful plastics produced by the silver, yellow, and red fabrication machine. By embracing colour technology in such an emphatic way, *Clangers* secured a lasting place in the popular imagination.[19] Even at a time when many other shows were being produced in colour, the colourfulness of *Clangers* stood out. This is confirmed in the promotional mailer produced by their marketing agent Roy Williams, which emphasized, in uppercase, that the show was 'IN COLOUR', while also rereferring to the fact that they lived in 'a labyrinth of yellow caves' inside a 'blue planet'.[20] TV guides at the time also noted that *Clangers* was a colour production, with the *Reading Evening Post*, on the eve of the series debut in November 1969, featuring the show in their 'Programme Highlights' section: 'The Clangers is a series of 13 colour films created by Oliver Postgate. Who the Clangers are and where these strange creatures live is revealed in the first story.'[21] Furthermore, the colourfulness of *Clangers* – namely their bright pink appearance – stands out as a prominent feature of the press coverage that announced their return in 2015.[22] Clearly, colour television technology played a profound role in shaping both the production and reception of *Clangers*.

Technology and invention

Reviewing the survey data, it is clear that technology, and the associated themes of inventiveness and imagination, represent strong sources of appeal within the show. For example, when asked why they liked *Clangers*, a number of responses commented explicitly on these aspects: 'Most imaginative' (R46); 'Its eccentric humour and its sheer imagination' (R5); 'For its sheer imagination, and probably because it's so multimedia: it's the mixture of sound (and talking in sounds), the craft creation, the creatures and settings, and the ideas explored' (R34); 'Just thinking about the sound of the clangers makes me smile. The combination of sound, texture and creative imagination was so distinctive' (R61); 'When I was a small child, the Clangers approached their world in the same way that I was exploring mine, everything was there to be discovered and investigated' (R109); 'There are many favourites for many reasons but I'd say that the original Clangers encapsulates all of the Postgate/Firmin values of immersive worldbuilding, achieved by eccentrically minimal means, while operating within the early 70s cultural landscape of interplanetary exploration and ecological concerns. Also, Soup Dragon and Tiny Clanger' (R174); 'It's incredibly sweet and calming, the introduction narration is so magical, i love the wonderful little inventions they make, how all the creatures are kind to one another. It's a very soothing show and the animation is incredible' (R319); and 'So imaginative! I loved all the creations in the programme' (R411). In addition to these audience responses, which reflect upon *Clangers* of the late 1960s and early 1970s, the press coverage of the 2015 *Clangers* reboot, which retains a strong emphasis on technology, also serves to confirm the importance of technological inventiveness within the show.

In a 2015 media briefing, the BBC included the following statement about the *Clangers* reboot:

> Great storytelling remains at the core of the show. Each episode centres on members of the Clanger family solving a problem, making a discovery, inventing something or greeting a new visitor to their small, blue planet. There are all manner of weird and wonderful objects and creatures that visit and they are often the catalyst for a brand new adventure for the Clangers and their friends. At the heart of the stories are universal themes of community, caring and resourcefulness with the aim of encouraging and nurturing a sense of wonder and natural curiosity.[23]

While the word 'technology' is not used, several closely associated themes are emphasized, such as problem-solving, inventions, weird and wonderful objects, resourcefulness and wonder. Additionally, to capitalize on *Clangers*' 50th anniversary celebrations, Coolabi, the show's rights holder since 2013, released a limited print-run illustration to mark the occasion:

> The 50th anniversary celebrations continue with the exclusive release of two limited-edition prints by the late Clangers co-creator, Peter Firmin. The two illustrations, which include a detailed sketch of 'Major Clanger's Workshop', a cave full of curious tools and quirky inventions, some harking back to previous adventures and even stories from the original series, and a rarely seen area of the Little Blue Planet, Major Clanger's 'Store for Inventions & Parts'.[24]

With only fifty copies of this print made available to collectors, the iconography of Major Clanger's Workshop, and the trope of technology, are transformed into highly prized emblems of the show more generally.

Fittingly, Firmin and Postgate frequently engineered their own solutions to the production challenges they faced. As noted above, Joan Firmin's crafting and maintenance of the knitted Clangers provides a good example of the way that technology adopts a range of shapes and forms when viewed through the prism of Smallfilms productions. Likewise, earlier chapters have revealed a similar appetite to find practical solutions in everyday materials: such as the cardboard cut-out animation process of their early productions, which relied on sticky tack for tension and placement; or the Pingwings, whose crocheted bodies provided flexibility and durability; or the hybrid environments of the Pogles, which used natural materials found in Firmin's garden and the nearby woods alongside butcher's grass and papier-mâché. These everyday technologies notwithstanding, the technological component that played arguably the greatest part in the production of Smallfilms works was Meccano.

Postgate and Firmin relied on Meccano from the outset, employing the versatile construction pieces to augment their camera equipment (as noted in Chapter 2) and to bring strength and precise articulation to their armatures. In episode three of *Clangers*, titled 'Chicken', Firmin and Postgate make Meccano a prominent part of the on-screen narrative. Not described as Meccano, but immediately recognizable as such to any viewer with a knowledge of the construction kit, we see a range of Meccano pieces fall on the Clangers' moon after they inadvertently blow-up an orbiting object. Confronted with the mysterious debris, the narrator proclaims: 'What an extraordinary lot of objects! Well, the only thing to do is to carry them down below and try to fit them together again. If there is one thing that Clangers are really good at it's putting together bits of machinery.'[25] Once rebuilt, the Meccano forms one of the show's most iconic characters: the Iron Chicken.

In addition to this clear in-joke, where the Postgate and Firmin essentially pull back the magician's curtain, there is also another famous – technology-centred – moment that features in this episode. At the start of the episode we hear Postgate's recurrent opening monologue:

> This planet, this cloudy planet is the Earth, it is home, it is the place where you and I live. Supposing we look away from here and travel in our imaginations across the last endless stretches of outer space. There we can imagine other stars, stranger stars by far than ever shone in our night's sky, and other stranger people too. People, perhaps, with civilization, skill and efficiency, maybe far in advance of ours.[26]

This narration is then promptly followed by a shot of the Clangers' main mechanical doorway struggling to open. Major, emerging from one of the creators, whistles in a seemingly frustrated manner, before giving the door a sharp kick, thereby restoring it to proper working order. The juxtaposition of this sequence, with the soaring vision of the narration and the awkward sight of malfunctioning technology, is a familiar trope of Postgate's writing. Behind the whistles lies a frequently embellished moment of *Clangers* history: Major's apoplectic remarks of 'Oh sod it! The bloody thing's stuck again!' On this occasion, it is tempting to see the Major's frustration as a knowing nod to the many occasions that Firmin and Postgate inevitably ran into difficulty with their bespoke production technologies.

In addition to the self-reflexive moments noted above (the Meccano-built Iron Chicken and the familiar frustrations of faulty technology), the mass-production technologies of consumer culture are also given the *Clangers* treatment. In the episode 'Goods' (BBC1, 22 February 1970), contemporary environmental concerns about mass-produced plastics are explored. This episode debuted at a time of increasing environmental concern in Britain, with the first edition of *The Ecologist* magazine being published in July 1970, while the British branch of Friends of the Earth (FOE) was established in September 1971.[27] Postgate's opening monologue sets the scene, noting how 'complex and convenient' the lives of the people who live on Earth have become, before reflecting upon how this reality is not visible from the vantage point of those looking down from outer space:

> One can see no factories, no roads, no cars or railways, no toothbrushes, no plastic mixing bowls, none of the millions of articles that man manufactures to comfort his short life. By comparison, we can imagine how dull and empty must be the lives of beings on other planets, which do not enjoy the benefits of a modern, industrial civilisation.[28]

With these words of dullness and emptiness still ringing in our ears, we cut to an image of the Clangers, colourful and certainly not dull, providing a moment of playful juxtaposition, before the sound of a falling object prompts the Clangers to take cover. Hearing a crash, the Clangers emerge to discover many colourful broken pieces littering the surface of their moon. In a sequence that treads similar ground to that discussed earlier in the chapter, when the Clangers rebuild the Iron Chicken after accidently blowing it up with a rocket, the Clangers quickly set to work piecing the mysterious object back together. The result: a machine (clearly made of Meccano) that can automatically fabricate plastic items (Figure 6.4). Upon completion, Major Clanger triumphantly pulls the lever, prompting the machine, after some chugging and clunking, to produce a plastic yellow spoon. Impressed, Mother Clanger remarks: 'Oh, isn't that lovely!'[29] Over the next couple of minutes, the machine delights the Clangers by producing a variety of plastic objects.

This sequence is rich with comedic reversals, as the descriptions provided by Postgate's narration frequently mischaracterize the objects, which is then followed by the Clangers' misappropriation of some objects, thereby adding a further layer of whimsy. After the yellow spoon we see: 'a plastic teapot' (which is clearly an plastic orange watering can), which Tiny Clanger then attempts to play as if it were a saxophone; 'a pretty hat' (which appears to be a red plastic cup); and then another hat, 'a hat for Major Clanger' (which appears to be a white plastic thimble). At this

6. *Technology and Inventiveness within Smallfilms Animation*   135

Figure 6.4 An example of the unashamed and self-reflexive use of Meccano in *Clangers* (1969–74).

point, the Soup Dragon retrieves a key that appears to belong with the machine. Using the key, the machine then begins to operate at high speed, producing: dozens of plastic cookie cutters (coloured red, yellow, and blue); flower pots; plastic boxes; plastic buckets; plastic toy cars; a plastic toy dog; a plastic spade; and what looks like a plastic net from the 1960s board game Mousetrap. These objects emerge from the machine so rapidly that the Clanger's cave is quickly filled with plastic detritus.

Unhappy with the cluttered situation, the Clangers try to dispose of the plastic objects by throwing them down the hole that leads to the cave where the Froglets live. Of course, the Froglets don't want the Clangers' plastic rubbish either and promptly eject the plastic cookie cutter that had been dropped down their hole. Eager to help, the Froglets bring a magic top hat from their cave and set up a conjuring trick, showing the Clangers how they can both materialize and vanish objects with the hat. Quickly understanding the situation, the Clangers dispose of all the plastic detritus, piece by piece, by throwing them into the Froglet's magic top hat. With the cave now clear, the Clangers and Froglets go to bed, leaving Postgate, through his narration, to have the last word: 'The place is going to look a bit empty without all those plastic things, but you know, I think Clangers may be better off without them.'[30] By offering this closing statement, Postgate provides clear confirmation of the episode's overarching goal: to critique our obsession with and reliance upon mass-produced plastics. While this critique is offered explicitly in *Clangers* and anchored in the show's repeatedly self-reflexive engagement with the theme of technology, it is also worth recognizing that Postgate and Firmin rarely favoured plastic artefacts within the work of Smallfilms as a whole, tending, on most occasions, to fabricate characters, props, and locations with more textured materials, such as fabrics, wools, woods, metals, cardboard, paper, and fresh cuttings from either the Firmin garden or one of the adjacent woods – which has the effect of inviting an almost tactile response when viewing their works on-screen.

Orbiting technologies: The space race

Close behind the themes of inventiveness and imagination is the theme of space. Unsurprisingly, given Firmin and Postgate's recognition of how the space race had captured the popular imagination,[31] and how the BBC amplified this association through their promotional materials for *Clangers*,[32] the survey data reveals a rich seam of space-based appeal. Explicitly referencing space or science fiction, the respondents noted the following as elements of appeal: 'Sci-fi at its finest' (R28); 'the universe's most wholesome sci-fi adventure' (R118); 'Fantastic animation, heart-warming togetherness and some incredible ideas e.g. a space boat powered by a musical scale!' (R461); 'In space – quirky characters – excellent storylines – IN SPACE !' (R43); 'Voiceover; sci-fi; "humanity"' (R248); 'Peaceful sounds, quirky animation. Space theme' (R197); 'Caught my attention as a small child fascinated with space, travel and music' (R631); 'Was an inspiration to delve into astronomy' (R407); 'The magic of the world that Oliver and Peter created. The story lines and the quality of the puppets. It also came at a key period for me growing up and interested in space and the Moon landings' (R183); and 'It chimed with the space race fever of the time' (R301). These responses suggest that some of the space-related appeal of *Clangers* is linked to Firmin's incorporation of contemporary Apollo mission iconography into the design process as well as Postgate's ability to capture within the narrative the popular sci-fi/astrocultural fascination with space in the late 1960s and early 1970s.

The concept of astroculture is an important one, and how it is both reflected within *Clangers* and how *Clangers* contributes to it are forces that deserve attention. Writing in 2012, Alexander Geppert introduced the neologism astroculture to help expand the framing of how the space age (from the late 1950s through to the early 1970s) was commonly understood:

> Hitherto predominantly treated as driven by either technological development or political imperatives, in particular during the Cold War, space travel and space exploration merit closer scholarly scrutiny, more comprehensive analysis and better integration into mainstream historiography, above all with a view to their cultural significance, societal impact, and imaginative dimension, within the broader frame of twentieth-century modernity and globalization.[33]

Geppert goes on to note that his motivation is to provide 'a culture-related equivalent to better known and long established terms such as "astrophysics," "astropolitics," and "astrosociology"', and defines astrocultre as comprising a 'heterogenous array of images and artifacts, media and practices that all aim to ascribe meaning to outer space while stirring both the individual and the collective imagination'.[34] Keen to distinguish the notion of astroculture from 'astrofuturism', which, Geppert acknowledges, some might view as related, he notes how astrofuturism can be seen as a 'specific subcategory of astroculture, emphasizing a close nexus between imperial expansion and utopian speculation, and expressing the belief that future space travel would define a distinct and higher stage of human development or even of human evolution'.[35] By comparison, Geppert proposes that astroculture is 'conceptually broader, as it includes manifestations of space-related culture that are neither necessarily utopian nor future-prone'.[36] By drawing upon this framework when thinking about how the space age is represented in *Clangers*, it becomes clear just how prototypically astrocultural the show is.

As the survey data highlights, the space-related aspects of *Clangers* that left a lasting impression were: the 'magic of the world', 'quirky animation' 'quality of the puppets' and 'quirky characters – excellent storylines – IN SPACE'; and the sense of 'humanity' 'heart-warming togetherness', and being 'wholesome'; and the fact that it featured 'a space boat powered by a musical scale'. Yes, at surface level there is the familiar sci-fi iconography of lunar modules, astronauts in spacesuits, and pink aliens (the Clangers). Yes, there is a heavy focus on technology, as noted above. However, the moon on which the space age action happens is a very unusual moon – being that it existed in the Smallfilms barn, and that its self-evident artifice consequently provided the foundation for very different space age narratives to unfold, narratives that had more in common with the wider themes of astroculture than the narrow hard science and military proxy of the real space race.

As the sentiment of these comments suggests, the astrocultural credentials of *Clangers* can be seen throughout the series. Most episodes orbit around the intrusion or creation of a mystery object, which, over the course of an episode, the Clangers attempt to either mend or understand. A common theme of these encounters is the way that Postgate and Firmin employ recognizable, everyday objects and materials, such as plastic plant pots, Meccano, magic top hats, and soup, thereby subverting the more common expectations of contemporary space-themed television shows, such as *Doctor Who* or Gerry Anderson's supermarionation productions, which while also offering up sci-fi and space on a very clearly limited budget, presented a steady stream of silver-coloured technologies, control dials, rockets, and various scientific elements rather than plant pots and Meccano.

If we look more closely at 'The Intruder' (1969) and 'The Rock Collector' (1971), two episodes that engage particularly overtly with the space age of the late 1960s and early 1970s, we find that this subversion is especially pronounced. 'The Intruder' features a silver lunar probe, which, much to the annoyance of Major Clanger, appears to be picking up pieces of the moon and shovelling them into its 'mouth'. Once the lunar probe has completed collecting surface samples, the probe turns to inspect Major Clanger with its telescopic attachment. Misunderstanding the situation, Major Clanger thinks the probe is trying to shake hands, and promptly grasps the telescope, but in doing so accidentally pulls it off. After the probe makes a hasty exit, the Clangers quickly realize what the telescope is, and Major Clanger is so impressed by the probe and its home planet that he sets the Clangers the task of building a rocket so that they can journey there immediately. Having rapidly built their rocket ship, Major Clanger boards the vessel and the countdown to launch begins. At the same moment, Tiny Clanger, who has been looking at the probe's planet through the telescope calls out in alarm, halting the launch. Leaving the rocket ship, Major Clanger comes to see what Tiny Clanger is anxious about and looks through the telescope for himself. Seeing what looks like the Manhattan skyline, Postgate's narration provides a translation of the Clanger's concern:

> **Narrator** (*translating Major Clanger's whistles*) Oh, oh dear. Yes, I see, what an unpleasant looking place!
> **Narrator** No, I don't think the Clangers will want to go there. No. No, no, what a good thing they were able to look at it first. Now they can put the rocket away and save it for something useful.[37]

Returning to the centrality of technology within *Clangers*, within 'The Intruder' we find both an enchantment with space age technology and then a refusal to be seduced by interplanetary travel. It is tempting to see in this reversal a reflection of the aborted potential of the UK's own space programme in the years leading up to the creation of *Clangers*. As Doug Millard writes, UK space activity 'had always struggled as a distinct policy area', failing to capture the imagination of successive British governments through the 1960s.[38] Unlike the national agencies that fuelled the space race in US and Soviet contexts, there was little desire in the UK to assign space 'its own coordinating council or agency', rather 'space activities – inherited or accumulated from the interests of other parties: defense, science, telecommunications – were considered piecemeal, as extensions and responsibilities of terrestrial departments and ministries with their respective heads and ministers always mindful of their own priorities'.[39] Major Clanger's decision to 'put the rocket away and save it for something more useful', chimes with the UK's own hesitance to fully embrace the space age agenda, and also represents, to paraphrase Geppert, a manifestation of space-related culture that is neither utopian nor future-prone.[40]

In the 'The Rock Collector' we see a similar setup to 'The Intruder', with the Clangers encountering a mysterious, shiny, silver space technology at the start of the episode. On this occasion it is a beeping beacon, which ushers the arrival of a lunar lander and its cargo: a spaceman. To begin with, Firmin and Postgate invest the narrative with familiar space age iconography: a lunar module resembling the Apollo 11 Eagle lander; an astronaut in a space suit that again mimics those worn by Neil Armstrong and Buzz Aldrin and seen on television sets in 1969; and a geological survey being conducted by the spaceman matching the types of activities conducted during the lunar landings. However, approximately three minutes into the episode the tone shifts, as an incongruous straw basket is used by the spaceman to gather his rock samples, and then a series of pratfalls that sees the Clangers covertly substitute the spaceman's rocks with Blue String Pudding, leading the unsuspecting spaceman to tumble out of his lunar lander covered in the stringy substance. At this point, Postgate, with his characteristically matter-of-fact style of recounting unusual circumstances, observes that the spaceman 'seems a bit puzzled'.[41] Understandably confused, the spaceman goes in search of the missing rocks, but instead of finding them he meets Tiny Clanger. Following Tiny Clanger's whistled greeting the spaceman runs away in a state of panic, having just encountered, we assume, alien life for the first time. Disorientated, the spaceman falls down an open creator and comes face to face with three Froglets, which only serves to heighten his bewilderment. Running dizzily through the subterranean caves, the spaceman then bumps into the Soup Dragon, at first staggering into a brief but beautifully surreal *pas de deux* (Figure 6.5), before tumbling into a soup well and passing out.

After fishing out the soup-covered spaceman, the Clangers bring him to the surface so that the rain from a musical cloud can be used to clean him up. Regaining consciousness, the spaceman runs off once more, this time running so fast that he leaves the surface of the moon and becomes stuck in a weightless orbit. For the final time the Clangers come to his aid, reeling him in with the aid of a magnet-based hook and line (Figure 6.6).

Figure 6.5 *Pas de deux* – Smallfilms-style as seen in *Clangers* (1969–74).

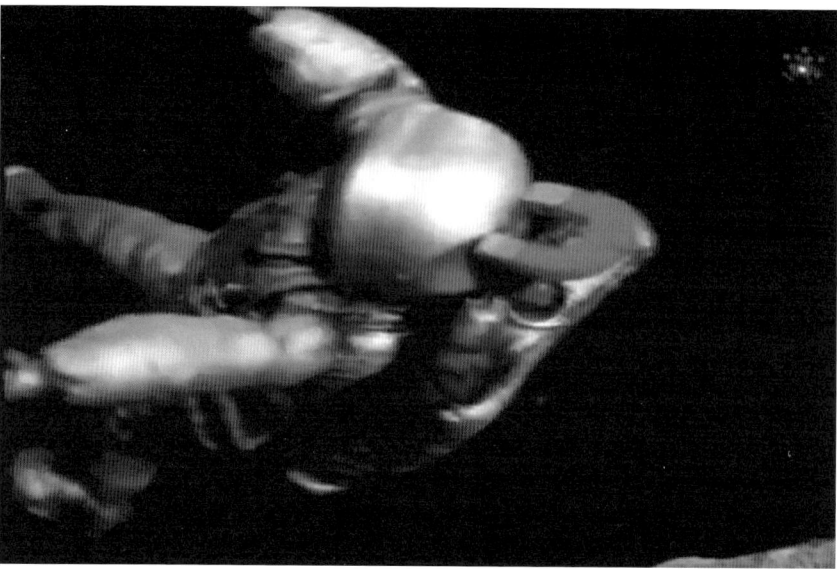

Figure 6.6 A bewildered astronaut discovers the magnetic appeal of *Clangers* (1969–74).

Worried that this unruly spaceman will get himself into more trouble, the Clangers bundle him into his lunar lander and bid him farewell. Postgate's narration paraphrases the Clangers' whistles as the spaceship departs: 'I wonder if he's aright, yes, there he is, look. Goodbye, come back soon, they shout. No, I don't think he will, I don't think he really liked it here.'[42]

Conclusion

As this chapter has demonstrated, technology represents a primary thematic concern within *Clangers*, and, through Postgate and Firmin's repeatedly playful representation of all things technological within the show, the themes of technology and inventiveness constitute a significant source of lasting appeal. Throughout *Clangers*, the technological takes a variety of forms, encompassing craft, elemental, magical, and malfunctioning devices and processes. In this regard, many of these ways of understanding technology, which are foregrounded in *Clangers*, repeat across Smallfilms' work more broadly. Of course, *Clangers* will appeal in many different ways to many different people, but in the context of this book, this chapter has simply served to emphasize a core element: the technological. After creating a solar system in the Smallfilms barn, and a space age story with little restriction beyond that of their own imaginations (and their ability to reappropriate everyday objects in fantastical ways), their next project saw Firmin and Postgate return to Earth. If we were to follow the established, popular accounts of Smallfilms' history,

6. Technology and Inventiveness within Smallfilms Animation   141

this return to Earth would lead us next to Emily's shop and her furry companion Bagpuss; however, these established histories overlook a sizeable project that Postgate and Firmin completed under the Smallfilms banner, prior to their work on *Bagpuss* (1974): *Sam on Boffs' Island* (1972–3).

Notes

1. Script for 'The Tablecloth', File: *Clangers*, Oliver Postgate Family Archive, UK, pp. 3–4.
2. Author's transcription from broadcast episode, available on DailyMotion.com, posted June 2017, https://www.dailymotion.com/video/x5v4jrh (accessed 20 May 2021).
3. Postgate, *Seeing Things*, p. 271.
4. Oliver Postgate, interviewed by Tim Jones, Canterbury, UK, 14 July 1993.
5. Postgate, *Seeing Things*, p. 272.
6. Postgate, *Seeing Things*, p. 274.
7. Postgate, *Seeing Things*, p. 273.
8. Esme Clemo, 'Peter Firmin: My Wife Knitted the Orginal Clangers and Dressed the Girls Like Twiggy', *Woman's Weekly* 15 July 2015.
9. Joan Firmin, interviewed by Chris Pallant, Canterbury, UK, 4 October 2019.
10. Joan Firmin, interviewed by Chris Pallant, Canterbury, UK, 4 October 2019.
11. Joan Firmin, interviewed by Chris Pallant, Canterbury, UK, 4 October 2019.
12. Joan Firmin, interviewed by Chris Pallant, Canterbury, UK, 4 October 2019.
13. Postgate, *Seeing Things*, p. 271.
14. Iain Baird, 'The Story of Colour Television in Britain', Science + Media Museum [blog], 15 May 2011, https://blog.scienceandmediamuseum.org.uk/colour-television-britain/ (accessed 10 June 2021).
15. See Justin Smith, 'Appendix I – Cinema Statistics, Box Office and Related Data', in Sue Harper and Justin Smith (eds), *British Film Culture in the 1970s: The Boundaries of Pleasure* (Edinburgh: Edinburgh University Press, 2012), p. 262.
16. 'A Pilot Survey of Colour Television Owners' produced by the British Broadcasting Corporation, October 1968, 'Audience Research Reports', File: R9/10/16, BBC Written Archives Centre (WAC), Reading, UK.
17. Leah Panos, 'The Arrival of Colour in BBC Drama and Rudolph Cartier's Colour Productions', *Critical Studies in Television* vol. 10 no. 3 (2015), p. 109.
18. Panos, 'The Arrival of Colour in BBC Drama and Rudolph Cartier's Colour Productions', p. 109.
19. See Chris Pallant, *Smallfilms: Audiences – data set*.
20. *Clangers* promotional mailer, *c*. 1966, File WW3/23/1, 'Clangers (The) – Owners Rights – Oliver Postgate & Peter Firmin', BBC Written Archives Centre (WAC), Reading, UK.
21. 'Programme Highlights', *Reading Evening Post* 15 November 1969.
22. See Ben Quinn, 'Souped-Up Clangers to Return to TV', *The Guardian* 15 October 2013, https://www.theguardian.com/tv-and-radio/2013/oct/15/clangers-remake-bbc (accessed 31 October 2021).
23. 'Clangers', *BBC Media Centre* 27 May 2015, https://www.bbc.co.uk/mediacentre/mediapacks/clangers (accessed 10 June 2021).

24 'Clangers Mark 50 Years since First Transmission with a Host of Birthday Surprises', *Coolabi* 15 November 2019, https://coolabi.com/clangers-mark-50-years-since-first-transmission-with-a-host-of-birthday-surprises/ (accessed 10 June 2021).
25 Author's transcription from *Clangers* episode 3, 'Chicken', viewed on DVD (Dragons' Friendly Society).
26 Author's transcription from *Clangers* episode 3, 'Chicken', viewed on DVD (Dragons' Friendly Society).
27 Brendan Prendiville, 'British Environmentalism: A Party in Movement?' *Revue LISA/LISA* vol. 12 no. 8 (2014). https://doi.org/10.4000/lisa.7119.
28 Author's transcription from *Clangers* episode 13, 'Goods', viewed on DVD (Dragons' Friendly Society).
29 Author's transcription from *Clangers* episode 13, 'Goods', viewed on DVD (Dragons' Friendly Society).
30 Author's transcription from *Clangers* episode 13, 'Goods', viewed on DVD (Dragons' Friendly Society).
31 Postgate, *Seeing Things*, pp. 271–272.
32 *Clangers* promotional mailer, *c.* 1966, File WW3/23/1, 'Clangers (The) – Owners Rights – Oliver Postgate & Peter Firmin', BBC Written Archives Centre (WAC), Reading, UK.
33 Alexander Geppert, 'Rethinking the Space Age: Astroculture and Technoscience', *History and Technology* vol. 28 no. 3 (2012), p. 219.
34 Geppert, 'Rethinking the Space Age', p. 220.
35 Geppert, 'Rethinking the Space Age', p. 220.
36 Geppert, 'Rethinking the Space Age', p. 220.
37 Author's transcription from *Clangers* episode 5, 'The Intruder', viewed on DVD (Dragons' Friendly Society).
38 Doug Millard, 'A Grounding in Space: Were the 1970s a Period of Transition in Britain's Exploration of Outer Space?' in Alexander Geppert (ed.), *Limiting Outer Space* (London: Palgrave, 2018), p. 94.
39 Millard, 'A Grounding in Space', p. 94.
40 Geppert, 'Rethinking the Space Age', p. 220.
41 Author's transcription from *Clangers* episode 15, 'The Rock Collector', viewed on DVD (Dragons' Friendly Society).
42 Author's transcription from *Clangers* episode 15, 'The Rock Collector', viewed on DVD (Dragons' Friendly Society).

Chapter 7

THE FORGOTTEN HISTORY OF SMALLFILMS: *SAM ON BOFFS' ISLAND* (1972–3)

Sam Samson   Sam? That's my name! Give me my name! Give!
Market seller   Well, I haven't got your name, mate.
Sam Samson   Oh, I'd forgotten all about my name. I'd better go back to Boffs' Island sometime and get it, hadn't I? Will you come too?[1]

This chapter constitutes a necessary and overdue recovery of Smallfilms history. The BBC show *Sam on Boffs' Island* (1972–3), which was produced by the BBC as part of its classroom-focused programming, is almost entirely missing from extant scholarship,[2] mentioned only briefly (in passing) in Postgate's autobiography,[3] and is omitted from most Smallfilms chronologies published in the public domain (which frequently give the false sense that Firmin and Postgate moved directly from *Clangers* to *Bagpuss*).[4] Yet, as this chapter will reveal, *Sam on Boffs' Island* was not a minor project, nor did it stray far from the stop-frame aesthetics that characterizes roughly half of Smallfilms' productions, and neither did it turn away from thematic constants such as collaboration (see Chapter 8), inventiveness (see Chapter 6), and whimsical authenticity (see Chapter 2), which bring a sense of coherence to the work of Smallfilms as a whole. Furthermore, the approximate total runtime of animation within *Sam on Boffs' Island*, which stands at roughly 102 minutes across the twenty episodes (see Appendix A – Fig. A.4), puts the show ahead of *The Seal of Neptune* (49 minutes), *Mermaid's Pearls* (51 minutes), and *The Pogles* (45 minutes).

Why then this omission? There is no singular answer to this question, but rather a number of converging factors that have resulted in the show's absence from the Smallfilms narrative. There is, of course, the prevailing view that this was purely a side project and not a fully badged Smallfilms production. However, while Postgate and Firmin were indeed contracted by the BBC to provide animated inserts into a show that was being written, directed, and produced centrally by the BBC, documentation held in the BBC's Written Archives Centre (WAC) reveals that invoices for this work were paid to Smallfilms.[5] Yet, as this chapter will highlight, even though the proposition at the outset was to simply outsource the animation production to Smallfilms, both Postgate and Firmin contributed creatively to the show in ways not initially anticipated.

The challenge of accessing *Sam on Boffs' Island* has also contributed to its exclusion. Since *Sam on Boffs' Island* was contracted as part of the BBC's Schools series 'Words and Pictures', which had a singular educational remit and less scope for primetime reruns (compared to many other Smallfilms productions), the show had less chance of reaching a broad audience, with its broadcast time suiting school schedules (being most commonly broadcast at 11.23 am and 2.05 pm), and thereby drastically restricting the opportunities for families of all ages to share the viewing experience (as was possible – and popular – for audiences of shows such as *Ivor the Engine*, *Noggin the Nog*, *Clangers*, and *Bagpuss*).[6] On top of the restrictive broadcast scheduling, *Sam on Boffs' Island* was only re-run once (23 September 1974–19 March 1975),[7] was never made available for private purchase by the BBC, and, at the time of publication, only one known surviving copy exists (held in the BFI Special Collections).[8] Consequently, only 2.5 per cent of the survey respondents confirmed an awareness of the show, with only *The Seal of Neptune* and *The Mermaid's Pearls* showing lower recognition (1.9 per cent).[9]

Thankfully, given these circumstances of audiovisual scarcity, the BBC's WAC holds a sizable file pertaining to *Sam on Boffs' Island*, affording insights into the show's inception, production, and reception. These files provide the spine of this chapter, with the goal here being to recover a place for *Sam on Boffs' Island* within the overarching historical narrative of Smallfilms. After establishing the details of the show's conception and pre-production, this chapter will then offer an abridged summary of the show's narrative, taking care to link insights gained from the archive to specific examples from the completed series. The chapter concludes by studying the show's reception in schools. At various stages throughout the chapter, newly gathered interview material will also be included to provide an additional point of reference when discussing the production.

Beginnings

At some point in November 1971, the precise date now lost to history, Firmin and Postgate met with Claire Chovil in London to discuss their next engagement with the BBC. Following up on this meeting, Postgate wrote to Chovil (31 November 1971) confirming that they 'would like to try and make some patches of film for your Reading series', before drawing Chovil's attention to the broadcast time of *Pogles' Wood*, which was airing on Thursday afternoons at the time of their correspondence, as a representative sample of their work.[10] Postgate also encouraged Chovil to 'make a Pilgrimage' to Smallfilms' base of operations in Kent, as, he notes, 'Ursula Eason would describe her visits here.'[11] In these words, we can see an effort to softly (re)establish his – and Smallfilms' – credentials, at the start of a new working relationship at the BBC with Chovil.

Like Eason and Doreen Stephens before her, Chovil was an influential force within her BBC department. While the public record confirms Chovil's professional achievements, serving as a producer on a variety of BBC shows, across television and radio, from the 1950s through to the late 1970s, biographical detail is largely elusive. Her obituary in the *Telegraph* from January 2008 states that she was a 'great lady', who was 'passionate about education' and 'an inspiration to friends, family, colleagues, and all who knew her'.[12] Of course, the convention of obituary writing is to highlight piecemeal aspects of the deceased's life, so these characterizations of Chovil can only take us so far. As part of the preliminary research for this chapter, I spoke with Tony Robinson, the actor who played the eponymous Sam (and more famously played Baldrick in the comedy series *Blackadder*), and the prolific actress of stage and screen, Miriam Margolyes, who played Sam's Mother and also voiced the adversarial Gran-Boff and several other characters in the show, and both spoke highly of Chovil. Robinson recalls:

> She was very, very smart. Really quite quiet, she really had that Roedean aura about her, whether or not she had been to Roedean, I didn't know, but she looked like the sort who had been to Roedean or Oxford […] She was a very good person manager. You always felt that she really admired your talent, that she understood what you were doing, and she gave people a lot of space, but, nevertheless, was very much the senior figure of the team.[13]

Robsinson's speculative characterization of Chovil's academic pedigree is unerringly accurate, as Chovil's obituary confirms her graduation from both Roedean School and St Anne's College, Oxford. Similarly, Margolyes reflects:

> I had quite a crush on her. She was a very English, rather reserved, rather Schoolmistressy type. Completely dedicated to her work and very pleased with *Sam on Boffs' Island*. We felt that it was a very good programme, everybody who worked on it liked it.[14]

Beyond the words of Robinson and Margolyes, another recollected snapshot of Chovil can be found in Charles Collingwood's book, *Brian and Me: Life on – and off – The Archers* (2009). Collingwood, who provided the voices of What-Boff, Tele-Boff, and Mr Gurgler for *Sam on Boffs' Island*, describes Chovil as 'a true bluestocking', before noting how she 'was a very serious woman who loved actors and show business, but she had headmistress written all over her'.[15] Beyond these descriptive fragments offered by Robinson, Margolyes, and Collingwood, Chovil's correspondence with Postgate and Firmin, held in the BBC's archive, also paints a picture of an individual at the top of her game, expert at managing people, and passionate about creating engaging educational content.

Working from the BBC's archive, it is evident that *Sam on Boffs' Island* took approximately four months to move from the initial meeting between Chovil, Firmin, and Postgate through to the commissioning and contracting of Smallfilms' contribution to the series. Given their established expertise, the terms under which Smallfilms was contracted by the BBC required the design and fabrication of puppets and sets, as well as the production of stop-frame animation, with the narrative and educational facets being the concern of the BBC's own creative division.[16] In a letter from Chovil dated 6 March 1972, she sets out the terms to be contractually agreed by the BBC's Purchased Programmes Department with Smallfilms. Chovil's letter separates the work being apportioned to Firmin and Postgate. Next to Postgate's name we find the obligation to 'make not less than 80 minutes of colour stop-frame film, at his suggested fee of £20 a minute', as well as references to additional 'rostrum camera work' to be paid at the same rate. Provision is also made in the agreement for the BBC to 'purchase the necessary colour stock in Eastmancolour [sic]'.[17] Regarding Firmin's work, the letter states that for 80 minutes of film the following is to be commissioned: '20 stop-frame puppets with 21 heads', '10 duplicate glove puppets with 11 heads to be used by the BBC in the film and the studio', '1 practical kite (studio and film use)', ten puppet sets 'all for stop-frame filming', and thirteen 'machines' (such as a 'word box', 'printing press', and a 'fog-making device') also for stop-frame filming.[18] Chovil closes with the request that, upon the signing of contracts, the first half of the fee be paid to Smallfilms in recognition of the fact that the actual work would 'stretch over quite a long period of time'.[19] These are important details to establish, since they help to reveal the parameters within which both Postgate and Firmin sought to exert creative influence over the series as a whole.

Evidence of Postgate's creative appetite can be found in an exchange of letters with Chovil that took place through December 1971. In a letter dated 8 December 1971, Chovil informs Postgate that she hopes to be in touch again soon 'with some ideas on paper' and states her intent to 'work out a story which will be satisfactory to you, as well as to us'.[20] Within these words is the implication that Chovil and Postgate have already discussed the story of *Sam on Boffs' Island*, in an embryonic sense, perhaps when meeting in person or on a telephone call in the intervening time between their first meeting and the writing of this letter. This is just an inference, of course, but the tone of the letter does appear to imply a clear desire on Chovil's part to satisfy Postgate's creative views. Two weeks later, Chovil writes again to Postgate, this time enclosing brief outlines of the draft story as it stood on 22 December 1971.[21] While these outlines are now lost, in the letter Chovil writes: 'I should emphasise that this is very much a first draft only. I think some of the episodes may be lacking in incident and they will get revised as soon as the script-writing begins.'[22] The letter from Postgate, written in response to seeing these outline drafts, which was sent to Chovil on 12 January 1972, reveals the scale of Postgate's creative investment at this early stage in the project's development.

Running over thirty-three lines and five paragraphs, Postgate is unflinching in his assessment of the show's early direction. For example, he opens his letter by voicing concerns that there is 'too much of the large general situations adventures expeditions and political manoeuvring for the sort of programme I imagine you are after'.[23] Postgate continues:

> There is marvellous rumbustious Treasure Island stuff here for a pure entertainment programme. I should say a programme about words, a teaching programme, should have its situations sort of connected with words and letters and the adventure should if possible have to do with words, though this isn't

essential and a certain amount of story stuff is essential but it's a matter of balance I suppose.[24]

Moving beyond these high-level critiques, Postgate then appraises the more granular details established in these early drafts (with 'Bods' being the name of the 'Boffs' at this early point in the show's development):

> I felt in our discussion on Monday we chewed our way down to quite a good basic situation with the Man in his box being of use to the ignorant Bods who were only underprivileged because some of their birds had flown and because they knew so few words. The Man can suggest more words to them which they can collect the letters of and feed into the Making Machine and produce consumer goods.
>
> I should have thought that basic situation was full of fun and could be squeezed for several programmes in a gentle wordy way. The process of their economy is interesting and mistakes and mis-spellings can produce fearful trouble (like 'comb' spelt with a B at the front. We and the man see it just in time but too late to stop the Bod putting it through the machine. It comes out a fizzing Guy Fawkes type bomb and has to be disposed).[25]

While Postgate is careful with this tone, a sense of frustration does permeate his critique, which is rooted in what he perceives as a movement away, in these outline drafts, from the ideas that he discussed with Chovil earlier in the development process. Postgate's reinforcing of the narrative opportunities afforded by the word-based economy, specifically the tensions that could be generated through misspellings, struck a chord with Chovil's BBC production team, and we find a scenario similar to that suggested by Postgate appear in episode 10 of *Sam on Boffs' Island*.

Postgate concludes his letter by appealing to Chovil's budgetary acumen:

> Later, perhaps when the Bods are equipped the Hairies come and reject the affluent society, life gets more subtle but even so I feel their lives should be simple and concerned with words and songs and singing and nonsense rather than escapes and imprisonments and plots.
>
> This is only my feeling. The only practical weight it has is that a simple life around a few machines will give you a simpler but much cheaper film than the big situations involving the Man being mobile.
>
> Peter and Sylvia are brooding pictorially about what we talked about.[26]

By quoting substantially from Postgate's letter it is possible to see the full extent of his creative investment in this project at a crucial moment in the show's early development. Reading these words, we do not get the impression that Postgate sees *Sam on Boffs' Island* as a side-project, something to simply pay the bills, or that he is working as a subcontractor who is being employed to deliver stop-frame animation in-keeping with the requirements of Chovil and the BBC. Rather, there is an acceptance on Chovil's part that both Firmin and Postgate will be keen contributors with significant sway over the creative shape of the show, and on Postgate's part there is a clear expectation that his creative input will be valued by the BBC's production team.

Regardless of its neglect, *Sam on Boffs' Island* represents an important part of Smallfilms history, given the creative talent that coalesced around the project, and how the show reveals Postgate and Firmin adjusting to – and excelling within – a different type of working arrangement to what they were used to. For *Sam on Boffs' Island*, instead of overseeing all aspects of production, as they had for their previous productions, Postgate and Firmin were tasked with contributing to a series that was being controlled at a higher level. In addition to Chovil, who was at the top of her profession at the time of the show's production, and Firmin and Postgate, who were also leading figures in British television animation at the time, there were also several individuals working on the show who were just starting their careers who would go on to be well-respected creative talents in their own right, such as the aforementioned Margolyes and Robinson, and writer Michael Rosen. Given that most readers of this book will be unfamiliar with *Sam on Boffs' Island*, the following section offers an abridged summary of the series narrative.

Sam on Boffs' Island: *The story*

Reviewing the documents held in the BBC's archive, we get an impression of a rather uneventful production, spread across the (mostly) agreeable letters exchanged between Chovil, Postgate, and Firmin, as well as the comprehensive shot list that portrays a largely straightforward phase of principal photography. Within the production documents, however, there is still evidence of Firmin and Postgate's desire to be more than just an outsourced production unit, responsible solely for stop-frame inserts and puppetry. In the summary of *Sam on Boffs' Island* that follows, such instances will be highlighted along the way, thereby revealing the gentle push-and-pull of creative influence that characterized the show's production. That these instances of creative exchange were accommodated in such a positive manner provides further testament to the skill of Chovil as a manager of personalities and a unifier of creative visions. This summary represents something of a reconstruction and recovery project since no complete broadcast copy of the show has been found to-date, so what follows is based on a combination of my own viewing of the BFI's pre-broadcast copy of *Sam on Boffs' Island* (which contains frequent blank screen sequences and incomplete sound), my study of the shot list that documents the BBC's principal live-action photography between 18 April 1972 and 13 June 1972, the correspondence between Chovil, Postgate, and Firmin that provides insight into the production of the animation, and my consultation of the brief episode summaries, which vary in accuracy, hosted on Ben Clarke's encyclopaedic *Broadcast for Schools* website.[27]

The first episode in the series focuses on establishing the main character, Sam Samson (Robinson) and the location of Boffs' Island, while placing less emphasis on the explicitly educational activity of practicing phonics – which is the production's underlying *raison d'être*. The shot list describes the moment that Sam sets foot on Boffs' Island for the first time:

> Master shot. Sam sitting on crunchy desert set, holding onto parachute with l. hand, milk bottle (half full) in r. hand., his zip bag in front of him. "Well, here I am. Sam Samson reporting from the sun-soaked island. I wonder what it's called?"
>
> <u>oov voice</u>: 'Boffs' Island. Boffs' Island.'
>
> <u>Sam</u>: "Did someone say Boffs' Island? I'd better take a look about her and see what's going on.[28]

This episode also establishes the recurrent daydream framing device that runs throughout the series, which, on this occasion, sees Sam fantasize about being a reporter, parachuting down onto a mysterious island. This occurs at his breakfast table, with Sam facing a box of crunchy cereal, so, despite his Mum's (Margolyes) best efforts to stop him, he slips into a cereal-inspired daydream.[29] This dynamic repeats throughout the series, with Sam's daydream excursions to Boffs' Island typically framed or informed by recent encounters in the real world.

Having had mixed fortunes on his first encounter with the Boffs, with the sleeping Sam being mistaken for a monster, the second episode sees Sam embraced by the Boff community and introduced to the 'Say-Birds' (Figure 7.1). As we learn, the Say-Birds perform an important function, both within the diegetic narrative and in support of the show's educational ambition. Firmin was responsible for designing the Say-Birds, and we can see his pre-production endeavour captured across pre-production documents held by the BBC. The final appearance of the Say-Birds closely matches the early design intentions established by Firmin in an undated handwritten note, but most likely dating from January 1972 (given the sequencing of the BBC's archive and by cross-referencing of details from Firmin's note with a letter from Chovil dated 21 January 1972): 'The birds are building bricks so that they can have their letter on.'[30]

The Say-Birds, as their name implies, are important because of their ability to literally say letters into existence. This ability provides the economic bedrock of the Boffs' society. By keeping the Say-Birds locked in cages and exploiting their ability to say individual letters, the Boffs' have created a Shopping Machine that can then harvest the letters to make full words, thus resulting in the production of corresponding physical commodities. The manner in which the Say-Birds utter their respective phonemes provides frequent opportunities for the intended young school-age audience to hear individual letters repeated, thereby providing the chance for phonics-based language acquisition activities to take place. Additionally, the appearance of the Say-Birds in their cages, and their exploitation at the hands

Figure 7.1 Our first sight of the Say Birds as seen in *Sam on Boffs' Island* (1972–3).

of the Boffs, also sets in motion a sub-theme of animal welfare that ultimately sees the Say-Birds liberated from their caged existence as a consequence of the Hairy Gurglers (who first appear in episode six), and who gradually change Boff culture for the better. Reflecting on the educational underpinnings of the show, and its value system, Margolyes reflects:

> We felt, because it was educational it was worthy, and I'm a great believer in worthy. I have a strong moralist streak because I was taught by Frank Leavis [F.R. Leavis] at Cambridge, so I think that things should have a moral quotient in them, and that [*Sam on Boffs' Island*] did! It was the sort of thing that the BBC should be doing – it was wholesome.[31]

Consequently, episode two focuses on establishing the utility of the Say-Birds for both the Boffs and the school-age viewer.

The next three episodes follow a fairly common pattern, with the prologue of each episode showing Sam in a specific situation (engaging with a newspaper seller in episode three, and doing his job as a pet shop worker in episodes four and five), thus inspiring thematically linked activities in the main narrative. For example, in episode three we see Sam discovering the Boffs' newspaper production line, overseen by Paper-Boff. During this episode Sam learns how the Say-Birds also provide the letters for each edition of the newspaper, and how the newspaper has a different name each day, with potential names including the likes of 'The Hanky-Panky Fantastico', 'The Rag Bag', and the 'Happy Nattering'. While in episodes four and five, the opening emphasis on animal welfare, inspired by both episodes opening in the pet shop where Sam works, foreshadows an emphasis within the two episodes on the Say-Birds – first on their escape (thus preventing the Shopping Machine from producing any goods) and secondly on the effects of their absence (with Sam coming to the Boffs' aid by handwriting new letters to feed the Shopping Machine).

On several occasions within episodes four and five, we see Sam's hands in close up, whether trying to catch the escaping Say-Birds or handing over the written letters. In Postgate's letter to Chovil, dated 10 June 1972, we can see the suggestion that this approach – of filming live hands – may have also been considered as a practical solution for the stop-frame animation of the Boffs, but ultimately was rejected by Postgate. Reflecting on the ongoing stop-frame animation, Postgate writes: 'No major troubles so far. I have overruled one or two small whims, mainly the appearance of live hands doing Boff's work as Boffs wear pink Boffskin gloves.'[32] Dated three days before the completion of principal photography, it is therefore likely that Postgate's words were intended as a reminder to Chovil, with much of the stop-frame animation still to be completed, rather than as an aesthetic ruling offered to shape the live-action filming. Although there is no correspondence confirming this, given Postgate's frequent presence at the Television Film Studios at Ealing, there is the possibility that creative suggestions were offered in person, and Postgate felt compelled to confirm his views by writing to Chovil.[33]

In episode six we are introduced to the Hairy Gurglers. These imagistically named characters live on another island, not far from the Boffs, and, it is revealed, they have often been at odds with the Boffs. The tension between the two cultures is rooted in their divergent value systems, a mismatch championed by Postgate early in the creative process, whereby the Boffs are an affluent, technological, and consumerist society, while the Gurglers represent a more equal society, with arts, crafts, and communal activities being central to their social fabric.[34] Discovering that the Say-Birds have flown to this island, and with their Gurgler prejudices firmly in place, Paper-Boff and Bird-Boff lead Sam on a rescue mission. Predictably, the rescue goes badly, and, with intolerance governing their actions, Sam and Paper-Boff flee, while Bird-Boff is seemingly held captive by the Gurglers.

The overarching story takes an important turn in episode seven, as we discover that the Gurglers are in fact harmless, caring, and fun. Returning to Bird-Boff, we find the Gurglers performing a welcome dance (Figure 7.2) to put their visitor at ease. Back on Boffs's Island there is panic at the news of Bird-Boff's apparent capture, and the Boffs are shown frantically jamming their telephone switchboard, desperate to find out what is going on; the Boffs' jamming of the telephone switchboard provides an example of the rostrum animation that Postgate also provided for the series (Figure 7.3).

Resulting from all this frenzied talk is the decision to rescue Bird-Boff and the Say-Birds. Consequently, episode eight begins with a scene of Sam sat in his house making a model boat, thus providing a thematic link to the activities

Figure 7.2 Friendly Gurglers as seen in *Sam on Boffs' Island* (1972–3).

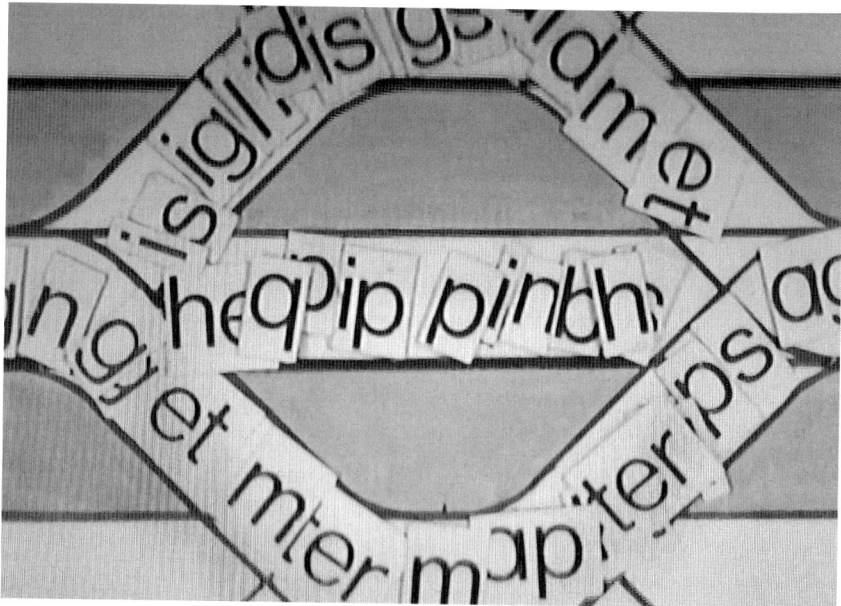

Figure 7.3 Crossed wires as seen in *Sam on Boffs' Island* (1972–3).

Figure 7.4 A crowd scene as seen in *Sam on Boffs' Island* (1972–3).

on Boffs' Island, where we find the Boffs putting the final touches to their own rescue raft (Figure 7.4).

This image of the Boffs and their raft, which was animated by Postgate in stop-motion, also shows the amount of fabrication work, such as prop- and model-making, undertaken by Firmin during the show's production. While all of this is happening on Boffs' Island, we learn that the Say-Birds, rather than being in grave danger at the hands of the Gurglers, are in fact being taught to speak complete words.

Episode nine is dominated by the difficult journey made by the Boffs as they sail through thick fog to the Gurglers' Island. This journey is intercut with scenes of the Say-Birds singing. While rather inconsequential within the narrative, these scenes of the Say-Birds singing, in this particular episode, provides an example of Postgate's own creative governance over what we see on-screen. Margolyes, who voiced many of the Say-Birds, confirms that a number of dedicated voice recording sessions took place in addition to principal filming sessions, and, crucially, it was Postgate who had oversight given that these voice tracks provided an important foundation for his stop-frame animation.[35] The creative latitude afforded to Postgate is evident in Chovil's undated letter (*c*. 3–10 July 1972), in which she offers only a loose steer for the O-Bird and F-Bird's singing: 'Easier perhaps. Start on: f-f-fff-f-f- (i.e. rhythmic f sounds). Then if invention flags: fa-fa-faffy-faffy-fef […] Similar from "p" combining discreetly, with short vowels but no more than desperation dictates.'[36] Although this example of creative autonomy within the production of *Sam on Boffs' Island* is a far remove from the richly layered narratives created by Postgate in collaboration with Firmin across their other Smallfilms works, it is a revealing glimpse, nonetheless, of a less regulated space within this otherwise tightly governed BBC production.

In episode ten, having reached the Gurglers' Island, the Boffs witness the Gurglers staging a 'Fun-Day'. The phonic featured in this episode is the vowel 'u', which provides the basis for one of the best examples of wordplay featured throughout the series. Incorrectly summarized on the *Broadcast for Schools* website, which records a misunderstanding amongst the Boffs where the word 'gun' is falsely repeated in place of the word 'run', yet in the broadcast episode there is no mention of a gun. Additionally, there is no mention of a 'gun' in the shot list, which removes the possibility that the *Broadcast for Schools* website summary was based on a pre-production document. It is also worth noting that the 1973 *Sam on Boffs' Island* Annual also features no reference to a 'gun' or even to this amusing sequence of misheard words.[37] Given the misinformation circulating in the popular domain about this sequence – rather apt given the subject matter – it is important at this point to establish in full, by working from the shot list, the critical exchange that occurs when the Boffs, emerging from the Gurgler jungle, first see the 'Fun-Day':

(guide track) MC/U What-Boff ('It looks like it! I never knew that before. Gran-Boff!') whip pan to MC/U Gran for her dialogue ('Hello? What is it?') (all What-Boff's lines oov – 'Tell the others. Gurglers have fun.') (Gran 'What?') (WB – 'Gurglers have fun!') (Gran – 'Oh. Just a minute') She turns to call ('Sell-Boff')

[…]

(cut-in) (guide track) MC/U What-Boff (Gran's lines oov)
('Gran-Boff…… . Gurglers have fun')

MC/U Gran (guide track) ('Gurglers have bun') (Sell-Boff oov: 'What?') (Gran – 'Gurglers have bun')

MC/U Gran listening, she turns to shout to What-Boff, whip pan to 2-s Sam/What-Boff. What-Boff leaves shot r., Zoom in to C/U Sam looking 'incredulous' (Sell-Boff oov 'Boffs are on the run. Boffs are on the run')
(Gran: 'Boffs are on the sun. Boffs are on the sun')
Pan
(Sam: 'Boggs on the sun? How did they get there?')
(WhatB – 'Hold on. I can see Bird-Boff. I'll try and rescue him')

Tracking shot r. to l., starting 2-s What-Boff dragging Bird-Boff along r. to l., to 3-s Sam lying b/g, zoom in to C?U Sam for his speech
(BirdB – 'Help. Help.')
(What – 'It's all right. I've saved you from the terrible Gurglers')
(Bird – 'No, no, I don't want to be saved')
(What – 'Be quiet [pause] they'll hear you')

(Bird – 'But I –')
(What – 'Shut up')
(Sam – 'Well. At least he's rescued Bird-Boff. Now all we need are the Say-Birds')[38]

There are several important threads to unravel within this sequence. By working directly from the shot list, in the absence of any surviving script material, we can see the effort taken by the series' writers, Rosen and Tulley, to establish the key tensions underpinning this pivotal episode within the series: xenophobia/tolerance (rooted in the Boffs dislike of the Gurglers), being a good listener (a key attribute to being a good learner, and shown by What-Boff's refusal to listen to Bird-Boff when 'rescuing' him), and the importance of practicing good diction (the key educational goal of the show as a whole).

This is the moment in the series when explicit confirmation is given that the Boffs have deeply misunderstood the Gurglers and have allowed their own prejudices to limit their understanding of Gurgler culture. Not only does What-Boff remark how he 'never knew that before', about Gurglers being fun and non-threatening, but Gran-Boff and Sam also reinforce this sense of surprise. Running in parallel with this cultural revelation, we also begin to see the rigidity of Boff thought with regard to their treatment of each other. This is hinted at throughout, particularly through Gran-Boff's frequent narrow-minded interactions with other Boffs, but is crystallized here through the unwilling – and quite uncomfortable – 'rescue' of Bird-Boff. With the undercurrents of the series revealed in this manner in episode ten, the second half of the series then sets out to convey how the two cultures, of Boffs and Gurglers, can learn from each other to find common ground and establish an expanded sense of community that is inclusive of Boffs and Gurglers alike.

Over the next few episodes the extent of the Boffs' prejudice is revealed, mainly through the actions of Gran-Boff, before ultimately being challenged and overcome, thanks to the unwavering positivity of the Gurglers and the subsequent Boff-Gurgler marriage. In episode eleven we see the Gurglers set sail for Boffs' Island so that they can reunite with Bird-Boff who they are missing. Consequently, episode twelve focuses on the Boffs' defence of their Island from what they perceive to be a hostile Gurgler incursion. The Boffs fire missiles at the Gurglers with peashooters before Bird-Boff intervenes and calms the situation. Despite Bird-Boff's best efforts to make peace, when he introduces the Gurglers to his Boff compatriots at the end of the episode, Gran-Boff addresses the crowd of Boffs and Gurglers, saying: 'I have this to say to you: I hate Gurglers.'[39] Set against the backdrop of increasing Boff and Gurgler interaction (seen in episode thirteen), Gran-Boff's prejudice remains undimmed. For example, after seeing Small-Boff play with a young Gurgler on swings erected by the Gurglers, Gran-Boff characterizes their playful antics as 'Silly Gurgler nonsense'.[40] Bleeding into episode fourteen and the 'Samboree' (a jamboree held to honour Sam), where we see large crowds of Boffs and Gurglers dancing together and sharing in the merriment as equals, Gran-Boff continues to voice her unease to anyone who will listen.

In the archival materials related to episode fourteen, we can find evidence of Firmin and Postgate relying upon their own creative problem-solving and agency, without waiting for approval form Chovil or the BBC, to ensure timely completion of their stop-frame work. For example, in a letter dated 24 August 1972, Postgate writes to inform Chovil of a changes they have made when faced with the challenge of animating a mole, which, in the script, was described as travelling under the surface of the ground, as well as how they have overcome a difficulty faced when attempting to animate the Boffs and Gurglers' maypole celebration sequence.

> About 14.
>
> Peter and I don't think we can do the travelling mole-bulge convincingly. Peter has an old mole which we can use without extra charge and I suggested we should pop him up out of the holes sort of instantly. So he goes down in one hole when boffed on the nose and immediately breaks ground and pops up somewhere else. I hope that is O.K.
>
> Incidentally, we can't fit the maypole on the Say-Birds' set but the North shore has the same colour floor so we can disguise the sides with boxes and junk and it will be anywhere in the Boff country. I will assume that's ok with you unless I hear to the contrary.[41]

There is no evidence in the archive of Chovil overturning these decisions, and the completed episodes match the intentions of Postgate and Firmin as articulated in this letter. This is not an attempt to overstate the creative input of Firmin and Postgate, but rather a reminder, rooted in a specific, well-documented example, that the production was supported by a number of talented individuals engaged in a process of frequent creative exchange.

Episode fifteen offers a symbolic resolution to the Boff–Gurgler conflict, as Tele-Boff and Purple Gurgler are married in front of a large crowd of Boffs and Gurglers. However, Gran-Boff continues to resist the goodwill that is spreading through the newly unified community. Then, in episode sixteen, we find that the Boffs are gradually – and unfortunately – beginning to take advantage of the good-natured Gurglers. For example, we see Tele-Boff giving instructions to Purple Gurgler, such as 'answer it will you sweetheart', when their phone rings; Bird-Boff relaxing while White Gurgler and Pink Gurlger tend to the Say-Birds; and Sell-Boff taking advantage of willing Gurglers who take on the responsibility for production.

Episode seventeen turns up the heat again, with Gran-Boff accusing Sam of being a Gurgler spy. Gran-Boff, having convinced the majority of Boffs that Sam is indeed a spy, then leads a mob in pursuit of the fleeing Sam. Having been captured by Sell-Boff and Paper-Boff, episode eighteen centres around a court case, with Sam being put on trial by the Boffs. Gran-Boff confronts Sam and assumes the role of Chief Interrogator, demanding to see the contents of his bag:

> **Gran-Boff**   Now what has he got in that bag, eh? Open it at once!
> **Sam**   There is nothing terrible in here. There can't be. See for yourself.
> **Gran-Boff**   Go on then.
> **Mrs-Boff**   I hope it doesn't explode!

> **Sam**   One pair of scissors.
> **Gran-Boff**   Careful! Just as I thought. A secret weapon!
> **Sam**   No, that's not dangerous.
> **Mrs-Boff**   Oh, who would have thought it!
> **Paper-Boff**   Oh dear, oh dear.
> **Sam**   One pair of shoelaces.
> **Gran-Boff**   For tying up his enemies!
> **Mrs-Boff**   Oh dear, whatever next?
> **Paper-Boff**   I knew it, it's a plot!
> **Sam**   And one tin of shaving cream.
> **Gran-Boff**   It's a bomb! It's a bomb!
> **Boffs**   [*Panicked noises.*]
> **Sam**   No it isn't, see for yourself.[42]

Refusing to accept Sam's innocence, Gran-Boff declares Sam to be under arrest and instructs the Boffs to lead him to the courtroom to face No-Boff. Ultimately, No-Boff refuses to sentence Sam. With Sam released from custody, Gran-Boff hatches her own plan:

> **Gran-Boff**   That trial was no good! Sam is a spy. If he can't be tried properly, at least he can be punished.
> **Paper-Boff**   How?
> **Gran-Boff**   He can be locked up.
> **Mrs-Boff**   Where can we lock him up?
> **Gran-Boff**   I've got an idea. See all this string, we are going to knit.
> **Paper-Boff**   Knit what?
> **Gran-Boff**   We are going to knit a net and there is no time to lose![43]

Sam is caught in the net, and, with the episode concluding, he begins to stir from his dream state.

Still held captive at the mercy of Gran-Boff, episode nineteen focuses on What-Boff, Bird-Boff, No-Boff, Small-Boff, and Little-Boff as they plot a rescue mission. Revisiting the items found in Sam's bag, they take the bomb (shaving foam), a parachute (umbrella), and a weapon (scissors) to help with their rescue attempt. After Bird-Boff sprays the shaving foam over Gran-Boff, Paper-Boff, and Mrs-Boff, rendering them incapacitated, Sam uses the scissors to cut himself free from the net. It is worth noting that the shot list reveals that the live-action production unit were unable to successfully stage the shaving foam attack, which was initially planned to be recorded on day two (18 April 1972) of principal photography at the Television Film Studio in Ealing. Instead, the shot list includes the following note:

> PROGRAMME 19 (p.14)
> We did shots 18 and 19, but then abandoned the idea of doing the shaving-foam sequence of ssf. Oliver Postgate will try to do it on stop-frame.[44]

Again, while this might seem a rather minor detail, when considered in the context of the production timeline, the confidence being placed in Postgate to deliver a solution so early in the principal photography, indicates how prominently – and respected – the Smallfilms-based production activities were viewed by Chovil and her team at the BBC. As the finished episode reveals, Postgate and Firmin successfully completed this sequence as stop-frame animation. With Sam successfully liberated, courtesy of the shaving foam attack, the Boffs then tie up Gran-Boff to prevent her orchestrating any more rebellious activity.

The final episode of the series implies that some time has passed since Sam escaped from Boffs' Island, with the opening scene showing a number of Boffs wondering if Sam is ok, where he is, and if he will ever come back. In a melancholic tone, Small-Boff confirms what they are all thinking: that they miss Sam. After discovering a printed telephone directory, or 'some sort of name book' as Paper-Boff describes it, the Boffs learn Sam's address and phone number and proceed to call him.[45] Telling him they are coming to visit him in his world, they discover a portal to Sam's live-action world hidden in a rather surprising location: inside a cereal box. Travelling via this portal they emerge during Sam's breakfast, prompting an episode that glosses over the Boff–Gurgler tensions of the series and Gran-Boff's propaganda and insurrection, and instead features the Boffs exploring Sam's world. At the end of the episode we see Sam take the Boffs on a trip to the local supermarket, and, as the Boffs begin to tire, they realize that they will be able to return to Boffs' Island if they can find a portal within one of the cereal boxes from the breakfast aisle. As the Boffs bid farewell to Sam, Sam once again emerges from a dream state, leaving the narrative open to interpretation: did Sam simply daydream everything? Whether he did or did not is open to debate, but to dwell on such a detail would distract from the fact that this series represents a hitherto neglected part of Smallfilms history.

Auntie knows best: Sam on Boffs' Island *in the classroom*

The activities behind the scenes of *Sam on Boffs' Island*, as captured within the BBC's archives, did not stop at the end of the show's production, since a dozen letters and documents exist that provide an insight into the show's reception in the classroom and the BBC's response to this reception. Beginning in an undated letter from Postgate to Chovil, but sent at some point between 23 September 1972 (the date of the previous correspondence between Postgate and Chovil) and 13 November 1972 (the date of Chivil's reply), Postgate passes on the details of a school teacher who had written to him about the show. Beyond stating the teacher's name (which will be kept anonymous here), Postgate doesn't provide the details of this correspondence, but does adopt a rather dry tone, writing: 'How stimulating it must be for you to have such an intense and critical audience.'[46] (Incidentally, this undated letter also records the beginning of the collaboration between John Faulkner, Sandra Kerr, and Smallfilms, with Postgate enquiring: 'Could you let me have the names and address of the people who did your beautiful Boff music? I would like to meet them.'[47] Faulkner and Kerr would go on to work with Firmin and Postgate on *Bagpuss*, composing a number of original songs and providing the iconic soundtrack to the series.) Responding to Postgate, Chovil (13 November 1972) thanks Postgate for his positive words about the series before noting, light-heartedly, that in response to the teacher's letter she'll 'put him right about the origins of the programmes by sending him a report card'.[48]

Over the next few months, Chovil received more letters criticizing the series, with two such letters surviving in the BBC archive, thereby prompting a change in mood and a more considered response by the BBC. Both letters in the archive are dated 15 January 1973, with one letter addressing the series as a whole, and the other targeting criticism at the first episode (broadcast 18 September 1972). Both letters, however, focus the bulk of their criticism around the vocabulary used and the presence of slang words. Given this common line of criticism and their identical postal date, it is tempting to speculate whether these two letters resulted from the ire of just one of the teachers in question, who, perhaps wishing to amplify their concerns to the BBC, encouraged a fellow teacher to write to the BBC with similar concerns. Of course, there is no hard evidence to support this speculation beyond the matching postal date and the commonality of their concerns.

The longer letter, written on East Suffolk County Education Committee stationery by an individual who shall remain anonymous, records a complaint from Occold Primary School in Eye. The letter, addressed to the BBC's Head of Schools Programming, articulates a 'strong protest at the standards of your programme 'Sam on Boff's [*sic*] Island', which, after acknowledging the typically 'high standard of schools' broadcasting from the BBC', highlights the perceived 'low standard of English in a programme specifically designed to help children with their speech' as a key point of disappointment.[49] Going on to note how the 'characters were scruffy and their speech incoherent', the author of the letter then returns to the key criticism, reiterating how 'what amazed my Headmistress and myself more than the poor presentation and content of the programme, was the choice of vocabulary'.[50] Providing an example from the show, the letter states:

> 'Slurp' and 'Ta-ta' are hardly words one encourages children to use when our language is so rich in choice, and it appears to us that this programme does nothing, absolutely nothing, to make our job any easier or to encourage children to widen their own vocabulary.[51]

While the shorter letter, written on Kent County Council stationery by an individual who will also remain anonymous, records a complaint from the Remedial Centre in Sheppey. Matching the strong tone of the longer letter, it begins: 'We were utterly horrified at the first programme of "Sam on Boff's [*sic*] Island". We would like some indication as to whether this low standard is to continue.'[52] Given the suspicion raised earlier regarding whether these letters were coordinated, it is worth noting the matching mispunctuation of the show's title as *Sam on Boff's Island* and not *Boffs'*. After this strongly worded opener, the author of the letter then writes:

> We spend a lot of our time encouraging our children to speak clearly and distinctly, to use handkerchiefs when they have colds and to refrain from using slang words. Surely it is possible to introduce sounds in an interesting way without having to descend to such a low level.[53]

The strength of the accusations in these two letters forced the BBC to adopt a more serious stance when responding to this criticism. The BBC's archives document a flurry of activity at the BBC through late January 1973, with Chovil and John Hosier, then an Executive Producer of Schools Television, exchanging three internal memos in quick succession (two on 19 January 1973 and one on 25 January 1973).[54] After which Chovil wrote directly to the two schools with the BBC's official response.

After opening with a sympathetic sentence, repeated in both letters ('I am sorry you feel that the standard of the programme was low'), Chovil then spends the bulk of both letters defending the values and objectives of *Sam on Boffs' Island* – a classic example of Auntie knows best.[55] Chovil begins her defence by explaining the thinking behind the show's use of phonics. Responding to the criticisms from both letters about incoherent speech and representation of an unwell Sam, Chovil writes about how they tried to pick seasonally appropriate phonic case studies, such as catching the flu shown in episode eleven (broadcast on 15 January 1973 – the date of the complaint letters), and how this temporarily impacts your speech.[56] The fact that Chovil replied with almost identical letters to both the Occold School, Eye and the Remedial Centre, Sheppey, hints that she might also have suspected some degree of covert coordination behind the complaints.

One noteworthy difference between the two letters centres around the need for Chovil to respond to the accusation from Occold School that the characters were 'scruffy'. In the passage quoted below in full, the first paragraph is repeated identically in both letters, while the second paragraph was sent only to Occold School:

> You also mention the use of slang – presumably referring to the made-up word 'Slurp'. Once again, the word was used for humour, because humour can assist memory. Lewis Carroll and others have done this to great effect. It would obviously not be sensible to use a great many 'made-up' words but surely an occasional one does no harm and may encourage children to believe the words can be used for fun (and incidentally in this case, for onomatopoeic effect).
>
> You mention also in your letter that the characters were 'scruffy'. I am not quite sure what you mean by this. Sam is not a presenter in the formal 'teacher' sense – he is simply the hero of the story. We wanted the less privileged children in the audience to be able to identify with him. So he comes from a very ordinary home and has a semi-skilled job; his accent and appearance are appropriate to his character and background. He certainly does not have 'short back and sides',

but very few young men do at present. His hair is clean and shaped, and not excessively long. The puppet characters vary in appearance and the accent in much the same sort of way as the people one meets in real life would do. Some of the puppets are smart and speak Standard English; others do not. But they all articulate clearly, whatever their accent. You may have noticed too that as soon as Sam arrived on the island the Boffs were anxious to cure his cold, so that he could speak more clearly.[57]

Chovil's highly literary rebuttal, which draws a comparison between the writing of Rosen and Tulley to that of Carroll, might have seemed fanciful at the time of writing in 1973, but looking back over Rosen's career now, with over forty-five years of literary activity, time spent as the British Children's Laureate between 2007 and 2009, and his frequent deployment of onomatopoeia (as exemplified in his 1989 award-winning children's book *We're Going on a Bear Hunt*), the comparison now feels rather apt. When Chovil tackles the 'scruffy' comment, her response becomes uncomfortably classist: 'We wanted the less privileged children in the audience to be able to identify with him. So he comes from a very ordinary home and has a semi-skilled job; his accent and appearance are appropriate to his character and background.'[58] Such a statement suggests a rather rigid view of class structures, and also troublingly implies – given that she is writing on behalf of the BBC – that an individual's class determines their aptitude to learn. Of course, all manner of historical concessions could be made to permit Chovil's words, such as the well-worn plea 'that was just how it was then', or that her elite, Roedean School education subconsciously enculturated certain classist values at an early age that proved hard to dislodge. Thankfully, Chovil returns to a more even-handed register when defending the design of the puppets – noting how their varied appearance is a positive factor and serves to represent the many different 'people one meets in real life'.[59]

Having received these letters of complaint, the BBC also commissioned a classroom survey to gain a better understanding of how *Sam on Boffs' Island* was being received through the months January to March of 1973. Taking place in schools in Birmingham, London, Manchester, and Sussex, the survey had the following objectives:

a. To assess the effect of the teaching points in each programme (phonics); to asses clarity of story, plot, characters and speech.
b. To assess usefulness of Pupils' Pamphlet.
c. To assess value of Teacher' Notes to teacher.[60]

Across the board, the report confirms the value of *Sam on Boffs' Island* as an educational show, both capturing the responses of the teachers and also noting the impact of the phonic sequences on the students' speech competence. For example, in the report for Robertsbridge Methodist School in Sussex, the word 'lemonade' proved challenging for the children (aged between four and six years old) before watching *Sam on Boffs' Island*, while after viewing the phonic breakdown in the show the report notes: 'Small number read this right, but a stubborn group still insisted it was "island".'[61] Furthermore, in a wonderful reversal of the report's – and perhaps BBC's – unconscious bias, with the Robertsbridge Methodist School being described as being in a 'rural community in countryside of great beauty' compared to Bishop Billsburrow School in Moss Side, Manchester being described as being in 'a pretty poor and dreary area, and designated EPA', the report shows the Manchester pupils had the best aptitude (with 'ALL GOT THIS' noted next to most of the words tested) and the teachers offered the most praise of all the schools surveyed.[62]

The positive responses to *Sam on Boffs' Island* – and, by extension, the work of Smallfilms – articulated in this schools survey are important to establish in the context of this Smallfilms history. While *Bagpuss* will be covered in more detail in the next chapter, given the doubts raised about *Sam on Boffs' Island* by the two letters of complaint, and given that by mid-December 1972 the BBC had opened early contractual negotiations with Postgate and Firmin about the production of *Bagpuss*, it is possible that as part of the BBC's evaluation of *Sam on Boffs' Island* performance and reception within the classroom, there may also have been an underlying desire to access the continued appeal of Firmin and Postgate's work. The fact that five teachers from Manchester described *Sam on Boffs' Island*, a show that employed a mix of live-action and stop-frame animation, as 'the most enjoyable television programme they had seen for some time' and that the 'children all love it', would surely have dispelled any doubts the BBC might have held about the continued appeal of Smallfilms' animation.[63]

Conclusion

As has been highlighted throughout this chapter, despite Postgate articulating some reservations about the show's development in early correspondence with Chovil, for the most part he adopts a convivial and positive tone about the show's production within his written correspondence dated between 1971 and 1973. Yet, speaking in 1993 to animator Tim Jones, Postgate adopted a different tone:

> We did some work for the BBC on *Sam on Boffs' Island*, which was some animation inserts, to some other, which was tangling with committees, which I hated. All the sort of conception of what one was doing was watered down by other peoples' conceptions of they were doing, so one finished up with a sort of lowest common compromise, which had no guts to it really. So, one of the virtues of which Peter and I have when working is although we collaborate a lot in the conception originally of what is going on, he has his department and I have mine.[64]

Within these words we can see a retrospective reinforcing of the Postgateian version of Smallfilms history, with *Sam on Boffs' Island* now reframed explicitly as a small piece of contract work, which, due to the creative compromises, frustrated

Postgate. This comment, in combination with his following remarks about the happy collaborations and creative freedoms that were at the heart of his work with Firmin under the banner of Smallfilms, serves to promote the significance of the autonomy they established and enjoyed when working independently as Smallfilms. By promoting this rather rigid, editorialized view of Smallfilms history, Postgate seeks to push *Sam on Boffs' Island* to the margins of his version of Smallfilms story – an agenda that was perpetuated with the publication of his autobiography in 2000. Hopefully, this chapter has gone some way to revising – and expanding – this narrative.

Notes

1. Author's transcription from *Sam on Boffs' Island* episode 1, viewed via the British Film Institute's Special Collections.
2. I can find only Joan T. Feeley's 1976 article 'Beyond Reading with TV: British and American Approaches' that offers any critical coverage of *Sam on Boffs' Island*. The fact that *Sam on Boffs' Island*, which employs puppets and stop-motion models made by hand by Firmin and aired during 1972 and 1973, slips completely under the radar in Rachel Moseley's otherwise excellent book *Hand-made Television: Stop-Frame Animation for Children in Britain, 1961–74* (2016), highlights just how forgotten the show has become within scholarly circles.
3. Postgate, *Seeing Things*, p. 294.
4. At the time of this book's publication, even the chronology presented on www.smallfilms.co.uk, a site created with the best intentions and with the permission of both Postgate and Firmin during their lifetime, omits *Sam on Boffs' Island*.
5. Correspondence from Claire Chovil to Senior Assistant (Sequences), Purchased Programmes Department, 6 March 1972, p. 2, File T69/54/1, 'Words and Pictures – Sam on Boff's Island', BBC Written Archives Centre (WAC), Reading, UK.
6. Broadcast times taken from BBC Genome and from evidence captured in the survey data about co-viewing habits.
7. Rerun schedule taken from BBC Genome.
8. A low-quality conversion of the first *Sam on Boffs' Island* episode can be found on YouTube (Jazz Whyman, 'Sam on Boffs' Island - BBC, 1972', YouTube, 20 September 2015, https://www.youtube.com/watch?v=6gKOv0fJYCY [accessed 5 November 2021]), but this provides only a small snapshot of the series as a whole.
9. Chris Pallant, *Smallfilms: Audiences – data set*.
10. Correspondence from Oliver Postgate to Claire Chovil, 31 November 1971, File T69/54/1, 'Words and Pictures – Sam on Boff's Island', BBC WAC.
11. Correspondence from Oliver Postgate to Claire Chovil, 31 November 1971, File T69/54/1, 'Words and Pictures – Sam on Boff's Island', BBC WAC.
12. 'Telegraph Announcements – Deaths: Chovil', *Telegraph Online* February 2008, http://announcements.telegraph.co.uk/deaths/73301/chovil (accessed 1 November 2021).
13. Tony Robinson, interviewed by Chris Pallant, telephone call, 13 May 2019.
14. Miriam Margolyes, interviewed by Chris Pallant, video call, 6 July 2019.
15. Charles Collingwood, *Brian and Me: Life on – and Off – the Archers* (London: Michael O'Mara Books, 2009), p. 113.

16. Correspondence from Claire Chovil to Senior Assistant (Sequences), Purchased Programmes Department, 6 March 1972, pp. 1–2, File T69/54/1, 'Words and Pictures – Sam on Boff's Island', BBC WAC.
17. Correspondence from Claire Chovil to Senior Assistant (Sequences), Purchased Programmes Department, 6 March 1972, p. 1, File T69/54/1, 'Words and Pictures – Sam on Boff's Island', BBC WAC.
18. Correspondence from Claire Chovil to Senior Assistant (Sequences), Purchased Programmes Department, 6 March 1972, p. 1, File T69/54/1, 'Words and Pictures – Sam on Boff's Island', BBC WAC.
19. Correspondence from Claire Chovil to Senior Assistant (Sequences), Purchased Programmes Department, 6 March 1972, p. 2, File T69/54/1, 'Words and Pictures – Sam on Boff's Island', BBC WAC.
20. Correspondence from Claire Chovil to Oliver Postgate, 8 December 1971, File T69/54/1, 'Words and Pictures – Sam on Boff's Island', BBC WAC.
21. Correspondence from Claire Chovil to Oliver Postgate, 22 December 1971, File T69/54/1, 'Words and Pictures – Sam on Boff's Island', BBC WAC.
22. Correspondence from Claire Chovil to Oliver Postgate, 22 December 1971, File T69/54/1, 'Words and Pictures – Sam on Boff's Island', BBC WAC.
23. Correspondence from Oliver Postgate to Claire Chovil, 12 January 1971, File T69/54/1, 'Words and Pictures – Sam on Boff's Island', BBC WAC.
24. Correspondence from Oliver Postgate to Claire Chovil, 12 January 1971, File T69/54/1, 'Words and Pictures – Sam on Boff's Island', BBC WAC.
25. Correspondence from Oliver Postgate to Claire Chovil, 12 January 1971, File T69/54/1, 'Words and Pictures – Sam on Boff's Island', BBC WAC.
26. Correspondence from Oliver Postgate to Claire Chovil, 12 January 1971, File T69/54/1, 'Words and Pictures – Sam on Boff's Island', BBC WAC.
27. Broadcast for Schools, 'Words and Pictures: *Sam on Boffs' Island*', 26 July 2011, http://www.broadcastforschools.co.uk/site/Words_and_Pictures/Sam_on_Boffs%27_Island (accessed 5 November 2021).
28. Shot List – Words and Pictures: *Sam on Boffs' Island*, 13 June 1972, p. 1, File T69/54/1, 'Words and Pictures – Sam on Boff's Island', BBC WAC; the acronym 'oov' is used throughout the shot list to denote 'out of vision' narration or commentary that will be combined with the on-screen imagery either via live delivery or post-production editing.
29. Shot List – Words and Pictures: *Sam on Boffs' Island*, 13 June 1972, pp. 66–68, File T69/54/1, 'Words and Pictures – Sam on Boff's Island', BBC WAC.
30. Correspondence from Peter Firmin to Claire Chovil, no date, File T69/54/1, 'Words and Pictures – Sam on Boff's Island', BBC WAC.
31. Miriam Margolyes, interviewed by Chris Pallant, video call, 6 July 2019.
32. Correspondence from Oliver Postgate to Claire Chovil, 10 June 1972, p. 1, File T69/54/1, 'Words and Pictures – Sam on Boff's Island', BBC WAC.
33. Miriam Margolyes, interviewed by Chris Pallant, video call, 6 July 2019.
34. Correspondence from Oliver Postgate to Claire Chovil, 12 January 1971, File T69/54/1, 'Words and Pictures – Sam on Boff's Island', BBC WAC.
35. Miriam Margolyes, interviewed by Chris Pallant, video call, 6 July 2020.
36. Correspondence from Claire Chovil to Oliver Postgate, *c.* 3–10 July 1972, p. 1, File T69/54/1, 'Words and Pictures – Sam on Boff's Island', BBC WAC.
37. John Tully and Michael Rosen, *Sam on Boffs' Island Annual* (London: Polystyle Publications, 1974).

38. Shot List – Words and Pictures: *Sam on Boffs' Island*, 13 June 1972, pp. 12–13, File T69/54/1, 'Words and Pictures – Sam on Boff's Island', BBC WAC.
39. Author's transcription from *Sam on Boffs' Island* episode 12, viewed via the British Film Institute's Special Collections.
40. Author's transcription from *Sam on Boffs' Island* episode 13, viewed via the British Film Institute's Special Collections.
41. Correspondence from Oliver Postgate to Claire Chovil, 24 August 1972, File T69/54/1, 'Words and Pictures – Sam on Boff's Island', BBC WAC.
42. Author's transcription from *Sam on Boffs' Island* episode 18, viewed via the British Film Institute's Special Collections.
43. Author's transcription from *Sam on Boffs' Island* episode 18, viewed via the British Film Institute's Special Collections.
44. Shot List – Words and Pictures: *Sam on Boffs' Island*, 13 June 1972, p. 3, File T69/54/1, 'Words and Pictures – Sam on Boff's Island', BBC WAC. It is unclear what 'ssf' means, but it is possible that is either a typo or an acronym used within the production to denote 'Sam's Shaving Foam'.
45. Author's transcription from *Sam on Boffs' Island* episode 20, viewed via the British Film Institute's Special Collections.
46. Correspondence from Oliver Postgate to Claire Chovil, no date, p. 2, File T69/54/1, 'Words and Pictures – Sam on Boff's Island', BBC WAC.
47. Correspondence from Oliver Postgate to Claire Chovil, no date, p. 2, File T69/54/1, 'Words and Pictures – Sam on Boff's Island', BBC WAC.
48. Correspondence from Claire Chovil to Oliver Postgate, 13 November 1973, File T69/54/1, 'Words and Pictures – Sam on Boff's Island', BBC WAC.
49. Correspondence from Occold Primary School to Head of Schools Broadcasting Programmes BBC, 15 January 1973, p. 1, File T69/54/1, 'Words and Pictures – Sam on Boff's Island', BBC WAC.
50. Correspondence from Occold Primary School to Head of Schools Broadcasting Programmes BBC, 15 January 1973, p. 2, File T69/54/1, 'Words and Pictures – Sam on Boff's Island', BBC WAC.
51. Correspondence from Occold Primary School to Head of Schools Broadcasting Programmes BBC, 15 January 1973, p. 2, File T69/54/1, 'Words and Pictures – Sam on Boff's Island', BBC WAC.
52. Correspondence from Remedial Centre Sheppey to Head of School's Programmes BBC, 15 January 1973, File T69/54/1, 'Words and Pictures – Sam on Boff's Island', BBC WAC.
53. Correspondence from Remedial Centre Sheppey to Head of School's Programmes BBC, 15 January 1973, File T69/54/1, 'Words and Pictures – Sam on Boff's Island', BBC WAC.
54. All of these memos are held within File T69/54/1, 'Words and Pictures – Sam on Boff's Island', BBC WAC.
55. Correspondence from Claire Chovil to Occold Primary School, 26 January 1973, p. 1, File T69/54/1, 'Words and Pictures – Sam on Boff's Island', BBC WAC; Correspondence from Claire Chovil to Remedial Centre Sheppey, 26 January 1973, File T69/54/1, 'Words and Pictures – Sam on Boff's Island', BBC WAC.
56. Correspondence from Claire Chovil to Occold Primary School, 26 January 1973, p. 1, File T69/54/1, 'Words and Pictures – Sam on Boff's Island', BBC WAC; Correspondence from Claire Chovil to Remedial Centre Sheppey, 26 January 1973, File T69/54/1, 'Words and Pictures – Sam on Boff's Island', BBC WAC.

57 Correspondence from Claire Chovil to Occold Primary School, 26 January 1973, pp. 1–2, File T69/54/1, 'Words and Pictures – Sam on Boff's Island', BBC WAC.
58 Correspondence from Claire Chovil to Occold Primary School, 26 January 1973, p. 2, File T69/54/1, 'Words and Pictures – Sam on Boff's Island', BBC WAC.
59 Correspondence from Claire Chovil to Occold Primary School, 26 January 1973, p. 2, File T69/54/1, 'Words and Pictures – Sam on Boff's Island', BBC WAC.
60 Results of Survey on 'Words & Pictures' – 'Sam on Boffs' Island' Programme in Schools in Sussex: Birmingham: Manchester: London. Jan/Feb/Mar 1973, no date, p. 1, File T69/54/1, 'Words and Pictures – Sam on Boff's Island', BBC WAC.
61 Results of Survey on 'Words & Pictures' – 'Sam on Boffs' Island' Programme in Schools in Sussex: Birmingham: Manchester: London. Jan/Feb/Mar 1973, no date, p. 2, File T69/54/1, 'Words and Pictures – Sam on Boff's Island', BBC WAC.
62 Results of Survey on 'Words & Pictures' – 'Sam on Boffs' Island' Programme in Schools in Sussex: Birmingham: Manchester: London. Jan/Feb/Mar 1973, no date, p. 7, File T69/54/1, 'Words and Pictures – Sam on Boff's Island', BBC WAC; EPA, standing for Educational Priority Area, was a term established by Lady (Bridget) Plowden the 1967 report for the Central Advisory Council for Education (England) entitled 'Children and their Primary Schools' – colloquially known as 'The Plowden Report'. The report put forward the argument that a practice of positive discrimination should be adopted to help enhance the prospects of students studying in areas of social and economic deprivation (pp. 57–60).
63 Results of Survey on 'Words & Pictures' – 'Sam on Boffs' Island' Programme in Schools in Sussex: Birmingham: Manchester: London. Jan/Feb/Mar 1973, no date, p. 8, File T69/54/1, 'Words and Pictures – Sam on Boff's Island', BBC WAC.
64 Oliver Postgate, interviewed by Tim Jones, Canterbury, UK, 14 July 1993.

Chapter 8

CREATIVE COLLABORATION AND THE BRICOLAGE OF *BAGPUSS* (1974)

We will find it.
We will bind it.
We will stick it with glue, glue, glue.
We will stick'll it, every little bit of it.
We will make it like new, new, new.

—Mouse refrain[1]

As the opening chords of the *Bagpuss* (1974) title theme ring out, we see a young lady standing alone in an opulent room surrounded by antique furniture. This is not Emily of Bagpuss & Co., but rather Lady Diana Spencer (Emma Corrin) as portrayed in *The Crown* (Netflix, 2016–present). After the sequence cuts to the TV screen, showing the *Bagpuss* title, we then see a melancholic Spencer distractedly watching the show (Figures 8.1 and 8.2).

As well as serving as a point of historical orientation, the brief glimpses of *Bagpuss* that feature in the episode 'Fairytale' (season 4, episode 3, available

Figure 8.1 The ongoing cultural capital of *Bagpuss* as seen in *The Crown* (2016–present).

Figure 8.2 Lady Diana Spencer (Emma Corrin) escapes into the realm of *Bagpuss* as seen in *The Crown* (2016–present).

15 November 2020) function suggestively, with audiences possessing knowledge of the 'saggy, old cloth cat' and his imagined world full of broken objects in need or fixing, being invited to draw parallels with Spencer's own plight at this point in the series narrative. With the young Spencer perhaps yearning for some magical force to enter her own life to fix the many internal fractures concealed by the public fairy-tale narrative of her impending royal wedding.

Despite Smallfilms securing international distribution for some of their productions, Postgate and Firmin's works only achieved lasting renown in the UK. In the case of their colourful, mixed-media animation series *Bagpuss*, the online fact-finding by international audiences of *The Crown*, desperate to learn more about this 'completely unknown' show, offers anecdotal proof of this dynamic.[2] Furthermore, a Google search of popularity polls that either have an international focus or were conducted by publications based outside of the UK, such as, but not limited to, *The New York Times*, *IndieWire.com*, and *Vulture.com*, reveals the complete absence of any Smallfilms production, thereby providing further evidence of the lack of lasting appeal (or even awareness) of Smallfilms' work on the global stage.

However, within a UK context, the works of Smallfilms enjoy lasting recognition and celebration – none more so than *Bagpuss*. As Rachel Moseley notes, 'the BBC Audience Reports between 1954 and 1976 repeatedly show the popularity of puppet programmes, as well as children citing stop-motion animations from *Camberwick Green* [1966] to *The Herbs* [1968] and *Bagpuss* as favourite children's programmes.'[3] Then, some years later, when the BBC conducted a poll to find the nation's favourite children's show, as part of their New Year's Day TV Special 'Are You Sitting Comfortably?' (BBC1, 1 January 1999), over 40,000 people participated and *Bagpuss* proved the eventual winner.[4] While the poll of 1999 limited respondents to selecting shows that had aired on the BBC, a Channel 4 poll of 2001 adopted a wider perspective, by asking viewers to vote for their favourite children's television programme of all time across all channels. *Bagpuss* finished fourth in this poll, beaten only by *The Simpsons* (1990–present) in first place, *The Muppet Show* (1976–81) in second, and *Dangermouse* (1981–7) in third.[5] To add a little more context to this achievement, *Bagpuss* finished above several hugely popular and long-running shows, such as *Grange Hill* (1978–2008), *Scooby Doo* (1969–91), and *Dr Who* (1963–present). In 2008, to mark the launch of a new CBeebies magazine, the BBC asked viewers to vote for their favourite children's TV animal of all time, with *Bagpuss* once again taking the number one spot. In 2014, *Radio Times* teamed up with the British Film Institute to conduct a poll (receiving over 40,000 votes) that sought to establish a new top 50 of 'the nation's best-loved BBC children's characters'.[6] Although *Bagpuss* didn't rank in the top three characters overall, *Bagpuss* did rank third in the 1970s subcategory, which, given that this poll was conducted forty years after the show was first broadcast, demonstrates the lasting appeal of this particular Smallfilms production.[7] The combination of the BBC's own internal audience research with these popular rankings provides a good indication of the sustained popularity enjoyed by *Bagpuss* within the UK.

Beyond the visible markers of popularity, such as these TV polls, or the fact that *Bagpuss* (along with *Ivor the Engine*) was selected for inclusion in a special edition print run of children's TV stamps by the Royal Mail in 2014,[8] or the thousands of items of Bagpuss-themed merchandise that continue to be produced (such as hot water bottle covers, pyjama sets, cushions, mugs, and, of course, soft toys), *Bagpuss* also ranked as the most popular Smallfilms production in the survey conducted for this book, with 43 per cent of respondents selecting it as their favourite – putting *Bagpuss* quite some distance ahead of *Clangers* (1969–74), which was rated the second most popular Smallfilms show by respondents with a selection rate of 24 per cent.

Why then has *Bagpuss* proven so popular over such a long period of time? The answer to the question is, of course, a combination of many factors: whimsical-authenticity, tightly structured standalone narratives, a variety of animation styles, iconic characters, and offering the most developed soundscape of any Smallfilms production. This layered textuality, the bricolage of *Bagpuss*, if you will, is rooted in the deeply collaborative working arrangement that underpinned the show's production. 'Bricolage' is a freighted, if not overdetermined, term. Popularized by Claude Lévi-Strauss, the term is now used widely across disciplines with varying degrees of connotative meaning.[9] My intended use of 'bricolage' here is relatively straightforward, building on the view that bricolage refers to 'the construction or creation of an artwork from any materials that come to hand'.[10] Augmenting this perspective, the views of Christopher Johnson offer a useful expansion of this starting point, as Johnson suggests that not only is bricolage the 'creation from a diverse range of materials or sources' but also it could be argued 'that it is bricolage which thinks, or operates, through the bricoleur, rather than the reverse'.[11] This final point clearly evokes Richard Dawkins's influential writing on the meme.[12] Here, bricolage is used to describe the particular material and conceptual construction of Smallfilms' many works, and in particular *Bagpuss*, whereby Postgate and Firmin persistently – and instrumentally – draw upon a range of artists (that were already 'to hand'), thereby giving their productions a rich mixed-media aesthetic.

While creative collaboration was a mainstay of the Smallfilms oeuvre, the desire to draw upon additional expertise, both from within the domestic realm and from individuals external to the Firmin and Postgate families, reached its peak during the production of *Bagpuss*. Therefore, the overarching thematic focus of this chapter is collaboration. Pushing beyond the received Postgate–Firmin creative dyad, this chapter sets out to achieve three things: to provide a detailed account of *Bagpuss*' conception, to expand the picture of *Bagpuss*' visual production, and in doing so establishing in greater detail the contributions of Linda Birch, Joan Firmin, and Charlotte Firmin, and to consider the ways that Sandra Kerr and John Faulkner's songwriting played an active role in helping to shape Postgate's own writing.

Conceiving the cat

As might be expected, given the lasting popularity of the show, certain details concerning the inception and creation of *Bagpuss* have circulated widely via print publications such as Postgate's autobiography and Jonny Trunk and Richard Embray's *The Art of Smallfilms*, and also through the frequently rehearsed anecdotes recounted, over the years, by Firmin and Postgate at various public events, and, at the time of writing, Wikipedia. The first of these popular *Bagpuss* origin stories centres around the cat's iconic pink and white fur. Having started work on *Bagpuss* in late 1972, Firmin was initially unable to find suitably soft stripey material, so he turned to Dunbar Fabrics of Folkestone to produce some. Firmin, addressing the London Animation Club in 2013, recalls how he asked for 'big marmalade cat material with big, inch-and-half wide stripes'.[13] Things didn't go according to plan, and a very apologetic employee of Dunbar Fabrics, a Mr Beaugia, was forced to present the faulty fur to Firmin, who offers the following account of this exchange:

> 'I'm terribly sorry, there has been a bit of a mistake and we did try to get this orange, but I'm afraid it has turned out pink.' And he brought four-square of furry material with pink and cream stripes, so I thought, you know, this is meant to be, because I would never have thought of that myself.[14]

Embellishing upon the standard format of this anecdote for his London Animation Club audience, Firmin noted how the same Mr Beaugia had recently re-established contact, claiming the rights to *Bagpuss*, 'because it was his mistake that led to the pink stripes'.[15]

In another of these frequently repeated anecdotes, Postgate tells the story of Professor Bogwood's evolution into Professor Yaffle. Writing in his autobiography, he describes Bogwood's demeanour as 'dark' and 'shadowy', and acknowledges how both Firmin and the BBC shared his own concerns about this initial characterization:

> We weren't sure we cared for him. Nor was the BBC, mainly because he was a human-type character. Also he had no sense of humour and wasn't a bit ridiculous. But all the same I still liked the idea of a distinguished academic personage who could claim to know everything; one who was dry and thinly-voiced and would go 'Nerp, nerp, nerp,' in a birdy way.[16]

This account is repeated verbatim in Trunk and Embray's *The Art of Smallfilms*, where it is also accompanied by a side-by-side comparison of the early (rejected) design of Bogwood and the approved design of Yaffle.[17] While the bespectacled Bogwood had a rather beaky nose, there is little else in his design to indicate the direction that Firmin would go when reimagining the character as Yaffle. Postgate concludes: 'I saw him as being a mixture of Professor Bertrand Russell and my uncle G.D.H. Cole. That was it! A bookish bird, a bird bookend, a wooden woodpecker called, naturally, Professor Yaffle.'[18] With the concept agreed, Firmin redesigned and carved the intricately detailed Yaffle that we know today.

The third of these popular origin stories concerns Gabriel the toad. Recalling how they frequently 'pinched from somewhere else', Firmin tells how 'Gabriel was a toad, a real toad' encountered – and befriended – when he and Joan lived in Twickenham.[19] Occupying a basement flat on the banks of the River Thames, Firmin recalls how the toad came to live in their garden, and how they came to name him: 'I said "he looks like Walter Gabriel from the Archers, or what I imagined Walter Gabriel would look like", so we called him Gabriel.'[20] This toad became the inspiration for a puppet for one of Firmin's animated nursery rhymes, which were screened as part of the *Musical Box* series: 'I made a little Gabriel puppet that sat and played banjo, and Wally [Whyton] would sing the song and we'd speed it up [the puppetry – to match the sync]. So that was his [Gabriel's] first appearance on television.'[21] Naturally, when the idea of having a toad character be part of the *Bagpuss* ensemble occurred, Firmin's mind returned to his *Musical Box* creation. Working from the same basic design, Firmin made a larger version for *Bagpuss*, noting:

> He was a bit bigger, but he's still worked from under with levers and string and things, and he's the only thing in the *Bagpuss* films that is actually recorded live, because animating songs single frame is quite tricky. So, Oliver played the tape and I animated [manipulated] him live to the tape, and then it was inserted into the film – so there is a slightly different feel to that bit of animation.[22]

Again, as with the preceding anecdotes, emphasis is placed on an inward-facing creative process, by which I mean the collaborative problem-solving and invention of Postgate and Firmin giving shape to the world we see on-screen.

After noting how 'all the other characters fell into place very easily, the mice and the cat – cats and mice, obviously, they live together in enmity always – and the shop window, and the things coming in that needed mending',[23] Postgate adds an additional layer to this inward-facing account of *Bagpuss*' genesis, remarking:

> Of course, *Bagpuss* had a whole series, and he had to have a new idea for each programme, and this was the proposition, which did make life easier, in the sense that the page was not totally blank, since we started with a thing to bring in. [...] Peter would come up and give me something, and somewhere in the toy box was this raffia elephant, and I thought 'that's got a history', and it was in a terrible state, so I kept that in mind, and there was the ship in the bottle, that's got a story too, so it was rather like giving the children their first essay to do, like to come up with a story of a shilling.[24]

In this account, we can clearly see Postgate's desire to recognize the equal contributions of Firmin to the creative process, ultimately offering this striking metaphor: 'A lot of this stuff doesn't come from me, it came from Peter originally. He threw down the bone and we chewed it.'[25]

Despite Postgate acknowledging the contributions of others in his autobiography, for example, mentioning how Sandra Kerr and John Faulkner both influenced the sound of *Bagpuss*, it is the anecdotes recounted above that have circulated with the greatest durability. On the one hand, these anecdotes serve to reinforce values often associated with the works of Smallfilms, such as: local production (sourcing materials from Folkestone and finding inspiration in the garden), handmade craft (working with faux fur, creating bespoke mechanisms, and carving wood), whimsical characterization (Yaffle), and finding inspiration in everyday objects (the broken 'things' that give purpose and structure to the world of *Bagpuss*). On the other hand, these anecdotes promote a rather closed, inward-facing impression of the creative environment within which *Bagpuss* was formed, which does not tally with the more collaborative arrangement hinted at in Postgate's autobiography and recorded within the show's on-screen credits, Table 8.1 lists the individuals and contributions from the on-screen credits.

Table 8.1 The rather limited screen credits associated with *Bagpuss* (1974).

Name	Episodes	Screen Credit
Sandra Kerr	All	'Told by' and 'Music by'
John Faulkner	All	'Told by' and 'Music by'
Babette Cole	(9) 'The Giant'	'Pictures'
	(11) 'The Fiddle'	
	(12) 'Flying'	
Linda Birch	(1) 'Ship in a Bottle'	'Pictures'
	(5) 'The Hamish'	
Charlotte Firmin	(3) 'The Frog Princess'	'Pictures'
	(13) 'Uncle Feedle'	
Joan Firmin	(2) 'The Owl of Athens'	'Pictures'

8. Creative Collaboration and the Bricolage of Bagpuss

What follows then is an attempt to expand the received *Bagpuss* production narrative by moving beyond the popular anecdotes and these ambiguous – and unreliable – screen credits, to establish in more detail the contributions of those identified in Table 8.1.

The layered realm of Bagpuss

Returning to the theme of bricolage, if we are to better recognize the numerous individual contributions to the collective project that was the making of *Bagpuss*, we must inspect more closely the individual layers that gave the show its mixed-media quality. In this regard, Rachel Moseley has already made headway, drawing on the work of Helen Bromley to help outline the multilayered nature of *Bagpuss*. In Bromley's view, '*Bagpuss* might be described as the original multi-modal text', given its combination of 'cartoon animation, puppetry and film' that affords viewers 'a multiplicity of points of access'.[26] While Moseley writes primarily of the textual experience of *Bagpuss* as a television series with a multilayered aesthetic, she also hints at the importance of the collaborative practices employed during the show's production, noting how 'Peter chose different styles and artists to give variety.' Building upon Moseley's initial work, and informed by fresh insights gleaned during the researching of this book, we will now look more closely at the contributions of Birch, Charlotte Firmin, and Joan Firmin.[27]

Ship in a bottle

Birch started working with Smallfilms in 1969, after impressing Firmin with the strength of her portfolio. Initially, Birch was employed to provide illustrations for the *Pogles' Wood* annuals, but she quickly proved herself and became a regular Smallfilms collaborator. Notably, Birch also worked on *Clangers*, designing and fabricating the iconic spaceman that made several appearances throughout the series, before she commenced work on *Bagpuss*.[28] Working nine-to-five in the studio alongside Peter Firmin, Birch recalls how Joan Firmin kept things ticking over with frequent rounds of hot tea and coffee, as well as bringing freshly prepared meals. As noted throughout this book, and later in this chapter, Joan Firmin also made significant contributions to the creative labour of Smallfilms, a point that Birch reinforces: 'Joan is a real unsung heroine, because Joan made a lot of costumes and she's never given the right credit.'[29]

Reflecting on her own place within the Smallfilms team, Birch notes how both Firmin and Postgate conducted themselves in a humble manner, creating an environment that encouraged collaboration. Working more with Firmin than Postgate, Birch remarks how their day-to-day interaction hinged on relaxed work-related conversations:

> I didn't see Oliver that much at all, actually. I mean he would pop over, but not specifically to see me, it would be the technical side of things with Peter.

> So, it was mainly Peter that I worked with, and he didn't prescribe. He'd say: 'I want you to do a story about tigers, so bring me some ideas of what you're thinking', and mostly he approved. I don't think he criticized anything. He wasn't prescriptive in that way, he enabled me to keep my own style.[30]

This style to which Birch refers evolved over the course of several Smallfilms productions, with her preference for gouache and ink giving way to line and wash watercolour by the time she worked on *Bagpuss*. Birch goes on to explain the advantage of using the line and wash technique:

> If you were shooting for camera you did it all on quite large boards, full Imperial size, and you had to do it in this specific way, since the camera could be tracking, or zoom outs and zoom ins, for close-ups, so it had to be quite detailed and specific. I was more watercolour then [at the time of *Bagpuss*], than I was with the earlier work. I used to use gouache and ink, but I quickly realized that gouache is quite an opaque medium and it doesn't print well, so I tended to use line and wash more after that.[31]

Put into practice, Birch's contribution and style can be seen quite clearly in the first episode of *Bagpuss* called 'Ship in a Bottle' (BBC One, 12 February 1974).

In this episode, viewers are immediately confronted with the layered aesthetic that would characterize the series as a whole, with Postgate's stop-frame model-based animation (Figure 8.3) running alongside the lyrical invention of Kerr and Faulkner's songs, punctuated from time to time by the cut-out illustrations by Firmin (Figure 8.4) and watercolour images by Birch (Figure 8.5).

As you might expect, even if you have not seen it, 'Ship in a Bottle' tells the story of how Bagpuss, Yaffle, Madelaine, Gabriel, and the mice restore the titular trinket. Structured in standard *Bagpuss* fashion, after we learn the details of the broken item, on this occasion the ship, Gabriel responds to the suggestion that the ship is much too tiny for anything to sail upon it by singing a song about two-dozen white mice who sail under the command of a duck. Gabriel's song thereby serves to encourage the group to think more imaginatively about the possibilities to hand. As Gabriel finishes singing, Yaffle quickly interjects: 'Nerp, nerp, nerp, what a silly song!' To which the mice reply: 'No, no, it's not a silly song, it's a nice song.' After Yaffle argues that the song 'doesn't even make sense', the mice, protesting that they love the song, gather around their 'Marvellous Mechanical Mouse Organ' and place a roll of sheet music into the device. This then triggers a sequence depicting the scenes as sung by Gabriel. Animated by Postgate, using cut-out illustrations created by Firmin, alongside cardboard rigs – such as the chorus line of mice – that could be manipulated in real time, this scene presents a carefully considered and clearly visible departure from the overarching narrative world of stop-frame model-based animation. The interior logic here being to create a distinction between the different layers of whimsy, which are: the fantastical realm where inanimate toys become animate; the imagined realm conjured by song; the magical realm of remedy, actively summoned by Bagpuss when thinking, which

8. *Creative Collaboration and the Bricolage of* Bagpuss 175

Figure 8.3 Professor Yaffle holds court – an example of stop-motion model-based animation in *Bagpuss* (1974).

Figure 8.4 The hand-drawn cut-out Captain Duck as seen in *Bagpuss* (1974).

Figure 8.5 Linda Birch's watercolour depiction of Captain Bagpuss as seen in *Bagpuss* (1974).

serves to fix the broken objects; and the sepia intro and outro sequences, which suggests a higher level of memory-based framing, whereby all the activities of each episode occur in the mind of the little shopkeeper, Emily (played by Emily Firmin), who's poetic incantation serves to bring Bagpuss to life at the start of each episode. Additionally, throughout the series, Yaffle functions as a proxy for our own disbelief, thereby repeatedly attempting to deflate, interrogate, or authenticate the numerous whimsical interludes that punctuate each episode. As noted above, as well as the self-contained scenes triggered by song (via Gabriel, Madelaine, or the Mouse Organ), when Bagpuss put his thinking hat on this also served to shift the narrative from a model-based to a drawn aesthetic.

Not always animated, many of these hand-drawn sequences were made up of dozens of still images, cut together to match the narration, and often giving the impression of greater dynamism by virtue of the roaming camera, which tracks, zooms, cuts, and fades between distinct areas of the same image. Taking inspiration from Postgate's script, Birch's sequence depicts, via twenty line and wash watercolour paintings, Captain Bagpuss on a seafaring adventure (Figure 8.5). With the wind failing to blow, Captain Bagpuss finds his two-masted ship rendered motionless, upon which Bagpuss reflects, as the scene cuts back to the stop-frame model realm to show his narration: 'when the wind doesn't blow, the ship doesn't go! But I was Captain Bagpuss, I knew the thing to do! I tied a pearl to the end of the string and baited it with glue, that way I caught a mermaid.'[32] With the mermaid agreeing to provide a westerly breeze in exchange for the pearl, the scenario quickly gets out of control as the breeze that was promised quickly develops into a gale, causing the ship to be wrecked. Apologizing for the mix-up, the mermaid calls her friends to help salvage the wreckage, before playing a magic song (Figure 8.6) to put the ship back together again.

Recalling the production of these images, Birch remarks: 'When I drew the mermaids I put all their anatomical features in on their chest, and Peter said, "I don't think that will get through the BBC, they're not allowed to put things on like that", which you weren't, you couldn't put nipples on, but they got through.'[33] Firmin's hesitance about the likelihood of the BBC allowing the mermaids' breasts to go uncensored, perhaps stemmed from his earlier experience of illustrating mermaids (Figure 4.1) in a similarly natural manner for *The Seal of Neptune* (1960) and *The Mermaid's Pearl* (1962), or his anticipation of editorial control being flexed by the BBC due to the early afternoon broadcast time (with *Bagpuss* immediately preceding a package of programming for schools and colleges). That Birch was proven right, and neither Firmin nor Postgate took any pre-emptive censorial action, again confirms the democratic and supportive nature of the creative and collaborative processes that underpinned Smallfilms' work at the time of *Bagpuss*' production.

'The Frog Princess' – Part 1

The layered bricolage of *Bagpuss* is taken to another level in the episode 'The Frog Princess' (BBC One, 26 February 1974), where the individual on-screen elements serve as a neat reflection of the off-screen creative contributions of Charlotte and

8. *Creative Collaboration and the Bricolage of* Bagpuss   177

Figure 8.6 Linda Birch's mermaids as seen in *Bagpuss* (1974).

Joan Firmin. The episode tells the story of some crown jewels, which, after being brought to the shop as loose pieces, provide the impetus for the standard deductive pattern of *Bagpuss* storytelling. After Yaffle completes his first inspection of the jewels, he remarks: 'bits and pieces of metal, enamelled by the look of it. I haven't the slightest idea what they are, Bagpuss, what do you think they are?'[34] To which Bagpuss responds, in speculative fashion: 'Oh, I really don't know, I think one of them looks a bit like a bird, yes, and the other one, I think it's a cat.'[35]

Looking at Figure 8.7 (which is a composite of twelve frames from this sequence), we can see the impact of Bagpuss' words, for when he says 'bird' and 'cat', the jewels move, as if in response, and adopt these forms more recognizably. Watching this sequence, it is tempting to see connections with certain Norman McLaren short animations, namely his works *Boogie-Doodle* (1941), *Blinkity Blank* (1955), and *Le Merle* (1958), which may well have been known to Firmin and Postgate when they cast around looking for inspiration for *Bagpuss*' many playful narrative diversions. The 76-second sequence in 'The Frog Princess' sees the enamelled jewels intermittently adopting and rejecting their imposed white bird and yellow cat form, and, through the process of their metamorphic movement, they also give the impression of a white dragonfly orbiting a yellow sun, a yellow snake, and a body of yellow water upon which the white bird floats. The tension that runs throughout this sequence is rooted in the question of whether the cat will catch the bird. Ultimately, the bird avoids the cat's efforts and, after a final

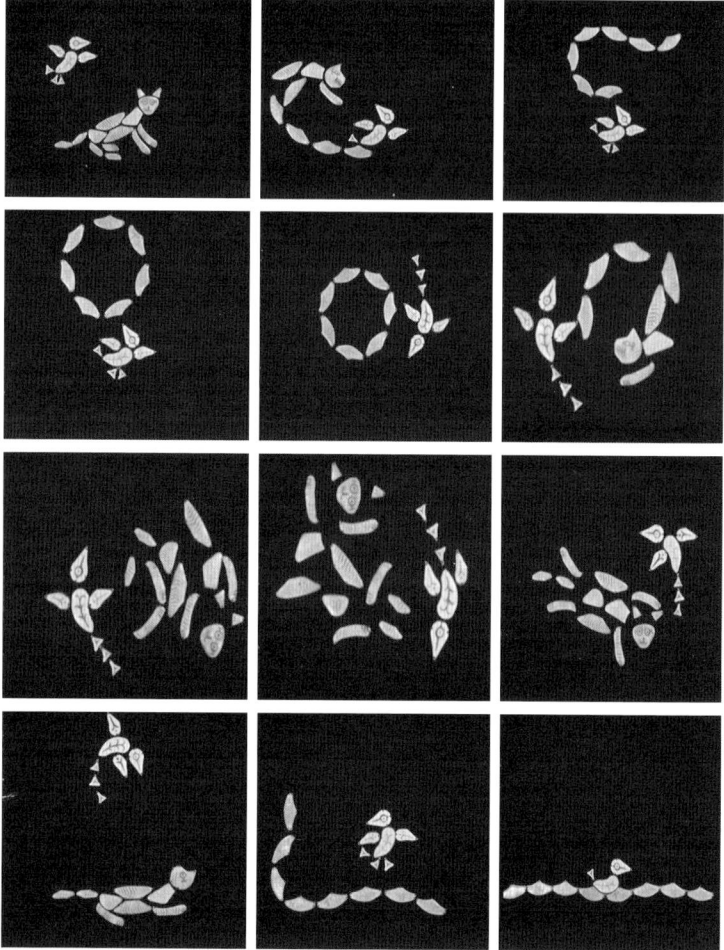

Figure 8.7 A sequence of metamorphic animation as seen in *Bagpuss* (1974).

unsuccessful pounce, the white and yellow jewels become intermingled, before falling, piece-by-piece, back onto the blue cloth that rests between Bagpuss and Yaffle.

While this sequence was animated by Postgate, it was Joan Firmin who created the enamelled jewels that Postgate worked with. Describing the creative skill of her mother, and how she found the time to juggle everything, Charlotte Firmin observes:

> She is a very creative person, and a textiles person, and by the time *Bagpuss* was being made I'd left home, and Emily, the youngest, was about nine, so everyone was at school or had left home, so she would have had more time to be creative in the day. She was always into doing evening classes, and would end up teaching them, so she was always going off and doing things, like silver smithing and

enamelling. Then after one or two of us had left home and she had more time, she was always doing stuff and making stuff, and knitting, and making rugs and cushions, so she was a very creative person and the TV bits were just other things that she did.[36]

While it might seem rather mundane to labour the point that Joan Firmin made the enamelled jewels, to move past this detail too quickly runs the risk of contributing to the elision of Joan from the Smallfilms story, and, in particular, from the production of this particular *Bagpuss* episode. With no screen credit for this episode, recognition of her contribution to this sequence is limited to a single sentence that appears in Postgate's autobiography: 'Joan also made the enamel pieces that were the jewels for the frog princess.'[37] Such limited recognition feels rather unfair, given the intricate, yet carefully minimalist detailing of the enamelwork, which helps facilitate the oscillation between concrete and abstract forms that plays out within Postgate's animation.[38]

Charlotte Firmin, who is credited on-screen, worked on *Bagpuss* while home from Art College during the summer of 1973. As well as working with textiles to create Uncle Feedle and his reversible house, Charlotte also created illustrations for *Bagpuss*. For the sequence where Madelaine sings about a Water Princess who is being forced to choose a Water Lord to marry, Charlotte created eleven watercolour paintings to provide the visual counterpoint for this mid-episode interlude. After finishing the first part of her song, Madelaine remarks: 'There you see, that was the rule: a Water Princess had to marry somebody. The trouble was she didn't like any of those proud, stupid Water Lords, she just couldn't bring herself to choose one of them.'[39] Madelaine then reveals how the Water Princess came up with a plan to avoid marrying the unappealing Water Lords, telling how the Water Princess threw her crown high up into the sky, and imposing the condition that only the Water Lord who retrieves the crown will be eligible for marriage. Consequently, the Water Lords magically turn into dragonflies to search – without success – for the crown. For this sequence, Charlotte used 'Dr Martin's concentrated watercolour', recalling how even though they were expensive, you could use just a tiny drop to achieve a very vibrant colour.[40] Seeing the finished work on-screen, it is clear that Charlotte's judgement was well founded as the concentrated watercolours served to enhance the aesthetic of this watery tale.

Unhappy with the story, Bagpuss demands to know what has happened to the crown, which prompts Gabriel to offer his account of the fairy-tale's conclusion. He tells of how a nearby frog accidently eats the crown, but then realizing his mistake returns it to the Water Princess. Inverting the usual fairy-tale trope, whereby a princess kisses a frog to turn it into a marriage-ready prince, in this retelling the frog refuses the Water Princess' advances, and instead transforms the Water Princess, by virtue of a kiss to her brow, into a frog. Gabriel finishes his froggy fairy tale by noting that they are both pleased with this new arrangement, so choose to get married and live happily ever after.

This final sequence employs cut-out animation provided by Peter Firmin. That the aesthetic detailing of Charlotte's and Peter's sequences correspond so closely, highlights the skill of Charlotte to adapt her own style to match that of her father's. It is worth noting that they both used Dr Martin's Ink, which would also have helped to link their work. Charlotte describes the dynamic of working alongside her father:

> Well, Dad worked at home, so he wasn't inaccessible, so I could pop into his studio and say 'what do you think if this one?' and I'd work with whatever feedback he gave. It was a very enjoyable arrangement. The process relied on a lot of trust. Dad just told us to do things and we'd do it, and he'd criticize, and we'd take the criticism – so it was great training for art school.[41]

By drawing upon the expertise surrounding him, namely that of Joan and Charlotte, as well as employing external artists, such as Birch and Cole, Peter Firmin ensured that *Bagpuss* offered viewers a rich and varied on-screen aesthetic. Beyond the flexible, collaborative arrangements that supported the show's visual development, we now turn our attention to the work of Kerr and Faulkner, whose songwriting shaped not just the sound of *Bagpuss* but also the narrative work of Postgate.

We will fix it: Scoring Bagpuss

Arguably, it is the soundscape of *Bagpuss* that has contributed most of all to the show's lasting renown. As noted in this book's introductory chapter, memory is malleable and it is possible that both individual memories and collective memories of *Bagpuss*, recalled – and reconstructed – over time, have served to amplify the significance of *Bagpuss*' sound. As Sandra Garrido and Jane W. Davidson note, music has the potential to shape our 'inner world' – our memories – in powerful ways:

> Since music can be extremely emotionally evocative, key life events can be emotionally heightened by the presence of music, ensuring that memories of the event become deeply encoded. Retrieval of those memories is then enhanced by contextual effects, in which a recreation of a similar context to that in which the memories were encoded can facilitate its retrieval. Thus, re-hearing the same music associated with the event can activate intensely vivid memories of the event. Memory is therefore closely intertwined with how our musical preferences develop and the personal significance that music holds in our individual lives.[42]

As the survey data highlights, the lasting appeal of *Bagpuss* is closely linked to its acoustic appeal, with both 'music' and 'songs' amongst the top ten words most frequently used by respondents identifying *Bagpuss* as their favourite Smallfilms production. Whether these responses reveal individual preference, collectively constructed values, or a bit of both is beyond the scope of this book, but what is clear is that the sound of *Bagpuss* deserves greater attention.

Having worked closely with Vernon Elliott and his ensemble from *Ivor the Engine* through to *Clangers*, Firmin and Postgate turned to Kerr and Faulkner after hearing their music in *Sam on Boffs' Island* and realizing that their wide-ranging folk repertoire would be perfectly matched to the bricolage world of *Bagpuss*. Kerr recalls how working for Smallfilms, namely with Postgate, immediately settled into a lively and collaborative rhythm: 'It was an interesting period before we started recording and coming up with ideas for songs and adapting songs and suggesting instrumentals and so on.'[43] By embedding the co-design of the show's sound more deeply within the pre-production process, Postgate opened up a creative space that has yet to be adequately considered.

Kerr gives a clear sense of this collaborative arrangement, it is worth quoting from Kerr at length:

> By the time that John and I came on the scene, I don't think Oliver had really any idea what the music was going to be like, or the extent to which it was going to contribute to the overall package, as it were. So, for instance, when John and I turned up at Red Lion House with dozens of instruments and lots of enthusiasm and ideas, not because we were exceptionally overwhelmed by the whole idea [of *Bagpuss*], I think we weren't actually, I don't think we knew much about children's television, at the time we didn't have children of our own, we were rather earnest messianic folkies, with, however, a lot of experience and very large repertoires of traditional songs and instrumental tunes, and some fairly useful skills musically and vocally. So, I don't think when we went into it that either Oliver or us had any idea about the magnitude of what we were going to be involved in, both in terms of its longevity and effect over the generations, and the way that it's been loved so much over generation, but also I'm convinced that once we started playing and singing to Oliver and he began – and this is his vision, creativity, and his imagination – I think Oliver began to see the potential for what we could bring to the films. I'm not convinced, because he hadn't cast any actors for Madelaine and Gabriel at that point, I'm not convinced that they were going to be doing much as far as their characters were concerned, vocally I mean, but I'm convinced that once he saw what we could contribute that he then bumped up their characters and the nature of what they could contribute musically – such as the mouse rounds, the songs, and the banjo playing.[44]

Kerr concludes: 'There was a freedom, there was no side to Oliver which was like "I am the great writer, and thou shalt not mess with my material", quite the reverse. He gobbled up suggestions that we made and adaptations that we suggested.'[45] What is clear from Kerr's words is that Postgate created a democratic collaborative space, where improvisation was encouraged, and early narrative ideas were flexed and refined.

To fully appreciate the influence of Kerr and Faulkner, we must turn our attention to the written materials that survive from the show's original production. Given the scholarly activity that has taken place within Screenwriting Studies in recent years, it is worth taking a moment to establish several useful ideas that will help to shape our reading of the *Bagpuss* production dynamic. First, we return to Ian W. Macdonald's pivotal concept of the 'screen idea', discussed in the Introduction of this book, which helped to move Screenwriting Studies beyond the tensions of textual and material specificity. Macdonald writes:

> The screen idea exists in the minds of all those involved in its production (screenwriter, producer, director and others), though of course it can never be exactly the same idea and it will never be complete. It can, however, be discussed in terms common to the shared understandings of this group; and these may emanate from the beliefs, the practices and conventions of those producing the film, and from the habitus and dispositions of those who discuss it. The screen idea can be recorded, formally or informally, though it need not be; and, as filmmaking is a dynamic process, the screen idea undergoes change throughout this process. The screenplay is one record of the shared screen idea, re-drafted in stages as the collaboration proceeds, a location for, and partial description of that shared idea, representing a framework within which others will work. As a concept whose essence is impossible to describe in toto, the screen idea exists only as the focus, at a given moment, of a dynamic and collectivized thought process.[46]

By promoting a more inclusive and fluid vision of the production process, which situates screenwriting as an activity within the progression of a screen idea, Macdonald's work brings together both the common objective of developing a story and the many diverse approaches to screen-based storytelling that exist in the world. Looking back at the many varied pre-production documents produced by Postgate and Firmin, as well as the project-specific formatting employed by Postgate when engaged in the act of scriptwriting, the inclusivity of the screen idea proves especially useful.

In a narrower sense, when thinking about the written screenplay document itself, which remains an important object of study within the broader framework of the screen idea, as both Steven Price and Paul Wells have highlighted, it is impossible to define a singular, conventional style.[47] While the master scene format has achieved popular currency within the screen industries over the past hundred years, there are many productions that necessitate a different presentational format, and there are just as many individuals working on screen projects who have developed their own idiosyncratic approaches to scriptwriting. Here, Postgate's work (see Appendix B) provides a good example of how such idiosyncrasies can pull the formatting of a screenplay in non-standard directions.

Macdonald's screen idea, when coupled with Rosamund Davies's writing on the palimpsestic nature of screen idea development, provides an ideal framework with which to interpret the surviving *Bagpuss* screenplays. Davies, discussing the process of adaptation in the broadest sense, describes the activity as a 'layered process of reading, rewriting, and reinscribing', before calling attention to the fact that the 'material deposits' of the archive, such as screenplays, should not be viewed as 'an exhaustive record or mirror of this process'.[48] Furthermore, Davies is careful to highlight the importance of retaining an open mind, or even working against the grain, stating: 'Gaps and absences in the material records, for example, may point to presences rather than absences in the background creative process.'[49] As we dig deeper into the collaboration between Postgate, Kerr, and Faulkner over the pages that follow, it is helpful to keep these notions of the screen idea and the palimpsestic nature of creative ideation in mind. These foundations are important when looking at the writing of *Bagpuss*, as captured through the surviving script iterations, because we can see an approach adopted by Postgate that contains some formal constants, but which ignores master scene style. Furthermore, comparing the different drafts, we can also see how much Kerr and Faulkner contributed to the development of *Bagpuss*, with their songwriting, on occasion, establishing story details not previously imagined by Postgate.

'The Mouse Mill'

A good example of this can be seen in the script drafts for the episode 'The Mouse Mill' (BBC One, 10 April 1974), where the song writing of Kerr and Faulkner not only superseded the songwriting of Postgate but also the lyrics of Kerr and Faulkner's song also prompted editorial changes to the surrounding narrative elements, helping to improve the flow of the script overall. Noting how 'The Miller's Song' was one of Postgate's favourite pieces of music, Kerr reflects on how the song developed quite organically: 'I'm immensely proud of that tune, I don't know where it came from. Many of the melodies that we created I can trace their line, as it were, from the origins to what they became, or what inspired them. But with that I have absolutely no idea where that came from.'[50] Comparing pages from the working script (Figures 8.8 to 8.10) and the clean scrip (Figures 8.11 and 8.12), we can see how Kerr and Faulkner's song shifts the narrative focus over the course of the pages in question.

Beginning with the song, and working outwards from that, we can see how Postgate's version (in Figure 8.8), which is to be sung by Gabriel and Madelaine and is circled by hand, differs substantially from the Kerr and Faulkner version seen in Figure 8.11. Postgate's song focuses on the personal circumstances of a miller who lives alongside the River Dee, and tells of how, despite working 'from morn till night', he still finds joy in his life: 'I love my mill she is to me / Both parent child and wife / I would not change my station / With anyone in life.'[51] It is unusual to find such literal references to the real world in the works of Smallfilms, with layers of fantasy and whimsy usually serving to destabilize the concreteness of any reference to the known world. Additionally, the decision to narrow the focus of this song and to make it more about an individual (the miller), rather than the found object itself (the mill), also feels out of step with the overarching storytelling conceit that unifies *Bagpuss* as a series. Whether it was these considerations, or possibly others that we can't glean from the surviving documentation, that encouraged Postgate to jettison his song in favour of that written by Kerr and Faulkner, we will never fully know, but what we can see from the surviving documents is the impact Kerr and Faulkner had on this particular sequence.

Looking at the song in Figure 8.11, we can see that Kerr and Faulkner shifted the emphasis away from the personal circumstances of the imagined miller from Dee and placed the mill at the heart of the activity. Still conveying a sense of the toil involved with milling, they present this through the seasonal repetitions contained within the chorus structure and the multiple stages of farming, milling, and baking described through the verses, rather than via the more literal and personal

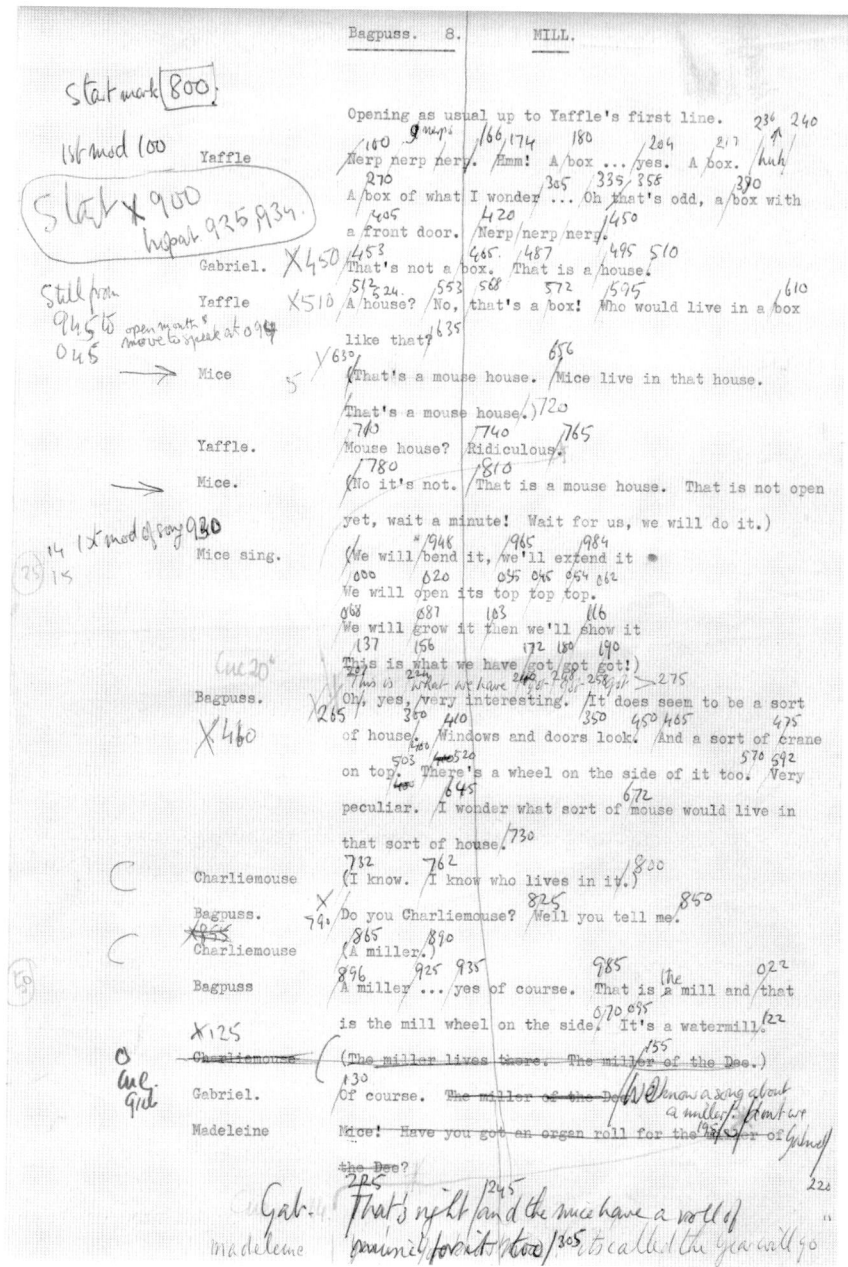

Figure 8.8 Page 1 of an early draft of a *Bagpuss* (1974) episode called 'Mill'.

8. Creative Collaboration and the Bricolage of Bagpuss

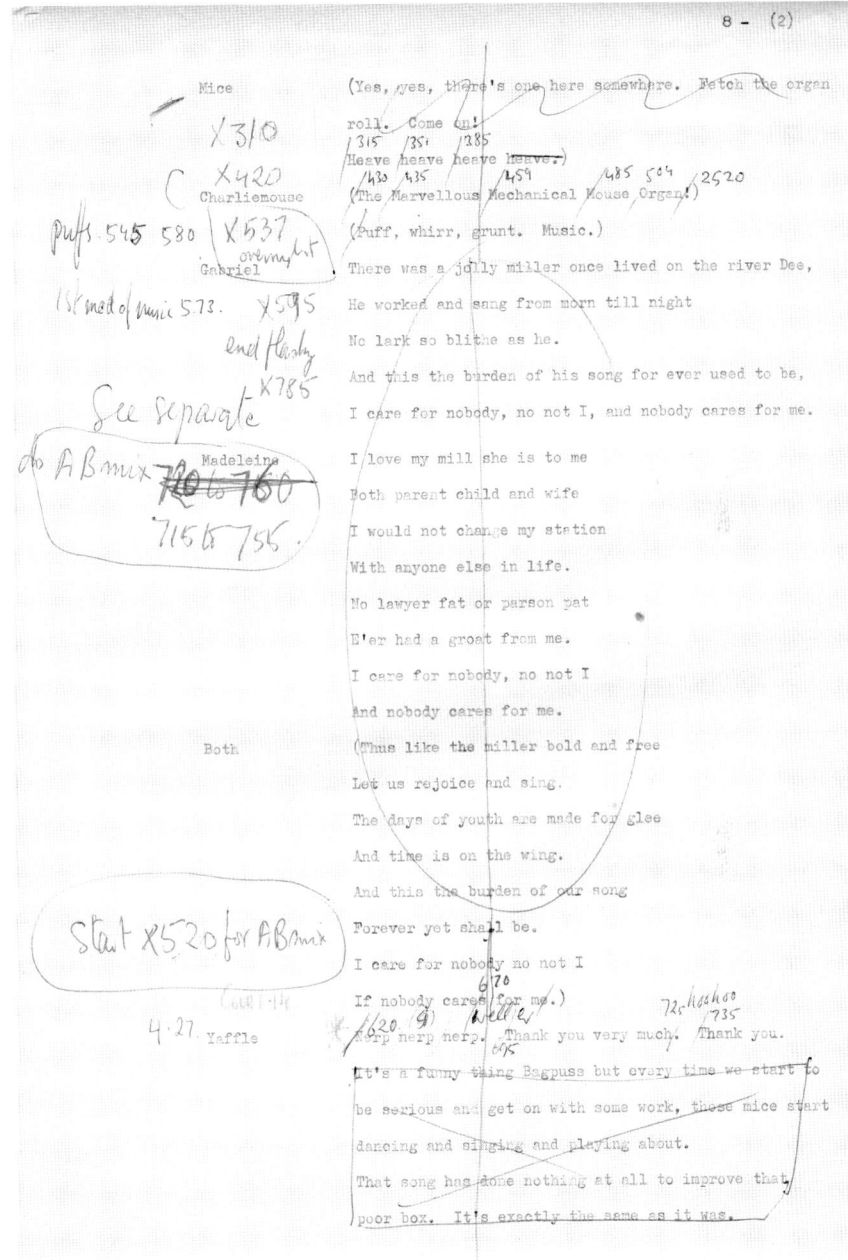

Figure 8.9 Page 2 of an early draft of a *Bagpuss* (1974) episode called 'Mill'.

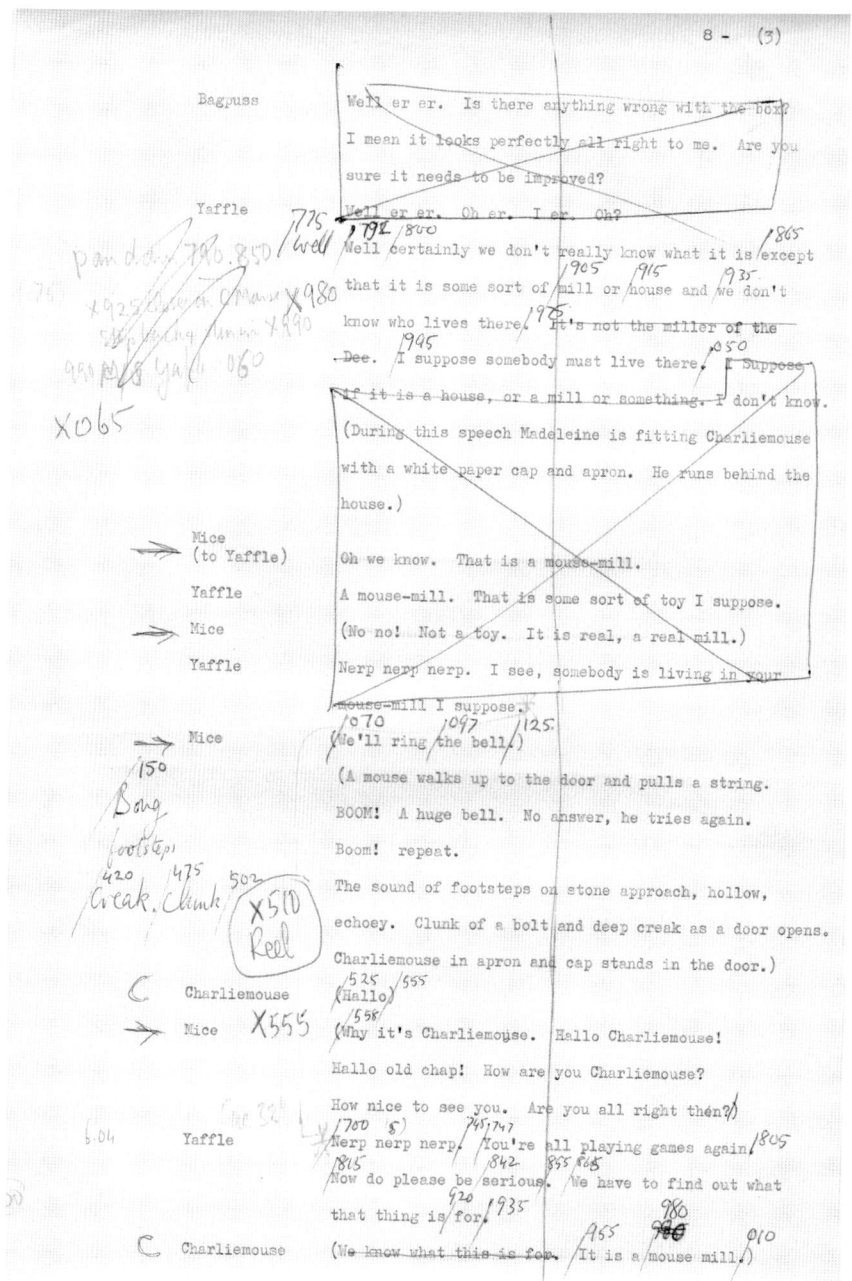

Figure 8.10 Page 3 of an early draft of a *Bagpuss* (1974) episode called 'Mill'.

3

BAGPUSS 8

The MOUSE MILL

                      Opening as usual up to YAFFLE's first line.

YAFFLE   Nerp nerp nerp. Hmm! A box ... yes. A box. A box of what I wonder ... Oh that's odd, a box with a front door. Nerp nerp nerp.

GABRIEL   That's not a box. That is a house.

YAFFLE   A house? No, that's a box! Who would live in a box like that?

MICE   That's a mouse house. Mice live in that house. That's a mouse house.

YAFFLE   Mouse house? Ridiculous.

MICE   No it's not. That is a mouse house. That is not open yet, wait a minute! Wait for us, we will do it.

MICE   (sing)
We will bend it, we'll extend it
We will open its top top top.
We will grow it then we'll show it
This is what we have got got got!

BAGPUSS   Oh, yes. very interesting. It does seem to be a sort of house. Windows and doors lock. And a sort of crane on top. There's a wheel on the side of it too. Very peculiar. I wonder what sort of mouse would live in that sort of house.

CHARLIE-MOUSE   I know. I know who lives in it.

BAGPUSS   Do you Charliemouse? Well you tell me.

C MOUSE   A miller.

BAGPUSS   A miller ... yes of course. That is a mill and that is the mill wheel on the side. It's a watermill.

MADELEINE We know a song about a miller don't we Gabriel.

GABRIEL   That's right and the mice have a roll of music for it too.

MICE   Heave heave heave.

                      The marvellous mechanical mouse organ. Music.

Figure 8.11 Page 3 of a revised, clean draft of a *Bagpuss* (1974) episode called 'The Mouse Mill'.

4

Song for BAGPUSS 8

Ploughman ploughman plough me a field
Turn me an acre of land
Ploughman ploughman harrow the ground
Drill in the seed and roll it down
For the year will turn and the spring come round
And the seed will grow.

Shine the sun and rain the rain
Fall the shivery snow
Frost and hail and wind again
As the year will go.

Farmer Farmer the field is ripe
Tall and straight they stand
Farmer Farmer it's time to reap
Time to combine the corn to keep
For the straw will blow and the chaff will leap
And the grain will flow.

Shine the sun and rain the rain
Fall the shivery snow
Fog and sleet and hail again
As the year will go.

Miller Miller take up the grain
Pour it out like sand
Miller Miller open the rill
To turn the wheel and work the mill
To grind the grain to flour and fill
The sacks below.

Shine the sun and rain the rain
Fall the shivery snow
Hail and wind and sleet again
As the year will go.

Baker Baker the flour is here
Soft and fine and bland
Baker Baker get out of bed
Put that silly old hat on your head
Bake me a loaf of golden bread
And then I'll go.

Blow the wind and rain the rain
Fall the shivery snow
Soon the sun will shine again
As the year will go.

Figure 8.12 Page 4 of a revised, clean draft of a *Bagpuss* (1974) episode called 'The Mouse Mill'.

approach adopted in Postgate's song. Following on from this song change, and embracing the broader visual possibilities established by the new lyrics, Postgate was able to adjust the dialogue of Bagpuss and Yaffle that bookends the song, to better set up the famous sequence where the mice comically demonstrate the workings of their mill. By removing the references to the miller of Dee by Gabriel and Charlie Mouse, which prompted the song in the working script (Figure 8.8), the song gains a more universal quality by virtue of not evoking a specific river originating in Snowdonia. Likewise, after the song concludes, Postgate again shifts the emphasis away from the individual grievances of Yaffle and Bagpuss, concerning the misbehaviour of the mice and the physical state of the object, instead moving more rapidly to Yaffle's confirmation of the object as a mill and the all-important question of whose mill it is. (This foregrounding of the mill paves the way for one of the most iconic and much-loved sequences from the entire Smallfilms oeuvre – our introduction to 'The Mouse Mill' which is capable of producing chocolate biscuits from just two ingredients: butter beans and breadcrumbs. This sequence interlaces themes of whimsical-authenticity, inventiveness, technology, low-angle persons, and the handmade to great effect, and I encourage readers who have not seen this episode of *Bagpuss* to watch it as soon as possible.)

The impact of Kerr and Faulkner's lyrics is also evident on-screen. Instead of a series of establishing shots of the River Dee, alongside a study of the work of one particular miller, the illustrations credited to (Peter) Firmin respond directly to the seasonal structure of the new song, depicting the sowing, reaping, milling, and baking described across the song's four verses. Collaboration such as this exists both within the material records created and kept by Firmin and Postgate, and yet also beyond these material pages, being recalled on this occasion via the memories of Kerr.

'The Frog Princess' – Part 2

Returning to the enamelled jewel sequence from 'The Frog Princess', but this time considering it from an acoustic perspective, the true collaborative nature of this sequence becomes apparent. Having already established the contribution of Joan Firmin, it is worth considering the ways that Kerr and Faulkner contributed to the sequence in question. Consulting both the working script and the clean script, we find only a four-word reference offered up to describe what would become the 76-second sequence that we see in the finished episode (Figure 8.7). Given the instrumental quality of this sequence, and the repetition of the statement 'Musical animated film sequence' in both versions of the script at the point where the sequence was to be inserted, Postgate clearly felt that nothing more was needed by way of description (since such a description was intended to serve as a note-to-self). However, this rather innocuous four-word statement conceals a hive of collaborative activity.

Rather than narrowing the production scope to just the mental notes of one individual, the statement 'Musical animated film sequence' served to expand the possibilities of this production moment. To return to Macdonald's notion of the screen idea, in this instance Postgate's pithy words take on a Schrödingerian quality, simultaneously pointing towards a confidence in his own already conceived ideas for this sequence and also his understanding that this sequence offered a perfect opportunity to experiment and improvise: representing, therefore, a moment of profound pluralistic potential. Looking at the words 'Musical animated film sequence' in this way prompts a comparison with the way that writers of classical Hollywood musicals incorporated the contributions of famed choreographer Busby Berkeley. Discussing the writing of *42nd Street* (1933), Price notes how 'Berkeley's celebrated designs operate in an autonomous fantasy realm that belongs to neither the front nor the back stage story, and requires no substantial input from writers.'[52] Consequently, Berkeley's work is 'barely anticipated' across various script versions, with responsibility for realizing the dance sequences 'passed to Berkeley', thereby 'creating a lacuna in the script'.[53] All that exists in the final script to indicate the contributions of Berkeley is a single word, written in pink within the margin: 'Buzz'.[54] Postgate's four words function much in the same way.

When speaking with Kerr about this particular sequence, she offered a rather surprising account of its early development:

> The only remote work that we did, where Oliver would send storyboards through the post, was the cat and bird little montage. He'd sent a storyboard in a long joined-up strip of card, so John and I sat at the music stand and just played around with the fiddle and the whistle, and then we just reproduced that when we went to the studio. So, there was that kind of remoteness, in the sense that ideas would come through the post or down the phone or in script form, but the recording was all done quite formally in the studio in north London.[55]

What is surprising about this revelation is learning that Postgate used storyboards in this relatively conventional manner, given the almost complete absence of formalized storyboard materials across the various, scattered Smallfilms-related archives.

What Kerr's words reveal is an interlocking journey of co-creation. Starting with Postgate's initial idea, and the four words ('Musical animated film sequence') that he placed in the script to carve out space for a screen idea that was not yet fixed, he then gave a rough drawing to Joan Firmin so that she could start work on the enamelled jewels.[56] Given that Kerr and Faulkner received storyboards that depicted an approximation of the sequence that we see on-screen, Postgate most likely waited for Joan to finish her enamel work, anticipating that the detailing of the jewels that she would produce would influence his approach to the animated sequence. Therefore, with the jewels in hand, Postgate would have been well placed to rough-up the storyboard sequence for Kerr and Faulkner. By not supplying a precisely timed animatic sequence, but instead posting only a storyboarded version of the sequence in question, he relied on Kerr and Faulkner to make a series of independent judgements regarding the musical composition, such as what notes to accentuate, when to change tempo, and how best to deliver the cadence at the end of the sequence. It is possible that Postgate worked in parallel to Kerr and Faulkner, animating the sequence without the music, with the expectation that their audio and visual rhythms would align serendipitously when edited together; however, the tight choreography of the sequence, with the jewels moving in time with the music, suggests that Postgate worked from the music. Consequently, Kerr and Faulkner's musical composition provided the foundation for the animated sequence that appears on-screen. Why, though, should we care so much about this? Well, as this discussion has highlighted, behind this lacuna, to return to Price's work on 'Buzz', or this gap, to invoke Davies, there is a wealth of collaboration that in the existing accounts of *Bagpuss*, or Smallfilms more broadly, is at best addressed in a marginal sense, but at worst remains hidden. The objective of this chapter, and more acutely in this case study of the enamelled bird and cat, has therefore been to better reflect the dynamic and deeply collaborative production history that underpinned the making of *Bagpuss*.

Conclusion

As we have seen throughout this chapter, *Bagpuss* constituted the most collaborative of all the Smallfilms productions, and consequently offers the most layered aesthetic. With confidence gained from having both survived and carved out a unique space within the television industry for over fifteen years, Postgate and Firmin clearly provided the creative foundations upon which *Bagpuss* was built, there is no doubt of this, yet, at the same time, they also had the confidence to open their production to a range of co-creators, in a fundamentally democratic manner, and to embrace the push-and-pull of the screen idea as it took shape. Although the phase of Smallfilms production that followed *Bagpuss* is often cast as a period of 'winding down', to quote Postgate himself, as we will see in the next chapter that is not the full story.

Notes

1 Author's transcription from *Bagpuss* episode 1, viewed on DVD (Universal Pictures).
2 'shuttlecocktails' Reddit user comment, posted January 2021, https://www.reddit.com/r/TheCrownNetflix/comments/k1n8qh/thoughts_on_bagpuss_s04e03/ (accessed 10 June 2021).
3 Moseley, *Hand-made Television*, p. 21.
4 'Bagpuss Cream of Television', *BBC News* 1 January 1999, http://news.bbc.co.uk/1/hi/entertainment/246080.stm (accessed 10 June 2021).
5 'The 100 Greatest TV Kids' shows Results', *BBC News* 28 August 2001, http://news.bbc.co.uk/1/hi/entertainment/1513234.stm (accessed 10 June 2021).
6 Paul Jones, 'Shaun the Sheep Voted the Nation's Best Loved BBC Children's TV Character', *Radio Times* 15 July 2014, https://www.radiotimes.com/news/2014-07-15/shaun-the-sheep-voted-the-nations-best-loved-bbc-childrens-tv-character/ (accessed 10 June 2021).

7   Danny Walker, 'Shaun the Sheep Voted Top Children's Character Beating Sooty, Teletubbies and Postman Pat', *Mirror* 15 July 2014, https://www.mirror.co.uk/tv/tv-news/shaun-sheep-voted-top-childrens-3862943 (accessed 10 June 2021).
8   'Royal Mail's Children's TV Stamps – in Pictures', *The Guardian* 4 January 2014, https://www.theguardian.com/artanddesign/gallery/2014/jan/04/royal-mail-childrens-tv-stamps-in-pictures (accessed 10 June 2021).
9   Claude Lévi-Strauss, *La Pensée Sauvage* (Paris: Plon, 1962).
10 Tate, 'Art Term: Bricolage', https://www.tate.org.uk/art/art-terms/b/bricolage (accessed 17 June 2021).
11 Christopher Johnson, 'Bricoleur and Bricolage: From Metaphor to Universal Concept', *Paragraph* vol. 35 no. 3 (2012), pp. 355–372.
12 Richard Dawkins, *The Selfish Gene* (Oxford: Oxford University Press, 1976), p. 189.
13 Martin Pickles, 'Peter Firmin at London Animation Club', Vimeo, 17 December 2013, https://vimeo.com/82087379 (accessed 17 June 2021).
14 Pickles, 'Peter Firmin at London Animation Club'.
15 Pickles, 'Peter Firmin at London Animation Club'.
16 Postgate, *Seeing Things*, p. 296.
17 Trunk and Embray, *Art of Smallfilms*, p. 179.
18 Postgate, *Seeing Things*, p. 296.
19 Pickles, 'Peter Firmin at London Animation Club'.
20 Pickles, 'Peter Firmin at London Animation Club'.
21 Pickles, 'Peter Firmin at London Animation Club'.
22 Pickles, 'Peter Firmin at London Animation Club'.
23 Oliver Postgate, interviewed by Tim Jones, Canterbury, UK, 14 July 1993.
24 Oliver Postgate, interviewed by Tim Jones, Canterbury, UK, 14 July 1993.
25 Oliver Postgate, interviewed by Tim Jones, Canterbury, UK, 14 July 1993.
26 Helen Bromley, 'Pandora's Box Or the Box of Delights? Children's Television and the Power of Story', in David Buckingham (ed.), *Small Screens: Television for Children* (London: Leicester University Press, 2002), pp. 208–226, at p. 214.
27 Babette Cole died in January 2017, before I began the main programme of key informant interviews, and given the objective to expand the Smallfilms narrative through the combination of archival research and oral history, amongst other methods, Cole's contributions fell beyond the scope of this work.
28 Linda Birch, interviewed by Chris Pallant, video call, 22 September 2020.
29 Linda Birch, interviewed by Chris Pallant, video call, 22 September 2020.
30 Linda Birch, interviewed by Chris Pallant, video call, 22 September 2020.
31 Linda Birch, interviewed by Chris Pallant, video call, 22 September 2020.
32 Author's transcription from *Bagpuss* episode 1, viewed on DVD (Universal Pictures).
33 Linda Birch, interviewed by Chris Pallant, video call, 22 September 2020.
34 Author's transcription from *Bagpuss* episode 3, viewed on DVD (Universal Pictures).
35 Author's transcription from *Bagpuss* episode 3, viewed on DVD (Universal Pictures).
36 Charlotte Firmin, interviewed by Chris Pallant, video call, 13 October 2020.
37 Postgate, *Seeing Things*, p. 298.
38 It should also be noted that Joan's screen credit for 'The Owl of Athens' relates to the intricate embroidered works that she created for that episode.
39 Author's transcription from *Bagpuss* episode 3, viewed on DVD (Universal Pictures).
40 Charlotte Firmin, interviewed by Chris Pallant, video call, 13 October 2020.
41 Charlotte Firmin, interviewed by Chris Pallant, video call, 13 October 2020.

42 Sandra Garrido and Jane W. Davidson, *Music, Nostalgia and Memory: Historical and Psychological Perspectives* (Cham, Switzerland: Palgrave, 2019), p. 3.
43 Sandra Kerr, interviewed by Chris Pallant, video call, 17 September 2020.
44 Sandra Kerr, interviewed by Chris Pallant, video call, 17 September 2020.
45 Sandra Kerr, interviewed by Chris Pallant, video call, 17 September 2020.
46 Macdonald, *Screenwriting Poetics and the Screen Idea,* p. 5.
47 Steven Price, *A History of the Screenplay* (London: Palgrave, 2013) and *The Screenplay: Authorship Theory and Criticism* (London: Palgrave, 2010); Paul Wells, *Basics Animation: Scriptwriting. Basics Animation* (Lausanne: AVA Academia, 2007) and *Screenwriting for Animation* (New York: Bloomsbury Academic, 2020).
48 Rosamund Davies, 'Don't Look Now: The Screenwork as Palimpsest', *Journal of Screenwriting* vol. 4 no. 2 (2013), pp. 164–165.
49 Davies, 'Don't Look Now', p. 165.
50 Sandra Kerr, interviewed by Chris Pallant, video call, 17 September 2020.
51 Script for 'Mill' episode 8, File: *Bagpuss*, Oliver Postgate Family Archive, UK, p. 2.
52 Steven Price, *A History of the Screenplay* (London: Palgrave, 2013), p. 136.
53 Steve Price, *A History of Screenplay*, p. 137.
54 Steve Price, *A History of Screenplay*, p. 138.
55 Sandra Kerr, interviewed by Chris Pallant, video call, 17 September 2020.
56 Joan Firmin, Charlotte Firmin, Emily Firmin, and Daniel Postgate, interviewed (as a group) by Chris Pallant, Canterbury, UK, 18 April 2019.

Chapter 9

SMALLFILMS AT THE END OF THE ROAD? *TOTTIE* (1984, 1986), *LIFE ON EARTH PERHAPS* (1985), AND *PINNY'S HOUSE* (1986)

> I enjoyed the *Pinny* films but, even as I was making them, I knew in my heart that this was the end of the road for single-frame filming, the end of my having to sit in the shed for hours on end pushing pieces of card about with a pin.[1]
>
> I looked out of the window and saw that the trees and the houses and the people could all be burned away one afternoon (in a legitimate first-strike action to eliminate the strategic threat posed by the widely distributed mobile launching sites of the cruise missiles). I contemplated and was appalled by this prospect for a moment… for an hour… but I had to go to the shops. I had to write a piece for a children's comic.[2]
>
> —Oliver Postgate

When Postgate sat down in the late 1990s to write his autobiography, when he came to summarize this part of his life, given the limited impact of the shows in question here, *Tottie: The Story of a Dolls' House* (BBC, 1984), *Life on Earth Perhaps* (1985), *Tottie: The Doll's Wish* (BBC, 1986), and *Pinny's House* (BBC, 1986), which struggled to achieve the same level of visibility and, most importantly, the same degree of lasting recognition as other Smallfilms productions,[3] he very reasonably focused his attention on other major life events that were happening at the same time, such as the death of his wife Prudence, his increasing public activism, and new beginnings with his second partner, Naomi Linnell. In doing so, however, Postgate's marginal engagement with these shows only serves to perpetuate the view that they are lesser works.

Other factors, beyond how these shows are framed by Postgate in his autobiography, have also served to undermine the standing of *Tottie*, *Pinny's House*, and *Life on Earth Perhaps* as important Smallfilms works in their own right. First, there is the ten-year delay between the 1974 release of *Bagpuss* and 1984 release of *Tottie: The Story of a Dolls' House*, with the intervening years seeing Smallfilms return to the already popular *Ivor the Engine* (1975–7) and *Noggin the*

Nog (1982) to produce new colour episodes (see Chapters 2 and 3). Given the life experiences accumulated by both Firmin and Postgate over the decade between the release of *Bagpuss* and their shows of the mid-1980s, this lengthy break before undertaking new work resulted in the latter shows diverging tonally from those works conceived pre-*Bagpuss*. The darker tone of the works in question, with danger and death proving recurrent themes, serves to set them apart from the rest of the Smallfilms oeuvre, where the more melancholic moments (of which there are many) are evenly counterbalanced by passages of positivity and whimsy.

Second, there is the problem of access. Compared to earlier Smallfilms productions that enjoyed extensive repeat programming, both *Tottie* series received only limited repeat broadcasting, with *Tottie: The Story of a Dolls' House* repeated three times (1985, 1988, and 1991) and *Tottie: The Doll's Wish* repeated just once (1987).[4] In contrast, *Pinny's House* was repeated eleven times (1987, 1988, 1989, 1991, 1992, 1993), but since then public access to the show has proven almost impossible, with the only known surviving copy of the series only recently rediscovered within the Firmin family archive as a result of the research activities undertaken to support this book.[5] While *Life on Earth Perhaps* was never broadcast on TV, the United Nations Association (UNA), who commissioned Smallfilms to make the 27-minute nuclear disarmament featurette, ensured that it was 'seen fairly frequently at UNA branch meetings […] and several times at Peace Group meetings'.[6] Like the other Smallfilms productions of the mid-1980s, public access to the film was only made possible after a substantial period of inaccessibility, when, in 2014, Concord Media acquired it for digital distribution. This picture of mixed impact when first broadcast, coupled with limited public access for the best part of three decades, has directly contributed to these productions being marginalized – or completely overlooked – within extant accounts of Smallfilms history.

Thirdly, there is the hesitancy, specifically regarding *Life on Earth Perhaps*, of whether it should even be considered a Smallfilms production. Despite the unambiguous end credit (Figure 9.1), which clearly identifies the film as a Smallfilms production, and also the fact that Postgate, Firmin, and Sandra Kerr teamed up again, the film is not included in *The Art of Smallfilms* coffee-table book or the otherwise excellent Smallfilms Treasury and Dragons' Friendly Society websites. This is a similar occlusion to the one identified and challenged in Chapter 7 of this book, regarding *Sam on Boffs' Island*. The above factors have, over time, combined to reinforce the status of these shows as Smallfilms outliers, a status that is borne out in the survey data, with only 10 per cent of respondents having any recollection of the *Tottie* productions and just 4.3 per cent recalling *Pinny's House*.[7]

As we have done repeatedly throughout this book, we must again reconsider how a particular period of Smallfilms activity is characterized and understood. As the title and the epigraph of this chapter suggests, which paraphrases Postgate's own subheading ('Ends of Roads') used to define this era in his autobiography, Postgate's account of his Smallfilms work in the mid-1980s conveys a sense of winding down. With *Clangers* and *Bagpuss* representing, by a number of measures, a peak within the Smallfilms oeuvre, the works that followed failed to reach those same heady

Figure 9.1 The unambiguous attribution of *Life on Earth Perhaps* (1985) as a Smallfilms work.

heights. However, as the twin epigraphic statements that open this chapter reflect, rather than this period being one of fallow, creative stagnation, the works featured here reveal the shifting interests and appetites of Postgate and Firmin. With that in mind, we now encounter Smallfilms at its most mature. Taking inspiration from the work of Rumer Godden, *Tottie: The Story of a Dolls' House* peels away the layers of whimsical authenticity to offer their darkest series since *The Pogles*; while *Life on Earth Perhaps* brought Postgate's nuclear activism in-house, prompting Smallfilms to embrace the featurette format; and through the conception and production of *Pinny's House* we see Firmin, for the first time under the banner of Smallfilms, take the writing credit in addition to his usual 'pictures' credit, and in doing so his writing and illustrative detailing sees Smallfilms offer their most progressive (yet ultimately flawed) response to the changing sociocultural landscape of the UK.

Tottie: The Story of A Dolls' House (1984)

From their earliest days working together, Postgate and Firmin found inspiration in the world around them, whether that was a recently washed knitted animal hanging from a line to dry, broken toys, or the pages of history. These sources of inspiration served to spark Firmin and Postgate into action, resulting in newly created characters, worlds, and stories. When approached by Goldcrest to adapt Rumer Godden's *The Dolls' House* (1947) as an animated television series, this was the first time that Postgate and Firmin were handed a readymade story, which also included a large selection of illustrations across the several editions published between 1947 and 1971. After agreeing terms with Goldcrest, Postgate then set about persuading Godden to approve the project. Godden's long-standing literary agent, Michael Shaw, notes how Godden and her publisher Kaye Webb (founder of Puffin) initially 'disliked the idea of Postgate messing around with her book', but that Postgate met Godden 'and persuaded her that it could be done, and their doubts were not merely removed, but were replaced with such enthusiasm that Godden herself took part'.[8]

Of course, as the extensive scholarship on the subject of screen adaptation attests, it would be foolish to view Firmin and Postgate's adaptation of Godden's book as a simple, faithful conversion from one format to another, rather the objective here is not to appraise fidelity but, given the marginalized status of the two Smallfilms *Tottie* series, our objective here remains to establish a fuller account of this work, with a particular emphasis on *Tottie: The Story of a Dolls' House*.

As Lucy Le-Guilcher and Phyllis Lassner write, 'despite her creative breadth and complexity, despite her continuing broad appeal', Godden has failed to secure critical recognition.[9] Across her sixty books, Godden 'combines a variety of narrative experiments and genres with a commitment to the representation of the political and social history and conditions as shaping forces of character, society, and fiction'.[10] Having lived in India for many years, Godden returned to England in 1945, and it is possible to see how her expatriate experience granted her an outsider's perspective that enabled her to dissect the social tensions that permeated post-war Britain. Two of these tensions, rooted in social class and domestic life, provided the foundation for *The Dolls' House*.

Although impossible to know for certain, it may have been the darker themes of *The Dolls' House*, coupled with Godden's detailed descriptions of the dolls' materiality, that appealed to Postgate and Firmin, given that both Firmin and Postgate placed a high value on the handmade, and that Postgate was dealing with difficult domestic circumstances at the time he took the project on. Whatever the motivations, Postgate and Firmin draw heavily from *The Dolls' House*, at times working verbatim from Godden's text, while also allowing their screen adaptation of *Tottie: The Story of a Dolls' House* to establish its own narrative rhythm.

Episode one begins by establishing Tottie's backstory: her status as a modestly priced antique doll, who was originally sold for a farthing, and how she is presently owned by Emily and Charlotte Dane, but how she used to be owned by Emily and Charlotte's Great Grandmother and Great, Great Aunt. Next, we learn that she is made of wood, 'good wood' as Tottie remarks, and this is reason that she has proven to be so durable. Amplifying Godden's original description, Postgate's voiceover notes how Tottie's 'hair was painted glossy black, her cheeks were glossy pink, her eyes were painted with bright paint, blue and very determined – firm as the tree she was made of'.[11] After introducing Tottie, we then meet Mr Plantaganet and Mrs Plantaganet, or 'Birdie' as she is informally known, which then leads into Postgate's narration detailing the material construction of Mr Plantaganet, Birdie, their son Apple, and their dog Darner. Having, established the dolls' own awareness of the constructedness of their family unit, Postgate narrates how 'Apple was made of plush, which is kind of velvet. She also knew that Darner the dog had pipe cleaners for legs and a darning needle for a backbone, which meant you had to be careful how you touched him.'[12]

Postgate's narration then turns to the dangers faced by dolls, offering a softened, paraphrased account of Godden's cautionary words:

> It is an anxious, sometimes dangerous thing to be a doll. Dolls cannot choose; they can only be chosen; they cannot 'do'; they can only be done by; children who do not understand this often do wrong things, and then the dolls are hurt and abused and lost; and when this happens dolls cannot speak, nor do anything except be hurt and abused and lost. If you have any dolls you should remember that.[13]

While Postgate softens this passage, changing 'abused' to 'misused', he ensures that the weight of Godden's original wording is conveyed, as this information serves to establish the foundations of the narrative world in which the dolls exist, foreshadowing the very real dangers they face throughout the series. To reinforce this point, Godden then offers the example of how Mr Plantaganet's suffered abuse at the hands of careless children before he found safety in the care of Emily and Charlotte. Following the book closely, Postgate notes how Mr Plantaganet had a 'china face, brown glass eyes, and real hair', and how, many years earlier, he had been dressed up as a Highland Bagpiper.[14] Postgate offers an account of the abuse he suffered at the hands of his original owners:

> They broke off his bagpipes, taking some of the painted skin from the palm of his hand as well. They tore his clothes off and let the puppy bite his foot until it was half nibbled away. One of the boys even drew a moustache on his top lip in indelible pencil […] Then they put him in a cold, dark toy cupboard, where he might have laine for years, had they not been told to tidy it up because some children were coming to tea.[15]

Finding him on the floor, eyes full of dust, Emily asks to keep him as her own and so he ends up in Emily and Charlotte's dolls' house. Pleasingly, as the narration notes, they cleaned him, 'gave him a sock for his foot, a new checked flannel suit, a plaster on the palm of his hand, a blue shirt, and tie of red silk ribbon'.[16]

We then get a much shorter account of Birdie's background and material construction, which focuses on her being a celluloid doll, an important detail, and we learn that she is a happy doll who is prone to burst into song at any given moment. The emphasis then shifts for the remainder of the episode to the fact that the dolls do not have a proper home. Tottie takes centre stage and tells the other dolls – and the audience – about a dolls house that she used to live in many years ago. Painting a highly detailed picture of this dolls house, Tottie notes how it even included a lamp that could be lit with a real flame, which prompts the dolls to remark how such a lamp would be dangerous for Birdie, given that her celluloid body is highly flammable.

Speaking to Josie Firmin about her work for this production, it became clear that visually they were not anchored to the look of one specific edition of Godden's book. Rather, the illustrations of Dana Saintsbury (from the 1947 Michael Joseph edition), Tasha Tudor (from the 1968 Viking Press edition), and Joanna Jamieson (from the 1971 Puffin edition) should be seen as providing an initial reference point for Peter Firmin, who then interpreted these visual ideas into a production brief for his work with Josie. Josie Firmin recalls: 'I was given instructions by my dad. He said it should be of the Edwardian era, and it should look like *this*, for example. From that brief I then found the fabric and made the elements.'[17] Josie is clear that there was an even share of the workload, with Peter Firmin also making a number of the dolls' clothes.

Episode two sees the arrival of the dolls' house, which it transpires is in dire need of TLC. The dolls set to work cleaning and mending the interior until it is almost entirely restored to its former glory. During the cleaning, Apple discovers the lamp, which prompts a reminder for the dolls – and the audience – of the danger that it potentially poses. However, some items can't be cleaned or fixed by the dolls. Dutifully, Emily and Charlotte explore the possibility of getting the dolls' furniture repaired, and decide to loan their Great Aunt's sampler (a piece of needlework completed to demonstrate skill) to Mrs Innisfree for a small fee so that she can include it as part of the 'Dolls Through the Ages' exhibition that she is helping to organize. The fee that the girls receive is then used to pay for the furniture repairs.

As part of the loan, Mrs Innisfree also takes Tottie to include in the exhibition, and episode three subsequently focuses on Tottie's experience of this excursion. Waking up at the exhibition, Tottie meets a fancy French walking doll, who is astonished to learn that Tottie is made of wood:

French walking doll   Wood, oooh la! I thought broom handles and clothes pegs were made of wood, not dolls!
Tottie   Well, some dolls are made of wood, and so are the masts of ships, and flagpoles, and violins, and trees. I am made from a piece of a tree.
French walking doll   Oooh la la. I am made of fine, white leather, how do you call it? Kidd and porcelain. Inside me I have a set of clockworks, wind me up and I can walk. I do not walk unless it pleases me, to do so.
Narrator   Well, of course, that was not true, because if anyone did wind her up she would just have to walk, and walk, and walk, until her clockwork had run down.[18]

We also meet the doll Marchpane for the first time in the episode and she quickly reveals her mean-spirited nature. As Tottie tells the other dolls about the old dolls house she is going to live in, Marchpane calls Tottie a liar, and claims that the house is hers alone.

Episode four shows Mr Plantaganet given the role of Postmaster by Emily and Charlotte. Marchpane and Tottie are then shown arriving back at the house, causing the harmony of the dolls' house that had been established over the previous episodes to dissipate. Marchpane immediately adopts a superior attitude towards the other dolls and, as the episode ends, we see the dolls arguing about who has lived in the house the longest: Tottie or Marchpane. This mood carries over into episode five, and we see Marchpane's influence over Emily and Charlotte grow. First, the children rearrange the house, giving Marchpane the bedroom once inhabited by Mr Plantanganet and Birdie, and, as a result, re-rooming Mr Plantanganet and Birdie in the attic. Tottie and Mr Plantaganet attempt to take a stand by out-wishing Marchpane, but Marchpane's influence over the children is too great, and as a result of their failed resistance, Emily and Charlotte recast the dolls as Marchpane's servants. Mr Plantaganet, stripped of his role as Postmaster is given the job of butler, while Tottie becomes the cook, and Birdie the housemaid. Apple, however, is exempt and Marchpane allows him to roam freely. Worryingly, Marchpane does not take on the duty of care for Apple, and, instead, sees him more as a plaything:

> **Marchpane** [*speaking to Apple*] You can play with me every day.
> **Narrator** So, Apple went into the sitting room with Marchpane every day. She let him sing to her, but she also let him climb on the furniture, and balance on the sideboard, and swing on the curtains, and do all sorts of dangerous and damaging things, because, to tell the truth, she did not care about Apple at all, she just wanted to take him away from the others.[19]

The dolls become increasingly worried for the well-being of Apple but are powerless to stop Marchpane. Furthermore, when the dolls eventually call out Marchpane for her bad behaviour, Emily and Charlotte recast Apple as Marchpane's son.

The episode culminates with a sequence that has gained a degree of infamy for its dark tone.[20] Hearing a song playing from the music box in Marchpane's room, Birdie becomes increasingly agitated and wants to be in the room too. The dolls open the door and peep inside. To their horror they find that Marchpane has lit the lamp and that Apple is stood on the table right next to it. Tottie tries her best to intervene but Birdie remains entranced by the sound of the music, while Darner the dog barks manically in the background. As Mr Plantaganet and Tottie begin to smell burning, Birdie becomes increasingly delirious, while the music and Darner's barking becomes increasingly prominent. Cutting to an extreme close-up of Apple's face next to the flame of the lamp (Figure 9.2), we hear screams from the dolls as they realize that Apple is starting to catch fire. Birdie, in a series of jump cuts, leaps to Apple, rescuing him from the flame, but setting herself on fire in the process.

We cut back to a wide shot, showing the reaction of the other dolls recoiling as Birdie burns away in a flash of light. Marchpane is unmoved, implying no

Figure 9.2 Apple, unsupervised by Marchpane, plays near the flame in *Tottie: The Story of a Dolls' House* (1984).

Figure 9.3 Birdie deliriously lunges to save Apple from the flame in *Tottie: The Story of a Dolls' House* (1984).

9. *Smallfilms at the End of the Road?* 203

Figure 9.4 Mixed reactions to the sight of Birdie's melted remains in *Tottie: The Story of a Dolls' House* (1984).

Figure 9.5 Despite the traumatic scenes, Marchpane remains unmoved in *Tottie: The Story of a Dolls' House* (1984).

emotional response and offering no words. Emily and Charlotte open the house in a panic and, seeing the dolls in disarray and the burnt embers of Birdie, they decide that Birdie must have given her life to save Apple. They realize that Marchpane has done nothing to help, and this brings Emily to the realization that she doesn't like Marchpane at all, so she is taken away and given a new life away from the house as a display doll.

The series ends with Mr Plantaganet and Tottie reflecting on Birdie's fate and the broader flow of life:

Mr Plant   Wasn't she beautiful in the flame? Like a firework.
Tottie   Like a fairy. She would have liked that.
[…]
Mr Plant   Things come and things pass
Tottie   Everything passes, from huge trees to tiny dolls.
Mr Plant   And times. Good times and bad times, they pass.
Tottie   They come and go.
Mr Plant   Have good times come back now, Tottie?
Tottie   Yes.
Mr Plant   May we be happy now, even without Birdie?
Tottie   Of course, of course. Birdie would have been happy. Birdie couldn't help being happy.[21]

Given the wistful conclusion, which speculates about the returning of 'good times', at the time that Godden originally published the book, this could be seen as a thinly veiled allusion to hopes for Britain following the end of World War II. While, in the context of Firmin and Postgate's 1984 adaptation, this story, and its bittersweet yet hopeful conclusion, perhaps appealed to on a personal level, given the trauma that Postgate had faced in particular (the death of his wife Prudence), as well as to his appreciation of sharp increase in nuclear disarmament-related public activism through the 1980s.[22]

Life on Earth Perhaps (1985)

Combining live-action footage (a mixture of original and archival B-roll) with cut-out stop-frame animation, *Life on Earth Perhaps* sees Postgate and Firmin adopt an aesthetic combination that, in the context of the Smallfilms oeuvre, gives the films a fresh feel. Beyond the aesthetic reinvention on display, *Life on Earth Perhaps* marks an abrupt departure in terms of narrative agenda. Whereas all of their preceding Smallfilms productions provide, to varying degrees, carefully crafted bursts of televisual escapism, when Firmin and Postgate set to work on *Life on Earth Perhaps*, they had a very different objective: to raise awareness of the threat posed by nuclear deterrence. From being uncomfortable with the government's nuclear policies of the 1970s, through to becoming an activist in the 1980s, Postgate had a wealth of knowledge to draw from when starting work on *Life on Earth Perhaps*, and it is possible to see how his two published pamphlets, *Thinking it Through: The Plain Man's Guide to the Bomb* (1981) and *Writing on the Sky* (1982) directly informed the structure and rhetoric of this Smallfilms featurette.[23]

In *Thinking it Through: The Plain Man's Guide to the Bomb*, which represents the culmination of Postgate's activist work up its publication in 1981, he focuses in on the contradictions of nuclear policy and seeks to establish the political foundations upon which resistance – and calls for nuclear disarmament – can be mounted.

> We choose the people we elect to public office. So we can ask them questions … in public, like:
>
> The governments of the world deploy huge arsenals of nuclear weapons. Would you or would you not be party to their use or the threat of their use in any aspect of human affairs?
>
> … and that person must know that if his or her answer is anything less than an unequivocal 'no', then no matter what other virtues they or their party may have, they will not have our vote.[24]

Published many years before the issue of nuclear deterrence twice proved a thorn in Jeremy Corbyn's side as he attempted, unsuccessfully, to beat Theresa May in 2017 and then Boris Johnson in 2019 when the UK staged General Elections, and before Donald Trump's US Presidency drastically eroded confidence in the truthfulness – let alone sincerity – of political discourse, Postgate's words feel very much of their time. Yet, at that time, political pressure remained a very real option for the CND, especially with rapid increase in active membership that occurred in the early 1980s, with membership increasing from approximately 9,000 in 1980 to approximately 100,000 in 1985.[25]

Defining nuclear weapons as the most recent addition to the landscape of human conflict, Postgate acknowledges how the human race has been 'busily inflicting inhumanity' for thousands of years, yet highlights how, with the development of nuclear weapons, the theatre of war of has been fundamentally changed:

> The sum total of man's injustices, oppressions, inflictions of misery, pain and murder is so vast as to be uncountable and yet, one piece of arithmetic is certain … by turning two keys and pressing a button, that total, the total of man's inhumanity to man since the beginning of time would be exceeded, probably many times over in a few hours of what would be called … 'Strategic Response Activation' … a sort of Do-It-Yourself Armageddon that would burn many millions of people to death in a flash, would condemn many millions to a hideous lingering death, scraping for scraps in the radioactive debris of our cities, and could, finally, leave this planet a dead dump, a lifeless poisoned poisonous waste, spinning uncounted years in empty space, a place where, to all intents and purposes, the human race never happened.[26]

By offering up such a powerful image of nuclear Armageddon, a tactic that he returns to on numerous occasions throughout *Thinking it Through*, Postgate establishes the high stakes that result from the global politics – and policies – of nuclear deterrence.

By confronting the underpinning political logic of the nuclear arms race, and twinning this with multiple, evocative descriptions of our shared worst case nuclear scenario, Postgate primes readers for action. Postgate concludes that, although asking candidates questions 'may not seem to be a very powerful form of action', 'it is one that politicians and the media can understand and evaluate', suggesting that once they come to see that 'the anti-nuclear vote is the "big one", they will respond accordingly'.[27] Postgate adds: 'Above all, we must not be exclusive! Peace movements are springing up everywhere. Their single purpose so transcends all other human purposes that their strength lies not in their unity but in their sheer diversity. In this the lion will walk with the lamb. That is its invincible power.'[28]

Recognizing that language was also inhibiting the CND cause, Postgate followed up *Thinking it Through* with *Writing on the Sky* a year later, which adopted a different frame of reference to support the call for nuclear disarmament. Shifting from the focus on politics and policies, in *Writing on the Sky* Postgate adopts military logic to argue the case for nuclear disarmament. Writing in November 1982, Postgate remarks:

> During the past two years of meetings and discussions I have found my own personal Pacifism to be irrelevant and confusing to any discussion of a peril that is not so much concerned with the ethics of war as the imminence of mass suicide and which arises from a misunderstanding that is essentially military in its origins. To be understood and resolved this misunderstanding has to be seen first in military terms.[29]

To that end, Postgate uses this second pamphlet to make a militarily reasoned case for multilateral nuclear disarmament.

First, Postgate interrogates the usefulness – and appropriateness – of the word 'weapon' to describe nuclear missiles. Postulating that weapons, in the pre-nuclear sense, are instruments 'which can be used to gain a particular advantage by threatening or inflicting a known amount of damage', Postgate suggests that before their use it was possible to apply a 'military equation which compared possible gain with probable damage'.[30] However, given the underpinning logic of mutually assured destruction, 'nuclear arsenals have a capacity for damage that has to be absolute and a capacity for gain that has to be nil'.[31] To which Postgate concludes, 'in terms of the military equation, the nuclear arsenals must be the final travesty … not weapons at all, but instruments of mutual suicide, the last word in useless self-immolation'.[32]

Postgate then considers the four positions that can be adopted when considering nuclear disarmament:

1. *Approver*: One who is in favour of keeping and using nuclear arms.
2. *Multilateralist*: One who is in favour of nuclear disarmament but only after

exact and verifiable equivalent gestures are agreed by the potential enemy *before* any action is taken.
3. *Unilateralist*: One who is in favour of nuclear disarmament and would do so, in part, without requiring exact equivalent gestures *before* taking such action.
4. *Absolute unilateralist*: One who is in favour of our nation, or any nation, simply putting down their nuclear arms forthwith.[33]

Concluding that positions 1 and 4 are rare, due to those favouring 1 being 'mad' and 4 creating political risk and military 'de-stabilisation', he confirms his own view that position 2 offers the greatest chance of persuading military and political minds to begin the process of nuclear de-escalation and disarmament.

Before moving on to make his final recommendations that the public must engage politically with this subject, they must vote conscientiously, and they should support their regional and national peace movements (recommendations that link *Thinking it Through* and *Writing on the Sky*), Postgate challenges the term 'disarmament' itself. Suggesting that the word '*dis-arm*ament is wrongly used', given that nuclear instruments are not arms, and, if used, they only really offer a short-cut to nuclear Armageddon. In response, Postgate writes: 'One could try another word… "*dis-junk*ment"? or "*dis-garbage*ment"? The word is not important once the implications of the crucial difference are fully understood.'[34]

Taking the rhetorical frameworks set out in *Thinking it Through* and *Writing on the Sky* as its foundation, the narrative of *Life on Earth Perhaps* explores the complex history of military conflict, being both a source of artistic reimagination (Figure 9.6) and human tragedy (Figure 9.7), before putting forward the case of multilateral nuclear disarmament. *Life on Earth Perhaps* goes beyond the scope of the two pamphlets by also providing a careful visual evaluation of pre-nuclear military weaponry, with the case being made for a return to a more measured deployment of non-nuclear offensive and defensive hardware.

While the principal photography and archival B-roll serves to connect the film, in a literal sense, with the everyday, the animation is deployed both as a way of visualizing things that would otherwise be impossible for Postgate and Firmin to safely access first-hand – such as nuclear missile silos – and also as a way of foregrounding the unhinged fantasy that is nuclear deterrence and the principle of mutually assured destruction. Drawing upon the interpretative framework established by Paul Wells, which maps an array of narrative strategies enabled by animation, we can see that *Life on Earth Perhaps* offers up multiple loaded examples of symbolic signification, condensation, and performance.[35]

Although Wells does not explicitly state as much, his engagement with the symbolic potential of animation loosely follows a Piercian framework, in so much as Wells privileges symbolic readings over indexical and iconic readings of signification.[36] Wells writes:

> The symbol itself can go through many transitions and eventually operate in a variety of ways. It is, therefore, useful to distinguish between the symbol and

Figure 9.6 The art of war as seen in *Life on Earth Perhaps* (1985) directed by Oliver Postgate.

Figure 9.7 The human cost of modern war as seen in *Life on Earth Perhaps* (1985) directed by Oliver Postgate.

the sign, and to engage with the idea that the symbol can function in different ways dependent upon its context and the specific historical moment in which the symbol is defined and, subsequently, called into the image system.[37]

This perspective is useful when considering the symbolic strategies employed by Firmin and Postgate in *Life on Earth Perhaps*. Figures 9.8 to 9.10, which show a sequence from the first half of the film, demonstrates how symbolism is used to visually reinforce a number of the broader conceptual arguments that are being articulated by Postgate's accompanying narration.

For example, in the first half of the film, we are presented with a short account of pre-World War I bellicosity, with Postgate's narration being accompanied by images of fine art (Figure 9.6) and live-action footage (Figure 9.7), culminating with symbolic sequence shown in Figures 9.8 to 9.10, which is accompanied by the following narration:

> **Narrator** Human history is a list of conflicts. Because, until fairly recently, war was generally recognized as being the usual way to achieve political ambition. War was seen as a respectable, and in some ways useful, part of a nation's life. It occupied the aggressive instincts of young men, uniting them in patriotic fervour, and, most important of all, being a fairly small-scale affair, a war could be conducted without seriously damaging the life of the nation. In a sense, one could say that in those days, nations were like people, able to fight with their fists. They could give each other nasty bruises and knock one another over, but they could not finally destroy each other. That is no longer true.[38]

Visually, the sequence shown across Figures 9.8 to 9.10 operates on several levels, which all help to reinforce the overarching point being made: that our experience of war has changed from a damaging but survivable exchange, as represented by the sequence in question, to a nuclear exchange of mutually assured destruction.

In Figures 9.8 to 9.10 we can see cut-out individuals, serving as symbols of entire nations, bopping each other on the head and fiercely gurning. Their two-dimensional – and lightly caricatural – appearance foregrounds how far removed these symbols of nationhood are from the lived reality of contemporary transnational identity. Their mutual head-bopping appears almost ritualistic, with each waiting to take their turn to deliver a single blow to their opponent's head. The ground upon which they stand is a map – similar in appearance to an Ordnance Survey Road Atlas – suggesting formally demarcated space, yet also flattening the landscape to that of symbolic space rather than the lived space of the live-action footage. Significantly, the mechanics of head-bopping necessitates that the two belligerents stand face to face, again symbolically evoking the proximity of early modes of military engagement. That they position themselves at their respective borders, gives the sequence a tactical overlay, with the symbolic suggestion being that this is a fight to gain ground in every sense of the word (politically, tactically, and literally). Finally, we see medieval architecture employed, namely fortified stone keeps, that are most likely intended to symbolically represent the capital

Figure 9.8 Red faces Blue in *Life on Earth Perhaps* (1985) directed by Oliver Postgate.

Figure 9.9 Red hits Blue in *Life on Earth Perhaps* (1985) directed by Oliver Postgate.

Figure 9.10 Blue hits Red in *Life on Earth Perhaps* (1985) directed by Oliver Postgate.

cities of each nation. Which, given their identical iconography, suggests the delusional mindset required to justify military expansionism. Again, by refusing a more literal visual reference, Postgate and Firmin cast capital cities as sites to be either conquered or defended. All of this symbolic layering is made possible by animation, both because it allows the filming of things that can only be imagined and therefore not achieved via strictly live-action means, and because it allows them to play puppet master, thereby acting out worst- and best-case scenarios for the viewer to consider.

The worst-case scenario depicted in *Life on Earth Perhaps* shows the predicted consequences of a large-scale nuclear exchange, whereby the multiple detonations (Figure 9.11) generate enormous dust clouds that block out the sun (Figure 9.12) and lead to what scientists at the time described as a 'Nuclear Winter'.[39]

Beyond the immediate deaths of up to 50 per cent of the global population,[40] those who survived the detonations would face the prospect of a severely challenging climate. R.P. Turco and colleagues map out several scenarios, taking into account different levels of nuclear payload, noting:

> Most striking are the extremely low temperatures occurring within 3 to 4 weeks after a major exchange. In the baseline 5000-MT [Mega-Tonne] case, a minimum land temperature of - 250 K (-23°C) is predicted after 3 weeks.

Figure 9.11 Mutually assured destruction as seen in *Life on Earth Perhaps* (1985) directed by Oliver Postgate.

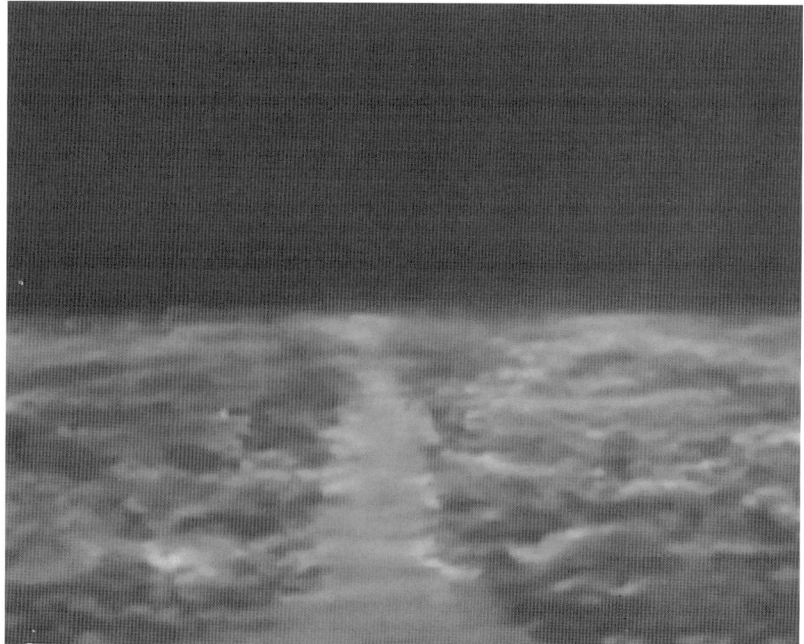

Figure 9.12 Nuclear Winter as seen in *Life on Earth Perhaps* (1985) directed by Oliver Postgate.

Subfreezing temperatures, persist for several months. Among the cases shown, even the smallest temperature decreases on land are - 5° to 10°C (cases 4, 11, and 12), enough to turn summer into winter.[41]

In this sequence we see a good example of what Wells terms condensation, which is the ability of animation to 'compress a high degree of narrational information into a limited period of time', and which enables 'the most direct movement between what may be called the *narrative premise* and the *relevant outcome*'.[42] Given the scientific validation of a potential 'Nuclear Winter' scenario, Postgate's animation and Firmin's illustration offers a shorthand visualization of such a scenario, by virtue of the rapid malleability of the animated form.

At the film's conclusion, we see Firmin and Postgate explore a more optimistic possibility: multilateral nuclear disarmament. Here, the decision to combine live-action with animation takes on extra importance. Given how their preferences shifted from 2D cut-out to stop-motion model-based over the course of their work, there is the possibility that their return to the cut-out method used in their earlier films, as well as being an aesthetic choice rooted in cost efficiency, was motivated by a desire to use the overt material quality of this type of animation to help reinforce a key argument set out in the film.

This is most powerfully felt as the film reaches its conclusion, with the careful reasoning of Postgate's narration serving as a sharp counterpoint to the blinkered nuclear stockpiling of the two-dimensional animated character/nation seen on-screen (Figures 9.13 and 9.14). Postgate's narration, which follows the military logic presented in his pamphlet *Writing on the Sky*, provides a direct address to the character/nation that highlights the wrong-headedness of viewing nuclear instruments as legitimate weapons, thereby prompting a moment of revelation:

Postgate Narrator The more of them [nuclear arms] we have the stronger we will be, is that true?
Character/Nation Oww-yup
Postgate Narrator No, that is not true. You have seen that it is not true! There are in fact three quite separate sorts of offensive instruments in the world, and only one of these is actually weapons
Character/Nation Ehhh?[43]

At this point, as seen in Figure 9.12, the character/nation turns to face the screen/voter, suggesting that our views – expressed by Postgate's narration – can influence the actions of our elected leaders.

Consequently, we see the character/nation reject the policy of nuclear stockpiling by chucking their nuclear missiles into a nearby bin (Figure 9.15) – providing a visual link back to Postgate's call for disjunkment. Via the narration, Postgate restates the democratic power of the audience, and the potency of lobbying groups such as the UNA:

As the fog of fear begins to clear, we shall at last be able to see what has been staring us in the face for years. That in a nuclear world, where each nation holds

Figure 9.13 Stockpiled nuclear weapons as seen in *Life on Earth Perhaps* (1985) directed by Oliver Postgate.

Figure 9.14 The penny begins to drop in *Life on Earth Perhaps* (1985) directed by Oliver Postgate.

9. *Smallfilms at the End of the Road?* 215

Figure 9.15 Disjunkment as seen in *Life on Earth Perhaps* (1985) directed by Oliver Postgate.

Figure 9.16 Future world peace as imagined in *Life on Earth Perhaps* (1985) directed by Oliver Postgate.

the key to the other's survival, true security can never come from the laying on of terror, but only from the willing sharing of safety. That will be the coming of age of the human race. After that we shall know that if life on earth is to have a future the nations are just going to have to do what people learned to do long ago: form and recognize a higher authority than their own. Make, and keep, and honour its laws, so that – *like people in slow motion* – nations will come to live in peace, together, safe in this small village that we call the world.[44]

Although ambiguous, it is possible that Postgate's reference to 'people in slow motion' is an idiosyncratic way of referring to the animated characters that feature in *Life on Earth Perhaps*, and, by drawing this comparison between the national leaders of the real world and their symbolic, on-screen counterparts, we are invited to share Postgate's hope that through democratic selection and focused lobbying we might see a similar outcome in the real world. After all, as the film closes, we see an image of these 'slow motion' animated characters sitting happily at the same table toasting their new peaceful coexistence (Figure 9.16). Sadly, as Postgate notes with resignation in his autobiography, although he offered the featurette to the television companies, 'none of them would show it because it was thought to be too "political"'.[45] It was perhaps this lack of broadcast pedigree that led Postgate to limit references to *Life on Earth Perhaps* to just one, four-sentence paragraph, in his entire autobiography, which in turn has prompted – up until this point – the featurette to be omitted from the Smallfilms historical narrative.

Pinny's House *(1986)*

Although they continued to work together under the Smallfilms banner into the 1990s, mainly focusing on repackaging their earlier works for VHS and audio cassette distribution or producing print-based spin-offs and annuals, 1986 was the last year that Postgate and Firmin worked together on original television productions. Alongside *Tottie: The Doll's Wish* (1986), which debuted in September 1986, and provided a follow-up to *Tottie: The Story of a Dolls' House*, once again drawing upon the tensions generated by the malevolent Marchpane for its narrative thrust,[46] *Pinny's House*, Smallfilms' final production, debuted in October 1986.[47]

Firmin traces the origins of *Pinny's House* to a doll exhibition that he had visited:

> I went to an exhibition in Tonbridge and they had a doll's house in there with the 'Smallest Doll in the World', so I saw that as a bit of a challenge. It was like half an inch tall and fully jointed, so I took on the challenge. […] I thought I'd make a doll as small as that, just because I like making Dutch Dolls. With Oliver, we had recently made *Tottie: A Dolls' House*, so it was about a year after that, and I thought it would be a nice idea to try to make a tiny Dutch Doll.[48]

Having found the right materials (cherry wood), as well as making his own tiny drill to achieve the desired joint sizes, he produced a tiny Dutch doll similar in appearance to Tottie. Given the small size of the doll it soon experienced a domestic mishap – being hoovered up during a bout of house cleaning. Postgate's version of these formative events diverges from Firmin's,[49] but only in so much as Postgate suggests that Firmin received a similarly tiny, broken Dutch doll in the post for him to repair, and it was this doll that experienced the unfortunate event. Firmin made no reference to this other doll when I interviewed him, and instead asserted that it was the doll that he manufactured that was hoovered up.[50] As Firmin and Postgate both recall: the loss of the doll resulted in Peter and Joan Firmin taking the hoover apart and combing through the contents of the bag to find the doll.[51] This incident is worth highlighting as it provided direct inspiration for one of Pinny's adventures, and also provided the impetus for Firmin to produce several *Pinny* books throughout 1985.[52]

Taking responsibility for the task of writing the *Pinny* television scripts, Firmin settled on a largely self-contained, episodic structure, with thirteen instalments detailing various domestic scrapes encountered by the two central characters, the Dutch dolls Pinny and Victor. The stories within each episode are entertaining, they always show Pinny and Victor getting themselves into a difficult situation and are usually resolved by one or more of the family members finding the dolls in a rather abrupt manner and returning them to safety. At the end of each episode we hear the narrator's anxious refrain, spoken by the rescuer, which ponders that had they not been found, 'something terrible might have happened'.[53] While the stories are competently plotted, despite the fact that we are presented with an animated world where dolls come to life – and, we might assume by extension, anything is possible – Firmin's storytelling style feels rather matter-of-fact compared to the more nuanced and layered storytelling of Postgate. When it debuted, *Pinny's House* was also the first production made solely by Smallfilms to be voiced by someone other than Postgate, with Matilda Thorpe reading all of the character dialogue and also providing the linking narration. Therefore, while *Pinny's House* looks like a Smallfilms production, as a consequence of Firmin once again providing the illustrations and Postgate directing the cut-out animation, if you were to simply hear the story and not see the visuals, you might struggle to associate the work with Smallfilms.

The show was well received by the BBC, and *Pinny's House* enjoyed eleven repeat broadcasts between 1987 and 1993. However, in the years since *Pinny's House* last broadcast, accessing the series has proved almost impossible. While small, incomplete fragments of the series are viewable on YouTube, at the time of writing, *Pinny's House* remains unavailable for purchase, and no access to the series is possible via the archival viewing arrangements of the BBC, the BFI, or the Dragons' Friendly Society. Thankfully, as part of the primary research for this book I was able to view the series via a private copy held by the Firmin family, which, to my knowledge, is the only surviving copy of the full series. It is of course possible that other privately held, off-air recordings do exist, but given the cult interest in this series that is evident via online forums, such private copies, if they exist, would surely have surfaced by now.

A striking feature of the series is the colour of the characters seen on-screen. As Figure 9.17 shows, while the two Dutch dolls share the same bodily construction, Pinny is white and Victor is black. At no point in the series does the narrative seek to exploit this difference in colour to facilitate stereotyping, nor do the characters speak with different accents (both being voiced by Thorpe in a rather RP manner), nor are their physical characteristics exaggerated beyond that necessitated by their representation as Dutch dolls. The starkness of Victor's black colouration matches the starkness of Pinny's white colouration – no attempt is made by Firmin to introduce any sense of graphical nuance in terms of the colour of their bodies. Victor is dressed in a Royal Navy Seaman's rank uniform, while Pinny wears a 1960s-style belted mini-dress. Being the first non-white leading character to feature in a Smallfilms production, Victor's appearance demands deeper consideration.[54]

It is helpful to place *Pinny's House* in the wider context of British television programming. From the late 1970s and into the early 1980s, Black characters enjoyed greater visibility on British television screens, especially through shows such as *Empire Road* (1978–9) and *A Hole in Babylon* (1979).[55] While Channel 4, which was founded in 1982, also contributed to this shift given its commitment to representing the multiculturalism of Britain on-screen – a drive that has been at the core of its public service charter since day one.[56] David Morely writes: 'By

Figure 9.17 Pinny and Victor as seen in *Pinny's House* (1986).

the time that Channel Four was launched, in the wake of the riots in black areas of many British cities in 1981, the connection between debates about the racialisation of geographical space and the racialisation of the airwaves had become much more apparent.'[57] While more widely, across the BBC and ITV, the white straightjacket of mainstream news coverage began to loosen. As Angela Barry notes: 'in that same year [1982], in those same organisations, a curious thing happened—Moira Stewart began to read prime time news; *Nationwide* seized upon a black female presenter, Maggie Nelson; on ITV, Trevor McDonald became more visible.'[58] In a frequently quoted line from Paul Gilroy's 1983 review of Channel 4's early Black programming, Gilroy notes how 'the wind which blew black TV onto our screens was part of the storm which swept through Britain's inner cities in July '81'.[59] Yet it is risky to reduce Gilroy's review down to just this comment, since his review posed important, far-reaching questions about whether 'the black TV bandwagon' would develop 'a momentum of its own, out of step with the pace of black struggles in less auspicious surroundings'.[60] What Gilroy drives home throughout his review of Channel 4's Black programming is that visibility is not enough, there also needs to be nuance, authenticity, and a relentless challenging of lazy stereotypes.

With this context in mind, while Firmin avoids stereotyping Victor, his decision to leave the character of Victor – and Pinny – underdeveloped, whose actions and words are voiced by the narrator, and whose adventures do not meaningfully contribute to – or reveal details about – the background of his character, falls short of the nuanced characterization sought by Gilroy. Given that *Pinny's House* was conceived in the mid-1980s, the decision to present Victor as a sailor who lives on his boat, is perhaps an attempt to make a connection with the children of the Windrush generation, who might have been watching children's TV at that time, but this is a tentative interpretation at best, as there is nothing overtly established in the narrative to advance this reading. What we see then in *Pinny's House* is an attempt by Firmin to contribute, in his own small way, to the sea change that he was seeing across television programming at that time. However, by failing to establish Victor's character in any meaningful way, Victor remains little more than a blank, black canvas, certainly contributing to the project of increasing Black visibility on-screen, but contributing in such a reductive way that the outcome is less productive than it could have been.

Sarita Malik offers a useful summary of the critical framing that must inform our current reading of *Pinny's House*. Reflecting on the 'Black Film, British Cinema' conference that was held at London's Institute for Contemporary Arts in 1988, Malik documents how the event provided a platform for four important responses to the 'new wave' of Black British film to be voiced:

> first, that Black audiences were heterogeneous, active and sometimes resistant to formal innovation; secondly, 'the recognition of the extraordinary diversity of subjective positions, social experiences and cultural identities which compose the category "black"' (Hall in Mercer, 1988, 28); thirdly, that we had transcended the 'siege mentality which says that anything we do must be good' (Henrique in

Mercer, 1988: 18); and finally, that the cinema had become, in Mercer's words, 'a crucial arena of cultural contestation' (Mercer, 1994: 73).⁶¹

While the event focused on Cinema, the insights are just as relevant when thinking about television, and, measured against the points referenced by Malik, it is clear just how limited – and limiting – the character of Victor was when *Pinny's House* hit television screens in 1986.

Despite the show's clear shortcomings, that Postgate and Firmin embraced this opportunity to change their representational register, in their final original production after over twenty-seven years making television under the banner of Smallfilms, should not be dismissed altogether. While they could surely have just returned to their greatest hits for their last show, that they once again took the opportunity to do something new provides a fitting final act for Smallfilms under the auspices of Firmin and Postgate.

Conclusion

Following the broadcast of *Pinny's House* this was very much the end of the road for Postgate and Firmin as a double act producing original television under the Smallfilms flag. While both Firmin and Postgate were naturally turning there attentions to other projects, with Postgate working on Thomas Becket-themed projects with Linnell, and Firmin spending more time invested with printmaking, the BBC also made it clear that times were changing. Postgate writes:

> Our films were definitely going out of fashion. The reasons for this were kindly explained to me by a member of department at the BBC. Apparently an edict had been issued by the powers-that-be to the effect that the *viability* of programmes (i.e., their worth and chance of continuing), was henceforth to be *ratings-led* (i.e., judged by the number of people watching). As the purpose of television was to entertain (as opposed to instruct or educate), the basic policy was to give the children exactly the sort of thing that they were already known to enjoy and deliver it in a form and manner that was especially exciting.⁶²

Postgate continues, adding wryly that 'impeccable American educational sociologists had established that in order to prevent a child switching channels (and thus transferring their rating to another channel), a programme had to have a *hook* (i.e., an incident sufficiently violent to re-attract the attention) every three and a half seconds'.⁶³ With their reliance on aesthetic stillness, carefully plotted whimsical-authenticity, and intricately detailed worlds, it is clear that the work of Smallfilms represented the exact opposite to what the BBC wanted. Looking at the final week's scheduling of *Pinny's House* during its May 1993 rerun, we can see this rationale being played out on a daily basis, with the following shows broadcast across BBC One and BBC Two: *Bananaman* (BBC One, 1983–6), *Alvin and the Chipmunks* (BBC One, 1968–present), *Pingu* (BBC One, 1990–2006), *Postman*

Pat (BBC Two, 1981–2017), *Noddy's Toyland Adventures* (BBC Two, 1992–2000), and *The Legend of Prince Valiant* (BBC One, 1991–3).[64] Clearly, the likes of *Noddy* and *Postman Pat* would not have featured the violent acts claimed by Postgate to be required every few seconds, but they are shows that rely more heavily on eventful happenings to drive the narrative along at a quick pace, setting them apart from *Pinny's House* and the traditions of Smallfilms storytelling. Although this was the end of road for Postgate and Firmin as Smallfilms, this is not the end of the Smallfilms story.

Notes

1. Postgate, *Seeing Things*, p. 397.
2. Oliver Postgate, *The Writing on the Sky* (London: The Menard Press, 1983), p. 26.
3. In 1980, Postgate also worked on the TV programme *What-a-Mess*, which aired on the BBC. There is debate within online forums, from viewers who remember the show and/or are Smallfilms superfans, regarding whether this show should be classified as a Smallfilms production, but I have found no evidence to support these calls to record it as a Smallfilms production. The TV listing from the time of the show's original broadcast only names Postgate, not Firmin nor Smallfilms, as playing a role in the show's production, with the book's original illustrator, Joe White, credited as the TV show's illustrator. Furthermore, from the only known surviving fragment of Postgate's contribution to this show, which can be found on YouTube (Retrobox, 'TVO What A Mess Film by D Owen (80's)', YouTube, 22 February 2016, https://www.youtube.com/watch?v=l29kda7UXjs [accessed 31 October 2021]), it is clear to see that he worked directly from the original book illustrations, panning, scanning, and zooming over these images to create a sense of dynamism in the absence of any actual animation.
4. Information sourced from BBC Genome.
5. Information sourced from BBC Genome; BFI Special Collections confirms no copy of the series is held in their archive.
6. Postgate, *Seeing Things*, p. 395.
7. Given the non-broadcast format and limited distribution of *Life on Earth Perhaps* I did not include it in the audience questions, to help reduce survey fatigue, and given the likelihood that the response would confirm an absence of audience awareness.
8. Michael Shaw, *DVD Sleeve Commentary – Tottie: The Story of a Doll's House* [DVD] (Dragons' Friendly Society, 2010).
9. Lucy Le-Guilcher and Phyllis B. Lassner, *Rumer Godden: International and Intermodern Storyteller* (London: Routledge, 2010), p. 1.
10. Le-Guilcher and Lassner, *Rumer Godden*, p. 6.
11. Author's transcription from *Tottie: The Story of a Dolls' House* episode 1, viewed on DVD (Dragons' Friendly Society); for Postgate's reference point see Rumer Godden, *The Dolls' House* (London: Puffin, 1971), p. 10.
12. Author's transcription from *Tottie: The Story of a Dolls' House* episode 1, viewed on DVD (Dragons' Friendly Society); for Postgate's reference point see Godden, *The Dolls' House*, p. 10.
13. Godden, *The Dolls' House*, p. 11.
14. Author's transcription from *Tottie: The Story of a Dolls' House* episode 1, viewed on DVD (Dragons' Friendly Society).

15 Author's transcription from *Tottie: The Story of a Dolls' House* episode 1, viewed on DVD (Dragons' Friendly Society).
16 Author's transcription from *Tottie: The Story of a Dolls' House* episode 1, viewed on DVD (Dragons' Friendly Society).
17 Josie Firmin, interviewed by Chris Pallant, video call, 24 November 2020.
18 Author's transcription from *Tottie: The Story of a Dolls' House* episode 2, viewed on DVD (Dragons' Friendly Society).
19 Author's transcription from *Tottie: The Story of a Dolls' House* episode 4, viewed on DVD (Dragons' Friendly Society).
20 See Andrew Brassealy, '7 of the most Terrifying Moments in the History of Kids' TV', *Metro* 7 February 2018, https://metro.co.uk/2018/02/07/7-of-the-most-terrifying-moments-in-the-history-of-kids-tv-7289468/ (accessed 1 November 2021).
21 Author's transcription from *Tottie: The Story of a Dolls' House* episode 5, viewed on DVD (Dragons' Friendly Society).
22 See Lawrence S. Wittner, *Toward Nuclear Abolition: A History of the World Nuclear Disarmament Movement, 1971–Present* (Stanford, CA: Stanford University Press, 2003), p. 131.
23 Oliver Postgate, *Thinking it through: Plain Man's Guide to the Bomb* (London: The Menard Press, 1981); Postgate, *Writing on the Sky*.
24 Postgate, *Thinking it Through*, p. 30.
25 See Wittner, *Toward Nuclear Abolition*, p. 131; Matthew Hilton, Nick Crowson, Jean-François Mouhot, and James McKay, *A Historical Guide to NGOs in Britain: Charities, Civil Society and the Voluntary Sector since 1945* (London: Palgrave Macmillan, 2012), p. 113.
26 Postgate, *Thinking it Through*, p. 30.
27 Postgate, *Thinking it Through*, p. 30.
28 Postgate, *Thinking it Through*, p. 30.
29 Postgate, *Writing on the Sky*, p. 5.
30 Postgate, *Writing on the Sky*, p.12.
31 Postgate, *Writing on the Sky*, p.12.
32 Postgate, *Writing on the Sky*, p. 12.
33 Postgate, *Writing on the Sky*, p. 30.
34 Postgate, *Writing on the Sky*, p. 31.
35 Paul Wells, *Understanding Animation*, 1st reprinted edn (London: Routledge, 1998), pp. 68–126.
36 See Paul Weiss and Arthur Burks, 'Peirce's Sixty-Six Signs', *Journal of Philosophy* vol. 42 no. 14 (1945), pp. 383–388.
37 Wells, *Understanding Animation*, p. 83.
38 Author's transcription from *Life on Earth Perhaps*, VOD via Vimeo (Concord Media).
39 R. P. Turco, O. B. Toon, T. P. Ackerman, J. B. Pollack, and Carl Sagan. 'Nuclear Winter: Global Consequences of Multiple Nuclear Explosions', *Science* vol. 222 no. 4630 (1983), pp. 1283–1292; and Paul R. Ehrlich, John Harte, Mark A. Harwell, Peter H. Raven, Carl Sagan, George M. Woodwell, Joseph A. Berry, Edward S. Ayensu, Anne H. Ehrlich, and Thomas Eisner, 'Long-Term Biological Consequences of Nuclear War', *Science* vol. 222, no. 4630 (1983), pp. 1293–1300.
40 Ehrlich et al., 'Long-Term Biological Consequences of Nuclear War', p. 1293.
41 Turco et al., 'Nuclear Winter', p. 1286.
42 Wells, *Understanding Animation*, p. 76
43 Author's transcription from *Life on Earth Perhaps*, VOD via Vimeo (Concord Media).

44 Author's transcription from *Life on Earth Perhaps*, VOD via Vimeo (Concord Media); my italics.
45 Postgate, *Seeing Things*, p. 395.
46 In episode two of *Tottie: A Doll's Wish*, Marchpane forcefully hits Apple in the face, which prompts heavy criticism and admonishment by Tottie and Mr Plantaganet for this act of child abuse. Given the intended child audience of this series, this moment of violence may have contributed to show's scarcity – or suppression – that, to date, means the show is only available to order on-demand via the Dragons' Friendly Society, where a single, faded VHS copy serves as the master copy.
47 Information sourced from BBC Genome.
48 Peter Firmin, interviewed by Chris Pallant, Canterbury, UK, 5 February 2018.
49 Postgate, *Seeing Things*, p. 396.
50 Peter Firmin, interviewed by Chris Pallant, Canterbury, UK, 5 February 2018.
51 Postgate, *Seeing Things*, p. 396; and Peter Firmin, interviewed by Chris Pallant, Canterbury, UK, 5 February 2018.
52 See Firmin's: *Pinny Finds a House* (1985), *Pinny and the Bird* (1985), and *Pinny in the Snow* (1985).
53 Author's transcription from *Pinny's House*, DVD copy supplied by Peter Firmin Family Archive. Postgate, *Seeing Things*, p. 395.
54 Other non-white characters do appear throughout Smallfilms' many productions, but these are all secondary characters who only feature for a few episodes of a given series. Sadly, some of the design and performance choices of these earlier non-white characters do stray into the territory of reductive stereotyping, such as the Indian circus owner in *Ivor the Engine* and Arabian baddie in *Noggin the Nog*. For completeness, it must also be noted that a Golliwog features in the live-action footage shown in episode 13 of *Sam on Boffs' Island*, but given the division of labour for that series, the decision to record and screen that image was taken solely by the BBC's production team, not Postgate or Firmin.
55 For more coverage of this period of expansion see Stephen Bourne's *Black in the British Frame* (London: Continuum, 2001), pp. 192–222.
56 Channel Four charter page: https://www.channel4.com/corporate/about-4/what-we-do/channel-4s-remit (accessed 19 December 2021).
57 David Morely, *Home Territories: Media, Mobility and Identity* (Oxon: Routledge, 2000), p. 120.
58 Angela Barry, 'Black mythologies—the representation of black people on British television', in J. Twitchin (ed.), *The Black and White Media Book* (London: Trentham Books, 1988), p. 9.
59 Paul Gilroy, 'C4—Bridgehead or Bantustan?', *Screen* vol. 24 no. 4–5 (July–October 1983), p. 131.
60 Paul Gilroy, 'C4—Bridgehead or Bantustan?', vol. 24 no. 4–5 (July–October 1983), p. 131.
61 Sarita Malik, *Representing Black Britain: Black and Asian Images on Television* (London: Sage, 2002), p. 165.
62 Postgate, *Seeing Things*, p. 403.
63 Postgate, *Seeing Things*, pp. 403–404.
64 Information sourced from BBC Genome.

Chapter 10

THE AFTERLIFE OF 'SMALLFILMS': ADAPTATION AND RENEWAL

> My dad, Oliver Postgate, left me in charge of his programmes and he said, 'you can look after them, and you can do what you like with them, as long as you don't muck them up'.
> —Daniel Postgate, 2015 BAFTA winner speech (*Clangers*: 'I am The Eggbot')

Unpicking the afterlife of Smallfilms is rather complex. There is the question of where to draw the line regarding Firmin and Postgate's active management of the studio. Do you draw the line when their TV work stopped? Or when they ceased working on spin-off products? The finality of Postgate and Firmin's deaths, of course, provides an unambiguous juncture where the Smallfilms studio becomes more than the core Postgate–Firmin dyad. However, even this measure is unhelpful, given the gradual transition of oversight for all Smallfilms matters to Daniel Postgate, with Firmin still playing an active role after Oliver Postgate's death (2008), alongside Daniel Postgate, until Firmin's death in 2018. Then there is the work of the Dragons' Friendly Society, which, from the time of incorporation in September 2002 through to its dissolution in January 2021, and under the Directorship of Ian 'Loaf' Warburton, helped shoulder the burden of remastering and distributing the works of Smallfilms. Beyond this official offshoot, there are also numerous Smallfilms-related projects that have ultimately gained official Smallfilms endorsement, but which began life as fan-driven ventures. And, of course, there is the new *Clangers*, which brought together, under the investment of Coolabi, creative input from Firmin, script and production oversight from Daniel Postgate (amongst others), and the expertise of the crew working at Altrincham-based animation studio Factory.

Despite these multiple, competing strands of Smallfilms-related activity, 8 December 2008 does serve as a useful date around which to make a distinction between two distinct historical periods of Smallfilms: the Oliver Postgate era and the post-Oliver Postgate era. Given the core objective of this book to expand the Smallfilms narrative beyond the Postgateian orthodoxy, the irony of suggesting a periodization that places Postgate at its very heart is not lost on me. However, explicitly anchoring this conceptualization around Postgate's contribution/absence also encourages further critical reflection on his pivotal role within the Smallfilms historical narrative, thereby supporting the overall aims of this book. For example, as this book has demonstrated, during the time that Postgate and Firmin were active, the idea of what Smallfilms as a studio stood for was perpetually being renewed, with Firmin and Postgate's actions, in combination with the actions of their many collaborators, serving to incrementally endow the Smallfilms brand with meaning through their various productions. Yet, after the death of Postgate, many of the creative intersections noted above, take inspiration not from Postgate or Firmin directly, but from the patchworked constellation of ideas and associations that constitutes the work of Smallfilms. Furthermore, with each fresh original interaction and new post-Postgate creation, the notion of Smallfilms is renewed again.

Linda Hutcheon's discussion of memes in her work on adaptation is useful here. Drawing on the work of Richard Dawkins, Hutcheon expresses her dissatisfaction with the unproductive nature of both the 'negative evaluation of popular cultural adaptations as derivative and secondary' and the 'morally loaded rhetoric of fidelity and infidelity used in comparing adaptations to "source" texts'.[1] Wishing to push beyond such frameworks, Hutcheon redeploys Dawkins's concept of the meme. Writing in his book *The Selfish Gene* (1976), Dawkins proposed that 'cultural transmission is analogous to genetic transmission in that, although basically conservative, it can give rise to a form of evolution'.[2] Dawkins consequently popularized the term meme, defining it thus:

> Examples of memes are tunes, ideas, catch-phrases, clothes fashions, ways of making pots or of building arches. Just as genes propagate themselves in the gene pool by leaping from body to body via sperms or eggs, so memes propagate themselves in the meme pool by leaping from brain to brain via a process which, in the broad sense, can be called imitation.[3]

Before offering the following qualification: 'Imitation, in the broad sense, is how memes can replicate. But just as not all genes that can replicate do so successfully, so some memes are more successful in the meme-pool than others. This is the analogue of natural selection.'[4] Hutcheon rightly acknowledges that Dawkins 'is thinking about ideas when he writes of memes', but persuasively suggests that 'stories also are ideas and could be said to function in this same way'.[5] Developing her argument, Hutcheon then notes how adaptation, 'like evolution, is a transgenerational phenomenon', before writing: 'Stories do get retold in different ways in new material and cultural environments; like genes, they adapt to those new environments by virtue of mutation—in their "off spring" or their adaptations. And the fittest do more than survive; they flourish.'[6] If we return to Dawkins for one final, important distinction, we find his recognition that unlike the 'all-or-none quality of gene transmission', he suggests 'meme transmission is subject to continuous mutation, and also to blending'. In this sense, the freedom to appropriate, adapt, and renew (with the blessing of Peter Firmin and both Oliver and Daniel Postgate) has ensured that the work of Smallfilms – in its most expanded sense – has become a memetic cultural touchstone, resulting in Smallfilms remaining a persistent feature of our small screen diet.[7]

Taking inspiration from Hutcheon and Dawkins, this chapter explores a number of contemporary Smallfilms offshoots and outgrowths. Following the concept of memetic evolution we will see that the projects discussed here did not require stimulation from Smallfilms management to develop, rather their genesis and progression was driven by a cross-fertilization of ideas, ideas that were undeniably Smallfilms-centric in nature, but ideas that emerged for the most part in a decentred way. First, we will consider the ways that Smallfilms texts have become sites of play, before concluding this chapter – and this book – with a discussion of two new television works: BBC Two Wales' redeployment of Ivor the Engine to help promote the roll out of digital broadcast, and the recent reboot of *Clangers*.

Playing the part – Staging Smallfilms

Several Smallfilms TV shows have been adapted for the stage, but of all the Smallfilms works, *The Saga of Noggin the Nog* has inspired the most sustained and diverse range of stage performances. This began in 1971, with the Birmingham Repertory Theatre's production of a new Noggin story, *The Rings of Nudrug*, which Postgate and Firmin created specifically for the company. Postgate reflects in his autobiography:

> The play I eventually put together was called *The Rings of Nudrug* and it was unashamedly derivative of the Noggin Sagas, which was exactly what the theatre was hoping for. As well as a wicked Emir with his cringing lackey and a most evil and plaintive Nogbad, it included a complete, working flying-machine, a magic carpet, an exploding barrel and some exploding dungeon-bars, a family of damp oppressed trolls, who, like the Firecake giants, finally defeat Nogbad and save the day, this gaining their freedom. It was all good standard Nogstuff.[8]

Debuting at Christmas, the show, which featured six songs and a four-piece musical ensemble, offered an energetic dose of pantomime adventure.[9] Reviewing for the *Coventry Evening Telegraph*, David Isaacs writes:

> As we might be entitled to expect from this company, there is a wealth of characterisation as Nogbad the Bad (Paul Chapman) is wicked enough to really frighten anyone.
>
> John Gill's Thor Nogson, the captain of the Royal Guard, is a sort of military version of Santa Claus and Bruce Bould doubles as Olaf the Lofty (inventor the flying machine) and the Troll King.
>
> The authors of 'Noggin', Oliver Postgate and James [sic] Firmin, have collaborated on a number of children's television series, and Mr. Firmin is responsible for the excellent design here, in which, for once, the false proscenium arch looks right.

> Michael Simpson's production never under-estimates its audience. It is unhurried but never slow to use the lilting and pleasant little tunes to good advantage.
>
> It is a sort of open secret that the Rep. feel they may be on a winner with this show – in the sense that it could become one of the most popular children's Christmas programmes for years.
>
> In another sense, they are already on a winner. The bookings are excellent, so if you want to see it, reserve your seats now.[10]

This 1971 production, like the 1983 adaptation of *Noggin and the Firecake*, which was performed by Unicorn Theatrical Group, featured a high degree of direct input from both Firmin and Postgate, with Postgate writing both plays and Firmin designing the sets, props, and costumes for both productions. Yet, this was not the only time that Noggin was adapted for the stage, as between 2013 and 2018 Third Party Productions and Mischievous Theatre toured their own 'The Sagas of Noggin the Nog' show around the UK, delivering over 150 performances.[11]

Tony Gleave and Clive Holland, two of the creative forces behind the 2013 to 2018 Noggin adaptation, highlight a number of ways in which they drew inspiration from the original TV series and also the ethos of Smallfilms more generally. Discussing the approach taken by Third Party Productions and Mischievous Theatre to the fabrication of sets and props, Gleave remarks: 'The homemade element was always one of the first things that Peter said, he often said "it looks homemade because it is homemade", and the good thing about that is that if a child is watching it they will think, "oh, I can do that myself", and I think that is very much part of our theatre.'[12] Continuing with this theme of accessible design, Holland describes how a similar attitude shaped their tour philosophy:

> We've both done quite a lot of community theatre, and rural touring, so you do end up going into strange little village and town halls, and school halls, to do a show, but what is really nice about those, and my philosophy of it is: we all go through the same door. So we went through the double doors a bit earlier than you, we put our set up, but we are going to go out the same door as you, whereas in theatres the audience go in the front and actors go in the back, and there is that barrier and you never meet, and so, even when we did Brighton, which was a huge thousand-seater, we came and sat on the front of the stage and people came down and chatted to us. And that sort of makes the event, it is like Peter is there with you, because it makes that event feel like we're all in it together, and yes you could make that hat prop.[13]

Beyond these complementary principles, which resulted in a positive blending of ideas between Third Party Productions, Mischievous Theatre, and the Smallfilms realm, this recent adaptation also found a way to present the original TV works within the theatrical space.

Reflecting on the process of adapting the first two Noggin sagas for the stage, Gleave notes:

10. *The Afterlife of 'Smallfilms'*

Figure 10.1 Third Party Production's interpretation of *Noggin*.

We thought it was important to retain the episodic nature of it, the repetition of it, the music comes back in, and the repetition of the opening lines. And we also thought it was Family theatre, so how long are the chunks? But the chunks were just the right size. We had this simple conceit, that they were sitting around the fire, because that is how it begins, telling tales. So the simple conceit was that we saw the tale in the fire, and through this magic jewel in the fire (which probably nobody got, but it was our reasoning), the story in the fire was projected onto this animal skin strung up at the back of the stage: that was our story [Figure 10.1]. So up there [on the animal skin] we saw a bit of the black-and-white original film, which we used, partly to establish locations, and partly to key into the original story.[14]

By rear-projecting sequences from the first two Noggin Sagas as part of their stage performance, Third Party Productions and Mischievous Theatre provided an opportunity for audiences to (re)encounter sequences of Smallfilms animation that had been first broadcast over fifty years earlier. Returning to Hutcheon, it is clear that the stage productions constitute particularly rich examples of stories being 'retold in different ways in new material and cultural environments'.[15]

Playing the game – Making Smallfilms interactive

Beyond the stage, *The Saga of Noggin the Nog* also inspired game adaptations, with a simple, dice-based castle climbing game being released in 1989, titled *Noggin the Nog* (designer: unknown), and, more recently in 2018, a richly detailed, multi-mechanism board game, called *Tales of the Northlands: The Sagas of Noggin the Nog* (designer: Nick Case), which sees players compete to defeat Nogbad and thereby save the Northlands. It is important to note that Firmin supported both board game adaptations through the production of original artwork. However, our focus shifts now, from Noggin to Ivor, because while the Noggin-themed game adaptations exist exclusively in the realm of the table-top board game, Ivor the Engine has inspired game adaptations spanning both analogue and digital realms.

It is testament to the lasting appeal of *Ivor the Engine*, that over fifty years after its TV debut, the stories inspired video game (*Ivor the Engine*, 2011, by John Thornewill) and board game (*Ivor the Engine*, 2014, by Tony Boydell) adaptations. Speaking to Thornewill and Boydell, it is clear that both grasped the importance of connecting with a dual audience, much in the same way that the original TV series did. Thornewill recalls that he wanted to create 'a game that would allow you to go and play around in Ivor's world. As much as anything, I wanted to create a game that was as much for adults as it was for the kids of those adults.'[16] While Thornewill identifies a desire to create a video game that would appeal to gamers of different ages, echoing Hutcheon's comments about successful adaptations being 'transgenerational',[17] Boydell recognizes another duality, highlighting the challenge of designing a board game that caters to players of differing ages as well as different skill levels:

> I play lots of serious board games and I love them and they are absolutely fantastic, but you can't have an *Ivor* game where people are going to buy the box and open it and go 'I have no idea what's going on here' and then put it away. If you read the Amazon reviews of the board game they are wonderful. And they are saying exactly what I wanted them to be saying: 'this game is really evocative of the theme, it's really easy to play, the kids love it, the grown-ups love it', and then I've got gamers who say 'we really like it because it's a bit nasty and you can play it like a game'.[18]

Beyond their shared focus on transgenerational appeal, Thornewill and Boydell also offer revealing insights into the process of translating the aesthetics of the series into game form.

Arguably, this was a more straightforward task for Thornewill, given that his adaptation for the iPad preserved the overarching audiovisual logic of the series, such as seeing the world through a 2D perspective, having the characters occupy well-established spaces in the world (such as Dai Station and Owen the Signal), and being able to recognize the voices and sounds of *Ivor the Engine*. Visually, Thornewill's Dreadnaught-Design team worked from the original artwork wherever possible, however, they were also forced to augment that with screengrabs from the actual films themselves.[19] The reason for this was, as Thornewill notes, when Postgate and Firmin 'were making the later parts of *Ivor the Engine*, when they did a lot of the winter episodes, the way they did that was they just took the summer episodes and drew snow on top', thereby making it impossible to recover those particular images.[20] The team were much more privileged when sourcing the audio for the game. Not only did they secure an agreement with the Elliott estate to use the original music, but they were also able to draw upon previously unpublished recordings of Oliver Postgate:

> Fortunately, Dan also had various different recordings of Oliver for his book, and there was also going to be an audio book version of some of the Ivor stuff that never got released, so we had a few of those files. We basically just pieced together as much stuff as we could that we could make a game from it.[21]

As Thornewill implies in this last statement, these limitations and discoveries actually served to focus the game's development. It is tempting to see further echoes of Dawkins and Hutcheon here, with the previously discarded elements – dormant textual DNA – being reactivated by later generations.

For Boydell, working in the medium of board games, offering the gamer an audiovisual or kinetic approximation of the original TV series (something the iPad game does well) was never an option. When designing the *Ivor the Engine* board game, Boydell quickly realized that he had to find a different way to bring Ivor's world to life for the gamer:

> The key thing was the stories. So, I sat down with the DVD and I literally played, paused it, wrote some stuff down, played, paused it, wrote some stuff

down. Every little tiny detail. […] All the cards on the top have got 'Fetch Prof. Longfellow's Lens cap from …', 'Fetch loom from Llanmad …', or something. Most people won't read that top bit, because they're playing the game, and they'll read the game bit, but those who know the stories will know who professor Longfellow is.[22]

It is this element of the original TV series that is prioritized in the board game: Ivor's utility – his role in moving objects, characters, livestock, and narrative all around the Merioneth and Llantisilly Railway:

> So that became about cleaning up all the sheep. Sheep are often referenced in the programme as getting in the way, they're either stuck in snow drifts or they're blocking the line, they're involved everywhere, and I wanted sheep to be through the game as well. For me it all came together once you start thinking about that map and picking up and delivering and being in the story. So, the stories themselves were the things that you delivered, just by being in that place when it was clear of sheep.[23]

While sheep were undeniably a recurrent feature of the original TV production, as this quotation highlights, it was Boydell who took the theme of sheep and developed this facet into something more fundamental to the experience of *Ivor the Engine* as a board game, and in doing so his work serves to reshape – or evolve – our collective understanding of *Ivor the Engine*. Capturing the experience of *Ivor the Engine* was just one of the challenges faced by Boydell, another was Firmin's changing aesthetic.

Discussing the packaging of the board game, Boydell offers a nuanced account of Firmin's *Ivor the Engine* visual style since his days of drawing the character for TV:

> When I chose the box art I was really keen to work from the library that was given to me, not to have Peter do a new piece, because the new artwork in the game is very distinct from the old artwork, Peter's style changed, just as much as it changed from the stuff he was doing in Pippin, and that was a very simplistic Ivor image, the characters were very lightly drawn compared to the detail in the TV series and the book illustrations. Then look at it now, they're much brighter colours and again they've gone back to a more smooth, less defined sort of structure. If you put them together you can see there is a lot of detail in that middle period, so I wanted a cover image that people could see across a room and go: 'That's *Ivor the Engine*'.[24]

Firmin's style shifted over time as a consequence of changing formats and varying levels of financial support. Studying Boydell's game, and the process of its creation, reveals how Firmin's illustration of *Ivor the Engine* was always evolving – meaning there is no singular, fixed Ivor style. By being alert to the shifting nature of Firmin's aesthetic, Boydell is able to bring different aesthetic phases of *Ivor the Engine* together within his board game design. Of course, simply having a strong aesthetic approximation is only half the challenge. Both Thornewill and Boydell also sought to bring out important thematic constants of the TV series through the gameplay mechanics of their respective games.

Lastly, the locomotive process and the navigation of Ivor's railway landscape were key mechanics that both of the designers worked hard to weave into their games. For Thornewill, this resulted in a two-step approach. When players interacted directly with Ivor's controls, the emphasis was placed on conveying the same level of detail that Firmin and Postgate had built into the TV show. For example, as discussed earlier in this book, before Ivor leaves his shed for the first time in episode one (1959), we first see Jones light Ivor's fire, then operate his controls (Figure 2.6). This moment is expanded for those controlling Ivor on their iPad, as this becomes 'a mini game where you had to set the controls in the right order', which Thornehill reveals was informed 'by looking at real episodes'.

In Figures 10.2 and 10.3, we can see the mini game that involves getting Ivor up to steam. While the first element requires a 'find and grab' approach by the player,

Figure 10.2 Starting Ivor's engine in the iPad game.

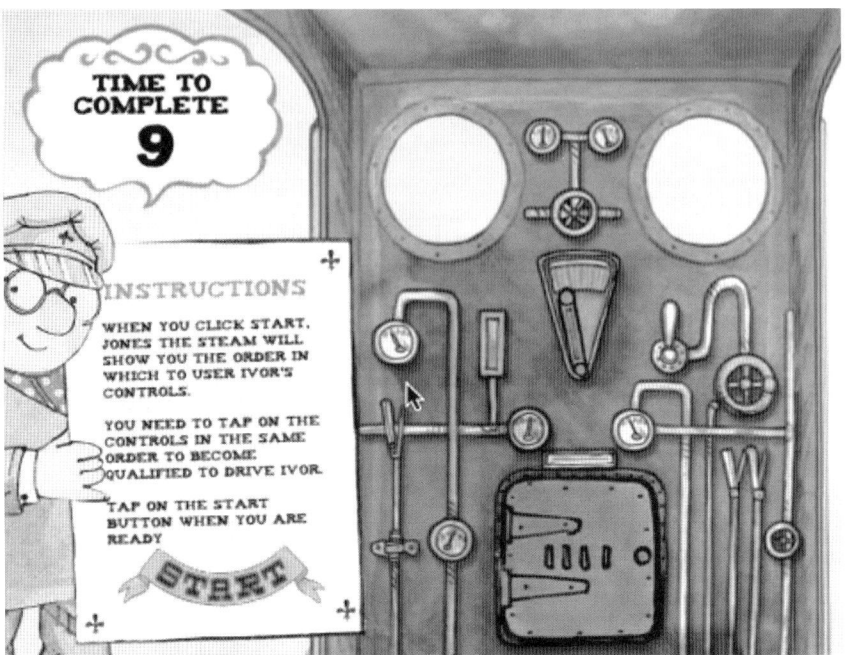

Figure 10.3 The minigame that challenges gamers to set Ivor's controls correctly.

akin to hidden object games, the second phase requires players to click specific controls in a set order. Only after these have been completed can the player reverse Ivor out of his shed and onto the railway line. This is a prominent element of the TV series, so there is a concerted effort made in the game to explore this facet in new ways. By placing this restriction on player movement, the Dreadnought team are encouraging players to recognize the importance of the mechanical process to the locomotive experience of *Ivor the Engine* – a creative choice that foregrounds the competing agendas of play and story, a tension that will be familiar to most gamers.[25]

The second step was how to evoke a sense of place. The answer for both Thornewill and Boydell was to make navigation of the map a detailed and rewarding process for players. Thornewill describes Dreadnaught's development process of the iPad Ivor map:

> Look at the way that Oliver navigated the various different characters throughout the world, and recognizing that there were various different cut-scenes where different characters would turn up and walk through bits of the scenery, and then looking at the scans we had got of the actual map itself, which never really existed, this was some of Peter's old artwork from when they were doing magazines and that, in the 70s. So, essentially, we just pieced together the *real*

map, and then looked at how Oliver got the various different characters to walk around in there, and we just took the next step.[26]

The challenge here was working from a composite sense of geography, whereby different versions of the *Ivor the Engine* map, which had been created at different times and for different purposes and media (Figures 2.13, 2.14, and 10.4), needed to be combined for the purpose of player navigation. Thornewill's provocative assertion that this process resulted in the *real* Ivor map being pieced together for the game is rooted in navigational logic. While the map had previously served a largely illustrative purpose, guiding continuity within the TV series and serving to provide Ivor's varied audiences with a graphic sense of place, both the video game and the board game forced the map to function differently: as a practical, instrumental, navigational tool. Thinking of this evolution through Ian W. Macdonald's framework of the screen idea, in the TV era of *Ivor the Engine*, the map was as much a dynamic conceptual guide as a documentary record of the narrative developments charted across the show's multiple series.[27] Yet, the function and format of the board game prompted the map to shift from being a potential fluid site of shared ideas to a fixed, singular space.

For Boydell, the map was the most important aspect of the entire game design process. It provided the literal platform for gameplay, it structured the fictional world of Ivor in such a way to make it concrete for real-world play, and it provided Firmin with an opportunity to lay out the definitive landscape of *Ivor the Engine*. Boydell recalls:

> Peter drew that map for us specially. That is the map for the board game, and he added Dyffryn Bridge, which wasn't there before, and that was added because I had a hex on the board map, because it was a hexagonal map overlaid onto the map, because you need to be able to differentiate your movement points and where you are going. So, there was this gap in the middle where you could move through but there was no name, and I needed a name for it, so he said 'just call it Dyffryn Bridge', because 'Dyffryn' means bridge apparently, so it's 'Bridge Bridge' in Welsh, so that was definitely something new for the game.[28]

Working from the 1978 map (Figure 10.4), Firmin's map for the board game (Figure 10.5) establishes the most up-to-date geography of *Ivor the Engine*.

Apart from Firmin's mistranslation (dyffryn means valley in Welsh), Boydell neatly captures Firmin's prevailing attitude towards the mapping of Ivor's landscape detail and, moreover, Firmin's detail orientation: whether policing Postgate's approach to continuity; or in his own illustration of the imagined world, scaling at macro level through the many iterations of the map to the micro level of individual background drawings (which correspond with the geographic logic of each iteration of the map); to the naming of a *new* bridge to ensure consistent navigation and reference from that point forth. Through these branch lines and sidings, audio

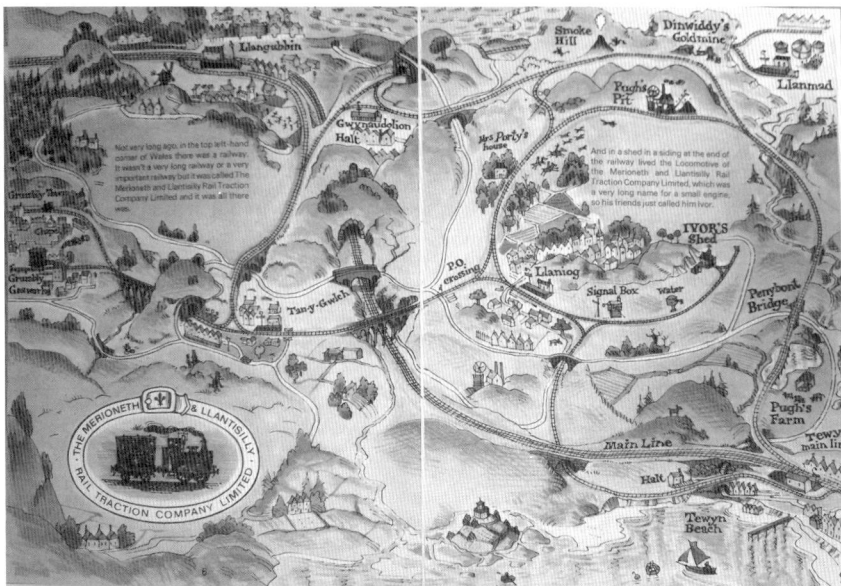

Figure 10.4 The Merioneth and Llantisilly Railway shown in the BBC's *Ivor the Engine* Annual of 1978.

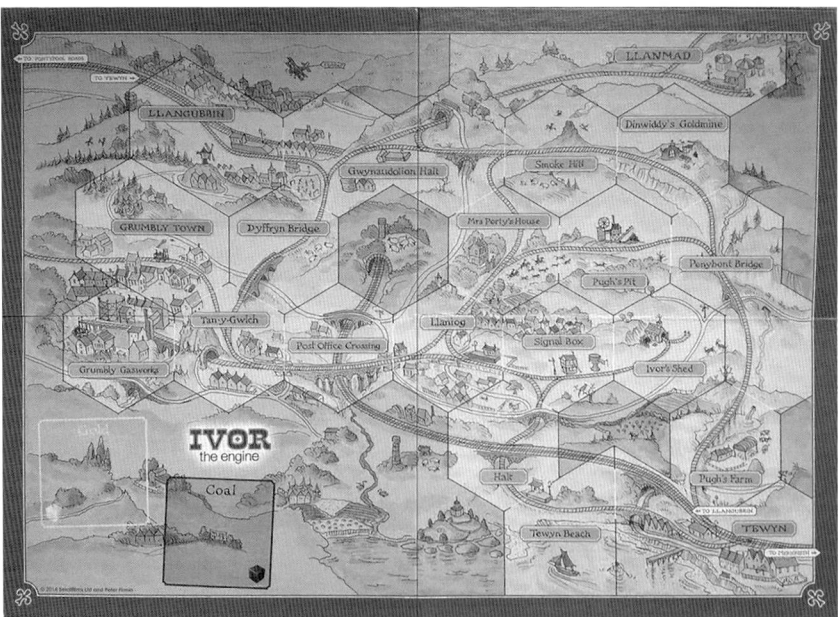

Figure 10.5 The final mapping of Ivor's Railway as drawn by Peter Firmin for the 2014 board game.

cassettes, digital trails, and games, the conceptual terrain of *Ivor the Engine* has remained consistent with that of the original TV shows, while, in various ways, extending that landscape in new directions.

Mynd adref/Going home

Having been set in a fictional Wales since its inception, in 2004 *Ivor the Engine* finally made it to Welsh soil in real life. Looking to promote the BBC Two Wales (BBC2W) digital switchover, Philip Moss, who at the time was Creative Lead for BBC Wales TV, Radio and Print Marketing, turned to one of the nation's most loved characters: Ivor. Although not officially listed in the 2003 '100 Welsh Heroes' poll (funded by the Welsh Assembly in response to the 2002 '100 British Heroes' poll), the survey conducted by the BBC in the build-up to the results being released recorded several nominations of Ivor the Engine.[29] Understanding the affection felt by many of his fellow countryfolk towards *Ivor the Engine*, Moss contacted Firmin and Postgate, and set about commissioning three short promotional trailers, which would promote the upcoming digital switchover. In an article published on *WalesOnline*, on the eve of the new BBC2W Ivor's broadcast, the excited tone confirms the lasting appeal of *Ivor the Engine*: 'thousands of viewers will remember the little Welsh engine fondly, as his adventures with Idris the Dragon and Dai Station were a staple of children's TV for decades'.[30]

Reflecting on the preparations for animating the BBC2W Ivor shorts, animator Jim Le Fevre talks fondly of having the opportunity to study the original work in close detail:

> These huge, wide landscapes, and the difference in brushes and pencil marks. Even with the characters, they are so wonderful, because they are very loose, but still all the characters are quite tight and recognizable, but you get a different brushwork with every different ink or watercolour, per hand or per arm, and I didn't change anything of that.[31]

With this in mind and understanding the widespread affection for the original TV works, the production team were acutely aware of the challenge facing them, working in a digital production environment, yet seeking to capture an authentic sense of the cut-out style animation utilized by Postgate and Firmin. Le Fevre, remembering the digital processes of the early 2000s, remarks: 'the terrifying horror of digital is that you lose sight of everything that was made wholesome by the process that they did, so anything that was animated was animated entirely on holds […] So it was really lovely to be able to properly animate walk cycles, or, to just think entirely through the process of hand-done animation.'[32] So how did this decision to animate entirely through 'holds' help to mitigate the then terror of a digital production process?

In animation production today, it is commonplace to talk of keyframes and in-betweens as a shorthand for implied automation. When a keyframe refers to a carefully designed still image that captures an important moment of activity, in a digital workflow, the in-between is then often automated, with the software creating the necessary images to move the scene from one keyframe to the next. To give a sense of labour, for every second of animation there is the possibility of having twenty-four (shooting on film) or twenty-five (shooting digitally) frames. Choices are then made, depending on the visual style, economic situation of the production, and time available to complete the work, with the decision typically resulting in animation either being captured every frame (animating on 1s), or every second (animating on 2s), or every third frame (animating on 3s). This means that for every one, or two, or three frames of animation there will be a new image. The more images per second of screen time, the smoother – and cost-/labour-intensive – the result. Le Fevre confirms that the BBC2W Ivor shorts were primarily produced on 2s, meaning that each second of screen time would require twelve unique images. Hypothetically, then, for a sequence of Ivor dialogue, in which very little changes from image to image beside the orientation of the head and perhaps a few arm gestures, keyframes could be designated every second or even every two seconds, meaning that the software could, if tasked to do so, generate eleven to twenty-two in-betweens for every one or two keyframes. This carefully managed production choice results in the new BBC2W Ivor shorts retaining the same sense of stillness that is an intrinsic quality of Postgate and Firmin's work under the Smallfilms banner.

The 'holds' that Le Fevre refers to are keyframes, so by actively resisting the automation facilitated by the software at that time, Le Fevre is choosing to animate every single frame that we see, still within the digital ecosystem of the software, but, crucially, manually by hand. The effect that this has on the finished animation is to ensure that the way the BBC2W Ivor characters move feels correspondent with that of the earlier series produced by Firmin and Postgate, with characters at times wiggling a little as they move, or Ivor jumping a little as he moves down the trainline. Le Fevre notes: 'If you're sitting there with your 16mm camera under the rostrum and your clicking away manually then there would be mistakes, and we didn't really ever go back and check because it all felt good to the eye [...] So, I guess it was just trying to embrace all those discrepancies.'[33] Rather than seeing these discrepancies as failings on the part of Postgate or Firmin, it is reasonable to see these as the signatures of their handmade process, their craft.

A surprising revelation to emerge from the research phase of this book was the discovery that much of the production materials generated for the BBC2W Ivor shorts have been rendered inaccessible due to the march of technological progress. Much of the work was completed using Adobe After Effects 6, and as part of the interview with Le Fevre it was planned to revisit his working process, given that he has kept all of the original After Effects files. Sadly, the current version of After Effects (18, at the time of writing), does not support the files and, despite our best efforts, we were unable to find another software that could open them. This is just one small example of the very real need to be proactive when it comes to digital archival practices, given how much can be lost through the well-intentioned, yet passive, storage of digital files.[34] It is tantalizing to think what insights could be gleaned by accessing the raw animation files from the BBC2W Ivor shorts, but until we are able to source a computer still running After Effects 6, this remains out of reach.

Clangers

It is fitting that the final point of discussion in this book should centre on the new *Clangers* series that debuted on the BBC's CBeebies channel on 15 June 2015. Having now run, at the time of writing, across six years and 104 episodes (series three: 52, series four: 26, series five: 26), it is perfect illustration of the durability of Smallfilms' appeal. Furthermore, with sixty individuals having worked on new *Clangers* across series three, four, and five, the fact that it has offered something self-evidently new, but has still been lauded for its ability to tap into many of the aspects that made the original series so popular,[35] confirms Hutcheon's view that stories 'get retold in different ways in new material and cultural environments' and that 'like genes, they adapt to those new environments by virtue of mutation—in their "off spring" or their adaptations'.[36] How then did the team at Factory accomplish this?

It is no exaggeration to state that the aesthetic coherence stemmed from an early contribution made by Firmin. Dan Maddicott, who served as the Series Producer overseeing the 2015 reboot, notes that when Oliver and Peter first made *Clangers*, 'they'd virtually made it up as they went along because there were only two of them involved', but recognizing the need for much greater levels of structure and oversight to ensure the success of their first 52-episode production run, he asked Firmin: 'Do you think you could come up with a sketch quickly for us of what the Clangers planet looks like? For example, how do you get from one bit to the other so that we can give a Bible to our writers so that they'll know what we're talking about.'[37] To the production team's surprise and delight, what Firmin produced was a highly detailed 'water colour of the interior of the planet, which had never been seen before', and, as Maddicott notes, enabled the team to have some large-scale prints made that could be mounted around the studio, 'and this gave us the overall design look for the clangers and at that point our production team really came into it and started working with that to create the new series'.[38] In this observation about the centrality of Firmin's early sketch to the world-building activity of the new *Clangers* production team, we can see a continuation of the commitment to world building that informed all of Postgate and Firmin's Smallfilms activity.

Building upon this, Chris Tichborne, director of almost half of new *Clangers* episodes produced to date, recalls how Firmin was 'creating these beautiful pictures right up until months before he passed away, in his late 80s, the most exquisite drawings, and we were still getting him to design sets and little bits of sets and props all throughout the you know the almost five years that we were making it'.[39] Recognizing the consistent balance that Firmin and Postgate struck between whimsy and authenticity, Tichborne details an important step in the pre-production research:

> At the very beginning, before we did any of you know any realization from the drawings, we looked at geology books because, in the original series the capabilities of what Oliver and Peter had, and the space that they had [informed their choices], we just thought we wanted to sort of create a bit more depth because we've got the capability to do that, so we looked at lots of different geology rock formations. So, the living cave is a bit like the Utah

National Park, very sandstone, and so Andy Farago [Production Designer] started to create these little dioramas like little plasticine sets and that helped us to visualize it.⁴⁰

The physical studio space available to the Factory crew constitutes an important distinction between the original and new *Clangers* productions, which, in turn, results in the key aesthetic difference between the two eras, identified by Tichborne: depth. Consequently, we see more detailed and more varied settings in the new *Clangers*, due to the crew's ability and desire to stage the action across – and pull focus between – different set locations (Figure 10.6).

While Postgate and Firmin's Smallfilms studio setup centred around one large planet surface set, with a few extra small-scale backdrops created when the narrative demanded, Factory's *Clangers* studio setup featured two living cave sets, a soup well set, four planet surface sets, and Major Clanger's workshop.⁴¹

An important quality associated with the work of Smallfilms, which we have discussed at various points throughout this book, is the explicit nature with which Firmin and Postgate embraced the handmade look of their work. Again, Firmin played an important early role within the development of Factory's *Clangers*. Tichborne recalls:

> Peter was with us very much all the way through the development of the set and he even brought up some of the doors to the bed caves. Part of when they were making

Figure 10.6 Distinct foreground, midground, and background focal points as seen in the new *Clangers* (2015–present).

it back in the 60s it was all found objects, and his original bed cave doors were Woolworth pie tins, they were literally silver foil pie tins, and he wanted to keep that idea of found objects and not just have everything tailormade and really slick.[42]

Tichborne goes on to note how Firmin even provided props for the production: 'He actually made this little satellite sculpture for one of the episodes, and we found it was a little bit too heavy, so we had it rigged, but it was essentially little bits of Meccano that he found and cobbled together in a very beautiful way.'[43] Firmin's desire to instil core Smallfilms values is clear to see, and this input coupled with the crew's general awareness of the original *Clanger* informed their own production.

Jo Chalkley, who has worked across all three of the new *Clangers* series, first as an animator and latterly as a director, also highlights another quality that can be seen to link back to the work of Postgate and Firmin. Paying attention to Chalkley's frame of reference, this similarity seems more serendipitous than consciously engineered:

> We had six animators in studio, so I think it was it was about two weeks per episode, and they were shooting twelve seconds a day, which is quite a lot for stop-motion, but because it's preschool the pace is quite slow generally. In 'The Visitor' episode and some of the others, sometimes they are faster, but generally there's about 100 hundred and 110 shots and there's a lot of pauses, and often the clangers will speak and then we give the narrator time to sort of tell us what they've just said, so it's about two weeks in studio.[44]

The slowness to which Chalkley alludes is evocative of the stillness of Smallfilms highlighted, in Chapter 1, as an important aesthetic quality of the studio's animation.

Having considered the conception, fabrication, and animation of the new *Clangers*, and how this new production can be seen to draw upon – whether intentionally or not – the characteristics associated with Firmin and Postgate's work under the banner of Smallfilms, one final observation is worth adding: how Firmin offered an early reminder about perspective. Discussing the creation of the title sequence, Tichborne recounts:

> It wasn't an easy process, because when we first started we did it on Post-it Notes and we presented it to the Board at Coolabi, who were like 'fabulous, wonderful and everything', and then we showed it to Peter and he gave us a bit of a telling off, well not telling off, but he slightly disapproved and he said 'no, no, this is too fast paced, it's got to be slower and it has got to be as if we're looking in through a window in the zoo, as if we're observing their life, and you need to slow it down', so we were quite humbled from having our first hurrah, to Peter sort of making us feel a bit like school boys but in a really nice way. That was a very important thing that he said: the idea that we're looking at them, not there with them too much, we're narrating about it is as if you're standing in a zoo watching the chipmunks.[45]

Reiterating the importance of stillness to the Smallfilms – and, by extension, *Clangers* – ethos, in this exchange Firmin also reinforces the need to remember that the Clangers represent what Postgate might have called low-angle characters. With Daniel Postgate, who was also attuned to the importance of this particular low-angle narrative perspective, being responsible for more than half of the screenplays across series three, it is hardly surprising then to find this final Smallfilms characteristic renewed and reimagined in the new *Clangers*.

Conclusion

It is only fitting to return at the end of this book to the very beginning: the title. How might we interpret the sentiment of 'Beyond Bagpuss' now? First, through an expansion of the Smallfilms historical narrative, bringing hitherto overlooked or marginalized works such as *The Seal of Neptune*, *The Mermaid's Pearls*, *Sam on Boffs' Island*, *Life on Earth Perhaps*, and *Pinny's House* more sharply into perspective, this book moves the reader beyond the iconic domination of *Bagpuss* – unquestionably the most high-profile of all the Smallfilms works. Second, the range of original interviews gathered throughout the preparation of this book has enabled new ways of looking at the work of Smallfilms and, more significantly, they have provided fresh insights about the deeply collaborative production process behind these works, thereby allowing us to move beyond the popular fetishization of the Postgate–Firmin creative dyad. Third, and following on from the first two interpretations, by considering the bricolage of Smallfilms, seen through the wide range of mixed-media aesthetics adopted across multiple decades, this book unsettles *Bagpuss* – and the narrow association of stop-motion model-based animation – as the key symbol of all things Smallfilms. Fourth, through the surveying of popular taste and interrogating the appeal of Smallfilms, this book offers a counterpoint to the common and casual associations of Smallfilms' work with nostalgia and homespun charm, associations frequently linked to discussion of *Bagpuss*. Seeking to push beyond these uncritical positions, this book has systematically scrutinized the themes of appeal that emerged from the survey data (such as whimsical authenticity, world building, bricolage, collaboration, inventiveness, and the importance of the handmade aesthetic), thereby expanding the terms by which we engage with specific shows and also the work of Smallfilms more broadly.

Ultimately, we have pushed beyond 'the end' of Smallfilms, being the 'end' rooted in a Postgateian view of Smallfilms history, to highlight the numerous Smallfilms adaptations that have continued to emerge in the years since Postgate and Firmin stepped back from the day-to-day running of Smallfilms. On this final point, it is fitting to discover that in the year 2021 the BBC's website, which for many represents the international face of the Corporation, enlists the help of two Clangers to help soften the pain of encountering a 404 error (Figure 10.7). Considering the vast range of BBC productions that could have provided inspiration for this light-hearted 404 page, such as Doctor Who using his sonic screwdriver to remedy the broken link or Bob the Builder proving that he can fix it,

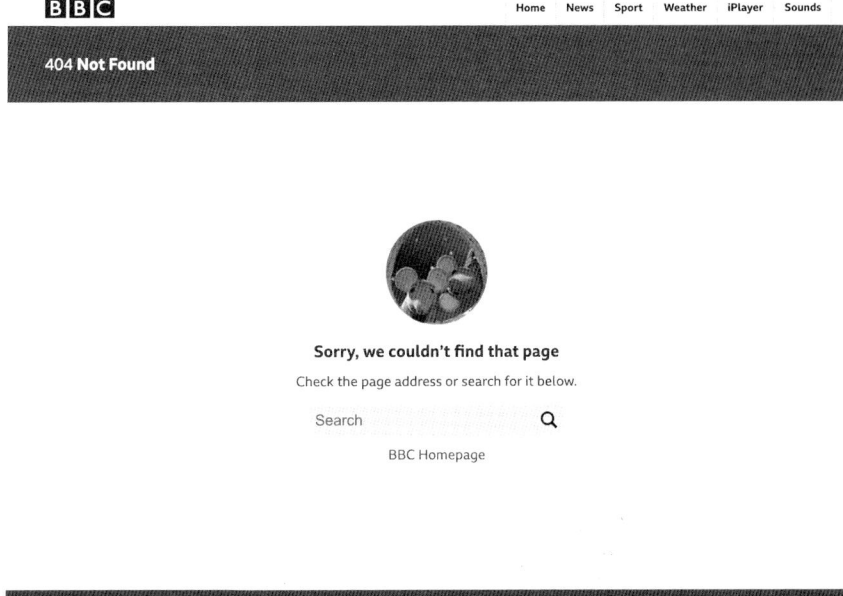

Figure 10.7 The BBC's *Clangers*-themed 404 webpage error screen (accessed in June 2021).

the fact that we find two Clangers stands as a testament to the lasting and pervasive appeal of Smallfilms' work.

Hopefully this book has provided some useful ideas, frameworks, and historical expansions to enable readers to continue their own Smallfilms journey in a more informed manner. We close with a reminder: 'Even Bagpuss himself, once he was asleep, was just an old saggy cloth cat. Baggy, and a bit loose at the seams, but Emily loved him.'[46] Therefore, my request to you, the reader, at the end of this book, is not to love Bagpuss any less, but just to remember that Bagpuss is only one of many Smallfilms creations, and when we allow ourselves to look beyond his pink and white visage, we find a world of Boffs, Froglets, Hairy Gurglers, Nogs, Pogles, and a legion of other low-angle persons in need of equal attention.

Notes

1 Linda Hutcheon, *A Theory of Adaptation*, 2nd edn (New York: Routledge, 2013), p. 31.
2 Dawkins, *The Selfish Gene*, p. 189.
3 Dawkins, *The Selfish Gene*, p. 192.
4 Dawkins, *The Selfish Gene*, p. 194.
5 Hutcheon, *A Theory of Adaptation*, p. 32.
6 Hutcheon, *A Theory of Adaptation*, p. 32.

7   At the time of writing *Bagpuss* is available to watch on Amazon Prime UK and the BBC's iPlayer service, while the new *Clangers* remains a primetime show on the BBC's CBeebies channel. Additionally, on Sunday 30 May 2021, BBC4 broadcast a mini Smallfilms retrospective, featuring episodes of *Bagpuss*, *Clangers*, *Ivor the Engine*, as well as the *Timeshift: Oliver Postgate – A Life in Small Films* documentary.
8   Postgate, *Seeing Things*, pp. 288–289.
9   Oliver Postgate and Peter Firmin, *Noggin the Nog: The Rings of Nudrug Brochure* (Holbrook Printing: Coventry, 1971), p. 7.
10 David Isaacs, 'Noggin Proves a Winner' Coventry Evening Telegraph, 24 December 1971, p28.
11 Tony Gleave, email correspondence with Chris Pallant, 22 November 2019.
12 Tony Gleave and Clive Holland, joint interview with Chris Pallant, Ramsgate, 22 November 2019.
13 Tony Gleave and Clive Holland, joint interview with Chris Pallant, Ramsgate, 22 November 2019.
14 Tony Gleave and Clive Holland, joint interview with Chris Pallant, Ramsgate, 22 November 2019.
15 Hutcheon, *A Theory of Adaptation*, p. 32.
16 John Thornewill, interviewed by Chris Pallant, Video Call, 14 June 2019.
17 Hutcheon, *A Theory of Adaptation*, p. 32.
18 Tony Boydell, interviewed by Chris Pallant, video call, 18 June 2019.
19 John Thornewill, interviewed by Chris Pallant, video call, 14 June 2019.
20 John Thornewill, interviewed by Chris Pallant, video call, 14 June 2019.
21 John Thornewill, interviewed by Chris Pallant, video call, 14 June 2019.
22 Tony Boydell, interviewed by Chris Pallant, video call, 18 June 2019.
23 Tony Boydell, interviewed by Chris Pallant, video call, 18 June 2019.
24 Tony Boydell, interviewed by Chris Pallant, video call, 18 June 2019.
25 This tension between play/story has provoked substantial debate in the field of Game Studies, where it is more commonly defined as a tension between ludology and narratology. For a summary of the debates across the ludology/narratology divide, see Antonio José Planells La Maza, *Possible Worlds in Video Games: From Classic Narrative to Meaningful Actions* (Pittsburgh: ETC Press, 2017); and Matthew Kapell, *The Play Versus Story Divide in Game Studies* (Jefferson, NC: McFarland, 2016).
26 John Thornewill, interviewed by Chris Pallant, Video Call, 14 June 2019.
27 Tony Boydell, interviewed by Chris Pallant, video call, 18 June 2019.
28 Tony Boydell, interviewed by Chris Pallant, video call, 18 June 2019.
29 'Who's Your Welsh Hero?' *BBC News* 9 September 2003, http://news.bbc.co.uk/1/hi/wales/3090076.stm (accessed 17 June 2021).
30 'Ivor the Engine Returns to TV', *WalesOnline* 25 April 2004, https://www.walesonline.co.uk/news/wales-news/ivor-engine-returns-tv-2442149 (accessed 17 June 2021).
31 Jim Le Fevre, interviewed by Chris Pallant, video call, 23 June 2019.
32 Jim Le Fevre, interviewed by Chris Pallant, video call, 23 June 2019.
33 Jim Le Fevre, interviewed by Chris Pallant, video call, 23 June 2019.
34 The British Library (https://www.bl.uk/digital-preservation/strategy) and the Library of Congress (http://digitalpreservation.gov/personalarchiving) (both accessed 15 November 2021) have both taken steps to promote digital preservation initiatives through the development of strategy and by supporting advocacy and collaboration.
35 A sentiment reflected in the survey data from those respondents that discussed the appeal of the new *Clangers*.

36 Hutcheon, *A Theory of Adaptation*, p. 32.
37 Dan Maddicott speaking during 'Lunch with the Clangers', BBC Digital Cities – Nations and Regions: Media Futures Event, Online, 22 September 2020, https://www.facebook.com/SalfordMediaFestival/videos/bbc-digital-cities-lunch-with-the-clangers/641758083143077/ (accessed 18 June 2021).
38 Maddicott, 'Lunch with the Clangers'.
39 Chris Tichborne speaking during 'Lunch with the Clangers', BBC Digital Cities – Nations and Regions: Media Futures Event, Online, 22 September 2020, https://www.facebook.com/SalfordMediaFestival/videos/bbc-digital-cities-lunch-with-the-clangers/641758083143077/ (accessed 18 June 2021).
40 Tichborne, 'Lunch with the Clangers'.
41 Tichborne, 'Lunch with the Clangers'; cross-referenced with author's own review of the screen texts and archival documentation.
42 Tichborne, 'Lunch with the Clangers'.
43 Tichborne, 'Lunch with the Clangers'.
44 Jo Chalkley speaking during 'Lunch with the Clangers', BBC Digital Cities – Nations and Regions: Media Futures Event, Online, 22 September 2020, https://www.facebook.com/SalfordMediaFestival/videos/bbc-digital-cities-lunch-with-the-clangers/641758083143077/ (accessed 18 June 2021).
45 Tichborne, 'Lunch with the Clangers'.
46 Author's transcription from *Bagpuss*, viewed on DVD (Universal Pictures).

APPENDIX A: SMALLFILMS – STATISTICAL PERSPECTIVES

The following statistics are grouped here for ease of reference, and to allow the main body of the book to flow in a narrative manner without unnecessary interruption. Statistics do not tell the whole story, they merely highlight patterns or points of potential interest, which must then be contextualized to understand their relevance or significance. The statistics presented here are drawn upon throughout the book and are used in service of the research methods outlined in Chapter 1.

Audience survey data

Total responses: 1,100 (F: 669; M: 405; Non-Binary: 5; Trans: 2; No response: 19)
    d.o.b of respondents: evenly distributed between the years 1946–2008
    Survey duration: June 2019 to December 2020
    Survey platform: Google Forms
    Distribution method: electronic (Twitter, Facebook, multiple public mailing lists, email)

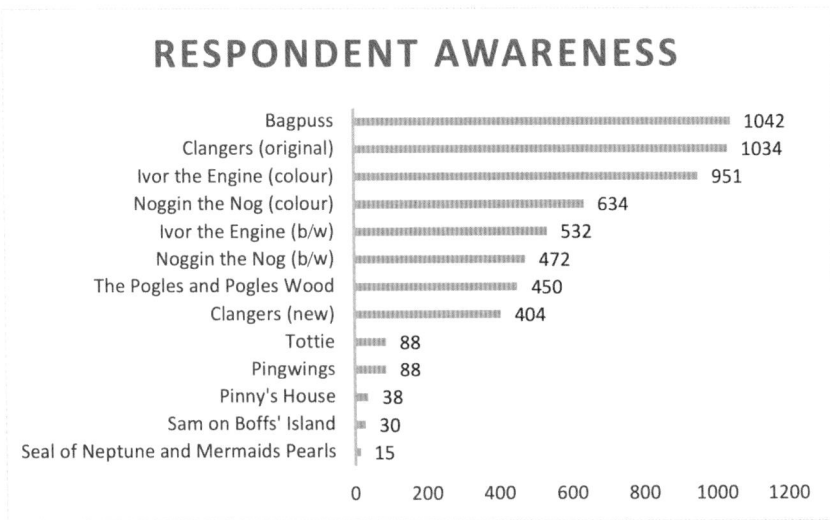

Figure A.1 Total number of responses to a multiple-choice question that asked: 'Oliver Postgate and Peter Firmin created many imaginative worlds, but how many of these Smallfilms TV shows have you seen?'

Appendix A: Smallfilms – Statistical Perspectives

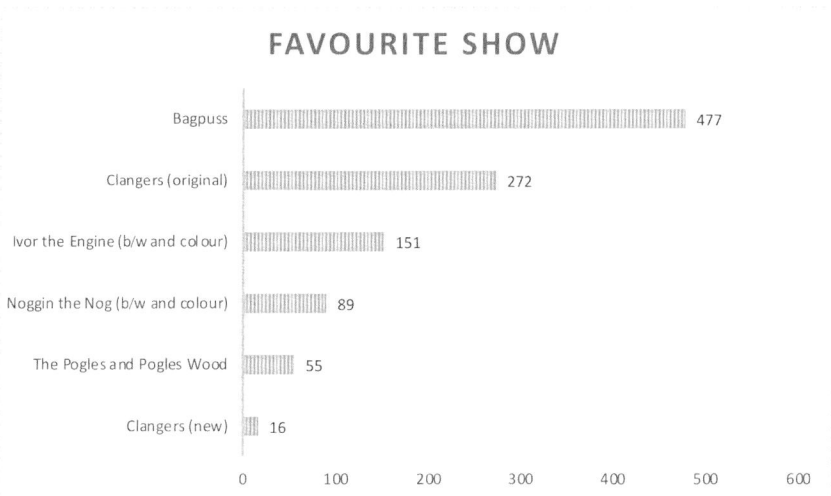

Figure A.2 Total responses to a single-choice question that asked: 'What is your favourite Smallfilms TV show?'.

Note: Shows that didn't register a response have been excluded.

Table A.1 After coding the survey responses to remove non-significant words, this table shows the most frequently used words of significance by show.

Frequency	*Ivor the Engine* (b/w and colour)	*Noggin the Nog* (b/w and colour)	*The Pogles* and *Pogles' Wood*	*Clangers*	*Bagpuss*
1	Characters	Characters	Childhood	Characters	Characters
2	Wales	Story	Tog	Made	Story
3	Story	Norse	Pippin	Soup (Dragon)	Childhood
4	Childhood	Childhood	Witch	World	Cats
5	Dragon (Idris)	Animation	World	Childhood	Mice
6	Steam/Engine	Setting	Nostalgia	Sounds	Songs
7	Train	Voice	Scary	Space	Music
8	Charming	Music	Small (Characters)	Story	Toys
9	Animation	History	Woods	Imaginative	Magical
10	Railway	Mythology	Accents	Funny	World

Table A.2 Comparison of approximate animation screen time.

Series	Average run time per episode (seconds)	Average animation time per episode (seconds)	Animation as percentage of total series screen time (%)	Total series animation time (minutes)
Ivor the Engine (b/w)	510	477	93	Presently unverifiable
The Seal of Neptune/The Mermaid's Pearls	540	503	93	100 (6th)
Noggin the Nog (b/w)	510	471	92	164 (3rd)
The Pogles	540	486	83	45 (8th)
Pingwings	540	441	81	132 (4th)
Clangers	570	445	78	192 (1st)
Pinny's House	270	157	58	34 (9th)
Pogles' Wood	870	486	55	170 (2nd)
Bagpuss	880	379*	43	82 (7th)
Sam on Boffs' Island	780	304	39	101 (5th)
Tottie: The Story of a Dolls' House	860	272	31	22 (10th)

Note: This data is drawn from the first five episodes of each series (to offer a more balanced picture given that some series are much shorter than others). Given the similar approach taken to animation for the colour *Ivor* and *Noggin* series these have not been included in this snapshot. The sampling method was rudimentary, involving a stopwatch and multiple viewings to gain a satisfactory sense of approximation. Animation was counted when consistent movement occurred on-screen, for poses held for more than one second the timing was stopped.

*While the recorded animation time may appear surprisingly low compared to other shows, this is a raw figure and belies the amount of pre-production work undertaken to deliver *Bagpuss*' mixed media aesthetic.

APPENDIX B: EXAMPLES OF OLIVER POSTGATE'S SCREENWRITING STYLE

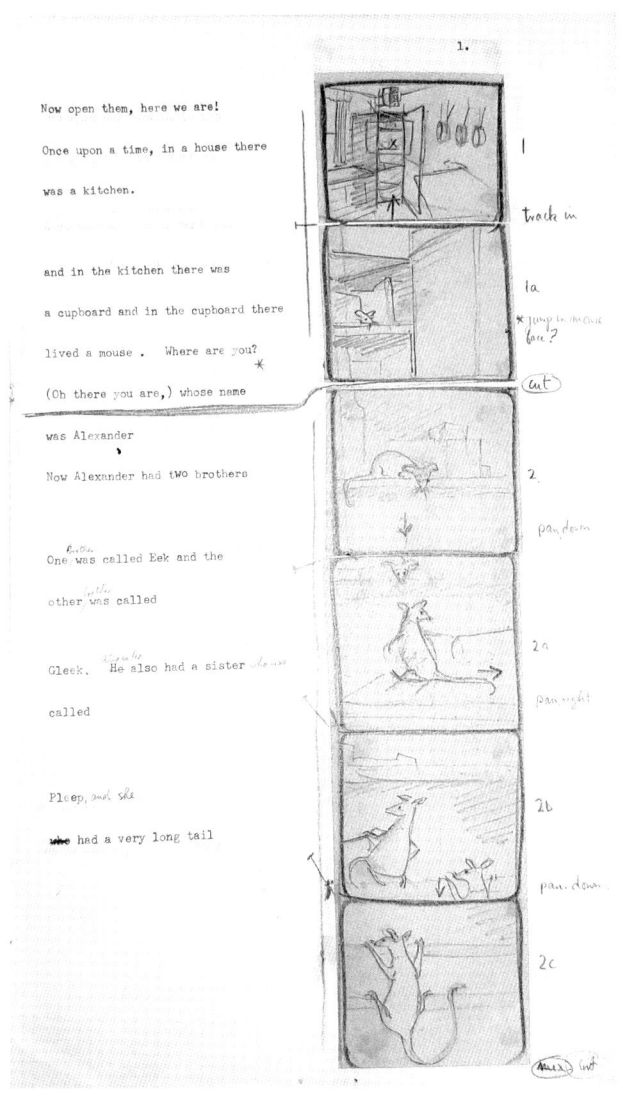

Figure B.1 A sample script page from the production of *Alexander Mouse*.

250 *Appendix B: Examples of Oliver Postgate's Screenwriting Style*

Figure B.2 A sample script page from the production of *Ivor the Engine*.

Appendix B: Examples of Oliver Postgate's Screenwriting Style

```
                    THE SEAL OF NEPTUNE
                    -------------------

Episode 1:  The Discovery:

              Far, far away a long way from here in the
         Western Sea, where the palm trees wave behind
         the golden sand and the coral reefs grow like
         gardens under the water, where the sun keeps
         the sea warm and clear and it is always summer;
         there was a rock.  It was a rock made of old
         sandstone, and the gentle ocean, flowing across
         and around it for thousands and thousands of
         years had worn it into shelves and caves,
         crevices and crannies.

              Now, on, in and under this rock, there
         lived sea creatures, shrimps starfish, sea-
         anemones, crabs, lobsters, oysters, limpets,
         and under one corner of the rock, where the
         shape of it formed a stable, there lived a
         family of seahorses, Mr. Seahorse, Mrs. Sea-
         horse, and their son Cyrus Seahorse.

              There they lived their seahorsey lives,
         grazing through the little fields of seaweed,
         eating the little sea berries that grow there
         on stalks, swimming in and out of the tops of
         the coral trees, chasing the bits of seagrass
         that catch in the coral as the sea goes past.

              There Cyrus played with his friends the
         shrimps, they played "He" in and out of the
         caves, they played hunt the starfish, and they
         teased the oysters to make them snap.

("Snap")

              It was a quiet gentle life and Cyrus grew
         to be quite a big seahorse.

              "Cyrus Seahorse" said Mrs. Seahorse one
         morning in a serious seahorse voice.  "Cyrus,
         you are growing up, you will soon be big enough
         to go anywhere you like - or almost anywhere,
         because there is one place you must not go.
         You must not go to the wreck that lies behind
         the rock, because that is a place where no sea-
         horse is allowed to go."

              Now Cyrus had never seen the other side of
         the rock, as it was a large rock, and seahorses
         are small creatures, so he just went back to
         play with his friends.

              "Shrimp, play hide and seek with me - I'll
         hide."

              "Why should you hide?"

              I know a new cave you don't know about,
         and you'll never find me".

              "Well if I'll never find you there's no
         point in playing, is there"?

              "Well you might find me, there's spiky
         seagrass over the door and it's near where the
         monkfish lives.  Come on, hide your eyes and
         count to a hundred.
```

Figure B.3 A sample script page from the production of *The Seal of Neptune*.

252 *Appendix B: Examples of Oliver Postgate's Screenwriting Style*

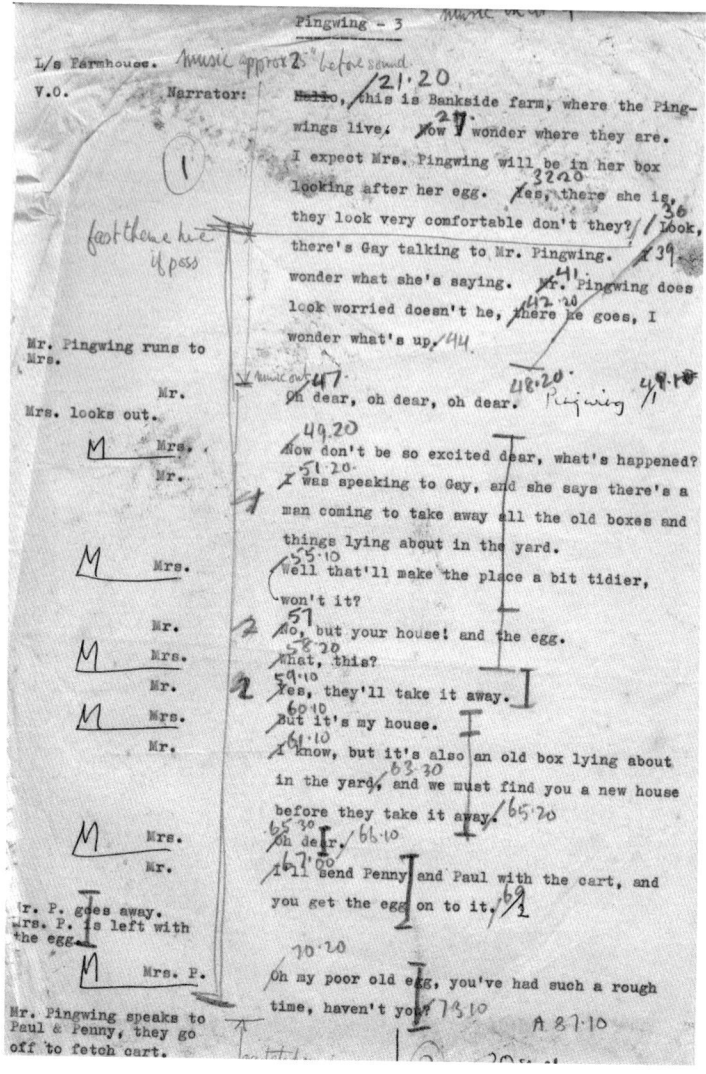

Figure B.4 A sample script page from the production of *Pingwings*.

Appendix B: Examples of Oliver Postgate's Screenwriting Style 253

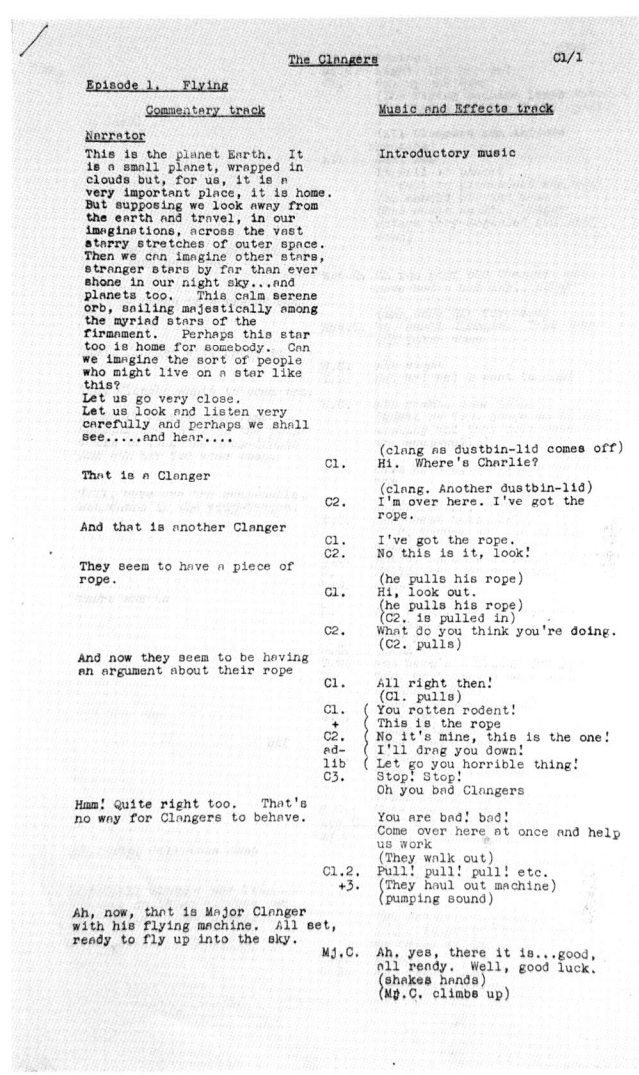

Figure B.5 A sample script page from the production of *Clangers*.

WORKS CITED

'The 50 Greatest Children's TV shows of all Time.' *Radio Times*, January 13, 2018.

'The 100 Greatest TV Kids' shows Results'. *BBC News* 28 August 2001. Available online: http://news.bbc.co.uk/1/hi/entertainment/1513234.stm (accessed 10 June 2021).

'1960s' Ivor the Engine Episodes Unearthed in Kent'. *BBC News* 26 October 2010. Available online: https://www.bbc.co.uk/news/uk-england-kent-11626470 (accessed 8 June 2021).

Ackermann, Edith. 'Amusement, Delight, and Whimsy: Humor has its Reasons that Reason Cannot Ignore'. *Constructivist Foundations* vol. 10 no. 3 (2015), pp. 405–411.

Alston, Katie. 'Episodes of Children's TV Classic Discovered'. *Kentish Gazette* 4 November 2010. Available online: https://www.pressreader.com/uk/kentish-gazette-canterbury-district/20101104/281835755078248 (accessed 10 June 2021).

Amidi, Amid. 'Pingwings Rediscovered'. *Cartoon Brew* 30 May 2007. Available online: https://www.cartoonbrew.com/classic/pingwings-rediscovered-3402.html (accessed 8 June 2021).

Andersson, Theodore M. *The Growth of the Medieval Icelandic Sagas (1180–1280)* (Ithaca, NY: Cornell University Press, 2006).

Atkinson, Robert. 'The Life Story Interview'. In Jaber F. Gubrium and James A. Holstein (eds), *Handbook of Interview Research: Context and Method* (Thousand Oaks, CA: Sage, 2002), pp. 121–140.

Atzbach, Rainer. 'The Legend of Hot Tar Or Pitch as a Defensive Weapon'. In Rainer Atzbach, Lars Meldgaard Sass Jensen, and Leif Plith Lauritsen (eds), *Castles at War* (Bonn: Hablet, 2015), pp. 119–134.

Baboulene, David. 'Knowledge Gaps in Popular Hollywood Cinema Storytelling: The Role of Information Disparity in Film Narrative' (University of Brighton, 2017).

'Bagpuss Cream of Television'. *BBC News* 1 January 1999. Available online: http://news.bbc.co.uk/1/hi/entertainment/246080.stm (accessed 10 June 2021).

Baird, Iain. 'The Story of Colour Television in Britain'. Science + Media Museum [blog], 15 May 2011. Available online: https://blog.scienceandmediamuseum.org.uk/colour-television-britain/ (accessed 10 June 2021).

Barker, Martin, Kate Egan, Tom Phillips, and Sarah Ralph. *Alien Audiences: Remembering and Evaluating a Classic Movie* (London: Palgrave, 2016).

Barker, Martin and Ernest Mathijs. 'Introduction: The World Hobbit Project'. *Participation: Journal of Audience & Reception Studies* vol. 13 no. 2 (2016), pp. 158–174.

Barker, Martin, Clarissa Smith, and Feona Attwood. *Watching Game of Thrones: How Audiences Engage with Dark Television* (Manchester: Manchester University Press, 2021).

Bell, Melanie. 'Movie Workers: Women's Labouring Bodies in Britain's Film Studios'. British Association of Film, Television and Screen Studies Annual Conference, 7–9 April 2021.

Bendazzi, Giannalberto. *Animation: A World History – Volumes 1–3* (Boca Raton, FL: CRC Press, 2015).

Birtwistle, Andy. *Cinesonica: Sounding Film and Video* (Manchester: Manchester University Press, 2010).
Boym, Svetlana (2001) *The Future of Nostalgia* (New York: Basic Books), pp, xiii–xix
Braithwaite, Rodric. *Armageddon and Paranoia: The Nuclear Confrontation since 1945* (Oxford: Oxford University Press, 2018).
Brassealy, Andrew. '7 of the most Terrifying Moments in the History of Kids' TV'. *Metro* 7 February 2018. Available online: https://metro.co.uk/2018/02/07/7-of-the-most-terrifying-moments-in-the-history-of-kids-tv-7289468/ (accessed 1 November 2021).
Brinkmann, Svend. 'Unstructured and Semi-Structured Interviewing'. In Patricia Leavy (ed.), *The Oxford Handbook of Qualitative Research* (Oxford: Oxford University Press, 2014), pp. 277–299.
British Broadcasting Corporation. *1927 Royal Charter* (London: British Broadcasting Corporation, 1927).
British Broadcasting Corporation. *1937 Royal Charter* (London: British Broadcasting Corporation, 1937).
British Broadcasting Corporation. *1964 Royal Charter* (London: British Broadcasting Corporation, 1964).
Broadcast for Schools, 'Words and Pictures: *Sam on Boffs' Island*', 26 July 2011. Available online: http://www.broadcastforschools.co.uk/site/Words_and_Pictures/Sam_on_Boffs%27_Island (accessed 5 November 2021).
Broadcasters' Audience Research Board (BARB) and the CLOSER Research Centre based in UCL's Institute of Education. 'Television ownership in private domestic households'. Available online: https://www.closer.ac.uk/data/television-ownership-in-domestic-households/# (accessed 31 October 2021).
Bromley, Helen. 'Pandora's Box Or the Box of Delights? Children's Television and the Power of Story'. In David Buckingham (ed.), *Small Screens: Television for Children* (London: Leicester University Press, 2002), pp. 208–226.
Burton, John W. and Caitlin W. Thompson. 'Nanook and the Kirwinians: Deception, Authenticity, and the Birth of Modern Ethnographic Representation'. *Film History* vol. 14 no. 1 (1 January 2002), pp. 74–86.
Byock, Jesse L. *Feud in the Icelandic Saga* (Berkeley: University of California Press, 1993).
Cairncross, Alec. *Managing the British Economy in the 1960s* (London: Palgrave, 2016).
Cavalier, Stephen. *The World History of Animation* (London: Aurum Press, 2011).
Chapman, Adam. *Digital Games as History* (New York and London: Routledge, 2016).
'Clangers'. *BBC Media Centre* 27 May 2015. Available online: https://www.bbc.co.uk/mediacentre/mediapacks/clangers (accessed 10 June 2021).
'Clangers Mark 50 Years since First Transmission with a Host of Birthday Surprises'. *Coolabi* 15 November 2019. Available online: https://coolabi.com/clangers-mark-50-years-since-first-transmission-with-a-host-of-birthday-surprises/ (accessed 10 June 2021).
Clemo, Esme. 'Peter Firmin: My Wife Knitted the Orginal Clangers and Dressed the Girls Like Twiggy'. *Woman's Weekly* 15 July 2015.
Collingwood, Charles. *Brian and Me: Life on – and Off – the Archers* (London: Michael O'Mara Books, 2009).
Coman, Alin, Adam D. Brown, Jonathan Koppel, and William Hirst. 'Collective Memory from a Psychological Perspective'. *International Journal of Politics, Culture, and Society* vol. 22 no. 2 (2009), pp. 125–141.
Davies, Rosamund. 'Don't Look Now: The Screenwork as Palimpsest'. *Journal of Screenwriting* vol. 4 no. 2 (2013), pp. 163–177.
Dawkins, Richard. *The Selfish Gene* (Oxford: Oxford University Press, 1976).

Diehl, Sarah J., James Clay Moltz, and Mildred Vasan. *Nuclear Weapons and Nonproliferation: A Reference Handbook* (Santa Barbara, CA: ABC-CLIO, 2002).
Dobson, Nichola. *Historical Dictionary of Animation and Cartoons*. 2nd edn (Lanham, MD: Rowman & Littlefield, 2020).
Egan, Kate. 'Memories of Connecting: Fathers, Daughters and Intergenerational Monty Python Fandom'. In Kate Egan and Jeffrey Andrew (eds), *And Now for Something Completely Different: Critical Approaches to Monty Python* (Edinburgh: Edinburgh University Press, 2020), pp. 207–225.
Ehrlich, Paul R., John Harte, Mark A. Harwell, Peter H. Raven, Carl Sagan, George M. Woodwell, Joseph A. Berry, Edward S. Ayensu, Anne H. Ehrlich, and Thomas Eisner. 'Long-Term Biological Consequences of Nuclear War'. *Science* vol. 222, no. 4630 (1983), pp. 1293–1300.
Ellis, John. *Visible Fictions: Cinema, Television, Video* (London and New York: Routledge, 2001).
Fetterman, David M. 'Key Informant'. In Lisa M. Given (ed.), *The SAGE Encyclopedia of Qualitative Research Methods* (Thousand Oaks, CA: Sage, 2008), pp. 477–478.
Fiddy, Dick. *Missing Believed Wiped: Searching for the Lost Treasures of British Television* (London: British Film Institute, 2001).
Frank, Hannah. *Frame by Frame: A Materialist Aesthetics of Animated Cartoons*. 1st edn (Oakland: University of California Press, 2019).
Frayling, Christopher. 'The Crafts'. In Boris Ford (ed.), *Modern Britain: Cambridge Cultural History of Britain* (Cambridge: Cambridge University Press, 1992), pp. 169–195.
Frosh, Stephen. 'Disintegrating Qualitative Research'. *Theory & Psychology* vol. 17 no. 5 (October, 2007), pp. 635–653.
Furniss, Maureen. *A New History of Animation* (New York: Thames & Hudson, 2016).
Garrido, Sandra and Jane W. Davidson. *Music, Nostalgia and Memory: Historical and Psychological Perspectives* (Cham, Switzerland: Palgrave, 2019).
Geppert, Alexander. 'Rethinking the Space Age: Astroculture and Technoscience'. *History and Technology* vol. 28 no. 3 (2012), pp. 219–223.
Geraghty, Christine and David Lusted (eds). *The Television Studies Book* (London: Arnold, 1998).
Godden, Rumer. *The Dolls' House* (London: Puffin, 1971).
Godfrey, Sarah and Su Holmes. '"Surely the most Natural Scenario in the World": Representations of "Family" in BBC Preschool Television'. *Critical Studies in Television* vol. 11 no. 1 (2016), pp. 59–77.
Gorton, Kristyn and Joanne Garde-Hansen (eds). *Remembering British Television: Audience, Archive and Industry* (London: BFI, 2019).
Gray, Jonathan. *Show Sold Separately: Promos, Spoilers, and Other Media Paratexts* (New York: New York University Press, 2010).
Groskop, Viv. 'Peter Firmin, the Man Behind Bagpuss and the Clangers.' *The Observer* 13 March 2016. Available online: https://www.theguardian.com/tv-and-radio/2016/mar/13/interview-peter-firmin-co-creator-bagpuss-the-clangers (accessed 1 November 2021).
Harris, Harry. 'The Christmas Animation: A Brief History'. *New Statesman* 19 December 2018. Available online: https://www.newstatesman.com/culture/tv-radio/2018/12/christmas-animation-brief-history (accessed 1 November 2021).

Hartley, Nick. 'Cartoons: Inside the Cow Shed Where Classics were Made'. *BBC News* 28 December 2019. Available online: https://www.bbc.co.uk/news/av/uk-wales-50906949 (accessed 8 June 2021).
Harvey, Colin B. 'Binding the Galaxy Together: Subjective, Collective, and Connective Memory in *Star Wars*'. In William Proctor and Richard McCulloch (eds), *Disney's Star Wars: Forces of Production, Promotion, and Reception* (Iowa City: University of Iowa Press, 2019), pp. 97–108.
Hatt, Christine. *The Peoples of North America before Columbus* (Milwaukee, WI: Raintree, 1999).
Hawkes, Alex. 'Bagpuss Licensee to be Sold for £4.2m'. *The Guardian* 20 September 2011. Available online: https://www.theguardian.com/business/2011/sep/20/bagpuss-owner-sold-venture-capital (accessed 1 November 2021).
Hayward, Philip. 'Whimsical Complexity: Music and Sound Design in the Clangers'. In K.J. Donnelly and Philip Hayward (eds), *Music in Science Fiction Television: Tuned to the Future* (New York and London: Routledge, 2013), pp. 72–86.
Her Majesty's Government. 'Sitting of 12 August 1966'. Available online: https://api.parliament.uk/historic-hansard/sittings/1966/aug/12 (accessed 8 June 2021).
Hermansson, Casie and Janet Zepernick. *The Palgrave Handbook of Children's Film and Television* (Basingstoke, UK: Palgrave, 2019).
Hilton, Matthew, Nick Crowson, Jean-François Mouhot, and James McKay. *A Historical Guide to NGOs in Britain: Charities, Civil Society and the Voluntary Sector since 1945* (London: Palgrave Macmillan, 2012).
Hutcheon, Linda. *A Theory of Adaptation*. 2nd edn (New York: Routledge, 2013).
'Ivor the Engine Lost shows found in Pig Sty'. *Express* 26 October 2010. Available online: https://www.express.co.uk/news/uk/207541/Ivor-The-Engine-lost-shows-found-in-pig-sty (accessed 8 June 2021).
'Ivor the Engine Returns to TV'. *WalesOnline* 25 April 2004. Available online: https://www.walesonline.co.uk/news/wales-news/ivor-engine-returns-tv-2442149 (accessed 17 June 2021).
Jencks, Charles. *The Language of Post-Modern Architecture* (New York: Rizzoli, 1991).
Johnson, Christopher. 'Bricoleur and Bricolage: From Metaphor to Universal Concept'. *Paragraph* vol. 35 no. 3 (2012), pp. 355–372.
Jones, Paul. 'Shaun the Sheep Voted the Nation's Best Loved BBC Children's TV Character'. *Radio Times* 15 July 2014. Available online: https://www.radiotimes.com/news/2014-07-15/shaun-the-sheep-voted-the-nations-best-loved-bbc-childrens-tv-character/ (accessed 10 June 2021).
Kammen, Michael. *Mystic Chords of Memory: The Transformation of Tradition in American Culture* (New York: Vintage Books, 1993).
Kapell, Matthew. *The Play Versus Story Divide in Game Studies* (Jefferson, NC: McFarland, 2016).
Kerrigan, Lisa. 'Stories that Never End: Television Fiction in the BFI National Archive'. *Critical Studies in Television* vol. 5 no. 2 (2010), pp. 73–76.
Lee, Stewart. 'The Clangers are Truly British'. *The Big Issue* vol. 51 no. 1123 (6 October 2014), p. 19.
Le-Guilcher, Lucy and Phyllis B. Lassner. *Rumer Godden: International and Intermodern Storyteller* (London: Routledge, 2010).
Lévi-Strauss, Claude. *La Pensée Sauvage* (Paris: Plon, 1962).

'Lost Ivor the Engine Reels found in a Pig Sty'. *WalesOnline* 26 October 2010. Available online: https://www.walesonline.co.uk/news/wales-news/lost-ivor-engine-reels-found-1893448 (accessed 8 June 2021).

'Lunch with the Clangers', BBC Digital Cities – Nations and Regions: Media Futures Event, Online, 22 September 2020. Available online: https://www.facebook.com/SalfordMediaFestival/videos/bbc-digital-cities-lunch-with-the-clangers/641758083143077/ (accessed 18 June 2021).

Macdonald, Ian W. *Screenwriting Poetics and the Screen Idea* (London: Palgrave, 2013).

Madden, Paul. *Keeping Television Alive* (London: British Film Institute, 1981).

Maza, Antonio José Planells La. *Possible Worlds in Video Games: From Classic Narrative to Meaningful Actions* (Pittsburgh: ETC Press, 2017).

McCrone, David. 'National Identity'. In Geoff Payne and Eric Harrison (eds), *Social Divisions: Inequality and Diversity in Britain* (Bristol: Policy Press, 2020), pp. 291–304.

McGown, Alistair. 'Oliver Postgate and Peter Firmin'. Screen Online. Available online: http://www.screenonline.org.uk/tv/id/562266/index.html (accessed 17 May 2021).

McGown, Alistair. 'The Saga of Noggin the Nog (1959)'. Screen Online. Available online: http://www.screenonline.org.uk/tv/id/562377/index.html (accessed 8 June 2021).

McGown, Alastair. 'Watch with Mother'. Screen Online. Available online: http://www.screenonline.org.uk/tv/id/445994/index.html (accessed 8 June 2021).

Miglbauer, Marlene, Susanne Kopf, and Veronika Koller (eds). *Discourses of Brexit* (Oxford: Routledge, 2019).

Millard, Doug. 'A Grounding in Space: Were the 1970s a Period of Transition in Britain's Exploration of Outer Space?' In Alexander Geppert (ed.), *Limiting Outer Space* (London: Palgrave, 2018), pp. 79–102.

Miller, Richard L. *Under the Cloud: The Decades of Nuclear Testing* (Texas: Two-Sixty Press, 1991).

Mills, Brett. 'Invisible Television: The Programmes no-One Talks about Even Though Lots of People Watch Them'. *Critical Studies in Television* vol. 5 no. 1 (2010), pp. 1–16.

Morely, David. *Home Territories: Media, Mobility and Identity* (Abingdon, UK: Routledge, 2000).

Moseley, Rachel. *Hand-made Television: Stop-Frame Animation for Children in Britain, 1961–1974* (London: Palgrave, 2016).

Mulvey, Laura. 'Visual Pleasure and Narrative Cinema'. *Screen* vol. 16 no. 3 (1975), pp. 6–18.

Newcomb, Horace. *Encyclopedia of Television*. 2nd edn (London: Routledge, 2004).

O'Sullivan, Tim. 'Researching the Viewing Culture: Television and the Home, 1946–1960'. In Helen Wheatley (ed.), *Re-Viewing Television History: Critical Issues in Television Historiography* (London: I.B. Tauris, 2007), pp. 159–169.

Palfreyman, Rachel. 'Life and Death in the Shadows: Lotte Reiniger's Die Abenteuer Des Prinzen Achmed'. *German Life and Letters* vol. 64 no. 1 (2011), pp. 6–18.

Pallant, Chris. *Animated Landscapes: History, Form and Function* (New York, USA: Bloomsbury Academic, 2015).

Pallant, Chris and Steven Price. *Storyboarding: A Critical History* (Basingstoke, UK: Palgrave, 2015).

Palmer, James. 'The Clangers Celebrate 50 Years since the Apollo 11 Moon Landing'. *The Sunday Times* 14 July 2019. Available online: https://www.thetimes.co.uk/article/the-clangers-celebrate-50-years-since-the-apollo-11-moon-landing-wr0h5nnlx (accessed 1 November 2021).

Panos, Leah. 'The Arrival of Colour in BBC Drama and Rudolph Cartier's Colour Productions'. *Critical Studies in Television* vol. 10 no. 3 (2015), pp. 101–120.

Payne, Geoff and Judy Payne. *Key Concepts in Social Research* (London: Sage, 2004).

Perry, Chris and Simon Coward. 'Swiped Or Wiped? Kaleidoscope's Part in the Recovery of Lost Television Programmes'. *Critical Studies in Television* vol. 5 no. 2 (2010), pp. 48–59.

Petter, Tashi. '"In a Tiny Realm of Her Own": Lotte Reiniger, Domesticity and Creativity'. *Animation Studies 2.0* 9 October 2017. Available online: https://blog.animationstudies.org/?p=2166 (accessed 1 November 2021).

Pickles, Martin. 'Peter Firmin at London Animation Club'. Vimeo 17 December 2013. Available online: https://vimeo.com/82087379 (accessed 17 June 2021).

Poland, Warren S. 'Whimsy'. *Psychoanalytic Quarterly* vol. 79 no. 1 (2010), pp. 235–240.

Postgate, Oliver. *Thinking it through: Plain Man's Guide to the Bomb* (London: The Menard Press, 1981).

Postgate, Oliver. *The Writing on the Sky* (London: The Menard Press, 1983).

Postgate, Oliver. *Seeing Things: An Autobiography* (London: Sidgwick & Jackson, 2000).

Postgate, Oliver and Peter Firmin. *Noggin the Nog: The Rings of Nudrug Brochure* (Coventry: Holbrook Printing, 1971).

Prendiville, Brendan. 'British Environmentalism: A Party in Movement?'. *Revue LISA/LISA* vol. 12 no. 8 (2014). Available online: https://doi.org/10.4000/lisa.7119 (accessed 19 December 2021).

Price, Steven. *A History of the Screenplay* (London: Palgrave, 2013).

'Programme Highlights'. *Reading Evening Post* 15 November 1969.

Price, Steven. *The Screenplay: Authorship Theory and Criticism* (London: Palgrave, 2010).

Quinn, Ben. 'Souped-Up Clangers to Return to TV'. *The Guardian* 15 October 2013. Available online: https://www.theguardian.com/tv-and-radio/2013/oct/15/clangers-remake-bbc (accessed 1 November 2021).

Retrobox. 'TVO What A Mess Film by D Owen (80's)', YouTube, 22 February 2016. Available online: https://www.youtube.com/watch?v=l29kda7UXjs (accessed 31 October 2021).

'Royal Mail's Children's TV Stamps – in Pictures'. *The Guardian* 4 January 2014. Available online: https://www.theguardian.com/artanddesign/gallery/2014/jan/04/royal-mail-childrens-tv-stamps-in-pictures (accessed 10 June 2021).

Ruddell, Caroline and Paul Ward. 'Introduction'. In Caroline Ruddell and Paul Ward (eds), *The Crafty Animator: Handmade, Craft-Based Animation and Cultural Value* (London: Palgrave, 2019), pp. 1–15.

'The Saga of Noggin the Nog First Transmitted'. History of the BBC. Available online: https://www.bbc.com/historyofthebbc/anniversaries/september/noggin-the-nog (accessed 24 May2021).

Shaw, Michael. *DVD Sleeve Commentary – Tottie: The Story of a Doll's House* [DVD] (Dragons' Friendly Society, 2010).

Sifanos, Georges. 'The Definition of Animation: A Letter from Norman McLaren'. *Animation Journal* vol. 3 no. 2 (1995), pp. 62–66.

Skeggs, Beverley and Helen Wood. *Reacting to Reality Television: Performance, Audience and Value* (London: Routledge, 2012).

Smith, Justin. 'Appendix I – Cinema Statistics, Box Office and Related Data'. In Sue Harper and Justin Smith (eds), *British Film Culture in the 1970s: The Boundaries of Pleasure* (Edinburgh: Edinburgh University Press, 2012), pp. 261–274.

Stabile, Carol A. and Mark Harrison. *Prime Time Animation* (Abingdon, UK: Routledge, 2003).

Stefanovski, Goran. 'Teaching the "Unteachable"'. Canterbury Christ Church University 30 June 2015.

Stewart, Garrett. *Between Film and Screen: Modernism's Photo Synthesis* (Chicago: University of Chicago Press, 1999).

Summerfield, Penny. *Reconstructing Women's Wartime Lives* (Manchester: Manchester University Press, 1998).

Sutherland, Patricia D., Peter H. Thompson, and Patricia A. Hunt. 'Evidence of Early Metalworking in Arctic Canada'. *Geoarchaeology: An International Journal* vol. 30 no. 1 (January 2015), pp. 74–78.

Tait, Derek. *1950s Childhood: Spangles, Tiddlywinks and the Clitheroe Kid* (Stroud, UK: Amberley, 2013).

Tate. 'Art Term: Bricolage'. Available online: https://www.tate.org.uk/art/art-terms/b/bricolage (accessed 17 June 2021).

'Telegraph Announcements – Deaths: Chovil'. *Telegraph Online* February 2008. Available online: http://announcements.telegraph.co.uk/deaths/73301/chovil (accessed 1 November 2021).

Thompson, Ethan and Jason Mittell. 'Introduction'. In Ethan Thompson, and Jason Mittell (eds), *How to Watch Television* (New York: New York University Press, 2020), pp. 1–9.

Timeshift, 'Oliver Postgate: A Life in Small Films'. Directed by Francis Welch (BBC Four, 2010).

Trunk, Jonny and Richard Embray. *The Art of Smallfilms* (London: Four Corners Books, 2014).

Tully, John and Michael Rosen. *Sam on Boffs' Island Annual* (London: Polystyle Publications, 1974).

Turco, R.P., O.B. Toon, T.P. Ackerman, J.B. Pollack, and Carl Sagan. 'Nuclear Winter: Global Consequences of Multiple Nuclear Explosions'. *Science* vol. 222 no. 4630 (1983), pp. 1283–1292.

Walker, Danny. 'Shaun the Sheep Voted Top Children's Character Beating Sooty, Teletubbies and Postman Pat'. *Mirror* 15 July 2014. Available online: https://www.mirror.co.uk/tv/tv-news/shaun-sheep-voted-top-childrens-3862943 (accessed 10 June 2021).

Wall, Tom. 'The Day Bristol Dumped its Hated Slave Trader in the Docks and a Nation Began to Search its Soul'. *The Observer* 14 June 2020. Available online: https://www.theguardian.com/uk-news/2020/jun/14/the-day-bristol-dumped-its-hated-slave-trader-in-the-docks-and-a-nation-began-to-search-its-soul (accessed 1 November 2021).

Weiss, Paul and Arthur Burks. 'Peirce's Sixty-Six Signs'. *Journal of Philosophy* vol. 42 no. 14 (1945), pp. 383–388.

Wells, Paul. *Understanding Animation*. 1st reprinted edn (London: Routledge, 1998).

Wells, Paul. *Basics Animation: Scriptwriting*. Basics Animation (Lausanne: AVA Academia, 2007).

Wells, Paul. *Screenwriting for Animation* (New York: Bloomsbury Academic, 2020).

Wheatley, Helen (ed.). *Re-Viewing Television History: Critical Issues in Television Historiography* (London: I.B. Tauris, 2007).

Whitehead, Mark. *Animation* (Harpenden: Pocket Essentials, 2004).

'Who's Your Welsh Hero?'. *BBC News* 9 September 2003. Available online: http://news.bbc.co.uk/1/hi/wales/3090076.stm (accessed 17 June 2021).

Whyman, Jazz. 'Sam on Boffs' Island BBC, 1972'. YouTube, 20 September 2015. Available online: https://www.youtube.com/watch?v=6gKOv0fJYCY (accessed 5 November 2021).

Williams, Raymond. *Television: Technology and Cultural Form*. 2nd edn (London and New York: Routledge, 2003).

Wittner, Lawrence S. *Toward Nuclear Abolition: A History of the World Nuclear Disarmament Movement, 1971–Present* (Stanford, CA: Stanford University Press, 2003).

Wood, Helen. *Talking with Television: Women, Talk shows, and Modern Self-Reflexivity* (Urbana: University of Illinois, 2009).

Wood, Tat. 'The Cult of Children's TV'. In Stacey Abbott (ed.), *The Cult TV Book* (London: I.B.Tauris, 2010), pp. 175–177.

FILMOGRAPHY

42nd Street (1933)
A Hole in Babylon (1979)
The Adventures of Master Ho (1958)
The Adventures of Parsley (1970)
The Adventures of Prince Achmed (1926)
Alexander the Mouse (1958)
Alien (1979)
Alvin and the Chipmunks (1968–present)
Andy Pandy (BBC: 1950, 1952, 1970)
L'Arroseur Arrosé (1895)
Bagpuss (1974)
Bananaman (1983–6)
The Band Concert (1935)
Benjy and Bolt (BBC: 1960)
Bizzy Lizzy (BBC: 1967)
Blinkity Blank (1955)
Boogie-Doodle (1941)
The Cabinet of Dr. Caligari (1920)
Camberwick Green (1966)
Captain Pugwash (1957–66)
Chigley (1969)
Clangers (1969–74)
The Crown (2016–present)
Dangermouse (1981–7)
Dastardly and Muttley (1969–70)
Doctor Who (1963–present)
The Dolls' House (1947)
Empire Road (1978–9)
Fantasia (1940)
Flower Pot Men (1952–3)
Game of Thrones (2011–19)
Grange Hill (1978–2008)
Hattytown Tales (1969–73)
The Herbs (1968)
The Hobbit trilogy (2012–2014)
Ivor the Engine (1959–64, 1975–7)
Jackanory (BBC1: 1965–96)
The Jungle Book (1967)

The Legend of Prince Valiant (1991–3)
Life on Earth Perhaps (1985)
The Little Island (1958)
Little Laura (1960)
The Lord of the Rings trilogy (2001–3)
The Magic Roundabout (ORTF: 1964–74; BBC: 1965–77)
Mary, Mungo and Midge (1969)
Le Merle (1958)
The Mermaid's Pearls (1962)
Muffin the Mule (BBC: 1946–55; ITV: 1956–7)
The Muppet Show (1976–81)
The Musical Box (1959–66)
Nanook of the North (1922)
Noddy's Toyland Adventures (1992–2000)
North by Northwest (1959)
Paddington (1975–86)
Pingu (1990–2006)
Pingwings (1961–5)
Pinny's House (1986)
The Pogles (1965)
Pogles' Wood (1966–8)
Postman Pat (1981–2017)
Roobard (1974)
The Saga of Noggin the Nog (1959–65, 1982)
Sam on Boffs' Island (1972–3)
Scooby Doo, Where Are You? (1969–78)
The Seal of Neptune (1960)
The Simpsons (1990–present)
Timeshift – Oliver Postgate: A Life in Small Films (2010)
Tom and Jerry (1940–67)
Tottie: The Doll's Wish (1986)
Tottie: The Story of a Dolls' House (1984)
Toy Story (1995)
Trumpton (1967)
Wacky Races (1968)
The Wombles (1973–5)
The Woodentops (BBC: 1955–7)
The Yogi Bear Show (1961–2)

INDEX

Activism 195, 197, 204–207, 216
Adaptation 3, 39–40, 46, 48–50, 55, 110, 195–196, 198–200, 204, 226–230
    Board Game 230–33
    Theatre 226–230
    Video Game 230–231, 233–234
Adventures of Master Ho, The 25–26
Adventures of Parsley, The 13
Alexander Mouse 25
Animation
    Armatures 91, 127, 133
    2D cut-out 2, 12, 27, 31, 55, 57, 69, 75, 77, 79–80, 83, 88–89, 92, 97, 133, 174, 179, 209, 213, 217
    3D, model-based, stop motion 2, 12, 26, 75, 77, 79, 88–93, 95, 97, 101–102, 106–108, 123, 143, 147–148, 151, 153, 158, 174, 195, 242
    Cel-based hand-drawn 11, 27
    Computer Generated 237–238
    depth, illusions of 29–31, 81, 83, 239–240
    and landscape 28, 38, 93, 96, 99n, 101–102, 105, 108–109, 124, 209, 233, 235, 239
    limited (aesthetic) 11–12
    mixed-media/bricolage 3, 79, 93, 107, 169–170, 173–180, 213, 242
    stillness 12–14, 73, 80, 109, 220–221, 238, 241
    watercolour 174, 179, 239
Archives/archiving 11, 15–17, 27, 33–35, 40–48, 51, 59–62, 78–79, 92–93, 98n, 102, 110, 128–129, 143, 145–48, 155, 182, 217
Associated-Rediffusion 10, 25, 39–40, 52, 56, 77–78, 88, 116
Astroculture 124, 136–140, 173

Bagpuss 3, 6–7, 13, 56, 88, 93, 102, 141, 143–144, 162, 167–191, 195–196, 242

Chocolate biscuits (see Mouse Mill)
    Marmalade fur 170
Benjy and Bolt 75n
Bizzy Lizzy 101
British Broadcasting Corporation (BBC), 2, 10–11, 27, 33, 39–40, 46–52, 55, 59, 74, 77–78, 102–103, 110–118, 125, 127, 129–131, 136, 143–144, 147, 154, 156, 158–162, 168–169, 176, 217, 219–220, 238
BBC2W 237–238

Camberwick Green 12, 101, 111–112, 168
Cartography 37–38, 232–237
Channel 4, 218–220
Chigley 12, 101
Clangers 3, 6–7, 10, 33, 58, 79, 88, 102–103, 105, 123–141, 143–144, 169, 173, 196, 225, 227, 239
Collaborators 1–3
    Birch, Linda 3, 170, 172–177, 180
    Chovil, Claire 144–145, 148–149, 151, 153, 156, 158–162
    Cole, Babette 172, 180
    Eason, Ursula 33, 74, 110, 112–114, 144
    Elliott, Vernon 36, 47, 49, 180, 231
    Faulkner, John 3, 158–159, 170, 172, 174, 180–183, 189–191
    Firmin, Charlotte 3, 56, 170, 172–173, 176, 178–180
    Firmin, Gloria 91
    Firmin, Joan 3, 56–58, 91, 94, 101, 125–130, 133, 170, 172–173, 177–180, 189–190
    Firmin, Josie 200
    Kerr, Sandra 3, 158–159, 170, 172, 174, 180–183, 189–191
    Stephens, Doreen 110, 144
Contexts
    Cold War 34–36, 56, 72–74, 195–197, 204–207, 209–216

Identity 218–220, 223n
Independence of the studio 31, 77, 111, 153, 163
national 3–6, 13, 15, 27, 32, 36, 38, 52, 56, 65–66, 73, 137–138, 168, 218–220
Craft 1, 5, 13–14, 53n, 57, 79–80, 127, 133
Arts and Crafts Movement 13–14

Disney 12, 112–113

Fairy-tale 38–39
FilmFair 6, 14

Gordon Murray Puppets 6, 14, 80, 101

Herbs, The 13, 101, 168

International reach 6, 118, 168
Inventiveness 125, 131–132, 136, 140, 143, 171, 189, 242
Heath Robinson 5, 20n
see also Mouse Mill
ITV 25, 39, 78, 219–220
Ivor the Engine 2, 10, 17, 25–52, 55–56, 69, 75, 77, 79, 81, 83, 88–89, 101–103, 105, 112, 116, 144, 169, 195, 227, 230–235

Life on Earth Perhaps 3, 195–197, 204–216, 221n, 242
Little Laura 97

Magic 38, 67, 107–108, 135, 174
Magic Roundabout, The 13, 101–102, 114
Mary, Mungo, and Midge 101
Materiality/material craft
Cardboard 2, 12, 59, 89, 96, 133, 136, 174
Crochet, 133
Embroidery 192n
Enamelling 178–179, 189–191
Fabrication 58–59, 91, 105–106, 117, 126–127, 131, 136, 145, 153, 228, 241
Found objects 86, 95, 126, 137, 241
hand-made aesthetic 6, 12, 14, 25, 57, 79–80, 85, 89–91, 93, 97, 126, 137, 242

Knitting 89–91, 94, 126–130, 133, 157, 179, 197
Meccano 25, 58, 91, 106, 127, 133–135, 137, 241
Mixed-media 107, 133
Plastics 90, 131, 134–137
Tactility 90, 136
Woodwork 103–105, 136
McLaren, Norman 177
Memory 3–4, 6–8, 36, 52n, 180
Merchandise 46, 50, 93, 110, 116–118, 169
Quality control 117–118
Mermaid's Pearls, The 2, 10, 77–80, 85–89, 102–103, 105, 143–144, 242
Mouse Mill
Breadcrumbs 189
Butter beans 189
Chocolate biscuits (see inventiveness)
Musical Box, The 25
Mythology 36–39, 49, 56, 59–60, 62, 85

Natural world 89, 95, 102, 105, 108–109, 136
Nostalgia 3–4, 6, 8
Nuclear Arms/Disarmament 73–74

Paddington 13
Pingwings 2, 77, 79, 88–97, 102–103, 106, 108, 112, 116, 125
Pinny's House 3, 11, 17, 88, 195–197, 216–221, 242
Pogles, The 2, 8, 79, 101–103, 105–110, 118, 143, 197
The Witch 8, 101, 105–110
Pogles' Wood 2, 7, 79, 101–105, 109–118, 130, 144, 173
Postgateian Smallfilms narrative, the 1, 2, 15, 20, 74, 126–127, 143, 162–163, 179, 195–196, 225–226, 242
Preproduction
Screen Idea 16, 181–191, 235
Scriptwriting 27–28, 40, 43, 46, 49, 57, 59–60, 74, 111, 146, 155–156, 176, 182–183, 185–189, 190, 206, 217, 225
Sketch work 59, 62, 126, 132, 239
Storyboarding 57, 75n, 190
Puppetry 25, 27, 112, 171, 173

Reiniger, Lotte 80
Roobarb 13

Sam on Boffs' Island 3, 11, 17, 141, 143–163, 181, 242
Saga of Noggin the Nog, The 2, 10, 27, 55–75, 77, 79, 88–89, 101–102, 105, 112, 116, 125–126, 144, 195–196, 227
   The Moon Mouse 126
Seal of Neptune, The 2, 10, 77–85, 102, 143–144, 242
Sound
   Composition 172, 174, 180–181, 183–185, 191
   Effects 124, 140
   Narration 27, 29, 32, 38, 81, 85, 93, 133–134, 199, 217
   Music 28, 32, 38, 159, 174, 180
   Soundscape 169, 231
Space exploration 3, 123
Storytelling
   dual appeal 27, 33, 53n, 61
   inspiration 26, 28, 59, 66, 89–90, 95, 125–126, 170–171, 216–217
   low-angle persons 102–105, 108–110, 189, 242
   narrative 5, 10, 33, 39–40, 56, 67, 93, 107
   setting 36–38, 56, 62–65, 88, 90, 96, 102, 105–106, 108, 240
   Whimsical authenticity 3, 26, 28, 31–32, 36, 38–39, 49–50, 52, 52n, 53n, 56, 67–68, 83, 85, 112, 143, 169, 242

studio space 56–58, 89, 93, 101–102, 105–106, 137, 140, 240

Tea drinking 5, 29, 32, 68–69, 134, 173
Technology 3, 5, 9–10, 28–31, 36, 90, 123, 140
   homemade 40, 58, 80, 91, 93, 97, 126, 133, 137, 241
   Low-tech 125
Television 4–5, 7–10, 13, 15, 88, 90, 106, 116
   Colour 129–131, 146, 162
   commissioning 26, 33, 40, 55, 74, 101, 110, 114–116, 143, 220
   television as the subject of television 96–97, 123, 131,
Tottie: The Doll's Wish 195, 216
Tottie: The Story of a Dolls House 3, 8, 195–204
   Apple's death 201–204
Trumpton 12, 61, 101

United Productions of America (UPA), 11

Watch With Mother 103, 105, 110–111, 115
What-a-Mess 221n
Williams, Richard 80
Wood, Ivor 13 101
Wombles, The 13
World building 3, 56, 65, 132, 136, 232–240, 242